SALTLEY FIRING DAYS

SALTLEY FIRING DAYS

Footplate memories, 1950-59

Terry Essery

Silver Link Publishing Ltd

ACKNOWLEDGEMENTS

Most literary efforts are not usually brought to a happy conclusion solely by the author - others are also involved, and so it is in this instance.

First I would like to thank my brother Bob whose idea it was to set down these chronicles and who was able to supply a wealth of detail and photographs from his vast library. Much appreciated too were unique photographs kindly provided by Messrs T. J. Edgington, P. Webb, J. A. G. H. Coltas, F. W. Shuttleworth and B. Jeuda.

Of course it would not have appeared at all had it not been for the marathon typing sessions of my wife Hazel, who not only learned how to decipher my hieroglyphics, but never even complained (well not much, anyway) when she permanently 'lost' her dining room.

First published in two volumes as Firing Days at Saltley and More Firing Days at Saltley by D. Bradford Barton Ltd in 1980
New edition, revised, enlarged and re-illustrated, first published by Silver Link Publishing Ltd in August 1994

All illustrations are by R. J. Essery or from the R. J. Essery collection unless otherwise credited.

British Library Cataloguing in Publication Data

A catalogue record for this book is available from the British Library.

ISBN 1 85794 017 2

Silver Link Publishing Ltd
Unit 5
Home Farm Close
Church Street
Wadenhoe
Peterborough PE8 5TE
Tel/fax (0832) 720440

Printed and bound in Great Britain

CONTENTS

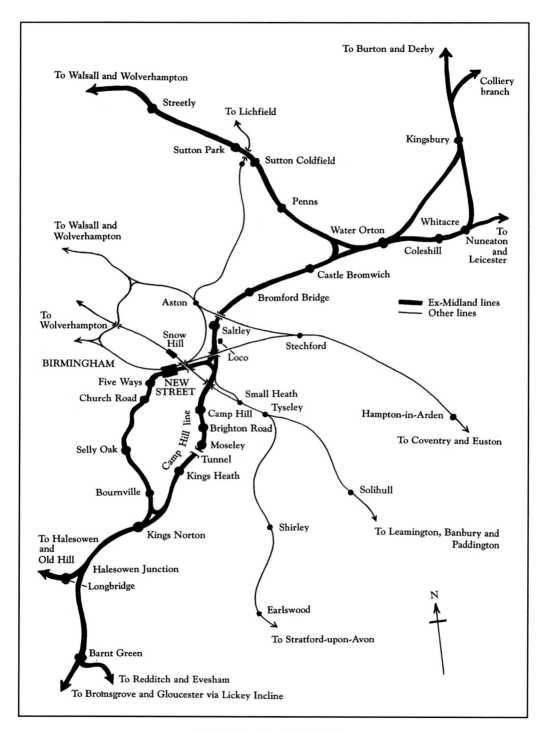

Midland lines through Birmingham

INTRODUCTION

It was the evening of one of those perfect days in early summer which unfortunately bless these Islands only too rarely. Two small boys wearing coats over their pyjamas crept downstairs, quietly unlatched the side door and scuttled the few yards from their front garden to a lineside fence. Climbing on to the top rail, they perched with ears cocked, listening for the first rumble of an approaching express. This operation was performed as often as circumstances would allow, since the 7.00 pm express from Worcester to Birmingham was the highlight of the day's 'spotting' on that section of ex-GWR track that winds its way through Shirley, Hall Green and Tyseley to Snow Hill station.

That first faint rumble, carried on the still air, rapidly grew to that once-familiar pounding roar that only a steam locomotive can produce. The two boys bounced up and down in excited anticipation as a gleaming 'Saint' - *Lady of the Lake* - exploded into view. A fleeting glimpse of flashing side rods, a friendly nod from an imperious driver, the pink tinge of fire on steam matching the glow in the western sky, the glorious crescendo of sound, then all was gone. The boys lingered a while, listening to the fading sound of wheels on rails, before quickly dashing home to the side door and swiftly sneaking back to bed to dream their own individual dreams of railways in general and locomotives in particular. It never seriously occurred to either of them in those days just before Hitler's machinations set Europe ablaze, that both would in time spend their early working days with British Railways and that the younger would indeed fire and, at times, drive over that particular section of track.

It was hardly surprising therefore that, living alongside the Worcester-Birmingham line, both boys were badly bitten by the 'railway bug' at an early age. These two youngsters belonged to a group of lads who showed a great enthusiasm for train spotting, and they travelled to as many vantage points as their limited pocket money in those austerity war years would allow. There were many such places in and around Birmingham, and interest was equally divided between the GWR and LMS.

As the younger brother of the two, I must admit that I did not at first relish the hours spent on cold, dirty station platforms or bleak windswept bridges. I merely tagged along with my elders so as not to be left out of things. However, my fondness for the GWR grew one day at Snow Hill station when I was first invited on to the footplate of a 'Hall'.

As a youngster, my blond hair, blue eyes and innocent expression quickly melted the heart of even the sternest of the old school of engine drivers. My ability to 'cab' engines became almost legendary in our circle of friends. I believe it was this early footplate experience, coupled with a few short rides, that created the desire actually to handle and master one of these magnificent beasts.

I very much favoured the Great Western in those days, mostly because its crews seemed friendlier, allowing me to 'cab' more engines, and both stations and locomotives were very much cleaner. The old 'Duke' Class locomotives were my great favourites, being so unlike the other GWR locos. Their appearance was as noble as their names, with their large domes, tall chimneys and all agleam with shining copper and brass work. Indeed, the highlight of my youthful cabbing career was when I finally 'cornered' *Duke of Cornwall* on Snow Hill station.

Gradually, though, interest in the LMS grew,

particularly after a day's spotting at Tamworth watching the 'Duchesses' hurtling past with their heavy loads. About this time we moved to the Small Heath district of Birmingham, which, by way of coincidence, was located about halfway between Tyseley and Saltley locomotive depots, the principal GWR and LMS sheds in the area. Visits to these on a Sunday afternoon were memorable indeed, and in the spring of 1948 I was delighted when brother Bob one day announced that he had signed on as a cleaner at Tyseley motive power depot.

Every day I required a full report on what happened during his shift, what engines he cleaned and how he did it. Despite the dirt and obvious hard work, he was gloriously happy, being a true Western enthusiast, so it was with some considerable surprise that after a few weeks he told me that he had transferred to Saltley. A friend of his had done this some six weeks earlier and was now enjoying firing turns as a Passed Cleaner. This, then, was the incentive, to be Passed Out in six to eight weeks, even if on an 'inferior' railway.

After this event, our interest and enthusiasm for the LMS developed, and has remained ever since. I was envious of my brother's adventures, and details of them only served to whet my appetite. He was quickly out firing and had acquired quite a bit of main-line experience before being rounded up to serve his King and Country for 18 months.

In the meantime, I was straining at the leash. Being nearly three years his junior the waiting seemed interminable, and it was therefore with great excitement that one day in February 1950, at the age of 16, I signed on at Saltley as a cleaner.

1
SALTLEY SHED

Saltley shed owed its existence to the need for the old Midland Railway to have a stable in the heart of the great rail complex that was interwoven throughout the Birmingham industrial conurbation. Such a stable should ideally be adjacent to the company's Derby to Bristol artery, and in this respect Saltley's location was near perfect, being only a short stone's throw from these illustrious if somewhat grimy tracks.

It was primarily required to supply freight engines for the numerous local workings involved in collecting and distributing the immense amount of industrial and other merchandise moving in the area. This traffic, having been concentrated and sorted in the major marshalling yards of Lawley Street, Washwood Heath, Bromford and Water Orton, had to be shipped farther afield, and suitable motive power also had to be provided. Though freight working was the major concern of Saltley, passenger engines were required too, but these were geared to the commuter traffic of the district rather than expresses.

Geographically speaking, Birmingham is roughly halfway between Bristol and the industrial area of Sheffield with its associated coalfields. It was, therefore, an ideal staging post for changing crews on passenger and faster freight traffic and changing or replenishing locos on the slower through freights. With so much activity, Saltley was obliged to provide a great many extra crews for the

Saltley shed. Of the three roundhouses, No 1 was the most modern. Its reconstruction had been initiated following a successful visit from the Luftwaffe during the war. Built in reinforced concrete with low-level ducting leading to extraction louvres in the roof, it should have been Saltley's pride. However, the absence of a roof on the adjacent No 3 shed is thought to have upset the surrounding air-flow. Whatever the reason, smoke extraction usually seemed to work in reverse, so the shed was nearly always full of choking fumes.

—— B. R.   BIRMINGHAM

RATIN

SCALE 40 FE

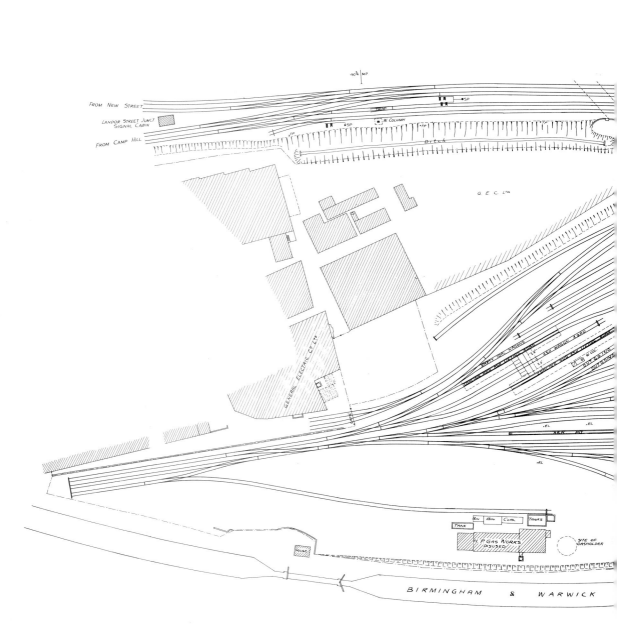

SALTLEY ENGINE SHEDS

LAN

AN INCH

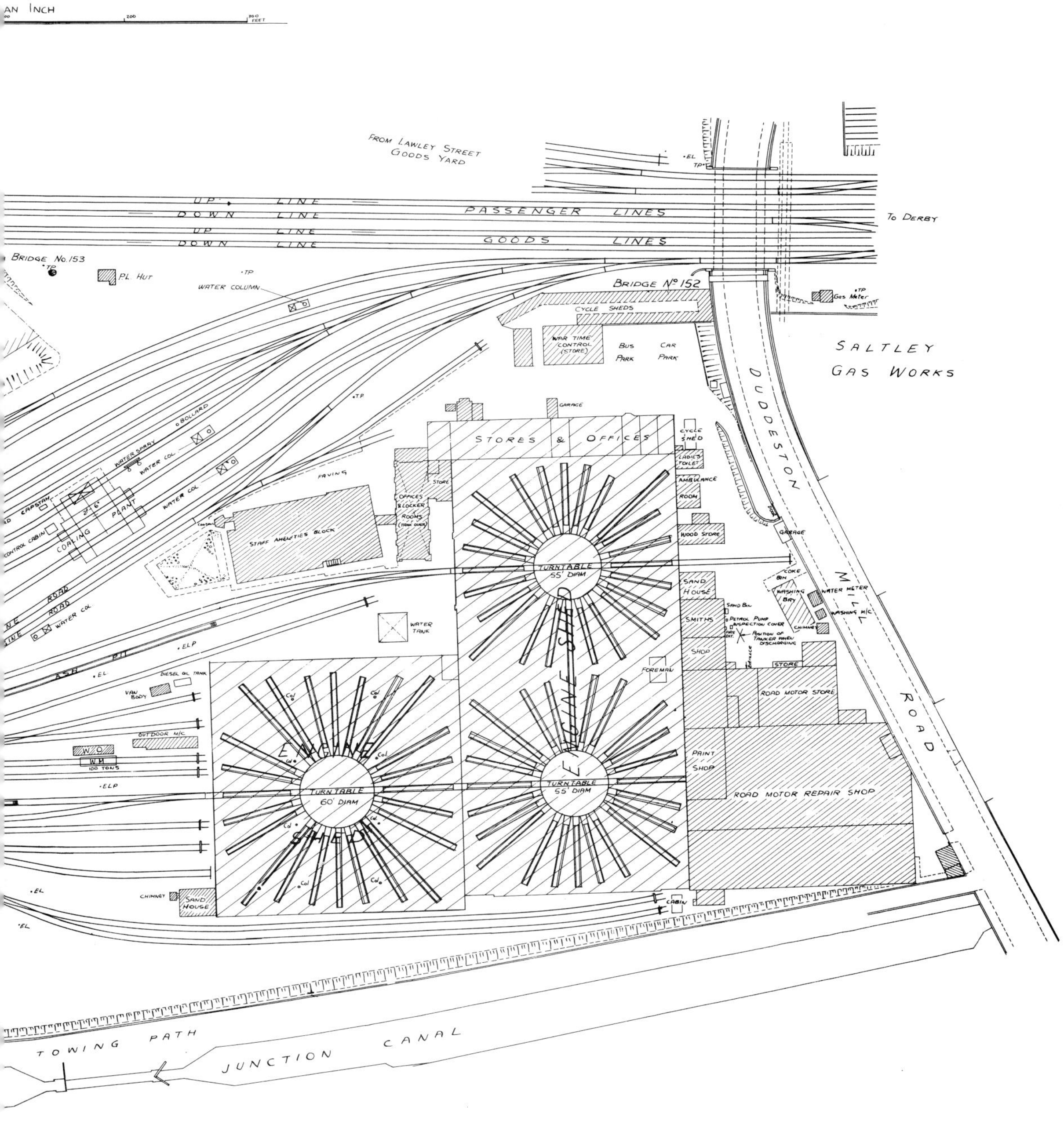

FROM LAWLEY STREET
GOODS YARD

UP LINE
DOWN LINE PASSENGER LINES
UP LINE
DOWN LINE GOODS LINES

To Derby

Bridge No.153

PL HUT

WATER COLUMN

Bridge No 152

Gas Meter

SALTLEY
GAS WORKS

CYCLE SHEDS

WAR TIME
CONTROL
(STORE)

BUS CAR
PARK PARK

GARAGE

STORES & OFFICES

CYCLE
SHED

LADIES
TOILET

AMBULANCE
ROOM

WOOD STORE

GARAGE

OFFICES
LOCKER
ROOM

STORE

WATER COL

PAVING

STAFF AMENITIES BLOCK

WATER COL

CAPSTAN

OIL
PLANT

CONTROL
CABIN

COALING

SAND
HOUSE

SMITHS

SHOP

SAND BIN

PETROL PUMP
INSPECTION COVER

BOTTOM OF
TRAILER HAND
DISCHARGING

WASHING
BAY

COKE

WATER METER

WASHING M/C

STORE

FOREMAN

ROAD MOTOR STORE

WATER
TOWER

ASH PIT

DIESEL OIL TANK

VAN
BODY

OUTDOOR M/C

W.O.
W.M.
100 TONS

PAINT
SHOP

ROAD MOTOR REPAIR SHOP

ENGINE

TURNTABLE
60 DIAM

TURNTABLE
55 DIAM

TURNTABLE
55 DIAM

CHIMNEY

SAND
HOUSE

CABIN

DUDDESTON

MILL ROAD

TOWING PATH

JUNCTION CANAL

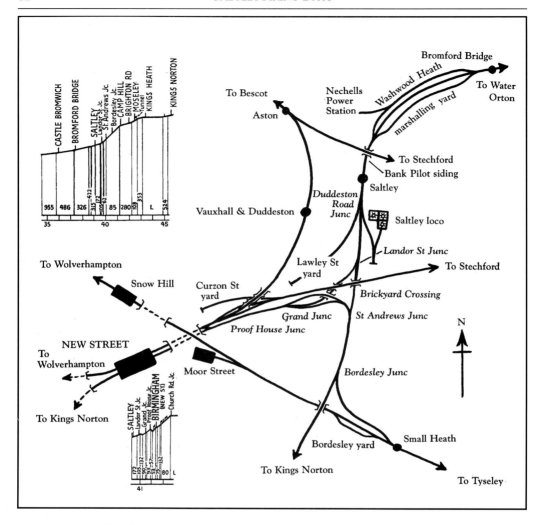

Simplified sketch map showing the lines around Saltley, together with gradient profiles

extensive amount of relief work necessitated by the control system. This system tended to keep crews operating in their own locality so that excessive hours need not be worked. Obviously this did not always occur as planned, but the link system at Saltley was based loosely on a progressively expanding field of activity commencing with shed and local shunting duties and terminating with the Carlisles.

In order of seniority the links ran thus:

Washwood Heath link: This was concerned principally with the disposal and preparation of engines, with a few odd turns such as marshalling and any local steam shunting duties that remained, thrown in to relieve the monotony.

Newly registered drivers and firemen cut their teeth in this link, but the firemen generally only had to endure at the most one full year, often less, since promotion was initially rapid. Drivers, on the other hand, were obliged to await a vacancy in the Control link, and established drivers did not leave BR very frequently. It was for them, therefore, often a case of waiting for a man or men (for they generally left in batches) to retire from the senior links, whereupon a general reshuffle would take place.

Firemen would move once a year to a different section of the same link and therefore to a different driver unless a vacancy occurred in a senior link, in which case they would be promoted directly into that vacancy irrespective of the time of year. The reason for this was to give firemen as much experience and route knowledge as possible.

Bank Pilot link: This was the next link in the promotion chain for firemen and was ideal for developing their firing prowess, since it could involve quite hard work banking westbound freights over the 4 miles between Washwood Heath west end and Kings Heath over the summit of Camp Hill bank.

There were six engines allocated for pilot duties, manned by 18 sets of crews working three shifts of approximately 8 hours, the crews keeping the same engine for a whole week. The engines used were '3F' 0-6-0s, but occasionally a Class '4F' 0-6-0 found itself on this duty, although they were not popular with the men. Long periods of waiting were unavoidable, and since the driver's seating arrangements were very much inferior to a '3F', the drivers objected. Moreover, they did not warm up as quickly as a '3F' and were more temperamental steamers, so this upset the firemen.

One advantage of retaining the same engine for a week was that the crews took a much greater interest in its mechanical condition and general appearance. This led to the rumour that if a '3F' was getting a bit run-down and frayed around the edges, seven days on the 'Bank' would certainly restore its condition.

Drivers had to apply for entry into this link and were therefore older men who might be also afflicted with some ailment or minor disability.

Control link: Having gained a reasonable amount of skills in the Bank Pilot link, firemen were then promoted into the Control link. This consisted of about 50 sets of men who had no booked work, only booked times, and were used by the Control to relieve crews who were required to work back to their own depots, or men who were on overtime, and so on.

If a driver had an extensive route knowledge, some quite interesting work could be had, particularly in the summer months when extra excursions and specials were run. Trips to Bristol and Sheffield were not unusual, while Gloucester, Derby or Leicester were fairly commonplace; even

Crewe or Blackpool could be visited if the driver was an ex-North West man.

However, the bulk of the work was mainly local relief, which was not particularly exciting and often meant disposing of the engine on arrival at the shed. Two or three such operations could be accomplished in an 8-hour shift, but by way of compensation it could be truthfully said that every day was different.

Special link: This was a senior Control link in which about 36 sets of men were used to cover booked work, when the booked crews were off duty or on rest days, holidays, etc. They also doubled up on Control work when required, but activity was usually more predictable.

Trip link: Having now gained a variety of experience, firemen then passed into the Trip link. This consisted of 12 sets of men covering the various local trips necessary to concentrate traffic in the major marshalling yards. It was a pleasant little link enabling firemen to acquire an intimate knowledge, through constant repetition, of local operations. Some interesting and obscure backwaters could be seen on these turns, which no other link allowed. As with the Bank Pilots, drivers applied for entry into this link and were therefore of a similar category, ie older men often nearing retirement.

Link Three, sections A-H: This was the bottom group of road links, and when the aspiring fireman arrived in this group he really felt that he was now out of the Baby Farm. Each section had 12 sets of men; that is to say there were 11 weeks of booked work with one set covering rest days. Therefore each crew completed the full section once every 12 weeks, or four times per year. Normally firemen would spend 12 months in each section of the link, then pass to another section with another driver until finally promoted to Link Two.

For example, a fireman might enter section C - the Redditch link - in, say, May 1951. In May 1952 he would pass into section B, the Little Bristol link, and in May 1953 he would go into section A. Theoretically he could pass through all the sections in turn, but in practice promotion would take him into the next group before the eight years had passed, which was the period necessary to accomplish this. Drivers stayed in this link until they

Much of the time, Control link work was nothing more exciting than local relief, usually terminating in disposal of the relieved engine. Occasionally, though, a run to Derby or Gloucester brightened the week, particularly when this was an express or 'fitted' freight. A ubiquitous '4F', No 44583, is shown here on the down main at Halesowen Junction in 1958 hauling a mixed freight train under 'semi-fitted' headlights (at least one-third of the train would be fitted with the continuous brake). With such a train the '4F' would be well extended on this 3-mile stretch of 1 in 301, and might possibly be a little breathless by the time it reached Blackwell at the top of the Lickey Incline. No 44583 was one of 20 built at Derby in 1939, 28 years after the first of its Class appeared.

either retired or a vacancy occurred in the Link One group. They could, however, apply for vacancies in the Bank Pilots, the Trip link or, surprisingly, Link Two - the Passenger Group.

Link Two - the Passenger Group: This consisted of three sections, A, B and C, colloquially known as the Top, Middle and Bottom Passenger links respectively. Each section contained the usual 12 sets of men, and although a normal promotion link for firemen from Link Three, drivers had to apply for it. The most plausible explanation for this would seem to be that generally less hours were worked because passenger trains ran more punctually than freight trains, and since much of the passenger work at Saltley could only be regarded as short-distance operations, pay packets at the end of the week would be lighter than those of their colleagues in the freight links. Of course there were compensations, since apart from the dubious status image,

social activities could be more accurately planned, more day working indulged in and, in the case of section A, mileage bonuses obtained on the runs to Bristol and Sheffield. There was also another plus, in that far less preparation and disposal work was required from passenger men.

Link One: Unlike many sheds, Saltley did not regard passenger work as the top link - this was the domain of the long-distance freights, of which the Carlisles and Glasgows were the elite. Again there were eight sections, A to H, and the experienced (for experienced they now were) firemen went annually into a different section until they were finally passed out as drivers.

The few remaining lodging jobs at Saltley were to be found in these links, and great efforts were made by the shed staff to ensure that the finest engines, with the best-quality coal, were allocated to these turns.

2
A CLEANER'S LOT

The function of an engine cleaner should be to clean engines, and there is really no better way of getting to know your way around a loco than by starting at the front buffer beam and working your way aft, along both sides, then over and under, while at the same time scraping off layers of filth to see what lies underneath. Discovering these bits and pieces and finding out their place in the scheme of things was all part of the training and, despite the obvious dirtiness of the job, most cleaners were at their happiest doing just this. It really made their day if one of the steam-raisers allowed them to shovel some coal into the firebox or put on an injector.

The method of cleaning engines was fairly straightforward. From the level of the footplate downwards, locomotives tended to be covered with a mixture of oil, soot, coal dust and general dirt. It was, however, reasonably soft where it was able to soak up a regular supply of oil, but could be literally inches thick. Most of this was removed with a metal 'scraper', the residue being rubbed with a lump of cotton waste soaked in paraffin, then wiped dry. The boilers and cabs were attacked by a liberal application of paraffin, then wiped down. Providing that the paintwork underneath was still in good con-

dition, quite a presentable job could be made in this way.

Unfortunately there were too many dirty engines and too few cleaners, and the cleaning foreman usually had to content himself with ensuring that engine numbers were rendered readable - but of course this only emphasised the dirtiness of the rest of the engine. Occasionally some special event would call for an all-out effort from the cleaning staff to bring a locomotive up to the required standard. At Saltley this would be the most recently 'shopped' 'Black Five', and understandably great enthusiasm was generated by all concerned, for the results were well worth the labour involved.

However, because of the acute shortage of shed labourers at that time, most cleaners after two or three weeks found themselves engaged on a vari-

It brightened a cleaner's day if one of the steam-raisers allowed him to fire some coal or put on an injector. Apart from being responsible for ensuring that steam pressure and water levels of stabled engines were adequate, they were also responsible for lighting up 'dead' engines. Some scrap timber and a few wads of oil-soaked cotton waste usually sufficed to initiate this. This posed photograph taken on a Class '3F' portrays a steam-raiser applying the lighted waste. He would not normally stand awkwardly on the driver's pedestal obstructed by the anti-glare shield, but since a section of the footboards is missing perhaps he has no alternative.

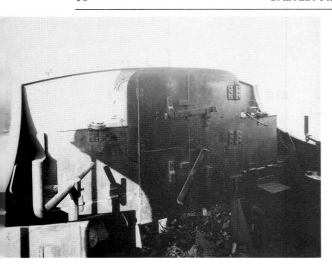

Cleaning locomotives was excellent training for an aspiring fireman. Not only did he gain confidence and expertise in climbing around and on top of the various types and engines and tenders, but he was also able to learn the names and functions of their many component parts. This photograph shows the tender front details of a Fowler tender. Access to the 5-ton coal space was via the folding doors, which could be hinged back and secured by the hook attached to the top of the driver's locker. The hand brake is on the left of the picture, while the water scoop handle, retained by a chain, can be seen to the right. Handles controlling the tender water cocks are located on either side of the shovelling plate support brackets.

ety of jobs. Many of these were very good for developing muscle - and, heaven knows, a lot of muscle was needed by a fireman at times - but they were not so good for morale. One had to be very dedicated to put up with weeks of shovelling ashes out of the disposal pits, picking up coal spillage, filling up sand bunkers and unloading stores. However, this made you familiar with all the operations of a motive power depot, and you certainly got to know your way around the shed.

My artistic aptitude was soon spotted, and I found myself armed with a 3 ft 6 in L-shaped paint brush, a gallon pot of black heat-resistant paint and a 'brief' to transform every rusty-looking Saltley smokebox to a Cherry Blossom shine. After this I had to get down to some really delicate work and whiten the shed and smokebox numbers. As long as I was on, in or under a loco I was very content, but then tragedy struck.

This took the form of being 'invited' to join the office staff in the shed's general office. I have always had a great aversion to office routine and having not long left school I was particularly sensitive to it at this time. I reacted violently at being kept away from 'my' locomotives. After two weeks of continual badgering I was transferred to the Time Office. Here at least I was in contact with enginemen and the more practical side of administration. During this period a new Firing Inspector was appointed to the shed and our training started in earnest. Now this was really interesting and

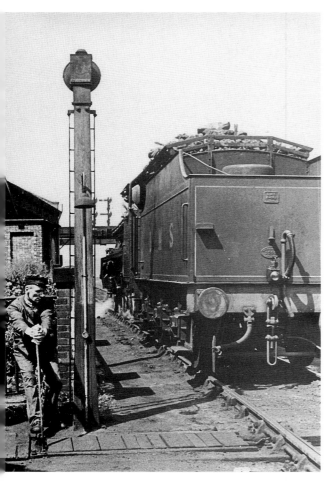

Firemen were rarely inactive when 'on shed'. Whether disposing or preparing, they had to precede the engine on foot checking that all was clear and pulling point levers so that engines could proceed in the intended direction. Most cleaners spent part of their limited spare time helping firemen with this strenuous operation; needless to say, the latter were only too willing to accept such assistance.

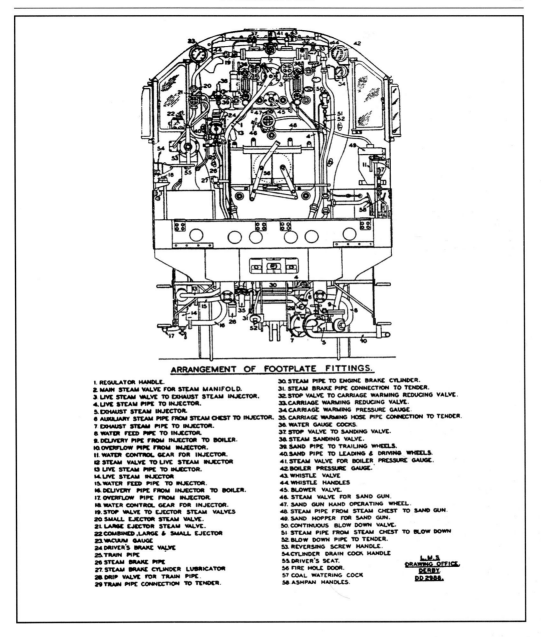

ARRANGEMENT OF FOOTPLATE FITTINGS.

1. REGULATOR HANDLE.	30. STEAM PIPE TO ENGINE BRAKE CYLINDER.
2. MAIN STEAM VALVE FOR STEAM MANIFOLD.	31. STEAM BRAKE PIPE CONNECTION TO TENDER.
3. LIVE STEAM VALVE TO EXHAUST STEAM INJECTOR.	32. STOP VALVE TO CARRIAGE WARMING REDUCING VALVE.
4. LIVE STEAM PIPE TO INJECTOR.	33. CARRIAGE WARMING REDUCING VALVE.
5. EXHAUST STEAM INJECTOR.	34. CARRIAGE WARMING PRESSURE GAUGE.
6. AUXILIARY STEAM PIPE FROM STEAM CHEST TO INJECTOR.	35. CARRIAGE WARMING HOSE PIPE CONNECTION TO TENDER.
7. EXHAUST STEAM PIPE TO INJECTOR.	36. WATER GAUGE COCKS.
8. WATER FEED PIPE TO INJECTOR.	37. STOP VALVE TO SANDING VALVE.
9. DELIVERY PIPE FROM INJECTOR TO BOILER.	38. STEAM SANDING VALVE.
10. OVERFLOW PIPE FROM INJECTOR.	39. SAND PIPE TO TRAILING WHEELS.
11. WATER CONTROL GEAR FOR INJECTOR.	40. SAND PIPE TO LEADING & DRIVING WHEELS.
12. STEAM VALVE TO LIVE STEAM INJECTOR	41. STEAM VALVE FOR BOILER PRESSURE GAUGE.
13. LIVE STEAM PIPE TO INJECTOR.	42. BOILER PRESSURE GAUGE.
14. LIVE STEAM INJECTOR	43. WHISTLE VALVE.
15. WATER FEED PIPE TO INJECTOR.	44. WHISTLE HANDLES
16. DELIVERY PIPE FROM INJECTOR TO BOILER.	45. BLOWER VALVE.
17. OVERFLOW PIPE FROM INJECTOR.	46. STEAM VALVE FOR SAND GUN.
18. WATER CONTROL GEAR FOR INJECTOR.	47. SAND GUN HAND OPERATING WHEEL.
19. STOP VALVE TO EJECTOR STEAM VALVES	48. STEAM PIPE FROM STEAM CHEST TO SAND GUN.
20. SMALL EJECTOR STEAM VALVE.	49. SAND HOPPER FOR SAND GUN.
21. LARGE EJECTOR STEAM VALVE.	50. CONTINUOUS BLOW DOWN VALVE.
22. COMBINED, LARGE & SMALL EJECTOR	51. STEAM PIPE FROM STEAM CHEST TO BLOW DOWN
23. VACUUM GAUGE	52. BLOW DOWN PIPE TO TENDER.
24. DRIVER'S BRAKE VALVE	53. REVERSING SCREW HANDLE.
25. TRAIN PIPE	54. CYLINDER DRAIN COCK HANDLE
26. STEAM BRAKE PIPE	55. DRIVER'S SEAT.
27. STEAM BRAKE CYLINDER LUBRICATOR	56. FIRE HOLE DOOR.
28. DRIP VALVE FOR TRAIN PIPE.	57. COAL WATERING COCK
29. TRAIN PIPE CONNECTION TO TENDER.	58. ASHPAN HANDLES.

L.M.S
DRAWING OFFICE,
DERBY.
DD 2988.

Typical arrangement of cab fittings.

took in theoretical work plus a certain amount of practical instruction actually on the footplate.

Classes were held in a lecture room set aside for this purpose at Saltley station. It was also the home of the mutual improvement group, so popular with senior firemen preparing for their driving examination, and contained many excellent models of engine equipment, diagrams, etc. Although we were overwhelmed with the amount of things to learn, we spent many very pleasant hours with

Mr Welch. He wasn't too concerned at this stage regarding our ability to generate steam, but he did emphasise the paramount importance of being able to keep boilers well filled. Maybe he had dropped a plug or two in his time, so the use and operation of injectors was pursued on a daily basis. We all acquired a little black book called *Questions for Enginemen*, which proved so helpful in bringing enlightenment after lengthy lectures in the soporific atmosphere of Saltley station. Most lads could follow the drift if equipment or models were used, but after an hour or so of pure theory on, say, the principles of combustion, the students would take on the appearance of a well-stocked fishmonger's slab. Those who had not actually nodded off had glazed eyes and open mouths.

To be fair, Mr Welch would always try and back up theory as soon as possible with a practical demonstration. A few minutes on the footplate with only a little bit of dialogue such as 'If you does this, you gets that, and if you gets that you does this' was much more effective in getting the various points home. It was during one of these demonstrations, which took place on the footplate of a Class '8' standing on one of the outside roads of the shed, that I saw Mr Welch dexterously 'fire' his bowler hat to the left front corner of the firebox. I was privileged to witness him perform this unusual feat on two further occasions; I rather

fancy he forgot about the appendage, which was of course his badge of rank, when carried away by the exuberance of firing. A slight tilt of the head cast it adrift, when even the action of the blast of a well-opened blower was sufficient to produce the inevitable result.

Much of the fireman's art will be already familiar to readers, and part only of our lectures need be given here; for example, how to deal with clinker. If this was allowed to form in large quantities it would block the air spaces in the grate and prevent the air supply being admitted through the dampers from passing through the fire, which in consequence would become dead, so that the steaming of the boiler would be affected. In this event it would be necessary to break up and dislodge the clinker by using the straight dart to lift it from the firebars and the pricker to clear out the air spaces in the grate. Incorrect firing and mismanagement of the dampers tended to accelerate the formation of clinker. (One also found that the stop-go type of running with which most slow freights were afflicted in those days - hours of inactivity in a lay-by, followed by a short spurt along the main line to the next block - clinkered the fire as much as anything.)

The best safeguard was to spread about a bucketful of broken clean firebrick or limestone over the grate before the fire was built up during engine preparation. These materials tended to collect the

Saltley station down platform, looking north. One of the waiting rooms had been set aside for the Saltley Mutual Improvement Classes, where keen drivers and firemen endeavoured to further their knowledge. As a cleaner, I and my colleagues spent many interesting hours in this MIC classroom learning our trade under the tuition of Firing Inspector Welch.

SECTIONAL VIEW OF BOILER

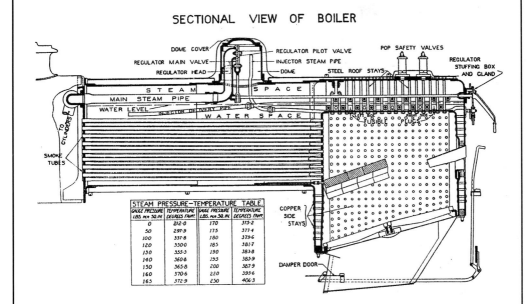

STEAM PRESSURE—TEMPERATURE TABLE.			
GAUGE PRESSURE LBS. PER SQ.IN	TEMPERATURE DEGREES FAHT.	GAUGE PRESSURE LBS. PER SQ.IN	TEMPERATURE DEGREES FAHT.
0	212·0	170	375·2
50	297·9	175	377·4
100	337·8	180	379·6
120	350·0	185	381·7
130	355·5	190	383·8
140	360·8	195	385·9
150	365·8	200	387·9
160	370·6	220	395·6
165	372·9	250	406·3

COMPLETE COMBUSTION

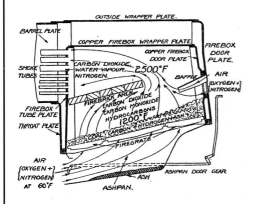

SECTION OF FIREBOX SHOWING THAT GASES ARE FORMED AND THAT TEMPERATURES OF UPWARDS OF 2500°F. ARE OBTAINED DURING THE COMPLETE COMBUSTION OF COAL.

INCOMPLETE COMBUSTION

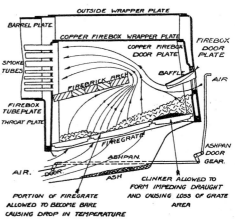

SECTION OF FIREBOX SHOWING EFFECTS OF MISMANAGEMENT OF FIRE.

clinker round themselves as it formed, and by so doing prevent it from adhering to the firebars.

A large quantity of air is required to ensure proper combustion, and this was drawn in by the blast and entered the firebox through the dampers, upwards through the firegrate, and also through the firehole door, to the top of the fire. Most ex-LMS engines had hollow firehole doors that allowed a certain amount of secondary air to be admitted even when the doors were closed. It was nearly always necessary to admit air through both the firehole door and the dampers. The air drawn through the firegrate was required to maintain an incandescent bed of fire, while the air admitted by the firehole door served to complete the combustion of the gases liberated from the glowing coal below.

However, all air admitted to the firebox over and above the quantity necessary for complete combustion of the coal would pass through the boiler unchanged, except that it would become heated in its passage. This meant that the surplus air robbed useful heat from the fire, which could otherwise be used to produce steam, and furthermore the loss of this heat from the fire lowered the temperature of the firebox.

Conversely, if insufficient air was allowed to enter the firebox, complete combustion of the coal was impossible because there would not be enough oxygen to combine with all the carbon in the fuel, and some of the carbon would pass through the tubes unburned, to appear at the chimney in the form of smoke. There was also the risk that the carbon consumed would only be burned to carbon monoxide, and that the hydrocarbon vapours would also escape unburned from the chimney, giving rise to a serious heat loss in addition to the production of smoke.

How then was it possible to judge when the correct amount of air was being admitted to the firebox to give correct combustion? One method was to set the dampers and firehole door so that a clear exhaust was obtained, but that when the firehole door was closed very slightly smoke appeared at the chimney. Another method was to adjust the dampers and firedoor so that there was just a perceptible discoloration of the exhaust at the chimney. This method had the advantage that there was something visible to watch, and there was no chance of admitting excess air. In either case, if combustion was almost perfect, each shovel of

coal fired would be accompanied by a dash of smoke from the chimney lasting perhaps one or two seconds.

I must say that as an experienced fireman I tended to prefer the second method, and found that I could accurately determine the state of the fire by watching the chimney exhaust. I've congratulated myself many times on placing a single shovel of coal dead on a target, which would be no larger than a teaplate and perhaps 10 feet from the firehole, with no more visual information other than the smoke pattern at the chimney. To be able to do this was particularly important when firing an engine very lightly.

Firing to the chimney exhaust, however, was rendered somewhat more tricky at night, when at times it was not possible to see even the end of the firebox, let alone what shade of grey was coming out of the chimney. At Saltley we seemed to work more at night, so other methods had to be adopted. For me, however, all these skills were many years in the future, so back to the Saltley station lecture room.

What is a brick arch for? During our labouring period we worked in the dark confines of a still hot firebox, helping the boilermen to rebuild them, but what were they for, apart from a temporary repository for some of Mr Welch's bowler hats? The brick arch served several useful purposes. It protected the tube-plate and tube ends from the direct flame of the fire. During intervals of firing when the firebox temperature fell, the brick arch radiated heat that tended to prevent rapid fluctuations in the tube-plate temperature. The brick arch also promoted thorough combustion of the gaseous products of the fuel by lengthening their path from the firegrate to the tube-plate, and at the same time, acting in conjunction with the firehole deflector plate, it caused these burning gases to be mixed ultimately with the supply of top air admitted to the firebox through the firehole door.

Much has been said and written on the best way of firing a locomotive, but the official method was known as Controlled Firing, and this is what we were taught. Controlled Firing can be described as firing at equal time intervals; a definite number of shovels of coal, well broken up, fired at short regular intervals, and the time between firings not altered by reason of speed or gradient. The actual number of shovels of coal fired depended, of course, on the work the engine had to do, and this had to be determined by experience, but as the firing was done on a time basis, variations in speed and gradient would not effect the rate of firing. An engine pulling a train up a bank will burn more coal per mile than on the level, but since it travels more slowly up hill, the coal burned per minute need not vary.

Controlled Firing saved coal because it was never added at such a rate that the gases it gave off could not be burned by the air passing over the fire from the firedoor. It also prevented waste due to excessive firing before or on a rising gradient. It is better to use the coal on the grate as a reservoir of heat to be drawn on when the engine is working hard, than to make a large increase in the rate of firing, bringing down the temperature in the firebox and causing black smoke. In Controlled Firing the reservoir was built up again on the down gradient by continuing to add coal at the regular 2-minute intervals. As stated above, the number of shovels of coal to be fired depended upon the work the engine had to do, and the fireman's guide to this was the maintenance of his boiler pressure on the gauge.

Controlled Firing, of course, did not dispense with the fireman's knowledge of the road, when to use the injector and when to cease firing, but it laid down sound principles that, when combined with his road experience, enabled him to fire an engine with efficiency and economy.

This, then, was the theory. However, there were certain difficulties in practice that require elaboration. To be properly executed, Controlled Firing required a high degree of skill, knowledge and confidence in oneself, one's driver and the locomotive. There were so many variables to be taken into account that even an experienced fireman could get into trouble before he realised it. Different engine classes obviously had different characteristics, and these had to be learned. To complicate things, no individual engine in the same class behaved in exactly the same way; some always steamed, or ran, better than others. Furthermore, the same engine would itself vary from month to month, week to week or day to day, depending on that particular period between 'shopping', its general state of repair, whether it needed washing out, the type of coal in the tender, and so on. This is what made every firing turn such an exciting challenge.

Apart from the actual locomotive, one had just as many variations with drivers. Some hammered engines mercilessly all the time, some occasionally, some never. Some worked them so lightly that anything but the thinnest of fires never had sufficient blast to burn brightly. Some drove inconsistently, seemingly at a whim of the phases of the moon, the weather, or the state of their livers, while a row with the wife could be detected by the position of the regulator or reversing screw. Some were very consistent, both good and bad, and some were downright geniuses, but no two drivers were ever the same. They, too, had to be learned. Then of course route knowledge was very important. Knowing just when the major effort was needed; where you didn't want much steam; where you could clean the fire if necessary; or where you could drag coal forward from the back of the tender, and when you could snatch a quick sandwich. It also helped to know what was going on around you with regard to other traffic, since this could either impede or hasten your progress.

Controlled Firing, therefore, could not always be strictly adhered to, since so many other factors influencing the modus operandi were not controllable, but it provided a sound guideline from which to work. However, I found that many old drivers tended to regard it with suspicion.

In the early 1950s some of the unpleasant hangovers from the war years were still very much in evidence - run-down equipment, poor fuel, congested lines, and a shortage of labour in nearly every department. This latter included firemen, and experienced men were at a premium. Although every effort was made to keep the inexperienced on the more lowly turns, sometimes a young Passed Cleaner found himself standing in for a top link man on a crack job, which could be embarrassing for all concerned.

Because drivers frequently had young firemen whose ability was an unknown quantity, they tended to play safe and instruct the fireman to get a good fire on; with the old Midland men this was in any case their habitual method of firing. The steeply sloping grates of the Classes '2', '3' and '4' goods engines responded well to a box filled up to the firehole, and these were the principal locomotives on which the old drivers fired, the doctrine being that it was better to have too much steam rather than too little. Unhappily this did not always work out. Understandably, many young firemen abandoned their Controlled Firing theory under the pressure of these influences and only some re-discovered its benefits in the light of their future experiences.

However, we were given the following advice about how coal should be put on during firing. This varied with different grates, depending on their shape, slope, etc, but in all cases the person firing had to aim to prevent the formation of holes in the fire. Generally it was advisable to maintain the fire thicker at the corners and sides, and to avoid placing much coal at the centre, which would cause smoke. In a sloping grate it was best not to fire much to the front except to prevent the formation of holes, because the coal would shake down forwards and feed the front of the box, and it was usually advisable to keep the back corners well filled.

It was most important to avoid the formation of holes in the fire because the air naturally tended to pass in at this spot since it was the easiest path for it. The rush of air through the hole would lift particles of glowing fuel, carrying them through the tubes and out of the chimney, while the remainder of the fire would become dead and the firebox temperature would fall due to imperfect combustion.

A rapid examination of the state of the fire over the entire grate could be made by resting the shovel blade on the firehole mouthpiece and using it to direct a stream of air on the part of the fire under examination. By moving the shovel blade it was possible to direct the air stream to each part of the fire in turn, and thus examine the whole fire. The fireman needed to endeavour at all times to avoid the use of fire irons since their excessive use tended to accelerate the formation of clinker and disturb the fire.

I personally found that examining the fire by the shovel blade method was easy and effective, but obviously one had to pick the right time and place, since a prolonged look at a white-hot furnace left the eyes somewhat lacking when trying to sight the dim glimmer of a distant signal on a black and murky night. I also found that the advice regarding the excessive use of fire irons was basically sound, although they could admittedly be very useful at times, but again this was an acquired art.

While still on the subject of examining fires, it is interesting to note that the temperature can be gauged approximately from its appearance and colour. Red, orange and yellow flames indicate temperatures ranging from 1,000° to 2,000°F. At about 1,800°F the fire will be glowing a brilliant red, while the fierce white furnace glow under good working conditions indicated temperatures from 2,000° to 2,500°F.

As I have previously mentioned, a great emphasis was placed on instructing us in the operation and working principles of injectors. Dropping a fusible plug could be a very expensive business, and we were all made well aware of the consequences. Fusible plugs are lead plugs set into the firebox crown sheet. Should these become overheated due to a fall in the boiler level, they would melt, allowing steam to fill the firebox and smother the fire. However, the crown sheet might well be scorched and damaged in the process. Therefore it is understandable why the question 'Explain the working principle of an injector' was so often asked. The official answer was as follows.

A jet of steam emerging at high velocity from the steam cone is brought in contact with the cold feed water which is admitted around the tip of the steam cone. Partial condensation of the steam jet takes place, a partial vacuum is formed, and the water is drawn forward at considerable speed into the wide end of the converging combining cone.

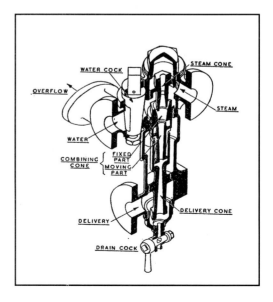

Cross-section of an injector, showing the arrangement of cones. The method of operation is as described in the text.

Passage through this cone completes condensation of the steam, producing a high vacuum, and the water emerges from the small end of the cone at greatly increased velocity. The water jet then jumps the overflow gap and enters a diverging cone known as the delivery cone. The shape of this cone causes the speed of the flow to be quickly and considerable reduced, which process converts the energy of motion in the water jet into pressure energy at the outlet end of the delivery cone.

The pressure developed in this way at the delivery end of the injector exceeds the boiler pressure sufficiently to enable the feed water to life the clack valve against steam pressure and enter the boiler. The vacuum developed in the combining cone when the injector is working is used to hold a moveable section of the cone up against the front portion, giving the effect of a continuous cone. If the action of the injector is interrupted, or the water jet upset, the vacuum in the cone is replaced by pressure, the moving section is forced away from its seating, and any surplus steam and water escapes through the gap so formed to the overflow jet. When pressure has been relieved, the working vacuum re-establishes itself and the injector will start again.

Needless to say, we were not expected to be word perfect in this description, but we were required to indicate the functions with the aid of a cut-away model. What is more to the point, we were encouraged to practise operating injectors as often as possible. This was a fairly straightforward procedure with an injector in good working order - merely a case of opening the water feed, opening the steam valve, closing the water regulator until steam blew back out of the overflow pipe, then opening the water regulator again the required amount, when a pleasant singing sound indicated that all was performing as it should. Unfortunately, not all injectors were in good condition and could be a constant source of anxiety to even the most experienced of crews.

Thus our training continued. We were taught basic rules, without which no railway system can operate successfully, and particular emphasis was placed on the important Rule 55 concerning the detention of trains on running lines. The Rule Book is a very complex piece of reading, and much went over our heads, but we were advised to read and re-read it and mark all rules applying to enginemen. It was expected of course that we would absorb these more readily when actually carrying them out on the road under direct instruction from our drivers.

Eventually our period of training came to an end and the happy day arrived, 12 weeks after joining British Railways, when, with some trepidation, we presented ourselves to Mr Welch for our Passing Out test. This consisted of oral questions on the basic workings of a locomotive, and some of the more important rules and regulations regarding enginemen. We were taken first to a Class '3F' in the shed and later to a Class '8F', and questioned on the names and functions of various parts of these engines. The examination was then conducted on the footplate where, individually, we were questioned on the controls. After this we were required to fire a few shovels of coal; it was considered adequate if you could get two out of three shovelsful through the firehole without letting go of the shovel. The most important part of the test was taken last - to operate both injectors. This accomplished, we joined our nervous colleagues to await the verdict. Most of us passed first time, so, full of elation, we were unleashed for better or for worse on the rest of Saltley.

3
BAPTISM

As Passed Cleaners, we were given a different works number and were required to book on and off with the rest of the enginemen. Since we were not yet matched with a regular driver and allocated to a link roster, the time of booking on and the job involved for the following day were obtained from the shed foreman's clerk on signing off.

My first firing turn began at the relatively civilised hour of 6.00 am, when I was assigned to the rather uninspiring job known as loco shunt. The requirements here were not very exacting, and were ideal for breaking in young Passed Cleaners. The whole operation was conducted in a quiet and leisurely way, which was just as well since the engine used was frequently fit for nothing else. This often took the form of the oldest Class '2F'; while it remained in the confines of the shed yard, all the parts that fell off during the day could be collected up and given to an apprentice fitter for re-assembly during the night; at least this was the conclusion I quickly arrived at. My mate, I found, was in a similar condition to the engine, being in the twilight of his railway career. He had, therefore, lost much of his boyish enthusiasm, but I none the less experienced the thrill of being asked to move the engine on my very first day.

Moving that old '2F' was also a leisurely operation. First one applied the steam brake. The control for this was a small brass wheel mounted centrally on the boiler face between the water gauges. It operated like a tap, clockwise to close, anti-clockwise to open - and it took a long time. However, a half-inch spanner was tied to the boss with a piece of twine and by flicking the spanner the wheel could be revolved at a fair speed; '2Fs' were fitted with this unofficial modification. As the brake valve was opened, a number of groans

and clunks from beneath the frames denoted that it had taken effect, thus enabling the tender hand-brake to be released. The reversing lever was pushed into the full forward position, and the brake valve closed. Loud hissings would result, and the cab filled with steam exhausted from the brake cylinder. This usually cleared from the cab in about the same time as it took for the brake blocks to release from the wheels, so that the regulator could then be opened.

The route from the regulator to the steam chest must have been more than somewhat complex, because for a time nothing happened. Eventually a hiss of gradually increasing volume announced its arrival at the other end, then after a heart-rending sigh the old girl would judder into motion and gently wheeze off, shrouded in its own little fog of steam. Nothing much to raise the blood pressure of an onlooker, but great stuff to me.

The duties of the shunt were varied, but they could be loosely described as moving anything that wanted moving. This might involve replacing a filled wagon with an empty one on the ashpit hopper or assembling coal wagons for feeding the coaling plant. The latter operation frequently caused great consternation, since it entailed actually moving off the shed limits and temporarily blocking traffic moving into and out of the depot. Even a dampish rail would cause loss of adhesion and I quickly developed the technique of walking alongside the engine sprinkling sand, clinker or ash on to the track with the firing shovel. However, it was all very instructive, and I soon became familiar with the various shed roads and the points controlling them. However, moving around the loco yard was always a strenuous occupation for a fireman as it meant haring along in front of the engine in order to pull the points over

Class '2F' 0-6-0 No 58230. In 1950 a few of these elderly '2Fs', whose lineage could be traced back to the 1870s, were still to be seen chuffing sedately around the area on local trip work. The one suffering most terminal complaints was allocated to the duty known as loco shunt. This was my first firing turn, and it proved to be a useful introduction to shed movements. My brother Bob, who was also a fireman at Saltley, is the left-hand figure on the footplate.

for the required direction, at the same time trying to keep one's feet on oil-soaked sleepers and avoid the numerous bric-a-brac and debris that always seemed to be lying around. As my week on the loco shunt drew to a close I realised that I had learned quite a lot more about shed routine, apart from gaining experience and confidence in actually firing and handling a locomotive, so I looked forward more eagerly to what the following week would bring.

It happened to be another shunting turn, but this time the real thing in Lawley Street marshalling yards, just across the main line from the depot. We booked on at 4.00 pm, so I enjoyed my first spell of operating an engine at night - much the same as operating in daylight except that you tend to rely more on touch than on sight. It was about this time that I became finally convinced that everything one touched on a locomotive was either very hot, very cold, very dirty or very rough. I therefore took to wearing leather gloves, and found them so satisfactory that I was never without a pair or two for the remainder of my firing career. The main advantage of protecting my hands was that I could instantly grab anything and operate or use it without fear of acquiring a first-degree burn. My days in the Time Office bore witness to the quite serious injuries inflicted on firemen's hands during the course of their normal work. After all, a hand flung out to save a stumble on a wildly oscillating footplate would leave another few square inches of skin sizzling away on the boiler front.

Preparing for the coming darkness at Lawley Street introduced me to the art of filling, trimming and cleaning the engine lighting equipment. To the layman these might appear incredibly primitive and a throw-back to the Victorian era, which of course they were. Nevertheless, one could argue that at least they were well tried, and suited to locomotives' requirements admirably. In any case, there was no alternative then available. Each engine was provided with two headlamps and a gauge glass lamp. The headlamps were really quite well designed, having an efficient inner draught shield with built-in reflector, a powerful bull's-eye lens and provision for conversion to a tail light by means of a red slide. The fuel for the lamps was paraffin, and if properly adjusted they would give a remarkably clear light for some 24 hours on one filling.

The gauge glass lamp on the other hand was a very simple rectangular box with a slit in one side. The designer had intended that this should be closed by a piece of heat-resistant glass, but very few lamps had these glasses, and even when you carried a spare, nine times out of ten it could not be fitted since the retaining frame was too battered and distorted. Generally speaking, then, they were not very reliable and prone to blow out if anything more than a breeze entered the cab. Running tender-first was therefore fatal to that diminutive glow, and an electric torch was resorted to. Because of the high operating temperatures obtained against the boiler front (the enginemen's term for the firebox backplate), rape oil had to be used, giving a duration of approximately 12 hours.

Shunting in Lawley Street could require some quite strenuous work from the locomotive, not to mention the crew, and for this we were provided with a Class '3F'. I soon discovered that these were a vast improvement in every way over the '2Fs'. They were of course somewhat larger, but the uplift in power seemed very much greater than the increase in size would appear to indicate, although this may have been in part an illusion caused by their crisp, raucous exhaust note. They were certainly much more comfortable. The boilers were higher-pitched, giving rise to a more spacious cab that afforded a considerably greater degree of protection from the elements. Later, when in the Bank Pilot link, I found that they could be made very cosy indeed with the aid of a tarpaulin or two. Large, wooden-topped boxes fitted on either side of the cab provided very adequate seats for both driver and fireman, and at the same time acted as storage lockers for the various impedimenta such as tools, oil cans, feeders, etc, that were normally carried. These boxes were of sufficient acreage to double up as beds when the opportunity presented itself to snatch 40 winks. The only drawback as far as the fireman was concerned was that the sight feed lubricator to the cylinders was located on the side of the cab above his head. If the drain plug was not a particularly good fit, a form of Chinese water torture could take place as hot emulsified oil dropped at regular intervals into one's eyes.

With a '3F', about 70 per cent of power would be developed on what drivers termed the first regulator. As the regulator was pushed across the quadrant, resistance was felt when the handle was in approximately the vertical position. Considerable effort - sometimes very considerable effort - was then required to move it right across to fully open. The final half of its travel was called the second regulator. Most shunting operations were generally accomplished by using the first regulator only. For one thing, performance was satisfactory, but the main deterrent to drivers who were relegated to shunting duties through lack of physical fitness, or who were anyway in their 60s, was the amount of extra muscle power that would be required.

Reversing, too, was a very speedy operation with a '3F', since they were equipped with a reversing lever rather than a screw; one mighty heave, or push, on this massive bar of steel was all that was required. During a busy shunting session the driver could be heaving, pushing or pulling something almost continuously for periods of up to an hour or so. It was little wonder that many were very pleased on these occasions to exchange places with the firemen who were, needless to say, only too happy to oblige.

Shunting usually came in bursts of intense activity followed by a period of rest. This, of course, was programmed to the arrival of incoming traffic, which seemed to present itself in bunches of three or four trains in quick succession. During these periods of work, quite a fair amount of steam was required, and this proved to be useful training in that it helped to improve my firing technique. I also had to make some attempt at cleaning the fire on this shift and, being my first introduction to this common chore, did so with some difficulty.

All locomotives carried three fire irons. These consisted of a shovel, either of the long or short variety, a rake, which likewise could be long or short, and a dart, which might be straight or bent into a curve so that the point could be at anything up to 90 degrees to the handle. On a '3F' it was usual to carry a short shovel, short rake and a bent dart, this combination proving most suitable for the locomotives' relatively short, steeply sloping grates.

In Lawley Street yard the specified place for cleaning fires was at the water column near the goods shed, and this was accomplished during a lull in the operations set aside for the purpose of replenishing the tank. Although considered stocky and well-muscled for my age, I was still far from the full development of manhood, and even though the fire irons were of the short variety, they seemed to me to weigh about a ton each. They were usually stowed on the back of the tender, so the technique was, having clambered topsides and put the bag - the leather hose attached to water columns - into the tank, that one scrambled forward over the coal, hauling the fire irons to a position easily reached from the footplate.

First, live fire was pushed away from the back corners of the firebox using the shovel or rake, so that it formed a sort of barrier under the brick arch. The clinker and ash thus exposed then had to be broken up and dislodged from the firebars. The bent dart was the implement for this job, being able to curl over the firehole mouthpiece and get right into the back corners. If the clinker was thick or hard, and it was often both, the work was really tough. Handling those heavy fire irons soon made my arms ache with such intensity that I thought the very sinews had been torn.

After breaking up and pushing the clinker forward, it then had to be ladled out of the firebox and thrown over the side of the footplate. The shovel was of course required for this, digging it in under the clinker using the coal barrier as a limit stop. Care had to be taken when withdrawing the shovel through the firehole, since any piece falling off would end up in precisely the same place whence it had originally come. I was very appreciative of my gloves at this stage. With iron being an excellent conductor of heat, the handle rapidly became nearly as hot as the blade, which was continually being dipped into glowing coals. Even so, I always supplemented the insulation provided by the gloves with a wiper folded up to form a thick pad of cloth.

Like the ship's cook at sea, it was advisable first to determine from which direction the wind, if any, was blowing. If not thrown out on the lee-side, a great cloud of hot, gritty ash would quickly arrive back on board again, only to settle on any sweaty exposed part of the crew. Having removed all the clinker from the rear half of the grate, live fire was then dragged back with the rake and the area under the brick arch attacked in a similar manner, the only difference being that generally less clinker formed here and it could be shovelled out without resorting to the dart. When thoroughly clean, the remaining live fire was spread over the grate area and fresh coal applied to build it up to a suitable working level. I was to endure this onerous task at regular intervals for the rest of my career. I suppose I became used to it - I certainly became better at it, but I must confess that I never at any stage grew to enjoy it.

With its relatively good fuel and water capacity, good visibility, adequately lively performance and crew comforts, the Class '3F' locomotives seemed as well suited to shunting as they were to the many other duties they were called upon to perform. They belonged to a small clan of locomotives that seemed to enjoy universal popularity amongst enginemen. The Stanier 'Black Five' and later, to some extent, the BR Class '9' were two others that spring to mind. I looked for a common denominator and found that primarily all were good steamers, their boilers being well capable of supplying all that was demanded from them. They also all rode well, were free-running, and their cabs were roomy or easy to work in.

My week at Lawley Street passed quickly by. Again I had learned a lot and wanted to know more. I could clean a fire, albeit somewhat slowly; I could generate enough steam for an hour's continuous shunting; I could clean and trim lamps; and what was more important, I had acquired a taste to see and hear a steam locomotive being worked hard.

The next fortnight brought a mixture of jobs, booking on at every odd hour round the clock. Fortunately none of them required a high degree of skill or stamina, and although I frequently pictured myself in a Walter Mitty-type situation performing heroic deeds on the main line, I was secretly grateful that this did not actually come to pass. After all, there was no joy in being the cause of a failure that might hold up scores of people and cost goodness knows what. Admittedly I was a little envious to learn of the exploits of some of my older and larger colleagues when chosen to stand in on some main-line duties, but every day I was acquiring fresh knowledge, seeing new places and gaining more skills.

As one old driver said to me, 'You'll get all the glamour you want later. Let the basic fundamentals sink in first - it takes a long time to become really good at this job.' He was right! While a fair bit of this mixture of jobs involved shed work, some of them did take me farther afield.

Leaving the loco yard and heading north along a sort of chasm between the two major parts of the gas works, one soon arrived at Saltley station, and a few hundred yards beyond this on both sides of the main line lay that great complex of sidings loosely known as Washwood Heath, divided into eight separate sections:

1 The up reception (Hill 60) leading into
2 Washwood Heath up sidings and through to Bromford,
3 Washwood Heath Junction up sidings,
4 Washwood Heath Junction down sidings,
5 Washwood Heath down arrival lines,
6 Washwood Heath old coal bank,
7 Washwood Heath down coal sidings, and
8 Washwood Heath goods sidings, better known as the West End.

Travelling north, the entrance to the up reception sidings was effected from the goods line under the shadow of the massive Washwood Heath gas holders, well-known landmarks on the Birmingham skyline. At the entrance the track divided into three roads, and you did not quite know which you would be directed along until the points were actually visible. Permissive block working was operated here, which meant that contact with the brake-van of the proceeding train could be made at any place, so extreme caution was necessary. These three roads were laid over what amounted to an elongated hump, halfway along which a gantry spanned the tracks carrying three stop signals and, under them, three calling-on signals. The hump dipped sharply at the far end, leading into the numerous sidings that ran right through to Bromford, the outlet for the north. The hump was colloquially known as Hill 60, after its notorious counterpart on the Western Front in the First World War.

My first contact with Hill 60 caused me some alarm. We had relieved a mixed freight from Worcester at Landor Street Junction (almost opposite the shed), which was hauled by a Class '3F'. Having rolled gently along the up goods line through the aforesaid chasm, past Saltley station, we were diverted on to Hill 60. I had not travelled so far before, so I was skipping from one side of the footplate to the other, all agog to see what new vistas of scenic wonder lay in store for me around each curve of the track. I was considerably surprised, therefore, to see all three roads blocked by trains and, finding that we were on the centre one, quickly calculated that we would be into the rear of that particular train in about 20 seconds. With rising panic, I rapidly drew my driver's attention to the fact for, although travelling at little more than a good walking pace, I had visions of soon being picked out of a heap of matchwood. His retort was a calm 'OK, mate, I've seen it'.

A few seconds later he closed the regulator and with barely a touch of the brakes, we eased gently up against the brake-van. I breathed a sigh of relief and sat down. This action provoked a frown from my driver, and his subsequent words contained a trace of annoyance.

'Carry on, then,' says he.

'Carry on what?' says I, frantically doing a mental scan of my training notes to think of something important I might have missed.

His voice broke in on my thoughts. 'Don't you know what to do? Never mind, son,' he said with gentle tolerance, 'I'll explain all about it. Just couple the brake-van to our engine, take the headlamp off the smokebox top bracket and put it on the tender, then come back here.'

I did as instructed and returned to the footplate, where my mate filled me in on this procedure. There were three arrival roads, and, if they were empty, trains were hauled through to the far end and halted at the shunter's cabin just before the tracks dipped sharply into the sidings. The locomotive was then uncoupled and set off to the shed or other duties as required. To save having an engine solely for the purpose of shunting this train, it remained on the arrival road until another train turned up behind it. The shunter then checked the destination labels, chalked a siding number on the front of the wagons and uncoupled them as appropriate. When he was ready, the calling-on signal was pulled off and the engine, having been attached as previously described, slowly pushed the original train over the hump, at the same time pulling its own train into position. The wagons trickled slowly at first, then with ever-increasing momentum into the dip, where a small horde of junior shunters and brakesmen leapt frantically hither and thither pulling points and dropping brakes, endeavouring to ensure that the right wagon entered the right siding at the right speed.

Sometimes the wagons moved over the top singly, when their motion could be easily checked, sometimes in twos or threes, and sometimes in great rafts of 20 or more! These fairly hurtled down into the sidings, and not even the most agile brakesman could do more than make a token gesture of dropping perhaps a single brake handle. So great was their momentum that they could run right through to the Bromford end if the road was empty; in later years I was to witness a number of these spectacular and dangerous instances.

More usually, though, they would finally come to rest against a train of wagons already standing on that particular road, when they would dissipate their energy in a most tremendous crash. At night these crashes and bangs could be heard for miles around - most irritating if you were standing in a nearby siding trying to get a spot of shut-eye. Needless to say, this method of shunting, while economical in motive power, was very heavy on the wagons and disastrous for their contents.

Wagons and vans could be seen with their end planking burst asunder by the violence of the impacts as their loads were transferred in the form of missiles to the next wagon in the train. A multitude of complaints arose from this form of vandalism, but the method persisted. Perhaps it was significant that the wagon repair shops were adjacent to these sidings, for they were certainly never short of business.

Now I knew all about the up sidings at Washwood Heath, that is except for one thing.

'Why did you get me to put the headlamp on the tender while we were still attached to the train?' I asked as we arrived at the shunter's cabin.

My driver smiled a benevolent smile. 'Merely to save your legs, my lad. You would only have had to do it now. As it is, we're all ready to go off to the shed.'

Economy of effort was always the byword of experienced enginemen.

Later that week I worked a local trip job as far as Water Orton, some 7 miles from Saltley and the farthest north of what can be considered the Birmingham area sidings network. This was the departure point of Saltley's premier jobs - the Carlisles! The crews for these crack long-distance express freights were treated with the reverence of royalty, and I watched with a mixed feeling of awe and envy as these beautifully turned-out 'Black Fives' blasted their way into the distance on their 226-mile run north. I never realised then that some eight years later I too would be receiving the red carpet treatment as one of the elite crews privileged to work the Carlisles and Glasgows. Nor did I realise that this would entail the hardest continuous physical effort I'd ever have to endure.

It must be admitted that I had enjoyed this fortnight's miscellany, particularly the local trip work that gave such a necessary insight into the workings of the area. It was therefore with some disappointment that I found I was booked to work the whole of the following week shunting at Water Orton, and, to make matters worse, I had to work not with a Saltley driver but one of three permanently stationed at Water Orton solely for this duty. Little did I know that this was to prove just about the happiest week I ever spent as a Passed Cleaner.

Water Orton sidings could be divided into four parts. The centre, with a capacity of 173 wagons, dealt mainly with traffic to and from Walsall,

Wolverhampton and points beyond. The marshalling sidings, capable of holding 918 wagons, had a long shunting spur at the west end. Here freight, both local and from the south and west, was sorted and assembled to form the northbound trains. The stowing sidings were unique in having flat rails (rails laid on their sides) and as the name implies were used only for this purpose. On the other side of the main line was a small siding known as 'Under the Wood'. Part belonged to the engineers' department, the rest being used to detach traffic destined for Walsall from through freight trains travelling south. The shunt was required to do all the sorting out that this busy marshalling yard demanded, and was therefore frequently called upon to perform a fair amount of very hard work.

In 1950 diesels had not infiltrated all the shunting turns, and although one would have suited the exacting requirements of this shunt admirably (single-manning, long duration and 24-hour availability), none had then been allocated. A ubiquitous Class '3F' therefore performed the function in its usual lively and raucous manner, being allowed a couple of hours off around mid-week to go back to the shed for stores and coal.

I was told to book on at 12.40 pm so that I could walk down to Saltley station and catch the 1.05 pm slow to Water Orton. For the first time since passing out, I felt lonely and somewhat worried as to how this week would work out. Also I had not been told by what means I was to return home after relief. However, I need not have concerned myself over this latter point. The system was simple. The signalman merely stopped a suitable passing freight long enough for me to hop on board and I then rode with it to within reasonable walking distance of the shed. With the goods line blocked with traffic, though, this reasonable walking distance could mean a 50-minute hike along the track from Bromford.

I duly arrived at Water Orton station and, after a few false starts, eventually located my engine, which was standing rather forlornly near to the shunter's cabin. She was No 3284, equipped with a 3,250-gallon Johnson tender without coal bulkhead. On these tenders a small partition about 3 feet high, on which the tool box was mounted, served to retain the coal. The number on the cab side was just discernible through the usual layer of dirt with which unfortunately most engines seemed to be ingrained in those days.

There was no sign of anyone about, so I clambered aboard, stowed my kit in the tender locker and did a quick check of boiler and fire. The water level was just out of sight in the top of the gauge glass and the fire, nicely thin under the arch, had a good body in the back corners and also looked relatively clean. The tender was well filled with coal of surprisingly good quality - so good, in fact, that I couldn't help feeling that someone had sneaked under the passenger end of the coaling hopper. I was, moreover, pleased to see that the footplate had been brushed and hosed down, indicating that the previous crew still had a pride in their job.

Feeling something like a member of the boarding party that discovered the *Marie Celeste*, I thought it would be prudent to see if I could find the missing crew. In later years experience taught me to look first in the nearest cabin, but on this particular occasion it took a few minutes before the logical deduction was arrived at. Once the penny had dropped, I trundled up to the cabin, knocked politely on the door and after a suitable pause, entered. I was greeted by looks of what can only be described as a mixture of blank amazement, anxiety and incredulity. It was, of course, usual for firemen to burst in unannounced. This knocking obviously had them rattled, thinking no doubt that they had been paid a surprise visit by the chief of the Operating Department. Mild annoyance quickly replaced their former expressions.

'Don't bloody well knock if you ever come here again,' growled a burly character who turned out to be Sam, the head shunter.

I apologised profusely and announced who I was. A lean, friendly chap in his mid-30s wearing enginemen's overalls immediately leaped up, made the brief statement that everything was OK, that in fact the old girl was quite a good 'un, that his mate was in the local with a pint already waiting for him, and that Joe (my driver) would no doubt be along in due course. He then departed hastily, heading in the general direction of the Dog & Duck, leaving me in sole charge. During my railway career I was to see many instances where, in order to expedite the job, rules - if not actually broken - were certainly severely bent. Only on the odd occasions when the various trade unions

thought it necessary to adhere strictly to the rules did operations come virtually to a standstill.

I eased out of the cabin with as much dignity as I could muster in the circumstances, and proceeded to conduct what I thought would be interpreted as a business-like inspection of our engine. Absorbed in this, I suddenly became aware that a rather high-pitched squeaky voice was addressing me.

'Are you my mate?'

I answered that if he was Joe, then I was indeed his mate.

'Is she all right?' said Joe, affably enough.

'I think so,' I replied. 'At any rate, the other fireman said she was.'

'Well, if Alan said so, that's good enough for me,' he squeaked. This statement was unusual coming from an engineman. Drivers tended to check everything for themselves where practical, no matter who had told them what. I therefore now regarded my mate closely for the first time.

Joe was of a very slight build that could only be described as generally bent. That is to say, his shoulders were hunched and his legs bowed, the combined effect of which reduced his height to about 5 ft 3 in. His face bore the marks of long exposure to the elements, and could be likened to that of a kindly walnut, for he looked much older than his actual 64 years. His demeanour was mild, gentle and considerate, and I couldn't help taking to him at once. This old chap, I thought, needs all the assistance I can give him. The first bit of help was not long in coming.

'We had better get aboard,' said Joe. He grasped the hand rails, laboriously hauled himself up to the second step and promptly stuck fast.

'Give me a bunk-up, mate. The rheumatism has got my knees again,' he panted.

I applied a shoulder to his rear end and projected him on to the footplate, wondering at the same time how he was going to cope with a hectic bout of shunting. Once on board, I opened the damper, turned on the blower and shot half a dozen shovels of coal down the front end of the firebox where the bars were now showing. Joe pulled out an ancient pocket watch and the myopic manner in which he studied this should have given me a clue as to the next brick-bat he was about to drop.

'We shall start shunting in ten minutes, so I wonder if you would mind clearing as much coal as you can from my side of the tender over to

Class '3F' 0-6-0 No 43284. At Water Orton during one memorable week with this locomotive, I learned the basic technique of driving a shunting engine while still only a Passed Cleaner. Four years later, in 1954, No 43284 was photographed on that very same duty, but shortly afterwards, as in other areas, diesels took over from steam. *Author*

yours. I can't lean out so easily with this rheumatism, and my eyes aren't what they were, so it helps if I can see over the top of the tender.'

This was, of course, a very sound practice which I often came across on the bank pilots and trip workings involving a fair amount of tender-first running. Vastly improved vision could be achieved by levelling the coal on the driver's side, and this was particularly effective on the low-built Johnson tenders. I had nearly completed this task when Sam, equipped with shunting pole, leaped on the bottom engine steps, thrust his head between the hand rails, and yelled in a powerful baritone, 'Right, Joe, let's get cracking.'

Everything about Sam seemed powerful. Although of only medium height, his chest measurements matched those of a gorilla. Massive arms led into even more massive shoulders, and the whole ensemble was emphasised by the somewhat comical long-sleeved waistcoat worn by shunters of that period. His dexterity was matched only by his boundless energy, and no one could work too hard or too fast for Sam. This man of action was without doubt the most skilful virtuoso of the shunting pole I ever had the privilege of working with, and as I watched Joe totter to his

feet and struggle with the reversing lever, I marvelled at how much the human body could vary.

We eased slowly back on to a long line of mixed vans and wagons, leaving a trail of steam spluttering from the open cylinder drain cocks. Sam coupled up at the instant the buffers touched, and scampered off down the train to check that all was well. In the meantime I took the opportunity to build up a good body of fire, since I wanted to see just how things were done in this particular yard. I soon discovered that practically all the shunting was accomplished from the driver's side, thereby relieving the fireman of that somewhat onerous duty of verbally translating the shunter's hand signals. This would have required constant vigilance achievable only by leaning half out of the cab and bellowing at the top of your voice such choice phrases as 'Hitemup!' or 'Whoa-up!'

Apart from ensuring that we had a good fire and keeping the boiler reasonably full, and with a Class '3F' neither of these requirements posed much difficulty, I thought that I was going to have a relatively easy time. However, it wasn't long before it became apparent that Joe was having difficulty in sighting Sam's signals. He called me over to his side of the footplate.

'Can you make out what Sam wants? I can't see him very well when he stands against a dark background,' said Joe, desperately wiping the moisture from his eyes.

I peeped over the side and was surprised to see Sam only some 150 yards away making frantic circular motions with his arm, indicating that he wished us to draw forward. Admittedly he was against a dark background, but he had a large piece of newspaper in his hand and I could clearly see that the expression on Sam's face was one of extreme exasperation.

Joe's eyesight was obviously worse than I thought, so for the next hour and a half I remained in station on that side of the footplate acting as his eyes and ears. I say ears as well, because Sam reinforced his hand signals with a bellow that could be clearly heard half a mile away. As we slammed the successive rakes of wagons backwards and forwards, I noticed that Joe's efforts became slower and more laboured. The old chap was visibly distressed; he could manage the regulator, which was quite free-moving on the first valve, without too much trouble, but the continual need to heave the heavy reversing lever to and fro was taking its toll.

Seeing him suffering thus, I was debating whether he would think it presumptuous of me to offer to take over when, during a brief lull in the operations, he suddenly gasped, 'Well, you've seen how it's done, mate. Would you like to have a go this side now?'

This was exactly what I had been itching to do for the past hour! Joe flopped on the fireman's seat, reaching for the tea can, and with as much control as I could muster I took up position on the driver's platform.

Sam was ready for us to draw ahead again, with a new train to be shunted. I would show 'em, I thought, flinging the reversing lever into forward gear with great gusto and pushing the regulator open in an equally sprightly manner. We puffed off in a lively fashion for a few yards when a terrific lurch sent me staggering and Joe's tea everywhere except the place he wanted it.

'Ease it open gently to start with, until you take up the slack in the couplings and feel the weight of the train,' Joe advised tolerantly. 'Then you can give it some stick.'

This was the first of many points I was soon to learn. We chugged forward gaining speed while I stared intently at Sam. Suddenly he flung up both arms. As quick as a flash I slammed shut the regulator and pushed the brake handle right across. Bang, bang, bang! A series of powerful buffets shot a couple of hundredweight of coal on to the footplate and more tea over Joe's overalls. Moreover, we ran well past the spot where Sam had wanted us to stop. I glanced anxiously at Joe.

'It's the same thing when you want to stop,' he said. 'Only the other way round. Give it a bit of brake to close up the couplings first, then when you feel the push of the train, give it the lot.'

It had all looked so easy when Joe was driving, but then an expert makes the most difficult things seem like child's play. I had a lot to learn yet, and the next lesson was soon forthcoming.

Sam's stentorian voice rent the air. 'Hitemup!' He was calling me back in his usual vigorous style. This time I eased the regulator open until I felt the wagons buffer up, then I gave it full first valve. We surged back in a grand spurt of acceleration. Sam deftly detached the couplings a few wagons from the end, then raised both arms into the air. I snatched the regulator shut and applied the brake almost in one movement - very slick, I thought. A violent pull again sent me reeling, while a loud crack and a cloud of brown dust drifted across the scene. To my horror I saw that we only had two wagons attached to the engine and the 30 or so that should have been there were trundling obediently after the six that Sam had detached. I had committed the cardinal sin of breaking the train.

Too late I realised that, as before, I should first have given a gentle check to stretch out the couplings, then, on feeling the pull of the train, rendered the final full application. Joe pointed this out, while Sam's only comment was, 'Just make sure that you don't break more than one shackle per wagon, otherwise I'll have nothing to hook on with.'

Having digested these basic shunting rules, I was gradually able to work faster and more effectively, and by the end of the shift both Joe and Sam seemed satisfied with my efforts. I did not break any more couplings and we were not getting thrown around the footplate. I was, therefore, feeling quite pleased with myself when I hitched a lift back to Saltley in the brake-van of a passing Class B freight. This was my first ride of any distance in the brake of a loose-coupled train; it was to prove very interesting and undoubtedly affected my approach to driving in the future.

The train was still stationary as I stumbled up the steps on to the rear verandah of the van. It was now quite dark and it took a little time before I managed to locate the position of the door and operate its unfamiliar handle. I groped my way inside the pitch black cavern, where nothing was to be seen but a small red glow indicating the position of the stove.

'Anyone at home?' I called. 'I'm the fireman off the shunt. Do you mind if I cadge a lift to the West End?'

'Not at all,' came the answer. 'Although you'll probably wish that you had picked someone else. It's Piggy Trotter driving.'

Here the voice paused, and I sensed that this name should have conveyed some significance to me, but, as it did not, I merely replied 'Oh'.

'You had better show the "bobby" a light,' said the voice, which turned out to belong to one Bill Bodkin, a goods guard of some seniority. 'Here, take my lamp, but hang on tight when we go.'

So saying, Bill pulled a hand lamp from where it had been wedged in a corner of the van and passed it to me. I leaned over the side and waved it in the general direction of the signal box. The signalman must have been looking out for this because almost instantly our signal was pulled off. I headed for the interior again and had just made the portal when the clank of tautening couplings could be heard rapidly approaching. I grasped the door frame, bearing in mind what Bill had advised, and the next moment found myself flying through the air to fetch up with an almighty crash, which knocked every bit of breath out of my body, against the back boards of the brake-van. We had instantly accelerated from a dead stand to 10 mph in about two yards! As I struggled to regain my feet, a violent bang shot me forwards this time, against the ashpan of the stove. Next came a series of minor tremors lasting about a minute, then quiet serenity reigned, broken only by the click, click of wheels over rail joints.

'Good grief,' I gasped. 'What happened?'

'That,' hissed Bill through clenched teeth, 'is Piggy's usual way of showing disapproval of being held up. Mind you, he's no more gentle at the best of times, so sit down and wedge yourself in like this.'

He again adopted a knees up, arms braced configuration. I did likewise.

'By the way, are you hurt at all?' said Bill. 'I'd offer you some tea, but you can't keep any in the can with this clown driving. Roughest twit that ever opened a regulator.'

That journey back to Washwood Heath was a real eye-opener, and showed me at first hand just what sort of treatment a thoughtless or unsympathetic driver could mete out to anyone travelling at the rear end of a loose-coupled train. Every check was accompanied by a series of buffets and surges, even slight changes in gradient giving a similar effect, while the starts were positively nerve-racking. One could not relax for a second, and I was very pleased indeed to escape from this torture chamber after only a few miles. How Bill and his colleagues stood it for 50 or more miles I will never know.

'Haven't you told him about it?' I asked Bill after a particularly powerful clout finally announced our arrival at the West End.

'Many times,' said Bill wearily.

'Well, hasn't it done any good?' I enquired, somewhat flabbergasted.

'On the contrary, it seems to make him worse. Why do you think he's nicknamed Piggy?'

We walked up towards the engine hoping to get a lift for the remaining half mile to the shed, but we were just in time to see the tender of a Class '4F', which was, incidentally, giving a pretty fair imitation of the up 'Midday Scot', disappearing under the road bridge archway.

'That's a nice friendly gesture,' I remarked with a trace of sarcasm.

'Ah, that's another of Percy's foibles - he doesn't like overtime. In fact, he tries to get finished before he starts,' said Bill laconically.

As I cycled home that night I vowed that if ever I came to drive trains I would concentrate on that very aspect of the technique. I did not know then that in time I would have a very much more intimate relationship with Percy 'Piggy' Trotter.

The following day I just could not get back to work at Water Orton soon enough. I had thoroughly digested the previous day's experiences, going over my mistakes again and again until I had at least mentally eradicated them. Joe had also intimated that for the rest of the week he would be quite happy to let me do the driving.

Now, it is one of the ironies of life that, when you desire time to pass quickly it just digs in its heels, so that seconds seem like minutes and minutes seem like hours. Ever since I had hopped out of bed that morning time had been behaving in this exasperating manner. Furthermore, the 1.05 pm slow was 15 minutes late at Saltley because its path had been used by a freight or two, and the 15 had become 20 by the time I disembarked at Water Orton.

With my feet barely touching the ground I legged it across to the centre, worried in case for some reason my engine would not be there. As it happened it was in exactly the same place as yesterday, but as I drew near I noticed that both Sam and Alan, the other foreman, were standing outside the cabin wearing anxious expressions.

'What ho?' I called when within earshot. 'Anything wrong?'

Alan spoke first. Joe hasn't turned up yet, and we were wondering what had become of you. I was just preparing myself for another 8 hours. Still, everything's OK, so I'm off. See you tomorrow.'

For a moment we watched Alan depart, then Sam turned to me.

'Well, as you can see we've got a full yard - are you ready to start? I reckon you'll be all right by yourself today.'

Pleased by this compliment, I replied, 'Just give me a minute to get some fire on, then we'll get stuck in.'

After a bout of hectic shovelling and a quick check around, I announced that I was ready to commence.

'Right, back up then,' called Sam, yanking over a couple of point levers. Steam brake on, wind the hand brake off, small ejector open, lever into back gear, steam brake off, regulator open! We chuffed backwards, leaving the cylinder drain cocks (known as the 'taps' to enginemen) open so as to clear any residual condensation from the cylinders. Without Joe on the footplate I felt remarkably at ease. Yesterday's training had certainly given me confidence and I was at that moment sublimely happy. It all seemed so natural that I might have been doing it for years and, although I admittedly needed the polish that can only be acquired through long practice, I had at least grasped the basic essentials. Clunk! With a deft wrist movement Sam hooked on.

'We've got a big one first,' he yelled. 'So you'll have to draw well forward - off you go then!'

I pushed the reversing lever into full forward gear, closed the taps, and eased open the regulator. Leaning well out, I could see each wagon gently rock into motion as the couplings tautened. I was also now sensitive enough to feel successive little checks as the weight of every individual wagon added its bulk to the strain, and I had to inch the regulator farther open to counteract this steadily increasing load. A faint wiggle from the last wagon was sufficient indication for me to pounce on the regulator and to thrust it on to full first valve. As that beautifully crisp blast rent the warm, still air, I was surprised to find how far I had already opened the regulator getting the train under way.

This was a heavy one indeed and called for sterner stuff than just full first valve. So far I had not worked the engine beyond this position. There had really been no need, but now, with something of an excuse, I pushed it right across! Very little difference could be detected initially, and I kept my hands on the regulator handle poised to slam it shut should she slip, but the old girl was very sure-footed and the rail was dry. Suddenly she seemed to get the bit between her teeth, the blast sharpened and it became obvious that we were accelerating this great load very vigorously indeed. I quickly kicked the firehole doors shut with the idea that this powerful blast would liven the fire up somewhat. It certainly did, for a towering column of black smoke rocketed skywards. Doubtless Mr Welch would have had something to say about that, but what the hell - if we sounded impressive, then we might as well look impressive too. . .

No other form of locomotion is as demonstratively powerful as a steam engine at full chat, and I was so enthralled at this spectacle that I almost forgot Sam. Looking back along the train I was just in time to see him throw up his arms. So, regulator shut, a touch of brake to close up the train, then full brake. There was an almighty surge as the weight came into us, but none of the crashing and banging of yesterday's shock tactics. Too late I realised that if you used second regulator you needed to shut off just that much sooner to stop at the required spot. Sam detached and called me back. If this 'right across' method gave more power to your elbow, I might as well use it as often as possible, I thought. Over went the regulator and we charged back in a veritable welter of sparks, smoke and noise. This time I anticipated Sam by a few wagon lengths and already had the brake on by the time he signalled me to stop. This was the secret then - anticipation!

As we pelted into rake after rake of wagons, I

gradually developed the technique, so that I was able to halt in just about the right place for Sam every time, and the minutes this saved added up to a sizeable amount by the end of the shift. I must admit that I was more than ready for a break when, after a couple of hours, Sam stopped me outside the cabin. Our mutual enthusiasm was undoubtedly infectious, for everyone had worked like blazes. Full regulator work had called for more firing than usual, and every brief pause found me with the shovel in my hands, apart from frequent use of the injector.

'Come and get a cup of tea,' called Sam. 'I reckon we've earned it.'

As I clambered down from the footplate, he addressed me in a quiet tone.

'Do you know, that's the fastest piece of shunting I've done in many a long day. These old fellows won't let 'em rip like that. Well done, kid!'

This compliment from a man who normally did not go out of his way to say much pleased me no end, and made me more than ever determined to work at maximum effort when conditions would allow.

Joe, who had been watching our performance from the cabin, had not really had the opportunity to join me during this frenzied spell. After the welcome tea, though, he took up station on the fireman's side.

'We've got to run down to the north end to pick up wagons now, but take it easy - the track's in a rare old state down there. Bill Wilson had her off the road all wheels last week!'

This procedure of running down to the north end was usually necessary at least twice a shift and was accomplished by using the empty outside siding - for me, a completely new experience.

To say that the track was in a rare old state was an understatement. The ballast had long since disappeared from under the sleepers, no two sections of rail were in the same plane, and with broken chairs and missing keys thrown in for good measure, the general condition was alarming. Fortunately travelling tender-first this was not too apparent. With an open stretch of track in front of me I gave way to a sudden impulse and notched her up to one out of mid-gear and opened up the regulator.

With a '3F', two types of gear quadrants were to be found. In one, an evenly spaced number of notches gave a progressive shortening of cut-off as the lever was moved towards mid-gear. The second and more common type had only three notches corresponding to approximately 50 per cent, 35 per cent and 20 per cent. Shortening the cut-off was easy enough when the regulator was only slightly open, but when on full first valve or more, with pressure high in the steam chest, even Hercules would have been a bit pushed to haul it into the desired position. No 3284 had the latter type and Joe, looking out of the fireman's side, did not notice my action, nor did he hear the clatter of valve gear that accompanied the notching up act until steam pressure in the chest built up again. Therefore, with just a sizzle of steam from the chimney we started to fairly gallop along, heaving and pitching uncomfortably. Joe stood this treatment until, with no more than half the complement of wheels in contact with the track at any one time, he turned towards me.

'Slow down, slow down,' he shouted, clinging desperately to the hand rail with one hand and the injector steam valve with the other. Even Sam, a confirmed speed enthusiast, was on the point of baling out from his position on the tender steps. Joe thoroughly ticked me off for this display of exuberance, and when we arrived at the north end took me down from the footplate to inspect the track. I immediately conceded that he had certainly good cause for anxiety, and our future travels along siding No 18 were at much more moderate speeds.

As the week progressed, so did my dexterity in handling an engine. I was able to achieve a delicacy of control with a loose-coupled train that stood me in good stead for my future driving activities, and which caused a certain amount of controversy with a particular driver I was to be booked with some years in the future.

Meanwhile, Joe seemed to spend more and more time in the cabin, only coming out to act as a deterrent to my record-breaking inclinations along siding No 18. This pleased us all, since apart from giving the old fellow a much easier time, I felt unfettered and more free to expand my boisterous technique. We were all slightly sad when I bade farewell for the last time at the end of the week. I had made many new friends at Water Orton, spent more hours at the regulator than I could ever have dreamed possible at this early stage in my career, and had developed a much better appreciation of the complicated chain of events that starts with a shovel of coal and ends when the last vehicle of a train jerks into motion.

4
NUNEATON PICK-UP

After that glorious week I was next required to book on at 6.00 am as a spare fireman. It was fairly common practice to ensure that a number of spare men were available at this time of the morning to cover for such contingencies as over-sleeping, sickness, specials and extra relief work. The more important jobs were of course allocated to the more senior firemen, so junior Passed Cleaners like myself were left with the dregs.

On the Thursday I was delighted to discover that the regular fireman of the Nuneaton pick-up had not arrived and I had to take his place. I was briefly introduced to my driver, a round, wobbly chap whose girth exceeded his height by quite a few inches and who, contrary to popular belief, was not at all a happy bundle of fun. Jack (for this was his name) looked at me with the expression of a gourmet who has just discovered something unpleasant crawling out of his favourite salad. He disliked junior firemen in general and Passed Cleaners in particular. This arose from the fact that as a fireman he had not been one of Saltley's brightest stars and, coupled with a pathological dislike for physical work, felt that should the fire-

man prove inadequate he would be unable or unwilling to put matters right.

'How long have you been out?' he demanded impolitely.

'Five weeks and four days,' I answered proudly.

'Good God,' he exclaimed, turning to the foreman's assistant. 'I'm not taking him, he's only a bloody kid.'

This left me absolutely stunned and not a little hurt. An argument flared up, ending only when the foreman's assistant told him that if he didn't take me, the job would have to be cancelled and the only alternative was shed duties. Jack grasped me firmly by the arm and hauled me through the lobby doorway to the engine board.

'That's our engine, 3435, and it's over there,' he said, indicating a '3F' just discernible in the gloom on the other side of the shed. 'Do you know how to prepare her?'

'Yes, I think so,' I replied, feeling about half the size I had a few minutes earlier.

Jack clicked his tongue impatiently. 'Make sure the sandboxes are full. We'll need them up the bank, and get me a good seat.'

The seat he referred to would be a plank or board of suitable size to serve as a substitute for the original locker lid. It was an unsolved mystery as to where these seats went, but they invariably disappeared almost as soon as an engine arrived

Class '3F' 0-6-0s were very tolerant of poor fuel and novice firemen, as I found on my first Road turn with No 43435 to Nuneaton. Despite problems of my own making, she saw me through on the 6-mile drag from Whitacre to Arley Tunnel. Because '3Fs' were relatively easy to operate and displayed no real vices, they were preferred to '4Fs' by many crews. Perhaps their most endearing feature, though, was a boiler that could easily produce all the steam the driver needed.

from shops. This 'disease' afflicted only Class '3F' and '4F' 0-6-0s and Class '2P', '3P' and '4P' 4-4-0s, all others being apparently immune. Rumour had it that steam-raisers used them for firelighting activities, but my own theory was that one of the shed staff manufactured rabbit hutches or the like as a sideline.

As we approached our engine, we met a Passed Cleaner friend of mine carrying a bucket of tools to the stores. This was a stroke of luck, since at that time of a morning tools were normally scarce. They had just disposed of an engine and had stabled it close to ours, so I quickly relieved him of the bucket and shovel and dashed over to strip it of the equipment I required; two headlamps, a gauge glass lamp, coal pick and the all-important seats.

Our engine was in a filthy state, with great clouds of 'green' smoke rolling lazily out of both chimney and cab. Holding my breath, I clambered on to the footplate, knocked the blower on and when the smoke had cleared somewhat took stock of the situation. Black smuts covered everything, of course, and I had to wipe both the pressure gauge and water gauge glasses before I could discern that we had 50 lbs per sq in on the former and that the water was out of sight in the top nut of the latter. I opened the firehole doors, which were of the old Midland pattern, ie a plate covering three-quarters of the firehole area, hinged at the bottom and secured when in position by a latch and chain; the upper quarter was closed by an adjustable flap hinged from the top.

I was relieved to see that quite a reasonable deflector plate was in position and the brick arch looked sound. A great solid mound of mainly unburned coal was heaped in the back corners of the firebox, so I decided that I had better spread this around first in view of the low steam pressure. I therefore required the rake, which was residing, together with a dart and clinker shovel, in their usual place on the back of the tender. As I scrambled over the coal, I noticed in the dim light that it consisted almost entirely of ovoids, briquettes and slack. It was not the type of fuel that exactly boosts confidence, but I was now aware of the steaming properties of '3Fs' and was therefore not too dismayed.

While on top of the tender, I ran through the normal drill of making sure that everything was secure and that no lumps of coal were likely to fall

off and injure any innocent bystander who might happen to be around as we moved off the shed. With rake in hand, I descended to the footplate and started spreading the fire over the whole area of the grate. In later years I never moved off the shed without checking to see if there was any clinker in the back of the firebox, since on many occasions I've had to do a quick cleaning job before departing. Very often the first indication that you had set out on a journey with a dirty fire was when the driver started to demand steam in quantity, and then it was too late to do much about it.

With the bottom flap of the firedoor closed, I left the fire to burn up and, armed with a seven-eighths spanner, climbed round the cab on to the framing. From here I was able to lift off the sand-box covers to check their contents before tightening the lugs on the smokebox door. After disposal it was common practice to leave only two lugs fastened, the remainder being the responsibility of the preparation crew. However, it was amazing the number of occasions that engines left the shed with insecure smokebox doors, and this oversight, needless to say, did not exactly enhance steaming properties. Fortunately the sandboxes only needed one bucketful each to top them up.

At Saltley, dried sand was to be found in ovens located in No 2 shed and adjacent to No 3 shed, so, depending on where your engine was stabled, a walk of only a few yards or as much as 50 was required to obtain sand. This was one of the most onerous tasks involved in preparation, since the sand was carried in what were termed buckets - similar in appearance to wide-necked watering cans and when full weighing about 60 lbs each. Half a dozen trips with a bucket in each hand resulted in a definite speeding up of the circulation, and arms feeling about 3 inches longer than when you started the exercise. The unwritten rule was that these buckets should be left on one end of the turntable where they could be seen by all, but human nature being what it is meant that not everyone complied, and much time was lost hunting around for them in the semi-darkness.

A series of grunts and much laboured breathing from under the engine indicated that Jack was trying to prise his oversized midriff into that inadequate space between firebox and big ends in order to attempt the oiling of the latter. Meanwhile I decided to do a spot of oiling on my own account, and turned my attention to the sight feed lubricator that served the cylinders. Jack had already left the bottle of thick black oil warming on the drip tray over the firedoor, so I only had to open the lower drain cock to run off the residual water and top up with oil through the filler plug. This was one of the first things my driver had shown me on the Lawley Street shunt, since, as he quite rightly pointed out, extra friction at the front end meant extra coal on the fire. It was, therefore, very much in the fireman's own interest to see that this little friend was kept filled and working properly.

The needle was beginning to move on the pressure gauge as the fire brightened under the influence of the blower and I now bent to the task of clearing up the layer of ovoids and slack that lay strewn over the footplate. There was still insufficient pressure to test the injectors properly, so I took the opportunity to sweep off the residual smokebox char from the framing. Quite early on in my career I developed a distinct dislike of having an eyeful of char every time I happened to look round the side of the cab, so I became very fastidious over this matter, even to the point of checking whenever possible engines I relieved on the road. Also, from the company's view, this practice was to be commended since this effective abrasive blowing into the motion did it a power of no good.

I had travelled down the starboard side of the framing, round the smokebox, and was heading for home along the port side when I came up against Jack's generous posterior protruding from under the boiler. It was quite obvious that his general topography was all wrong for this sort of work. He withdrew and, through the grease and sweat that smeared his face, I perceived that he regarded me now with a somewhat milder eye.

'You're a bit slimmer than me, kid,' he panted. 'See if you can oil the inner slide bar cups.'

I obliged with alacrity, only too pleased to show him that I was not quite as useless as he thought. Perhaps I'd given him a quizzical look prior to squeezing under the boiler, because he added by way of an explanation, 'My mate usually does the oiling.' That remark did not surprise me in the least, and I thought that this was probably another good reason why he didn't like strange firemen.

'If you are ready, I'll get the table,' he said in a tone that lacked the former aggression.

'Well, I haven't tested the injectors yet!' I answered.

'Never mind about those,' he shouted, walking over to the table. 'There's too much water in the boiler as it is. We can do that out in the yard.'

Having filled the last cup, I slithered to the floor and joined Jack on the table as he released the second of the two locking catches.

'These apologies for steam raisers, fill 'em up to the whistle, and then we have the responsibility of trying to stop 'em when they're priming,' he grumbled irritably.

Jack was of course referring to the condition of priming, the phenomenon when water is carried over into the cylinders via the regulator and main steam pipe. Apart from the possibility of knocking the ends out of the cylinders, since water is incompressible, the alarming spectacle of an engine charging away after the regulator had been closed usually resulted. Coupled with a cold brake and lowish steam pressure, even quite experienced drivers have effected a number of speedy demolition jobs on shed walls over the years.

With the table in position, Jack returned to the engine while I stood well clear at the end of the pit. Streams of water and steam spluttered from the taps as Jack eased open the regulator. Wumph! A muffled beat indicated just what was in the cylinders, then a veritable torrent of dirty water mushroomed out of the chimney, collected the surface layer of soot from the shed roof and descended on the immediate neighbourhood. I instinctively looked down as the deluge swept over me, and No 3435 shuddered forward on to the table to stop just about on the point of balance.

On the tables in Nos 1 and 2 sheds, it was important to position a locomotive so that the weight was evenly distributed over the centre pivot, otherwise hand cranking could be very strenuous indeed; No 3 shed's table, being more modern, was not so critical in this respect. Since we had to turn our engine through nearly 180 degrees so that it was pointing to the north, I coupled up the engine vacuum pipe to the table tractor motor, hoping that we could create sufficient inches of mercury for it to function adequately.

'Blow up,' I yelled at the top of my voice, and Jack tugged open the large ejector. More dirty water headed skyward, but when I pulled the control lever the motor settled to its distinctive chug, chug, chug and whine of straight-cut gears which always reminded me of a No 36 tramcar.

With the turning operation completed, I placed the headlamps in the light engine position, walked through the shed entrance, set the points for the departure road, and called Jack out. He did this cautiously, since the boiler was still very full; meanwhile I trotted ahead, setting the points in the yard and keeping a good lookout for other engine movements.

We needed to fill the tank so I stationed myself at the water column on one of the departure roads. Jack rolled gently up and stopped at exactly the right spot. When first passed out, I wondered how drivers always managed to be so accurate when halting engines at water columns without apparently looking back at the tender. This became abundantly clear when it was explained to me that at every column a marker, such as a lamp standard or the like, was selected. Some part of the locomotive cab was lined up with this marker, then it was only a case of remembering which part of each particular class of engine lined up with the marker. It sounds simple, but when you think of all the different types of engines then in service, plus all the columns one might visit, the number of permutations is quite staggering. No wonder enginemen never stopped learning.

Hopping on top of the tender, I pulled the column arm round by means of the chain provided and wrestled the stiff leather hose into the tank filler hole. 'OK, Jack,' I shouted, when satisfied that it was in position without any kinks. I had previously experienced having an unintentional shower, if shower is the right word when one receives 30 gallons of cold water travelling at high velocity square in the chest, because a bag had been hastily and incorrectly inserted.

'If you are all right,' called Jack when the water was running well, 'I'll go and mash the tea and ring out.'

I nodded my assent, being now capable of turning off the water and removing the bag from the tank. With him out of the way I could test the injectors and complete my cleaning down operations on the footplate. In addition to removing smokebox char from the framing I had also acquired a taste for having a clean and tidy cab, a task that was admittedly motivated in part by pride, but it developed into almost an obsession in later years and I became well known for this idiosyncrasy.

Nearly all engines were provided with a slaking

Putting the bag in, a regular chore to be undertaken anywhere at any time. Precise alignment was necessary, and crews had to learn the exact stopping point at every water column used. The slender pipe in the foreground is not part of the column, but the chimney of its attendant frost fire.

pipe. This was a flexible hose coupled via a valve to the fireman's injector and, depending on the setting of that injector, was capable of delivering either cool water at moderate pressure or an extremely powerful jet of scalding hot water and steam. This device was most suitable for disposing of every bit of dirt and dust from the footplate and quickly brought the footboards up to a very presentable scrubbed appearance.

With the tank filled and the housework completed, I awaited Jack's return. It was most important for us to 'ring out' at our prescribed time. If we did not, then any subsequent delays would be booked to the motive power department. Providing the controller at Duddeston Road signal box was advised that we were ready to depart on time, any delay occurring after this would be booked to traffic and would not be our fault.

As it happened, Jack was back at the checker's hut with some 5 minutes to spare, and within

Coal spillage on the footplate gave rise to dirty, uncomfortable and even dangerous conditions. However, a few moments with brush and slaking pipe soon restored that 'scrubbed deck' look.

moments of regaining our engine with the all-important can of tea, the signal was pulled off allowing our departure. We chuffed gently over Duddeston Road bridge, across the main lines and on to the up goods, to proceed at a leisurely pace to Bromford sidings where our train of empty hopper wagons was waiting. The shunter was ready for us and pulled over the appropriate points before calling us back on to our train. Our guard appeared a few moments later, coupled up, announced that we had 32 wagons, and if we were fit he would advise the Inspector.

'I just want to check the sanders,' said Jack, 'but we'll be OK by the time you've rung out.'

So saying, he climbed down from the footplate armed with a piece of wire and the coal pick. I already knew the drill. First the small cork in the base of the sand box was removed to see if the sand ran out freely. If not, the wire would be inserted and poked around to loosen any clogging obstruction. The cork would be replaced, and the sand valve in the cab operated. With a bit of luck, sand would then be blown in a steady stream directly between rail and wheels. Should the flow not be up to standard, a couple of sharp blows with the coal pick in the area of the sand trap at the top of the delivery pipe would generally suffice to do the trick. It was, of course, most important to ensure that the sanders on both sides of the engine worked simultaneously, for if only one side functioned, there would be a grave risk of broken coupling rods and crank pins. Jack quickly completed this task since none of the boxes caused any major problems. His main concern was that it was

one of those damp days with periods of intermittent drizzle - not a decent downpour that would wash the rails clean, but just enough moisture to mix with the dust collected over the preceding dry spell to form a slippery paste which certainly did not make for good adhesion. In the past he had rolled his train back through some trap points on an incline and did not wish to repeat this embarrassing experience ever again.

'Set your lamps at Class B,' he said on regaining the footplate. 'That is, one on the top of the smokebox and one on the centre of the buffer beam.'

I did as instructed and returned to the cab with a tingle of excitement. This was my first real road job and I wondered how I was going to make out. Jack's earlier attitude had done much to destroy what confidence I had in myself, but now it was gradually building up again.

A shrill whistle focused our attention in the direction of the shunter's cabin, where our guard was now calling us with an emphatic gesture. This was it then, I thought, as I sprang to release the hand brake, realising that the waiting was now over. Jack eased open the regulator while I quickly closed the firehole doors, turned up the blower and fully opened the damper. I was now familiar with the road and knew that I would not be overtaxed on the slightly falling gradient as far as Water Orton, but after that I had no idea what to expect, except that there was a goodish bank up to Nuneaton.

'Make sure that we've got the guard,' called Jack, who now seemed to be getting edgy again. Leaning well out, I watched our 32 wagons slowly snake from the sidings, over the crossovers and out of the yard. Yes, there was the brake-van, but no sign of the guard. I wondered where the devil he was. A dark shape suddenly appeared on the verandah as the brake passed the shunters' cabin - he must have waited for it there. A long arm holding a piece of white paper protruded from the side of the van and began slowly waving up and down. I in turn gave a quick flap or two with my wiper, a pop on the whistle and Jack the news that he was safely on board.

As we chugged easily along the up goods still in full gear and with partially opened regulator, Jack turned to me and shouted, 'You'd better get some more fire on! They usually turn us out on the main line at Castle Bromwich.'

I bent to the task, and had the uneasy feeling that he was closely watching every move I made. To create the right impression, I thought that I would try a bit of fancy stuff and bounce the shovel off the firehole mouthpiece. This is the normal technique for feeding the front end of a firebox with the minimum of effort, but not really necessary on the short firebox of a '3F'. I had started to get the hang of it on previous firing turns, but on this occasion Jack's intense scrutiny had put me off my stroke somewhat. What commenced as a smart deflection to the front right corner of the box terminated with the shovel squarely striking the edge of the firehole and depositing 10 pounds of slack and ovoids round Jack's ankles. This did nothing to improve his temper or my ego.

'Never mind the front. Get a good back on,' he grumbled irritably, shaking the slack out of his turn-ups.

I immediately dumped half a dozen shovels of bricquettes and ovoids in the back corners and under the door, flipped up the bottom flap, partially closed the top one, and turned my attention to the pressure gauge. It had dropped back to 160 lbs per sq in, but now a rich black column of smoke was billowing out of the chimney, so I felt that soon the needle would reverse its backward movement. In those days I was a little uncertain how much secondary air to allow through the firedoors, and tended in consequence to err on the side of too little rather than too much. Drivers also seemed to favour this method, based no doubt on the old philosophy that where there's smoke, there's fire. As long as they could see smoke coming from the chimney, then they could relax, happy in the knowledge that at least their mate had not let the fire go out, no matter what sort of mess he was making of the rest of his duties.

'You'll have to do better than that up the bank,' was Jack's next scathing comment. 'We're going downhill here!'

My confidence began to drain out through my boots again. The boiler level was showing about two-thirds of a glass, so I turned on my injector.

'Don't put it on now. Wait until I shut off.'

Half a minute later he closed the regulator, and I repeated the operation, at the same time dropping the bottom firedoor to eliminate some of the smoke that had been rolling in dense volumes from our chimney. I couldn't make up my mind whether Jack was trying to be awkward or trying to be helpful, but I did feel I was being robbed of all initiative and not giving of my best. As we moved gently up to the starter signal at Castle Bromwich, an express passenger hauled by a 'Black Five' flashed past.

'You'd better put some more on now,' he said, this time in a more moderate tone, since by now the pressure gauge needle was on the red line and the boiler had recovered to a full glass.

I spread another ten shovelsful around the box, concentrating as before on building up the back to the acknowledged classical slope, and had just completed this when we heard the points clank over and could see that we would indeed be turned out on to the main line. Injector off, bottom flap up, release the hand brake, and there we were all ready to go as the signal was pulled off. A few gentle puffs sufficed to tauten the couplings and then, as he felt the weight of the train, Jack jerked open the regulator. No 3435 gave a little half slip then surged forward with a healthy bark cracking back at us from the chimney.

'Wow!' I thought as I watched the train curving out over the points. I'm working on the main line at last! We could not, of course, dawdle here and as we accelerated to about 20 mph on the slightly falling gradient of 1 in 955, Jack suddenly almost closed the regulator and heaved the reversing lever back to the first notch on the three-notch rack. He then quickly opened up the regulator to the full first valve position and the exhaust settled down to that crisp but slightly irregular beat that Class '3Fs' give when working on a shortened cut-off. I glanced in the firebox and was glad to see that it was beginning to take on that white furnace glow. The smoke had now thinned to a light grey and the needle had not left the red line. As our speed increased, I was also happy to find that I had no difficulty in keeping my balance, but then of course Class '3s' always did ride well, so I relaxed for a few moments to enjoy the now familiar scenery rolling past, even though it was shrouded in mist and drizzle.

Our quick burst of effort was soon over, for the Water Orton Junction distant signal was against us, causing Jack to close the regulator, drop her into full gear and start checking our speed. I put my injector on and joined Jack on his side of the footplate so as to be in a better position to sight the home signal over that long sweeping right-hand curve. We saw it come off just before it was obscured by the smoke and steam from a fast approaching fitted on the down main. This must have been the cause of our check, since it had no doubt travelled over the fast at the station junction and had consequently crossed our intended path.

We were still rolling at a reasonable rate and Jack allowed us to continue coasting steadily towards the station junction where we would divert to the right along what was known as the slow. This is a loop some 3 miles in length via Coleshill and Whitacre, which rejoins the fast again at Kingsbury Station Junction. Two miles from Water Orton along the slow the track again diverts to the right at Whitacre Junction, whence it proceeds through Nuneaton, Hinckley and on to Leicester.

The distant for the station junction indicated that we now had a clear path, and as the facing points hove into view I wondered what sort of reaction we would feel crossing over them. I stayed on Jack's side of the cab in case there was an audience on the platform, but in this respect I was to be disappointed. The only animate object in sight was Ginger the station cat, who was huddled on one of the platform seats wearing a rather forlorn and somewhat pained expression on his normally handsome features. The weather had no doubt discouraged his lucrative hunting activities that morning, and a saucer of milk was poor compensation for a fat young rabbit.

We clattered through the station and under the road bridge, the points causing only a very slight lurch, then I suddenly realised as we headed for Coleshill that I had not the faintest idea what lay ahead. I noticed a gradient board showing that we were still going downhill at 1 in 346, but I thought it prudent to consult Jack.

'What's it like from now on?' I shouted in his ear.

'We won't use much steam until Whitacre Junction,' he replied. 'But after that we shall be on the collar all the way up to just this side of Arley Tunnel, about 6 miles. What's more,' he said, grimacing as if recalling past unpleasant experiences, 'the steepest part is the last 2 miles. You've got about 2 miles to Whitacre, so fill the box up!'

The safety valves were just lifting, so it was a good opportunity to build up a really big fire. The fresh coal would cool the box down for a while, preventing wastage of steam and obviating the possibility of over-filling the boiler by excessive use of the injectors. As I spread more fuel on the only partially burned mass already in the firebox, I did not realise that I was building myself a whole heap of trouble. One can get away with charging a firebox if one has good-quality coal such as South Kirkby Yorkshire hard. Nicely broken and properly applied, it will eventually burn through and give a glorious fire providing no excessive demands are made on the boiler during the initial stages. However, with a mixture of briquettes, ovoids and slack, heavy firing merely blocks all air spaces, causing the fire to become dead; and the fuel sets into a spongy mass that only an energetic attack with the fire irons can break up.

By the time we arrived at Whitacre Junction, I had all the makings of such a mass in the box, and the only silver lining to this particular black cloud was that it was lying on the top of a substantial amount of well-burned-through fire. Signal checks had slowed us to about 10 mph on passing over the junction, but as soon as we had cleared it Jack brought the gear lever back to the first notch and opened up the regulator to full first valve. Once again that distinctive raucous blast crashed out across the countryside as we started to tackle the 1 in 146 towards Shustoke and up to Arley, the location of the well-known North Warwickshire collieries. Once again an impressive column of black smoke rocketed skywards and then hung like a curtain in the calm, damp air.

The scenery here was very lovely, the track running between steep, heavily wooded banks of every shade of green imaginable, but my mind was on other things and I groaned inwardly at the sight of the pressure gauge needle dropping like a stone. I couldn't believe it. A whacking great fire in the box, clouds of black smoke from the chimney, but the pressure falling back! The explanation was simple, but my ignorance was such at the time that I did not realise that the layer of fresh fuel was acting as a screen and blanketing the heat of the fire beneath from the rest of the box. Until that layer became incandescent, the needle could only go one way.

With the train now on the 1 in 206 section of the bank just past Shustoke, Jack became aware of the falling pressure as the exhaust beat took on a more laboured note, and flashed me a look of disapproval as he dropped the lever into full gear.

'You'd better pull the rake through that lot,' he yelled.

I started to scramble over the tender, but his hand grabbed my jacket and pulled me back to the footplate.

'Wait until we get through this next bridge,' he shouted in my ear, 'or you'll knock your silly head off.'

Gosh! In my anxiety to comply I had not thought of that, for there was no doubt I might have received a nasty injury had I come into contact with that particular piece of ironwork, even though our speed was now only some 15 mph or so. Jack's stature promptly jumped a couple of points in my estimation. As the clouds of acrid smoke that had bounced down from the bridge cleared, I once again set off over the tender to obtain the rake. Our steam pressure had by now dropped to under 150 lbs per sq in and the water was showing about two-thirds of a glass when, with only the top flap of the firedoors open, I inserted the rake. The technique was to draw this implement through the fire, starting at the front end.

It was hard, hot work and I had completed five of the six strokes necessary when No 3435 slipped. Due to our falling pressure, Jack had edged the regulator on to the second valve, and as she started to slip he snapped the regulator shut. However, it had become gagged, this being the term used when, although the regulator handle is in the closed position, the actual valves have not properly shut and steam is still being admitted to the cylinders. It was quite a common occurrence, and many drivers developed the habit of fully opening the regulator before slamming it shut as a precaution.

This slip was a real beauty. An explosive roar erupted from the chimney, spewing a mighty column of steam, smoke and blazing cinders high into the air, while the wheels revolved at an incredible speed causing a most disconcerting up and down oscillation. I had been on slipping engines before, but this one seemed to go on and on, and I clung desperately to the rake which was still buried deep in the fire. Meanwhile Jack had acted with commendable alacrity, flicking the sand valve open and applying the brake almost in one movement.

Now, the official instructions point out quite clearly that the sanders should not be operated until slipping has stopped, since the sudden shock of regaining adhesion could cause considerable damage to the motion, but it was common practice to take advantage of the few seconds time-lag between opening the valve and the sand actually beginning to run, so that they would be operating at full flow as soon as the regulator was re-opened. The brake application, of course, also helped to slow the spinning wheels. Because the regulator had gagged, Jack was obliged to open it fully before again slamming it shut, and this action not only prolonged the slip but momentarily made it more violent.

I was still hanging on to the rake, with my face quite close to the boiler front, when this frantic blast of energy finally ceased. Instantly a great orange tongue of flame flared out through the firehole into the cab. I instinctively leaped back, but not before the major part of my eyebrows and eyelashes had disappeared in a quick puff of smoke. This was my first close-up of a blow-back, and I didn't like it. In fact, it impressed me to such an extent as to ingrain a lasting respect for this phenomenon, which I always tried to anticipate and avoid.

The cause on this occasion was the mixing of unburned fuel and hot fire occasioned by my efforts with the rake, followed by a tremendous blast for a few seconds that liberated great quantities of gases. This was quite all right as long as they were being drawn at high velocity through the fire tubes, but with the abrupt removal of this powerful draught they had to escape in some direction, and the line of least resistance was into the cab.

Jack had the regulator open again even as the flames rolled out of the firehole and, having contrived very successfully to shrink his rotund form into that small corner between gear lever and spectacle plate, suffered nothing worse than a pair of over-heated trousers. With a steady stream of sand under the wheels, No 3435 once more regained her feet and settled to the struggle up the bank, which had steepened to 1 in 136.

Having decided that it was now safe, I withdrew the red-hot rake, and quickly swung it up on the tender. That prodigious slip had certainly done the fire a lot of good, for the needle, having hit an all-time low of 140, had now crept up to the 150 mark. The water, on the other hand, was down to less than half a glass, and I glanced inquiringly at Jack.

'Better put it on,' he shouted, indicating the injector.

I did so, and was delighted to find that the needle was still slowly recovering. My spirits also rose with it, and I felt a distinct quickening of the pulse as I listened to that rough crisp bark as we hammered our way up to Arley & Fillongley station. Jack was operating the sanding gear intermittently, more as a precaution than a necessity, but what a good job, I thought, that he had checked their efficiency before starting. A little bit of forethought and a thorough knowledge of the road when properly applied made life so much easier on the footplate.

With 160 on the clock and the water an inch below the top nut, I dropped the firedoor with the intention of shooting a quick half-dozen around the box. I bent to grasp the shovel only to find that Jack had hauled up the flap again.

'Don't do it like that,' he yelled. 'Fire it over the flap. Like this,' he continued, brushing me aside, for I had greeted this remark with a look of blank amazement. He scooped up a level shovelful of slack and, with the handle held at a high angle, sprayed the fuel mixture in over the bottom door. He repeated the operation some six times in quick succession, thrust the shovel into my hands and shouted, 'Carry on then. You can fire almost continuously like that while we're working hard.'

I looked first at the pressure gauge, which was still showing 160, and then at the water, which was just in sight, and decided there and then that this could be the right answer. In fact, I found that this was indeed an excellent method of firing an engine fitted with the old Midland-type doors, providing that conditions warranted it; that is to say, if the engine was working hard, and the fuel was of a small size. A steam-shy engine does not like a lot of cold air going into its firebox, and this was a very good way of keeping it down to a minimum. The draught drew the fuel off the shovel, and by skilful angling of the blade the whole box could be evenly fired.

We were now more than halfway up the bank, and I was being kept pretty busy, for with the regulator on full first valve and the gear lever at maximum cut-off, fuel was disappearing into that white-hot slot as fast as I could shovel it. Through Arley & Fillongley the gradient eases slightly from 1 in 132 to 1 in 240 and, as our pace quickened, so our exhaust beat became crisper and more strident. I began to feel for the first time that complex mixture of emotion that was, in the course of time, to provide the ultimate sense of satisfaction when working a steam locomotive.

Between Arley & Fillongley station and Arley Colliery Sidings is the steepest part of the bank at 1 in 109. With only 2 miles to go to the summit I

On first acquaintance the old Midland-style firedoors appeared rather fussy and time-consuming to operate when compared to modern sliding patterns. The lower door or plate covered some two-thirds of the firehole area and was hinged at the bottom. This was raised by means of an attached chain, and secured with a latch on the left of the firedoor. The upper door or flap was hinged at the top and could be locked fully open by a catch over the drip tray. It could also be set in three intermediate positions so as to regulate the supply of secondary air. The design of door was well suited to the relatively short, steeply sloping Midland grates, since when working hard with the top flap open, suitably broken coal could be sprayed over the bottom door in the manner of a mechanical stoker.

was beginning to think that I had mastered this new technique of firing, for the pressure gauge was showing 170 lbs per sq in and the water was just in sight at the top of the glass. Even Jack seemed less tense, and as we crashed our way up past the colliery, he took the trouble to point out the position of his dreaded catch-points. I watched these clatter by under our wheels, and then glanced up at the pressure gauge for reassurance. My heart missed half a dozen beats as I blinked disbelievingly at it. The needle was dropping steadily and was already pointing at 160 lbs per sq in.

'Now what has gone wrong?' I said to myself as I quickly shut off the injector. I just could not think what might have caused this dramatic fall. The glare from the slot seemed as bright as ever, but the smoke at the chimney had thinned considerably. I re-doubled my efforts with the shovel and poured in more fuel. I was surprised to find that not as much smoke was being generated as before and, moreover, the needle had not stopped its downward swing. As the sound of the blast lost some of its former bite, Jack pulled his head in from round the side of the cab to investigate the cause. His voice now had a definite tinge of excitement in it and rose a couple of octaves in consequence as he eyed the gauge which had halted at 145 lbs per sq in.

'I can't ease up yet,' he screeched. 'We're the wrong side of the catch-points to stick,' and he pushed the regulator over on to the second valve as if to emphasise his statement. 'What have you done? What have you done?' he repeated three or four times while hopping up and down on his platform.

'I don't know,' I mumbled truthfully, while ruminating how amazingly light on their feet fat men could be. Finally the hopping ceased and Jack, having grabbed the shovel, made a quick inspection of the firebox by using its blade as a deflector.

'You've choked it under the arch,' he announced in a sour voice, snapping shut both firedoors. 'Get the rake down and pull it back, for heaven's sake, and be quick about it!'

He hopped back on to his platform. While I wrestled the rake into the firebox again, I noted that the pressure had, if anything, risen slightly, but the water level was steadily dropping. This time raking was much worse than before, since for one thing the surface of the fire was hotter, and for another, a great many more than six strokes

were required. The space underneath the brick arch was blocked by a mass of small, burning particles of fuel, which had arrived there by the action of the blast taking them from a shovel held at the wrong angle. I should have held the handle higher, so that the coal entered the box close to the firedoors instead of halfway to the front. Vibration had also assisted in shaking the fire forward, with the ovoids rolling downhill, and the result was a shape exactly opposite to what was desired and a typical consequence of over-enthusiasm and lack of experience.

My arms ached so much that I could hardly move them and the rake was too hot to hold anyhow, so with a last desperate effort I hauled the glowing implement from the fire and swung it on to the tender. I was momentarily exhausted, but at least the needle was once again travelling in the right direction, evidence that I had been partially successful in clearing the blockage.

'Get some water in the boiler,' shouted Jack. 'Otherwise we'll drop a plug when we go over the top.'

We were by then only about half a mile from the summit and from climbing at 1 in 125 we would abruptly start descending at 1 in 168, increasing to 1 in 126. Two inches of water in the glass would disappear from sight as soon as the boiler tilted downwards. I did not fully appreciate what Jack meant, but I had already learned to act first and ask for an explanation afterwards, so I put my injector on, somewhat relieved to see that the steam pressure had recovered to 155 lbs per sq in.

I then asked what he meant about dropping a plug. In a few brief sentences that contained more choice adjectives than I had heard in the whole of my life, he explained. Practical lessons like these are so much better learned on the footplate than in the classroom.

That last half-mile with the gallant old lady blasting away on second valve was an anxious period for both of us. She wasn't steaming well enough to leave the injector on all the time, so it was a case of trying to hit a compromise that would ensure sufficient water in the boiler as we breasted the summit, and sufficient steam pressure to get us there. Not quite knowing how far we had to go was a great handicap for me, so I had to rely entirely on Jack's judgment, and this, even in his excited condition, was logically to sacrifice water for steam pressure initially and then, as we approached the summit, allow the water to build up at the expense of steam. Fortunately No 3435 was game to the last puff and, although we struggled over the summit with only 135 lbs per sq in on the clock, we had 2 inches of water in sight when the regulator was closed. It had been a close thing, far closer than I realised, for a slip like our previous one would no doubt have brought us to a stand from which we would have had great difficulty in getting into motion again - not without a blow-up to regain a full head of steam anyway.

Jack visibly relaxed as we rolled gently down towards the rather foreboding black maw of the 995-yard Arley Tunnel.

'Screw the hand brake on, mate,' he said quite affably. 'It's downhill all the way to Nuneaton now, and we want to keep the train buffered up.'

He applied the steam brake, enabling me to get a good bite, knocked the blower fully open, and then with what might be construed as a grin said, 'Don't forget to keep your head in. It's wet and smelly in here, and keep the doors boxed up and the blower on.'

I had not been through a tunnel of this length before and wondered what it would be like. As the darkness closed over us I noted that the steam pressure was recovering nicely and there was certainly plenty of room in the boiler so I could safely leave the injector on. We of course wanted as much pressure as possible to ensure braking efficiency, but we certainly did not want the safety valves blowing off in the tunnel. With the firedoors closed and no gauge lamp lit, the blackness was virtually complete. I tried holding my hand in front of my face by way of experiment and, not being able to see a thing, groped my way to the tender. The air was certainly smelly. It had a stale acrid flavour, which I found in due course was typical of a great many tunnels and, since breathing became more difficult, concluded that it was low in oxygen content. I looked up in an endeavour to view the tunnel lining, but after receiving an eyeful of dirty water, decided nothing was to be gained by this notion and returned unsteadily to my seat.

We rumbled on, every sound being greatly amplified in the confines of the tunnel, while Jack kept our speed in check by regular applications of the steam brake. I wondered how he managed to gauge our speed so accurately while not being able to see a thing, and then I noticed a small circle of light far ahead. It was so clear and perfectly formed that at first I did not recognise it for what it was - the end of the tunnel. This circle steadily grew in area and intensity until at last we were out into broad daylight once more. I took a deep breath of fresh air and felt relieved that I could again see everything on the footplate.

The pressure was back to 170 lbs per sq in and the water was showing three-quarters of a glass. On observing this check, Jack, now quite cheerful, responded with, 'We'll roll all the way to Abbey Street, so you can tidy up and put some water in the bucket for a wash.'

Not wishing the relieving fireman to see the unevenness of the fire, I once again got busy with the rake and pulled the remains of the heap under the arch back to quite a respectable shape. Satisfied with this, I then cleared the spillage from the footboards and dropped it into the back corners of the firebox, leaving the doors open so as not to generate too much steam. A quick swish round with the slaking pipe soon had the rest of the dust and debris washed overboard and the footplate was transformed to a very presentable appearance. All through my career I could never understand why some men seemed content to hand over an engine in a deplorable condition, when only a few seconds' work with brush and slaking pipe could give it that 'scrubbed deck' look. I could forgive a chap for having a dirty fire, no coal brought forward, low steam pressure and a half empty boiler, but never a dirty footplate.

Jack managed to complete his ablutions by setting the steam brake on a partial application which, together with the tender brake still operating, kept our speed in check on the 1 in 135 gradient. In true oriental custom I had second dip in the bucket and had just finished as we approached Abbey Street station, where we rumbled gently to a halt at the water column at the far end of the up platform. Our relief crew, two senior Leicester men, were already walking over to us as we collected our kit together, and we exchanged the usual pleasantries and information about our respective engines and trains.

The one we were to take back to Birmingham was standing across the line on the down loop, and consisted of a mixed freight of 42 wagons headed by Class '8F' No 8319.

'She's a bit of a rattlebox, but apart from that, quite all right,' said the other driver as we bade farewell.

Stockingford station in 1950. After struggling with a Class '3F' 0-6-0 on the outward run to Nuneaton, I had no problems with '8F' No 43819 steaming in the opposite direction, despite a 4-mile climb through Stockingford to Arley, mainly at 1 in 126. During the early 1950s Stockingford Sidings was very busy handling the output of local collieries, and even had its own loco depot. In this photograph, taken from the down platform, some of this activity can be seen beyond the goods shed on the up side. The loco shed is out of sight to the left of the down platform.

On climbing aboard I was glad to see that the footplate had been left in a clean and tidy condition, and that we had a good supply of 'real' coal in the tender. The boiler was nearly full, while the firebox contained a substantial bed of well-burned-through fuel. It looked somewhat dead, but this was because both dampers were in the shut position. Jack pulled his watch from his waistcoat pocket.

'We usually follow the slow,' he said. 'So that gives us about 40 minutes in which to have our food.'

With this announcement I suddenly realised that I was ravenous and quickly disposed of my packet of sandwiches, while I watched with increasing fascination Jack's preparations for his lunch. His generously proportioned abdomen should have indicated to me that he was an enthusiastic trencherman, but it wasn't until I saw the quantity and variety of food he brought out from his haversack that the point went home. It soon became obvious that he was very experienced in the art of footplate gastronomics and quickly transformed the cab of that '8F' into a makeshift kitchen in which he performed his tasks with the accomplished ease of a hotel chef.

First he heated the firing shovel by placing the blade just inside the mouthpiece ring. This was

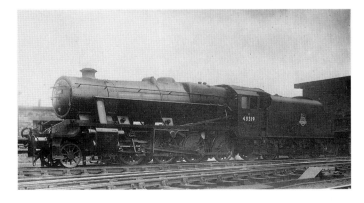

Class '8F' No 48319, which I fired on the return journey from Nuneaton with a mixed freight. As a 16-year-old Passed Cleaner I at first found it difficult firing the front of the grate, but this became easier with practice. Like 'Black Fives', '8Fs' were held in high regard by footplate crews, that is until they were eclipsed in every respect by the superlative '9s'.

then blasted spotlessly clean with a jet of steam and water from the slaking pipe. Several large rashers of best streaky bacon were placed on the blade and quickly fried, again by holding it just inside the mouthpiece. When cooked to his satisfaction, these were removed and placed on three enormous slices of bread laid out for the purpose. He next dropped a knob of butter into the hot shovel and added a good handful of button mushrooms and, although I had just eaten, the smell soon had my mouth watering. The mushrooms were added to the bacon and these in turn were followed by three fried eggs. Finally some tomatoes were fried, and the resulting pulp poured over the whole treat, while so as not to waste the residual fat in the shovel a further round of bread was fried.

Any one of those three open sandwiches would have satisfied the average man, but Jack, having gobbled them down at an astonishing speed, seemed almost disappointed that there were no more. Looking up for the first time after starting this feast, he actually grinned broadly.

'By jingoes, I feel better for that,' he exclaimed, reaching out for the tea can, quite oblivious to the fact that I had watched every move.

Footplate fry-ups, I discovered later, were quite commonplace with many drivers, but I was never again booked with anyone who was able to cook such a variety and quantity of food so quickly and with such skill.

A semi-fitted hauled by a new-looking '4F' 0-6-0 clattered past on the down main, and could be heard for some considerable time snorting heavily as it laboured up the bank towards Arley Tunnel.

'The slow will be along in about 10 minutes,' said Jack, 'so I'd open the rear damper and get the fire warmed up if I were you.'

I turned the blower on slightly and pulled up the left-hand damper, somewhat surprised to find that he was now advising me rather than telling me what to do. Had the breakfast worked the miracle, or had he more confidence in me now? I could not decide, but I certainly preferred this new attitude.

'I've never worked an "8F" on a train before,' I said a little apprehensively, thinking that this pronouncement might cause a reversion to his former self.

'Don't worry, lad, we shouldn't have much trouble with this little lot. We've bags of power and they're good steamers, but you'll probably have trouble reaching the front when we're on the move, so bang some up there now and just keep the back damper open.'

I took up the shovel, still shining from its recent culinary episode. It was of the long-handled type and, as one might expect, ideally suited to the long firebox and roomy cab of a Class '8'. Firing shovels came in two sizes, long-handled and short. Engines with short, steeply sloping fireboxes such as '2Fs', '3Fs' and '4Fs' did not require a powerful swing to fire the front of the box. This was just as well since these engines had small cabs, making such an action difficult. Although some tank engines, such as 2-6-4 passenger tanks, had rather larger boxes, their cab layout again prevented a lengthy swing, and the short-handled type was generally preferred. However, on most of the larger tender locomotives, and indeed all the BR Standard engines, long-handled ones were most suitable, and you soon noticed the difference if supplied with the wrong type.

With a great deal of concentration and a lot of wasted energy I managed to place a suitable quantity of coal in the front half of the firebox and was just hanging my head out of the side window for a breather when a 'Compound' hauling six coaches rolled briskly past and came to a halt in the station. This must be the slow, I thought, and turned to Jack for confirmation. He nodded.

'Right, you can build up the back now,' he said, knocking the blower wide open and winding the gear lever down to the full forward position.

I quickly plied more coal to the back half of the grate and had just closed the firedoors to the halfway position when a shrill whistle from the station indicated that the slow was about to depart. I hurried over to my window to watch it pull out. It blasted away in fine style for a few yards, then went into a spectacular slip, shooting up a plume of smoke and steam while its 7-foot drivers clattered round at a fearsome rate. Then, with sanders on, it settled down and its healthy, crisp exhaust could be heard accelerating away as it attacked the bank, working on simple engine. 'Compounds' were usually very quiet exhaust-wise, when compounding, but were as crisp as any other Midland engine when working on simple.

As that thrilling sound died away in the distance, I once more turned my attention to the state of our own locomotive. Steam pressure was on the 220 lbs per sq in mark, the water just in sight at the top of the glass, and the fire was burning up brightly. It seemed an awful lot more engine than the little '3F', and I felt more than a little excited at the prospect of working her back to Saltley.

The points clattered over and Jack applied the steam brake.

'Take the hand brake off, mate,' he called and, as he opened the small ejector, so the signal controlling our siding dropped.

Jack eased open the regulator and after a few revolutions of the wheels, closed the taps. We clanked slowly out on to the main line. One of the cylinder cocks on my side was obviously sticking, since each stroke of the piston was accompanied by a powerful hiss from the outlet pipe. Also both piston glands were blowing moderately, which was a further indication that she had run up a fair mileage since her last shopping. I put the live steam injector on in order to prevent blowing off as we trundled through the station, but now the starter showed that we had the road and Jack hauled open the regulator. The exhaust suddenly became audible as a deep-throated, slightly muffled woof, the hisses at the front end became louder and more penetrating while a very distinct thump could be felt through the footboards once every revolution.

With the cab doors open, I leaned out of the driver's side in order to make sure that the train was intact and that the guard was in his van. Having exchanged hand signals with him, I advised Jack, who merely nodded and opened the regulator to about full first valve. The exhaust crashed out, a much deeper full-bodied sound than the '3F', and Jack wound back the reversing screw two or three turns. As he did so, the thump from below took on a new dimension, just as though a steam hammer was attacking the underside of the footboards. I was fascinated to watch the tea-can leap about half an inch clear of the drip tray at each mighty blow. Jack scowled, partially closed the regulator and wound the screw down a couple of turns. The violence subsided somewhat.

'Crikey,' he commented. 'She's a bit rough. Can't pull her up much, that's for sure!'

I later learned that should the big-ends of an engine be worn to such an extent as to produce a powerful knock, the condition would become progressively worse the wider the regulator was opened and the shorter the cut-off used. Worn big-ends usually went along with worn everything else, looseness in the axleboxes, etc, and conditions on the footplate particularly at speed could be quite intolerable if the engine was worked normally. By using a smaller regulator opening and longer cut-off it was possible to smooth out some of the bangs, rattles and thumps, so making life a little less of a misery. Even so, on many occasions I have found it quite impossible to sit down while an engine was in motion.

We clumped and clanged our way back up the 1 in 123 gradient from Abbey Street with little apparent effort and, since the safety valves were beginning to lift, I opened the firedoors and commenced shovelling. I was not very adept in those early days at firing from the right-hand side, but with an '8F' there is quite sufficient room in the cab to stand behind the driver and still get a good swing with a long-handled shovel, provided that the tender doors are not open. My attempts to reach the front of the grate were not altogether successful, since when I put all possible effort behind the swing I tended to lose direction and occasionally struck the mouthpiece ring. Apart from the damage to my ego, I received a stinging shock through the full length of my right arm and coal ricocheted all round the cab like so much shrapnel. However, the '8F' was very tolerant as to where the coal was placed in the grate, and the needle barely left the red line even when I used the exhaust injector.

Another very noticeable difference between the '8F' and the '3F' was that because of the greater boiler capacity, one travelled much farther before there was a marked drop in the boiler water level. This, together with the locomotive's excellent steaming qualities, did much to restore my confidence, which had sunk so low earlier in the day. Jack also seemed more confident and relaxed, and even indulged in some idle gossip when climbing towards the tunnel. As we thumped our way steadily up the 1 in 126 gradient, he turned to me and shouted, 'We've only got about a mile to go before we reach the summit, so you needn't fire her any more. We don't want to choke ourselves going through Arley Tunnel, and we'll need steam on this time. We're OK now,' he added, indicating the full boiler and the pressure gauge still showing 225 lbs per sq in, 'and you'll want some room to stop her blowing off down the bank.'

By this, of course, he meant that it was good

policy to work the boiler level down somewhat so that the injector could be used when coasting to prevent wasting steam by blowing off, yet without the risk of overfilling the boiler.

I was initially doubtful whether we could travel that far without further attention to the engine's needs, but as we approached those massive stone portals the water was still showing two-thirds of a glass; I was amazed at the reserve capacity of an '8F' when compared to the small engines I had been used to.

Once more the inky blackness closed over us, and the pounding exhaust reverberated from the tunnel walls, partially masking the amplified clank of side rods. This time we left the firedoors slightly open so that a shaft of intense white light illuminated the clouds of steam that billowed round the rear of the cab. As we penetrated farther into the tunnel, the atmosphere became progressively more foul, and acrid smoke fumes began to irritate our lungs. Obviously the 'Compound' had not been so meticulous about emitting smoke when passing through. I squeezed myself as far as possible into the front corner of the cab, and watched with fascination the flow of steam and smoke as it poured round the trailing edge of the roof and moved in a succession of jerks corresponding to the exhaust beats towards the firedoors; I had always imagined that it would travel in a steady flow. Suddenly the noise subsided as we burst out into daylight. I quickly slid forward the side window and hung my head out, taking in gulps of fresh air while I observed the vast cloud of steam and smoke that rolled upwards over the tunnel mouth, sucked out by the motion of our train.

Jack closed the regulator and, without being told this time, I put the exhaust injector on. Despite being on a downgrade of 1 in 125 the water was still showing a third of a glass and the safety valves were just beginning to lift, but I now had plenty of boiler room to keep her quiet. Kicking the firedoors open on the way, I moved in anticipation over to the hand brake.

'Yes, wind it on a bit, mate,' he said, seemingly pleased that I had been alert to this intended manoeuvre.

We now had 5 miles of downhill coasting to Whitacre, so I studied the fire to see what mistakes I had made. The rear half of the grate was reasonably even and well filled, but the front half was just the opposite. Humps and ridges were interspersed with valleys and depressions where the fire was so thin that holes were beginning to form. I quickly realised that there was a lot to be learned about this firing business, particularly when physical strength had to be combined with skill and accuracy.

As our speed increased under the influence of gravity, a peculiar buffeting motion set up between the engine and tender, which was only checked when Jack made a steady application of the steam brake. It was decidedly unpleasant, but had the advantage of tending to shake down coal ready for use on the tender shovelling plate. I cocked an enquiring eyebrow in Jack's direction.

'Weak springs, I reckon,' he muttered by way of explanation.

I sat down on my seat, which on a Class '8' is merely a spring-loaded wooden flap, listening contentedly to the rhythmic clanking of the motion and the whistle of air through the jammed exhaust cocks, and reflecting that nearly all sounds from a steam locomotive are very beautiful sounds - even when they indicate a fault.

Our descent of the bank was uneventful and I was able to repair the fire at leisure with fresh coal, filling in the holes that had formed. By leaving the firedoors wide open, I was able to prevent generating excessive smoke as the coal ignited; at the same time the cooling effect of the secondary air prevented blowing off. My intention was to arrive at Whitacre with a full boiler and a bright fire, ready for a quick dash to Washwood Heath. However, when all too soon the Whitacre Junction distant became visible against its backcloth of bright May greenery, it was seen to be on. Jack brought our speed right down on the still falling gradient of 1 in 146, with lengthy applications of the brake, and as we hissed and clanked up to the home signal we could see that a local trip engine was drawing out of the down sidings.

We waited a few moments before being allowed to draw up to the starter and then, after a further interval of some 10 minutes or so while the trip engine cleared Coleshill, we were allowed to proceed. I had filled the boiler well above the top of the gauge glass, but even so Jack was able to use such a small regulator opening in getting our train moving up the 1 in 735 gradient to Coleshill that no trace of priming was noticeable.

We did in fact reach Water Orton station junction, 2 miles further on, before the water came

The old Midland practice of double-heading was perpetuated by the LMS until larger and more powerful engines became available under Stanier's regime. Seen on the down line at Whitacre in 1931, Class '3F' No 3729 and '4F' No 4432 are drifting easily along after their descent from Arley. With a coal train of this size they will now have a steady 3-mile haul at 1 in 735 to Water Orton.

into sight again, where once more we were brought to a halt while a mixed freight passed in front of us from the down fast on to the slow. Our signals indicated that we were also to travel up the slow and, just as we hissed gently to a stand at Water Orton Junction home signal, so it too came off. As we clanked towards the signal box, a green flag was thrust out of the nearest side window and, on spotting this, Jack reached up and gave a short hoot on the whistle.

We still called them whistles on a Class '8', but the instruments fitted by Sir William to his locomotives were pitched (acoustically speaking) rather low, and tended most of the time to sound like an asthmatic bullfrog. Hence, while the term 'croaker' might have been more accurate, it never caught on, nor for that matter did 'hooter', so 'whistle' it was. I always felt that the timbre and pitch of a whistle should suit the size and characteristics of the engine it was attached to. For example, the shrill, clear bell-like tones of a '3F' were very appropriate, and very feminine. The deep-throated hoot of the larger Stanier engines was again in keeping with their size, power and masculinity, while the high-pitched piping of a BR Class '9F' seemed absolutely ridiculous - a giant with a midget's voice. Nothing less than an ocean-going liner's siren would have satisfied me for this magnificent piece of locomotive engineering. That they were so equipped seems all the more a pity since the Riddles design team experimented with whistles in their early days, and fitted a beautiful triple-tone chime whistle to the Standard Class '5'. We all thought these a wonderful novelty, and I recall continually playing 'tunes' on them at every opportunity. Even the

most staid of the senior drivers seemed to be bitten with the same bug and, when only moving around the shed yard, managed to give a pretty good impersonation of the Santa Fe Express. Maybe this was one reason why the idea was abandoned, apart from cost.

On passing the junction signal box we waved to the bobby, who held up two fingers. I thought that this was a rather unfriendly gesture, and was about to reply in a like manner when Jack grunted, 'There's two in front of us then.'

I asked him to explain, and was it anything to do with the green flag business? It seems that this was another instance of permissive block working, which allowed two or more trains to be on the same section of track at the same time providing that the crews had been properly advised. This only applied to the goods line, but it did mean that a great number of trains could be accommodated on that 4-mile stretch between Water Orton Junction and Washwood Heath Junction. In the early 1950s it was by no means an uncommon sight to see it full from end to end with waiting trains. I have personally relieved a train at Castle Bromwich and have been relieved again 8 hours later at Washwood Heath, having travelled less than 2 miles during that period. No wonder this condition was known to all as 'on the block'. The two fingers had indicated the number of trains in front of us on the section to Castle Bromwich, a useful tip when visibility was bad.

We chugged steadily along the goods line, keeping an eye open for the brake-van of the preceding train. The drizzle had now stopped and the sky was brightening considerably, making the lush grass in the meadows to our left look greener than ever. We found only one train in front of us at the Castle Bromwich home signals, and this was allowed to proceed after we had halted for only a short while. Ten minutes later we followed suit, again being advised by the bobby that we were in a queue. This time we moved only at walking pace, since the goods line curves round the back of the down platform at Castle Bromwich station before passing under the Chester Road bridge and forward vision is severely limited.

On clearing that road bridge, we saw that the now familiar brake of the train ahead was only a hundred yards away but apparently still on the move, judging by the little puffs of steam, like so many balls of cotton wool, rising lazily into the air from above the line of wagon roofs. We crept forward like this for a few hundred yards and then came to a standstill for half an hour. This was followed by another few hundred yards of movement, then a further halt.

It was about this time that I realised that, although an '8F' has many advantages over a '3F', the seating layout was certainly not one of them. Providing that one had a suitable piece of wood on a '3F', one could quickly arrange a very comfortable couch and a pleasant 40 winks might follow. The 1-foot square flap seat on an '8F' did not allow any more relaxed an attitude than sitting upright, and my legs were too short to even reach the footboards comfortably. I could achieve a sort of reclining position by putting my feet up on the drip tray or the tops of the damper handles, but since my legs were just about at full stretch, they tended to slip off as soon as the muscles relaxed. Unless I was desperately tired not even a light doze was possible.

While I was still contemplating this shortcoming in the '8F' design features, Jack again drew out his watch, studied it with his usual care, then turned to me with a smile and said, 'Well, mate, at least we won't have to put her away. We're on overtime now.'

I had not realised that it was more than 8 hours since we had booked on, and now that our official day was up, we would not have to dispose of our engine even if we went straight to the shed. Not that there was much hope of that, since there was still another train in front of us before we reached Bromford Bridge station home signals. Forty minutes later found us under the station starter signal,

and I had just changed my seating position for the 49th time when a friendly voice called to us from the trackside.

'Hold on, we're after you.'

I opened the cab doors on Jack's side and a relief crew from the Control link climbed on board. Greetings and information were rapidly exchanged and both Jack and I, now feeling the need for further refreshment, grabbed our respective empty lunch bags and set off to hoof the 2 miles or so to Saltley shed. We were allowed 50 minutes walking time from Bromford, but Jack was not disposed to walking any more than was strictly necessary. Not that he could be blamed on this particular jaunt, since clumping over ballast, sleepers, point rods, signal wires and general bric-a-brac for more than 2 miles was certainly unpleasant. The official and correct route lay through the slum streets of east Birmingham, but even on a bright May afternoon such a journey brought no sense of pleasure.

Fortunately the train in front started to move as we reached the ground and I was amazed at Jack's speed and agility as he bounded after that retreating brake-van. Needless to say, I was close on his heels as he tumbled inelegantly on to the van's verandah, but, as he so rightly observed, a bad ride was better than a good walk. By hopping from one train to another we managed to get to the West End in reasonable time, from where even Jack was able to stroll to the loco without too much distress.

As we entered the enginemen's lobby, I noticed an unusually large crowd of chaps jostling around the notice board.

'What's all the excitement about?' I enquired of a Passed Cleaner colleague who was standing nearby.

'We've been registered now,' he said, grinning from ear to ear as he swelled with pride. 'You're booked with Ronnie Jackson,' he added, pointing to the lists of links. 'Nice chap. I was with him last week.'

There it was then, in black and white: 'Washwood Heath link. Driver R. Jackson. Fireman T. Essery.'

A full-blown fireman at last. But who was this Ronnie Jackson? No matter, I would find out at 2.00 pm Monday afternoon, for that was the time scheduled to book on for disposal work.

5
THE FIRST RUNG OF THE LADDER

At 1.30 pm on Monday afternoon I was to be seen racing over the cobbled sets of Duddeston Mill Road on my trusty bicycle, before charging up the slope across the shed forecourt and through the car park to drop it into a vacant slot in the cycle racks. On my first day as a registered fireman, I had no intention of being late, for I still had to find out what Driver Jackson looked like. I entered the enginemen's lobby more confidently than ever before, feeling that I was now part of the elite. Drawing my card from Peter the clerk, I asked if Ronnie Jackson had booked on yet. Peter glanced at the clock.

'Good lord, not yet,' he said. 'You're a bit early, you know. He'll be in, though, about five to two.'

'Give me the tip when he arrives,' I said over my shoulder as I moved off to read the notice boards.

Another of the lads I had been cleaning with bowled in full of exuberance and also nearly half an hour early, so we soon became engrossed in relating our exploits since passing out. While still deep in conversation, I felt a tap on my shoulder, and on turning found myself confronted by a chubby, baby-faced driver in his early 30s. His rosy round features were split by a cheerful grin, and I noticed with growing approval a deeply dimpled chin and twinkling blue eyes.

'Are you Terry Essery?' he said.

I nodded. 'You must be Ronnie Jackson.'

'That's right,' he said. 'Let's go round to the cabin and get acquainted.'

The cabin to which he referred was a large cavernous room located under the water tank adjacent to No 2 shed, and served as a mess room for enginemen until being replaced by a far more grandiose affair that was erected in the mid-1950s, known officially as the Staff Amenities Block.

The mess room as such (pictured on page 78) was not very elegant, having high arched windows (always semi-opaque), a stone-flagged floor and zinc-topped tables with rather uncomfortable benches attached. One ancient and stained porcelain sink, along with three more modern but equally stained hand-basins, provided the only washing facilities, but set in the middle was a gigantic combustion stove capable of roasting all the inhabitants even in the depth of winter. To supplement this heating, one wall sported an open fireplace large enough to do justice to any baronial hall, while in the corner of the room stood a great cast iron urn of water perpetually on the boil. Anyhow, it was home to us and there was always an open forum running where many and varied subjects were hotly debated. What was going to win the 3.30 at Cheltenham, the merits of Beethoven's piano sonatas or the state of the fire irons on the disposal pits, could all crop up in 5 minutes flat.

Ron had collected a tea-can from his locker on the way to the mess room, and as we entered he suggested we had a cup of tea first. The mashing operation completed, he guided me to a quiet corner and, when comfortably seated, opened a most enlightening conversation.

'OK, mate,' he said. 'You've got a lot to learn, so we might as well start off by giving you an idea of what happens in the link. As you probably know, we are mainly concerned with the preparation and disposal of engines on the shed, with the odd bit of marshalling thrown in. We used to have some shunting turns as well, but these have been taken over by diesels now, so it's unlikely that we will ever go past the loco signal. Now then, since we're on disposal, I'll explain all about this first. We operate two systems here; we can either volunteer for the quota system, which means that each crew has to dispose of six engines as quickly as possible, then they are finished for the day, or we can wait for the yard foreman to allocate engines to us as and when required.

'The advantage of the quota system is, of course, that it is possible to go home after four, three or even two hours and still be paid for eight hours, but to take full advantage of it the driver has to deal with one engine, while the fireman takes another. Believe me, it can be very hard work doing the lot yourself, and you have to work without a break. You also require sufficient engines to go at, and there are certain times of the day when very little comes on the shed, so you have to choose the time carefully. Furthermore, the fireman has to be sufficiently strong, skilled and trustworthy to carry out these tasks without supervision, because if anything goes wrong it's the driver who carries the can.'

I conceded this point.

'Although it often suits me to work the quota system,' he went on, 'I do not propose to try it until we've been together for a while. For one thing, I don't think it would be fair to you, and for another, I would have grey hairs wondering what you were getting up to.'

'OK,' I replied with a smile, since Ron said this in the nicest possible way.

'The yard foreman will give the quota men all the available engines first, so we'll have to wait a while, but we shall probably get our first one about 3.30. In the meantime, I'll run through the procedure so that you'll have an idea of what to expect.

'Engines are normally left on one of the two arrival roads, that is the ones leading under the coaling plant. If the tanks are less than half full, we top them up, otherwise we don't usually bother. The foreman will tell us whether to just clean the fire or whether to drop it completely. This happens if the engine is required for repairs or washing out. He will also tell us where to stable it and if it requires turning.

'Normally we coal the goods engines at the far end of the plant since this contains the poorer grades, unless advised otherwise, and passenger engines, 'Black Fives' and 'Crabs' at the near end. I'll show you how to operate the plant when the time comes. After coaling, we move down to the ashpit, and if the road is empty we clean the fire at the ash hopper. The road is usually full, though, so we have to throw out the fire on the side of the pit, but you'll see when we get there.

'When we're over the pit, you can get underneath and rake out the ashpan, and when that's done you finally clear the smokebox of char. I will have completed my examination by then, so after that it's only a matter of dropping it in the shed and returning the tools to the stores, OK?'

I had, of course, an idea of disposal procedures,

Saltley was always busy, and the complex manoeuvres over its numerous roads needed to be mastered as soon as possible. All movements into and out of its three roundhouses passed over the two tracks in the foreground. These joined the arrival (ashpit) roads behind the camera and led to a dead end. In this view, looking north, No 2 shed is to the left and No 1 shed lays behind the roofless No 3 shed directly ahead, while in the far distance can be seen the roof and chimneys of Saltley gas works.

but I was grateful for having it spelled out in detail. During the next hour or so I discovered that Ron was a very entertaining chap to talk to, and well able to discuss a wide range of subjects in which we both shared a common interest.

Some weeks previously, after working an early morning turn on a Kingsbury trip job, I had been given a lift by the head shunter on the pillion of his BSA 350cc motor cycle from Kingsbury to Water Orton station. This had been a real piece of silent movie stuff since we had to race the slow passenger in order for me to catch it back to Saltley. The ease with which this had been accomplished had so impressed me that I was determined to purchase a motor cycle as soon as I could afford one, and since Ron was the proud owner of a BSA 500cc Combination, we were soon discussing the merits of the various makes and sizes.

Motor cycles in those days were a very popular mode of transport for many enginemen, some of whom lived considerable distances from the shed. Being self-sufficient in this respect was most important because even in Birmingham there was a dearth of public transport at 3.00 am on a Sunday morning. Motor cycles, being fast, economical and relatively inexpensive, therefore proved to be an ideal solution. Popular opinion was that a 250cc machine would be most suitable to start with, but Ron's philosophy favoured the larger machines that generally had, as he put it, better acceleration to get out of trouble with, brakes to match their performance, and better road-holding. An added bonus was that you could always attach a sidecar later if so desired. I found his arguments so logical and convincing that I delayed the great day until February of the following year before acquiring a BSA M33 500cc machine, a decision I never regretted since this ultimately led me to becoming an ardent enthusiast, from which I derived countless hours of pleasure.

We seemed to have known each other much longer than a mere two hours when at 3.45 pm one of the foreman's assistants came up to Ron and asked him if he would care to dispose of No 4203, a '4F' standing on the front arrival road.

'Leave a bit in, and drop it in No 2 shed,' he added as he moved over to give instructions to another set of disposal men.

It was a humid day and, although a thin veil of cloud was drawn across the sun, I could feel its heat as we walked across to our engine. With the temperature in the low 70s, I had visions of some warm work ahead of us. Ron preceded me on to the footplate and his first action was to test the water gauge.

'Always check the water level first,' he said, 'and then make sure that there is plenty of steam. Sometimes they arrive on shed without much of either, in which case you have to raise more steam and fill the boiler up. If you don't, you may find yourself having to be towed off the pit, and that upsets everyone.'

He pulled open the firedoors, which were of the sliding pattern, and glanced inside.

'Hmm! Looks a bit rough! Still, I thought it might be, judging by the amount of coal used. I'm going to drop down to the water column first. We'll have to fill this one.'

As I scrambled on to the tender I noticed that the tank gauge was showing less than a thousand gallons, and that over two-thirds of the coal supply had been consumed; she had obviously been out some good while.

Class '4F' No 44203 was the first locomotive Ron Jackson and I disposed off together. Compared with later replacements such as the Ivatt 2-6-0 'Doodlebugs' (see pages 66 and 164) they did not have the same lively acceleration or free running, while both preparation and disposal could be a tedious chore. Inadequate axleboxes apart, they were, however, rugged engines and were to be seen on a wide variety of duties until 1966.

'Throw the fire irons into the back of the tender while you're up there, mate,' called Ron, as he opened the water column valve. I did as requested, realising that you could not very easily coal the tender with fire irons lying across the top of it.

While waiting for the tank to fill, I surveyed the shed yard from my elevated position. It was certainly a veritable hive of activity. To my front a queue of engines stood on both arrival roads, stretching underneath the towering, blackened concrete structure of the coaling plant. Beyond, this queue continued right down over the pits to the ash plant, where the engines were obscured in a haze of smoke and dust as the quota men did desperate battle with clinker and char. To my right, a train of coal wagons stood waiting to deliver their loads into the insatiable maw of the plant hopper, and standing behind these on the back departure roads were lines of prepared engines awaiting their crews. Over to my left there was the busy bustle of traffic moving into and out of the three roundhouses, while just before me engines were leaving for unknown destinations.

A frantic gurgling from the tank indicated that it was near to overfilling.

'OK, Ron, that'll do,' I yelled, and, as the flow ceased, I hauled the wet, slippery hose from the opening and pushed it aside before replacing the lid. I had already been instructed to make sure that the tank cover was in position before coaling, since a hundredweight of coal going into the water compartment every time the engine went under the hopper would soon severely restrict its capacity, to say nothing of the effect on the delivery pipes.

Ron eased forwards and, being a goods engine, we had to obtain our coal from the far end, but we were unable to get into the correct position straight away, for the queue was still blocking us.

'I'll show you how the plant works while we're waiting,' said Ron, as he skipped lightly on to the concrete platform that ran the full length of the hopper between the two roads. We entered one of the two little concrete huts that housed the control gear. These huts were substantial structures capable of withstanding the impact of the heaviest lump of coal that might bounce off an over-coaled tender and, although they had glass windows in either side, these were protected by heavy wire grilles.

Inside, two large metal levers mounted in slotted quadrants - looking not unlike the reversing levers of a Class '3F' - protruded from the floor.

A view across a typical modernised Motive Power Depot - this is Leicester on 23 April 1959. During the 1930s many principal depots were improved by installing automatic coaling and ash disposal plants, which not only speeded the servicing of locomotives but also reduced the man-hours involved. The arrival roads are those that pass beneath the coaling hopper and either side of the ash disposal units. *BR*

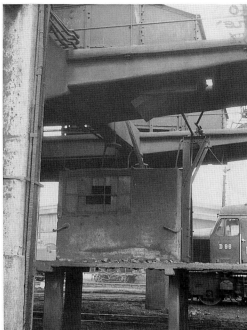

Above Saltley, too, was dominated by its automatic coaling plant. The two arrival roads led past water columns, then beneath the hopper and finally on to the ashpits. Coal supplies were shunted along the road behind the hopper upon which a '4F' is seen standing tender-first. Above and beyond this engine the ash plant can be glimpsed.

Above right This close-up of Saltley's coaling plant shows the protected cabin inside which engine crews operated the controls. By means of a lever the delivery chute could be angled as desired to give an even distribution when coaling.

These controlled the angle of the delivery chutes, one for each track, while mounted on the wall were two sets of water valves for the sprinkler systems and two switch boxes containing separate on and off buttons, again one set for each track. The principle was simple: coal from the hopper fed on to a metal plate which moved backwards and forwards like a shuttle when the switch was pressed. Coal dropping over the edge of this moving plate fell on to the chute, which in turn deflected it into the tender. The angle of the chute could be altered to distribute the coal more evenly, while the sprinkler system was intended to lay the often considerable clouds of dust generated from certain types of fuel.

Below At busy times the coaling plant operator was hard pressed to keep pace with usage. Coal wagons were drawn on to the hoist by means of an electric-powered capstan and rope. After being securely clamped into position they were lifted to the top of the hopper whereupon, being inverted, they delivered their contents to either the passenger or goods end, whichever had been selected. At Saltley the leading end supplied passenger coal.

Ron ran over the controls for my benefit, and then went on to give me a few tips. 'Always turn the water on first. It may take a little time, but it makes a heck of a difference if you want to keep yourself and the engine clean. Now, before you touch the lever, make sure that there is nobody around and that the engine is correctly positioned. Next, make sure that you know which way you want the chute and that you are already pulling hard in that direction before you release the catch. Sometimes a large lump of coal will be lying on the chute and the weight of this will pull the lever out of your hands, causing it to drop the opposite way to what you intend. You won't gain any laurels for putting half a ton of coal on the cab roof, believe me!

'Always switch off a bit on the light side. For one thing, a certain amount of coal still drops even when the motor has stopped, and for another you can always put a bit more on. So don't over-coal any engine. It's a danger to everyone, yourself included, and all spillage only has to be picked up again by some poor blighter. However, you will sometimes be asked to coal to maximum capacity, but this is a special technique and I'll show you how when the time comes.'

I never thought that there was so much to be learned about coaling engines, but taking this afternoon's activities as typical, I realised that I was going to get plenty of practise in during the next few months.

'I'll move her down a bit now,' said Ron, popping his head round the corner of the hut to confirm that the preceding engine was clear. 'Drop the chute so that it points towards the rear of the tender first. Doing it that way prevents coal from shooting out all over the footplate; when it's filled up a bit I'll draw down, and then you can tip it the other way so that it tops up the front part without making a mess.'

We proceeded as planned and I once more realised that there is nothing so effective as a practical demonstration for making a lesson sink in, and although it was some considerable while before I was accomplished in this art, I always took a great delight in doing a neat and tidy job under the coaling plant.

Down on the ashpit, Ron gave me further instructions.

'This is almost rough enough to warrant taking up the firebars,' he said, nodding towards the great heap of clinker and ash covering the grate, 'but I think we'll ladle it out on this occasion. Get me a long and a short shovel, a rake and a bent dart and we'll make a start.'

I jumped down on to the mounds of clinker, which were piled on both sides of the track, and began looking for the required implements. There was a short shovel lying a few feet away and I pounced on it eagerly. Almost immediately, heat struck through my leather gloves, causing me to release my grasp.

'Crikey,' I thought, 'what a good job I was wearing them.'

Lesson one: never pick up a fire iron from the ashpit without first spitting on it to see if it is hot.

I dragged it respectfully to a nearby standpipe and cooled it down with a jet of water before handing it to Ron.

'I see you're learning,' he said with a grin.

I obtained the other irons without any more trouble than a singed right boot and joined my mate on the footplate.

'Sit up on the driver's seat out of the way and watch for a while,' he puffed, for the sweat was already trickling down his face.

I noticed that he had removed the deflector plate and had placed this behind the hand brake column, so as to give more room for manoeuvre through the firehole. I also noticed that he was tackling the cleaning in the well-tried manner of pushing live fire to the front of the box and clearing the rear half first.

'It's generally the best way,' he commented, after I had brought this to his attention. 'Unless, of course, it's so choked under the arch that you've got no room, in which case it usually pays to pull four bars up and push it out through the ashpan.'

After breaking up the clinker under the doors and pushing it forward, he turned to me with a wave of his hand, indicating that we were to change places.

'Right,' he gasped, mopping his brow with a handkerchief. 'Ladle that lot over the side with the short shovel.'

I set to work with gusto, but after a few minutes the shovel grew rapidly heavier and hotter, and I grew heavier and hotter with it. My movements became slower and more laboured, and streams of perspiration gushed from every pore. The muscles in my arms and shoulders began to ache so that I could barely retain a grip on that ton weight of a shovel. Determined not to give in, I struggled on, staggering in a daze of agony and gritting my teeth so as not to shout out. Blinded by sweat and gasping for breath, I was nearing the end of my tether when Ron laid a kindly hand on my shoulder.

'That's enough, old fellow, let me have a go now.'

I fancy he had been testing me to see how far I would go before giving in, but my obvious distress had been too much for his sensitive nature, and he had thus put a stop to my self-inflicted torture. However, my efforts had at least cleared the rear half of the grate, so that he was now able to give a really first-class demonstration of how to clean the front out. Using the long shovel, Ron performed with a skill and swiftness that made my eyes bulge. Knowing exactly what to do, he wasted not one movement and, although he puffed and sweated in the intense heat, he showed no sign of the fatigue that I had been stricken with. I concluded that experience and practise notwithstanding, you also needed a lot of brute strength and stamina, and the sooner I got down to some serious exercise to improve my physique, the better. With the last shovel of clinker thrown over the side, Ron pushed the fire irons clear of the cab and slapped the dust from his overalls with his leather gloves.

'Drop two or three shovels of coal under the door now, but don't put too much on or you'll get choked when you come to do the smokebox.'

I did as requested and shut the firedoors, remembering that you should never move an engine after the fire has been dropped without first doing this, otherwise cold air will be drawn in and cause severe contraction stresses to be set up in the firebox and tube plates, etc.

'If you've got your breath back now,' he said with an impish smile, 'we'll do the ashpan. Get down and stop me so that the damper door is just in front of one of the slaking pipes. The wind's blowing the wrong way down the pit, so you'll get covered in dust if you don't soak it well.'

This accomplished, I slithered into the pit and, crouching well down, made my way towards the

pan. These pits were brick-lined structures about 4 feet wide and 3 feet deep. The floor was cambered like a road and a water drainage gutter ran down either side. Midway along the pit and set in the floor was a metal grid that allowed ash to fall through into a hopper below and, when full, this hopper could be raised to tip its contents into a wagon set aside for the purpose. On either side of the grid were two sets of slaking pipes fixed to the pit side walls. These took the form of 3-foot long L-shaped half-inch copper pipes, flattened at the outlet end to give a fan-shaped jet, and attached to a universal ball joint at the other. When in good working order, a very effective stream of water could be directed into the ashpan and, if one cared to take sufficient time, all the ash therein could be converted to a wet sludge.

Raking out the ashpan was generally considered the dirtiest task during disposal operations, particularly if the wind was blowing towards the operator. Fortunately slaking pipes, which can be seen projecting from the pit wall, could direct a spray of water into the ashpan, and this did much to reduce the inevitable dust clouds.

Although not on the same scale as coaling, the quantities of ash and clinker produced daily on the two disposal pits at Saltley were sufficient to warrant an automatic plant for its removal. Hoppers were located beneath grids on both pits and, when full, were hoisted so as to tip their contents into a wagon positioned on the centre road. As can be seen, spare wagons were shunted on to this road and could be partly filled with ash shovelled from the pit side.

As a cleaner I never relished going under an engine, but familiarity eventually banished my fears, and now I rather enjoyed it. However, I did not relish raking out ashpans, particularly if the wind was in the wrong direction or the slaking pipes inoperative. The odd spot of hot oil or water dropping down one's neck was not too bothersome, but it could be very wet when the universal pipe joints leaked and when ash blocked the drainage channels, causing small lakes to form around one's feet. It was so on this occasion and, as I directed the main jet of water over the damper door, a fine curtain of spray drifted towards me from the general direction of the control valve. As it happened, I quite welcomed the cooling droplets on my overheated brow, and my overalls were in any case already soaked with perspiration. The pan was full to the bars with ash, and by the time this had been cleared to my satisfaction I had an aching back to go along with my aching arms.

Emerging from the pit I saw that Ron was standing on the front framing holding a heavy spanner in his hand.

'I was waiting for you to finish before showing you this tip,' he called as I stood wiping sweat and dust from my face with a decidedly soggy handkerchief. 'Slacken all the nuts first, and then tap the lugs off except for the one furthest away from the hinge. Do that last, and then when the smokebox door swings open it won't knock you off the framing.'

So saying, he sharply smote the aforesaid lug, upon which the door swung back allowing a small avalanche of char to pour out, swirling on to the framing.

'Dig it out with the firing shovel and throw it well clear downwind, like this,' and Ron dextrously threw half a dozen shovels of the black, unpleasant substance on to a large heap some two yards from the smokebox. 'Come on up and have a go then,' he said, dangling the shovel before me.

I clambered up the front steps on to the framing and waded in. The first shovel of char was a well-heaped one, but as I withdrew it from the smokebox, a goodish portion fell from the blade, only to be whipped up in the airstream created by the blower. I seemed to be suddenly engulfed in a hot, gritty blizzard which got into my ears, nose and eyes, and penetrated every crevice of my clothing. I quickly realised that, unless I wanted to be smothered in the stuff, I would have to go very gently indeed and not get too much on the shovel. I suppose that cleaning out a smokebox required far less effort than cleaning either the fire or the ashpan, but I never did like the job, mainly because I could do nothing to lay the dust, and I also found the noise from the blower jet at close proximity physically painful.

Ron was watching my performance from a safe distance with some amusement, but he didn't say anything until I had finished.

'Now wipe the joint faces clean of char and close the door,' he instructed, adding as an afterthought, 'Only fasten the two outer lugs.'

I wrestled with the heavy smokebox door and nearly fell off the framing in the process. Why in God's name was everything so heavy on a locomotive, I thought, as I finally managed to secure the lugs. Even the spanner was over a foot long and weighed pounds! I rejoined Ron on the footplate and tucked a few more shovels of coal under the door as he prepared to move forward over the points that led into No 2 shed.

It was very necessary to keep one's eyes open when moving about the yard. Everyone seemed to be in such a rush and minor collisions were not at all uncommon even between experienced crews. We proceeded slowly towards the shed, each in our correct roles - Ron driving and myself walking in front, pulling over the appropriate points. The arrival and departure roads merged just outside the shed entrance, so great care had to be exercised at this point and it was always sound, and indeed official, policy for the fireman to walk in first in order to ascertain that no other engine was about to emerge and that the table was secured in the correct position. On more than one occasion an engine, possibly low on steam, has passed from the bright sunshine outside into the dark gloom of the shed without stopping, only to find that the table was set for another road. Eighty tons of metal down a 6-foot hole causes quite a nuisance for a while. . .

I found a Class '2P' at the far end of the arrival road and, since the crew were disembarking, enquired if they were leaving her there.

'I'm afraid the sheds are full at the moment,' said the driver. 'We've been told to park it here, so you'll have to do the same.'

I later discovered that this was a fairly common occurrence at busy periods, and this is why two sets of marshalling men were always on duty. Ron nodded when I advised him of the situation, and he gently brought our engine to rest against the buffers of the '2P'. We topped up the boiler, dropped some large lumps of coal in the back corners of the grate, shut the firedoors and left the damper open one nick. I collected our tool kit of four spanners and dropped them into the bucket along with the canister of detonators; then, with bucket and shovel grasped firmly in one hand, I slithered to the ground.

We normally left the two headlamps, the gauge lamp and the coal pick on the engine, but were obliged to return the rest of the tools to the stores, which was fortunately only a few yards away tucked into a corner of No 2 shed. Having done this, I suddenly realised that I felt as though I had been stranded in the desert without water for a couple of weeks. My mouth and my throat were so dry I could hardly talk. Ron must have felt the

same, because on entering the mess room we both dived for the taps over that old sink. Never had cold water tasted so good.

No sooner had we sprawled out on the bench and made ourselves as comfortable as our still steaming bodies would permit than who should appear but Frank, the foreman's assistant. He was in even more of a bustle than usual and, after a quick glance around the cabin, spotted us and came straight over.

'Sorry to give you another one so quickly, Ron,' he said with genuine concern, 'but we're on the block outside and the 2.00 pm men have gone.'

He referred, of course, to the 2.00 pm quota men who, with plenty of engines to go at, had after three hours either finished or were finishing their requisite six.

'OK,' sighed Ron, in a manner that would have been appropriate to a French aristocrat when mounting the steps to the guillotine.

'8608,' continued Frank, 'on the back road. She shouldn't be a bad cop.'

Ron prudently filled the tea-can with cold water before we set out once more to find our engine. The sun now shone brightly from a clear blue sky, and if anything it was hotter than ever. I noticed that there were three engines standing on each of the arrival roads, but it was deserted under the hopper and there were only two or three engines actually on the ashpits. Proof, if any was needed, that the quota men had indeed departed.

Our Class '8F' was the leading engine of three standing on the rear road. We clambered aboard and went through the usual check drill. A glance in the fire confirmed Frank's assumption that she was not a bad cop. The boiler was full, the pressure was showing 220, and the tank indicated 3,000 gallons.

'I'm glad we've got an "8F",' said Ron as he wound her into forward gear. 'I'll be able to show you how to clean a fire by getting the bars up.'

'Do you always get the bars up on these then?' I asked, out of genuine interest.

'Yes. "8s", "5s", "5Xs" and "Crabs" are best tackled by pushing it out through the ashpan. "Crabs" are the worst, though. They only have two sets of bars and they weigh a ton each. Because they are so difficult to get out, some men prefer to use a paddle, but I think that's even harder, and in any case there's no need to get underneath to rake out the front pan when you've already done it from the top.'

We drifted gently down to the hopper and, as before, obtained our coal from the goods end. Ron pointed out that it was even more important to start with the chute facing the rear of the tender on engines fitted with tender doors, since large lumps of coal travelling at high velocity could burst open the door catches and it was very easy for this to happen unnoticed. Some time ago, he himself had managed to deposit a ton of coal on the footplate in this manner. With the coaling completed we were then able to move right down the pit so that our front ashpan was over the grid.

'Right,' said Ron when in position. 'All I want is the firebar tongs, and an ashpan rake.'

Once more I set off to search around the piles of clinker and was fortunate to find the required tongs quite nearby. They must have weighed nearly a hundredweight, and with handles six feet long it was as much as I could do to even carry them. With some effort I propped the tongs against the engine steps, then jumped down into the waterlogged pit in order to retrieve the ashpan rake. Again, these rakes were all steel and, being 15 feet long, were awkward things to carry around. By the

time I arrived back on the footplate, Ron had laid bare the middle six firebars of the centre section with the aid of the engine's own short clinker shovel.

'Make sure that you pull some live fire into the back corners first,' he said as he noticed me peering into the firebox. 'You'll need it there if you want to save some.'

Ron returned the clinker shovel to the fire iron compartment on the tender, then with a mighty heave pulled the tongs on board.

'Give me plenty of room with these things,' he grunted as he wrestled the heavy implement through the firehole. 'The idea is to remove about four firebars from the middle of the grate - like this.'

He clamped the jaws on the rear end of one of the selected firebars and by grasping a massive handle in each hand he squeezed both inwards and downwards. At first nothing happened, so Ron bounced his whole weight on the handles so that the tongs became a sort of seesaw with the firehole mouthpiece ring acting as the fulcrum. Suddenly the end of the bar jerked upwards and

A typical shed ashpit scene (this is Wakefield), as the disposal crews try to keep the arrival roads clear. Note the usual clutter of fire irons at the side of the pit. Extracting four firebars from the rear of the grate of an '8F' eased the task of fire-cleaning; ash and clinker could then be dropped into the ashpan and pushed through the front damper opening by means of a long rake. Looking rather neglected by 1964, No 48608 was the first Class '8F' I disposed of using this method.

Ron was able to drag it backwards over the slope of fire and clinker so that it was lying just against the mouthpiece ring.

'Now this is the tricky part,' he grunted. 'If you are going to lose a bar in the ashpan, this is when it happens.'

'What are you going to do now then?' I said, wondering what form his next gymnastic exercise would take.

'I'm going to turn the bar over on its back and draw it out of the firehole,' and so saying he wound himself round the tongs and then performed a sudden sideways half somersault; the bar clattered on to the footplate.

'The next one should be easier,' he gasped, ramming the fearsome instrument back through the firehole again.

'I should hope so,' I retorted, retrieving my cap from the footboards and retiring to the furthest corner. I must admit the last three firebars to be extracted did not require quite as much effort, but even so, by no stretch of the imagination could they be called easy. In due course I was to try my hand at this king-size dentistry and eventually became quite expert, but not before dropping a few hundred bars into ashpans and down hopper chutes, removing a square yard or two of skin from my knuckles and straining just about every muscle in my body.

The gap left by the four extracted firebars enabled entry to be gained to the front compartment of the ashpan. This compartment extended in an upward slope to the rear of the second set of bars, while a similar but smaller compartment served the third set of bars. As Ron explained, we now had to clear the ashpan before starting on the fire, and this was accomplished by inserting the long rake through the gap, and ramming hard in the general direction of the front damper which was, of course, fully open. Unfortunately, one of the ashpan stays ran right across the line of fire, so to speak, so the rake had to be manoeuvred over or under this thoughtlessly placed obstruction. When properly cleared, daylight could be seen shining faintly through the open damper and work could then be started on dropping the mixture of fire, ash and clinker into the pan. It was advisable to drop only a small quantity at a time, so that this might be easily cleared from the ashpan. A larger amount tended to compact and this then became very difficult to dislodge.

We took it in turns and I found that, although I was soon a bath of perspiration again, it was not quite so tiring as working with a clinker shovel. This was mainly due to the fact that the weight of the rake rested on the mouthpiece ring, and only pulling or pushing movements were required. Having cleared the front two sets of bars, live fire had to be pushed forwards from the back corners and under the firedoors, so that it lay on either side of the gap. Care had to be taken here, since it was quite easy to inadvertently lose the fire in the ashpan as well. A short clinker shovel was best suited to this purpose, while a short slightly curved engine rake was used to lift the clinker still lodged in the rear of the grate. When Ron had dextrously pulled the remaining live fire back under the door, I placed a few shovels of fresh coal on it and closed the front damper.

'Right,' said Ron, 'you go and clean out the smokebox and I'll clear the rear ashpan.'

I found that he was able to do this with the curved engine rake while standing at the side of the track below the cab. Meanwhile, I made my way on to the front framing armed with the firing shovel. The smokebox door of a Stanier engine was secured by a dart that fitted into an elongated slot in a bar running across and inside the front of the smokebox. The dart was attached to a hefty handle which, when turned through 90 degrees, aligned the dart with the slot and so enabled the door to be opened. A similar handle attached to a lock-nut secured the whole assembly and, when in the closed position, allowed the door to be pulled very tightly on to its seating. It was a very much more convenient design than the circumferential lugs found on the old Midland engines, and only a sharp tap on the locking handle with the back of the shovel, followed by a few brisk turns, was required to gain access.

Pulling the door open was less of a hazard than on a Class '4', since the framing area was much more generous, but the size of the box on first acquaintance was quite staggering. I found that it was very hot indeed. The locomotive being so much longer than a '4F', I had to get my head and shoulders inside in order to reach the tube plate, even though I was using a long-handled firing shovel. However, in 10 minutes the task was completed and, feeling somewhat overcooked, I rejoined Ron.

'We've got to put her in No 3 shed,' he said as we ran down the pit towards the dead end.

Contrary to regulations, I jumped off the still moving engine as we passed over the points. This rather dangerous manoeuvre, together with jumping on to moving engines and riding on the tender or loco steps, was widely practised, mainly because it saved a lot of time and effort. Surprisingly few accidents resulted from these capers, which is probably why they were allowed to continue, but occasionally someone managed to sober the rest by putting his foot under a wheel. I recall being witness to such a drastic piece of surgery when a young fireman had three toes amputated on the spot. It was a gory sight and it certainly slowed me down for a while.

No 3 shed was the only one with a 60-foot turntable and the only one capable of turning and housing the larger engines. It was also the only one without a roof. Having been bombed during the war, no one had got around to replacing it, but the majority of enginemen preferred it that way since the absence of trapped smoke made conditions far more pleasant to work in - except during torrential rain and the odd blizzard. However, the absence of a roof apparently upset the draughting arrangements of the adjoining and reconstructed No 1 shed. A modern concrete structure had been built to replace the original so effectively removed by the Luftwaffe, but whatever the cause it was an undeniable fact that smoke generally hung in an asphyxiating layer down to about footplate level in this shed.

Skipping lightly from the rear tender steps, I galloped ahead into No 3 shed and ascertained that all was clear before calling Ron in. He stopped nicely on the centre of the table and, since we only had to turn as far as the second pit, I cranked it round by hand. A preparation crew were good enough to relieve us of the tool kit and, once again feeling very hot and thirsty, we returned to the cabin.

'I think we'll have a spot of supper now while we've got the chance,' said Ron when we had removed the sweat and grime with revitalising cold water. Over our sandwiches we discussed all manner of problems that might arise during disposal, and by the time we had washed the last crumbs down with generous quantities of tea, I felt that at least I now knew how to tackle most types of locomotives likely to come on to the shed.

We were shortly given our next engine, a Fowler 2-6-4 tank. Ron groaned. 'They're a bit of a pig. Quite a big firebox and no room to manoeuvre the fire irons.'

I had not been on one of these before and was interested to see what they were like. Climbing into the cab, I could appreciate what Ron meant. On other engines there is a convenient space between the cab and tender so that one can swing the handles of the fire irons practically without restriction, but on a tank engine this gap is closed by the rear of the cab.

Due to their limited water-carrying capacity, tank engines normally require watering on arrival at the shed, and ours was no exception. As we pulled up under the passenger end of the hopper, Ron told me to open the rear cab windows, since this prevented the possibility of breakage by any small pieces of coal that may penetrate between the bars of the protective grilles. He also instructed me to tilt the chute towards the cab since the bunkers on tank engines are too short to allow the other method without excessive spillage, and in any case the passage to the shovelling plate was too tortuous for much coal to fall on to the footboards.

Down on the pit Ron explained that again two methods of fire cleaning could be adopted. Four firebars from the front set could be removed and the fire dropped through in the same manner as a 'Crab' (which they resembled), only on this occasion the fireman had to get underneath to clear the pan since a long rake could not be used in the confines of the cab. Alternatively the fire could be paddled out, using first a short and then a long clinker shovel for the purpose. It was more laborious, of course, than on a tender engine because the shovel required skilled and delicate manoeuvring round all the built-in obstructions. However, in this instance Ron decided on the latter method since there did not appear to be much clinker in the firebox.

We started off in the usual manner of initially clearing the rear half of the grate, and Ron allotted me the first shift. I was immediately conscious of it being much hotter on a tank engine, and was in trouble straight away when I withdrew the first shovel of clinker. The ring that forms the end of the handle became hooked over the hand brake, and by the time I had got this clear again I had deposited the contents of the blade on the footboards. A nice little conflagration started up as the red-hot clinker and coal mixture made contact with well-worn oil-soaked woodwork. Ron came to the rescue with an accurately aimed bucket of water, and amid clouds of steam and dust I started again. Gradually I noted the disposition of all the pitfalls, but even so I found it much harder going than with a '4F'.

Long before the back half was cleared I was tottering, so Ron took over for a while. Working in turns, we ladled out a surprising quantity of ash and clinker, for the grate area on these '4P' tanks was very deceptive. Needless to say, Ron did the major share, which was just as well since I felt decidedly shaky when I dropped into the pit to rake out the ashpan. Caked with dust, and soaked from the combined effect of spray and perspiration, I crawled out to find that Ron was up on the front framing attending to the smokebox.

'What a grand fellow he's turning out to be,' I thought as I asked him if I should take over.

'No thanks, I've nearly finished now,' was the cheery reply, 'but you can go and set the road for No 1 shed, though.'

I did as requested, although I first had to wait for a couple of engines coming out on the departure road.

No 1 shed was always somewhat more difficult to enter, since one first had to travel through No 3 shed. By the time No 1 shed's table had been secured, someone wanted to come out of No 3 shed and preference was always given to engines leaving a shed. Then, when this matter had been dealt with, one could find that a similar situation had now developed in No 1 shed. Thus a fireman could become involved in an awful lot of running to and fro between the sheds before finally getting settled on a vacant pit. It was so on this occasion, and it took a full 10 minutes of haring backwards and forwards before I eventually managed to call Ron in. The turntable in No 1 shed was also the most sensitive of the three to balance. A few inches either way meant the difference between turning with reasonable effort and a desperate struggle. The shorter the wheelbase the more difficult it seemed to be to achieve this balance; however, Ron managed it on the second attempt and we were able to stable the engine on one of the short pits set at 90 degrees to the arrival road without too much difficulty.

The heat had now gone out of the day, but not out of our bodies, and as we made our way back to the stores Ron mopped his streaming face for the umpteenth time and said, 'Do you see what I mean about the big tanks now?'

I replied that I certainly did, but I was glad of the experience and in any case he must admit that at least we had seen some variety.

The 8.00 pm quota men were now setting about the incoming engines with some purpose, and we waited in the mess room for nearly an hour before being given our final engine of the day. Frank came over to Ron with a disarming smile.

'I've got an easy one for you to finish with,' he announced.

'Blimey, you've left it a bit late,' was Ron's comment.

'3014 on the back road. Coal it with best and

Turning upwards of 100 tons of locomotive by hand could be hard work, and balancing it correctly on the table was often crucial. Fortunately modern turntables were also equipped with vacuum tractor motors powered by the locomotive's ejectors.

drop it in No 2 shed,' continued Frank. 'That suit you?'

Ron's face brightened at this news. 'Ah! well, that's different,' he said. Then, turning to me, he explained that 3014 was a 'Doodlebug', an Ivatt Class '4MT' 2-6-0, and that these were equipped with rocker grates, hopper ashpans and self-cleaning smokeboxes. I had never been on one of these rather ungainly-looking engines, although of course I had seen them both around the shed and out on the road. With their high framing, exposed motion and angular enclosed cabs, their design showed a transatlantic influence and, although not pretty, they certainly had an appearance of utilitarian efficiency. However, from the gossip that I overheard in the mess room, their crews were not overimpressed, complaining of indifferent steaming and draughty cabs. During the next half hour, though, I was to become endeared to them for life.

The daylight was failing rapidly as we once more walked over to our engine. I clambered up unfamiliar steps to the footplate and found Ron already peering at the tank gauge in semi-darkness.

'We had better top it up,' he commented.

A short ladder ran up the back of the tender, and having climbed this and opened the tank lid, I suddenly felt a distinct feeling of insecurity. This I realised was due to the fact that the tank top was a turtle-backed affair with sides that sloped away like the roof of a house. Great for rearward vision, but not so very helpful if one happened to slip.

Not that I had ever heard of anyone falling off the top of one of these tenders, but the absence of a well left me a trifle nervous, particularly when pulling a stiff water column arm round.

While waiting for the tank to fill, Ron prudently lit the headlamps, since a surprisingly high number of incidents occurred on the shed precinct due to engines not carrying lights, and furthermore these were mainly at dusk. The Ivatt tenders carried their coal in high-sided bunkers that stood up proud from the rest of the tank and which were rather narrower than most; therefore extra care had to be taken during coaling operations. When Ron opened the regulator to move under the hopper I was quite amazed at the sudden surge of acceleration. I subsequently found out that these engines were incredibly lively and the regulator needed a very light hand indeed when moving around the shed. This faculty was, of course, a great asset on stopping passenger trains for which work they were eminently suited and, when I ultimately came into the passenger links, I thought them superb. On mentioning this point to Ron, he agreed that he knew of no engine quicker off the mark than a 'Doodlebug'.

'Do you know how a rocker grate works?' he asked when we had rolled down over the ashpit.

'Only vaguely,' I replied.

'Well, it's very straightforward really, and why all the more modern engines are not converted as a matter of routine when they go in for shopping I'll never know.'

Ivatt Class '4MT' 2-6-0 No 43014. My first experience of a 'Doodlebug' was on the ashpit at Saltley when Ron Jackson showed me on this very locomotive just how easy the task of disposal could be. These engines were fitted with rocking grates, hopper ashpans with bottom doors and self-cleaning smokeboxes, all of which reducing anything up to one hour's hard work to a few minutes of relatively easy work. Bearing a transatlantic appearance, their lines did not meet with everyone's approval, particularly those equipped with double chimneys; however, their functional simplicity and ease of servicing won favour with most of the men who worked with them.

A typical rocking grate with the forward section in the open position. Operated by a lever in the cab, the grate could function either in a limited stroke for breaking up clinker while running, or fully open for dropping the fire completely. The ashpan also had opening bottom doors, which, together with a self-cleaning smokebox, made the normally tedious work of disposal very easy indeed.

Ron pointed out the main features of the system in plain, easily understood terms. Just below the firedoor two short spigots projected out of the floor. On either side of these were two simple hinged limiting catches, the first allowing a short stroke to enable the fireman to break up clinker while actually running on the road, the second set allowing a full stroke and actually dropping the fire through the ashpan. The spigots were connected to levers running either side of the firebox, and these were attached to a number of slotted, narrow transverse sections that formed the grate. This in turn was divided into two halves, the front being operated by one spigot, the rear by the other. When in the long stroke position, the transverse grate sections turned nearly 90 degrees, allowing any residual fire to drop straight through the gaps thus formed. The bottom of the ashpan was likewise made up from a number of flaps that could be opened by removing a locking catch and then applying a lever supplied for this purpose to a spigot located behind the rear driving wheels. These flaps again turned through 90 degrees so that material dropping down from the grate passed straight through into the pit below.

Ron detached the 3-foot-long lever from its retaining clips, which were located on the side of the cab beneath the fireman's seat, and quickly climbed down to the ground. Pulling out a safety pin and flicking up the locking catch, he then placed the lever on the spigot and heaved upwards. The flaps in the bottom of the ashpan opened with a clank, disgorging its contents directly over the grid.

'Don't ever forget to open the hopper first,' he advised as we clambered to the footplate again, 'or you'll be in real trouble.'

With a short clinker shovel he pushed some live fire forwards just beyond the halfway mark. He then pulled up the limiting catches and, with the lever firmly in place on the right-hand spigot, vigorously rocked the grate backwards and forwards. I glanced over his shoulder to see what was happening and was just in time to glimpse fire, ash, and clinker disappearing through the gaps in the rear half of the grate. He then returned the lever to the midway position and closed the catches. Pulling some fire back under the doors was the work of but a few seconds, and he was then able to repeat this rocking operation on the front half of the firebox. Two minutes later, with the entire grate as clean as a whistle, I was shovelling fresh coal into the box while Ron was down on the ground once more to slam shut the ashpan flaps.

'That's all there is to it,' he said with a grin. 'The smokebox is self-cleaning, so we don't have to bother with that. All we do now is to put her in the shed.'

'Good Lord,' I said, still somewhat flabbergasted, 'no wonder you wished that every engine was a rocker.'

From then on I too was a rocking grate enthusiast, but unfortunately at that time only a few engines were equipped with this wonderful labour-saving device. Like Ron, I couldn't help thinking that the initial installation costs would quickly have been recovered by the vast saving in time.

It was now almost completely dark and the yard

lights had been switched on. These were not the tall batteries of brilliant lamps similar to those found in football grounds and with which we later became familiar, but an odd assortment dotted around at strategic points. Rather like some street lamps, they tended to throw pools of bright light with intervals of sharply contrasting blackness in between. Running about the yard in front of my engine, I found that I was jumping over shadows and tripping over unseen obstructions, so I was somewhat battered and confused by the time we arrived in No 2 shed.

Having parked on a vacant pit, I decided to top up the boiler and it was then that I discovered how efficient the injectors on these 'Doodlebugs' were. One could actually see the level in the gauge glass rising, and it did not require much imagination to guess that these would have to be used in only short bursts when out on the road. We were still on the footplate when another set of shed men clambered aboard.

'Leave everything where it is,' said the driver. 'We've got to prepare her for the Evesham.'

'Suits me,' replied Ron, and so saying he grasped me by the arm and guided me rapidly in the direction of the mess room.

A quick swill removed the surface traces of our day's toil and, after collecting our lunch bags, we walked round to the lobby to book off. It was still only 9.50 pm when I collected my cycle from the rack. Enviously I watched Ron kick his motorbike into life and after a cheery wave roar off up Duddeston Mill Road. I followed at a very much more leisurely pace, a peculiar stiffness seeming to have afflicted a great many muscles that up until then I did not realise that I possessed.

My home was nearly 3 miles (mostly uphill) from the shed, but this gave me time to reflect on the many events of the day. I was booked with a first-class mate, and I had the happy feeling that with his help and guidance I was going to get an excellent grounding for the better life to come.

I was not quite so early the following day and I still felt rather tender and stiff. However, this soon wore off as we tackled our first engine, a Class '3F' that was required in No 1 shed for a washout. Engines had the sludge washed out of their boilers at set intervals, and when disposing of those booked for this operation one had to be rather more fastidious than usual. The fire naturally had to be dropped completely and, while the engine

was cold, any repair work which could not be executed when in steam was carried out. The fitters, not unreasonably, objected to any deposits of char, ash or clinker left in the smokebox, ashpan or firebox respectively. These objections, of course, came back to us via the Shed Foreman, and it was no advantage to incur his wrath for this or any other reason.

The day followed roughly the same pattern as the preceding one except that we had different engines, and the weather was hotter than ever. A 'Black Five' came after the '3F', and the method used on this was exactly the same as with the '8F', since they were practically identical except for their wheel arrangements. Ron raised my spirits considerably by telling me that 'Black Fives' of the 4700 and 4600 number series were also fitted with rocking grates, but alas none came our way that day.

Another '8F', which gave the impression that it hadn't been attended to for the better part of a year, followed. It caused Ron and I more hard work than any two previous engines, for the entire grate was covered by a layer of hard tenacious clinker, every inch of which had to be literally chipped off. Luckily we were able to obtain a Western dart to use for this task, otherwise we would have been there all night. This formidable 12-foot-long chisel was the only fire iron on the shed capable of doing the job, and glory be to the gentleman who had the foresight to borrow it from the other Region. Apart from the clinker, the firebox was knee-deep in ash with precious little fire left on top of it and, despite Ron's skill, we were not able to save sufficient from which to light up. So long did we take with this engine that both steam and water levels dropped very low and, while I was digging my way through the solid bed of char that was nearly level with the top of the blastpipe, Ron negotiated with a colleague on the engine behind to secure a tow into No 3 shed.

Eventually the task was completed, and the yard foreman, who knew full well that he had given us a very rough cop, tried to make amends next by presenting us with a Class '3F' 0-6-0 tank. Although a dreaded tank engine, this 'Jinty' was so diminutive by comparison that it turned out to be a piece of cake, as the saying goes. The whole of the grate area was within easy reach of a short clinker shovel, while there was so little char in the tiny smokebox that a dustpan and brush would almost have been quite adequate. We ended the day with a Class '2P' 4-4-0 which, having been used only lightly with best-grade coal, also proved to be quite easy.

And so the week progressed; it was hot and dirty work, but we had a great variety of engines to deal with and by Saturday night I felt that I could now tackle with confidence just about everything that might come to the shed. However, knowing how and actually doing a job are poles apart, for I still did not possess the necessary strength or stamina to dispose of the average engine by myself without a rest. This no doubt would come in time, for after only one week my muscles had taken on a much harder feel and I was sure that my biceps had grown another half-inch.

The following week we were booked to arrive at 5.00 am for preparation duties, and since I liked to have a substantial breakfast before beginning a strenuous day, it entailed arising at about 4.00 am. Anxious not to oversleep, I seemed to wake up at 15-minute intervals from about midnight onwards. Although not conducive to a good night's rest, it at least ensured that I was wide awake by the predetermined time to show a leg. Later on, after years of practice, I developed the ability to awake exactly at the minute I wished, and although I always set my alarm clock, I was invariably ready to depress the stop button as it actually went off.

With the inner man well satisfied I was able to enjoy the ride to work through deserted streets. On summer mornings getting up early enabled one to see all the glories of the dawn, a pleasure not appreciated by the majority of the populace, but in the middle of winter it did have its drawbacks, and ploughing the first furrow through half a foot of snow on a bicycle could be both spectacular and not a little dangerous, particularly when descending the precipitous Ash Road hill near the shed. During the previous afternoon I had curled up for a quiet half hour with *Questions for Enginemen* and read through the section devoted to the fireman's duties when preparing an engine. It ran as follows:

'A fireman joining his engine on the shed should first examine and test the water gauges, notice the steam pressure and, if this is sufficient, at once test both injectors. If there is insufficient steam pressure he should at once proceed to level the fire in the box and commence to build it up in order to raise steam without delay so that the injectors can be tested as early as possible. If the

state of the fire is entirely unsatisfactory or the steam pressure and water level excessively low, no time should be lost in notifying the driver and the foreman who will then, if necessary, be able to provide another engine without incurring any delay.

'It is the fireman's duty to draw the tools and equipment from the stores. Clean, trim and fill headlamps, gauge lamp and handlamp. He must inspect the detonator canister to note whether the lid is properly sealed in position, and if the tape is broken he should obtain a sealed container from the stores. When using a coal of clinkering nature, he must obtain a supply of limestone or broken firebrick and spread this evenly over the firebars as early as possible after the fire has been levelled out. The fireman should also satisfy himself that the smokebox is properly cleared of char and afterwards must see that the smokebox door is securely fastened up, taking care to wipe the faces of the door joint clean of char before closing it. He must also be particular to sweep the front platform and foot framing clear of all loose char and sand which will be liable to blow about into the motion, and in any case present a slack and untidy appearance. The sandboxes and the container of the sand gun must be filled, and finally the fireman must pay special attention to the position of the fire irons and coal on the tender, and must see that all are properly stowed in accordance with instructions.'

To be forewarned is to be forearmed, so with this information firmly implanted in my mind I felt reasonably confident at being able to tackle the day ahead. Ron overtook me just before reaching the depot and was already in the lobby signing on when I walked in.

'Morning, mate, are you fighting fit?' he enquired, obviously in the best of spirits himself. I answered in the affirmative, and after collecting my card from the clerk, joined him at one of the several high writing tables that surrounded the lobby.

'That's what we've got to get through today,' he said, passing over a metal-backed wallet containing the relevant job card. It listed six engines and the jobs they were destined for, but very little other information.

'Come on round to the engine board and I'll show you how it works,' he continued, noticing my puzzled expression.

The board was located on the wall of No 2 shed and was unique in that it was the centre of the only well-lit area in the whole shed. In appearance it was not unlike a huge blackboard and listed all the permanent jobs in chronological order. Beside these jobs the foreman chalked the engine numbers allocated to them and whereabouts in the depot they were stabled, so that provided one knew the job and its time, one could quickly ascertain the engine and its location. Ron looked at his job card and then at the board.

'Well, we've got the first two anyhow,' he said, pointing out a couple of engines with his finger. 'As with disposing, a lot of chaps try to get through them as quickly as possible, the driver taking one and the fireman another,' he went on, 'but it will be a while before you are ready for that. To start with, it will be better to work together until you get the hang of everything.'

I nodded my consent. 'Is 4201 in No 1 shed the first then?' I enquired.

'Yes,' said Ron. 'See if you can find her and I will join you there when I've dropped my traps in the locker.'

I made my way round the table and entered No 1 shed; as usual it was very gloomy, with a great cloud of raw smoke hanging in a thick layer beneath the roof. It was quite impossible to make out the smokebox numbers of engines on the other side of the table pit, so I was obliged to walk round 12 of the possible 23 berths before spotting her. My first impression on gaining the cab was that of utter dismay. Coal lay strewn all over the footplate, and everything was coated in soot. She had obviously been in for a washout and had spent the last few days completely at the mercy of energetic preparation crews who had effectively stripped from her everything that was removable. Even one gauge glass protector and the driver's pedestal were missing. However, there was a good fire in the box, the boiler was just about full and there was 140 lbs per sq in showing on the pressure gauge.

My first task now was to draw the tools and lamps from the stores, and I set off hot-foot in that direction. On arrival I gave the engine number to

The arrangement board at Camden Town MPD on 1 September 1936. This is fairly typical of such boards to be found throughout the LMS system, and was similar to that at Saltley in BR days. The Shed Foreman would chalk engine numbers and their location beside the jobs listed so that train crews could immediately identify their particular locomotive and quickly find its position in the shed.

the storeman, who merely shrugged apologetically and said he could only furnish me with a firing shovel and a seven-eighths spanner. I scurried back to the engine bearing my trophies. Ron was just climbing down from the footplate.

'In a bit of a state, isn't she?' he murmured as I galloped up to him.

'They haven't any tools in the stores,' I gasped somewhat breathlessly.

'I'm afraid that's not unusual at this time of a morning. You'll just have to scrounge around the shed and rob another engine. The arrival road may be your best bet.'

Ron went on briefly to explain that in the good old days locomotives had their own tools and each was stamped with the engine number. However, when Josiah Stamp instituted his economies on the LMS in the 1930s, tools were kept in a common store, booked out to an engine for its turn of duty and then returned to the store when this was completed. The idea, of course, was that a considerable reduction in the number of sets required could be effected. Unfortunately, in the early 1950s such was the shortage of equipment that much time was wasted by crews running around trying to find some. Very often they were forced to wait for engines coming on to the shed before they themselves could depart. Regrettably, this deplorable state of affairs persisted for many years, and it was not until the late 1950s that sufficient tools became generally available. The situation was always at its worst during the early part of the day and at its best in the late evening, when a glut of engines seemed to arrive at the shed.

I looked desperately around No 1 shed for engines with lamps, but there were none to be seen. Being slightly nearer to No 3 shed at the time, I tried in there first, but again drew a blank. This is damned silly, I thought, beginning to feel a trifle ruffled, and dashed back across No 1 shed into No 2 where, wonder of wonders, I spied a '2P' with a lamp on its front bracket. I quickly gathered this up, together with the gauge lamp, rear lamp and coal pick. I was lucky. The engine had just been turned off, and no doubt in another minute this lot would have been whisked away by some other foraging preparation crew. Not daring to put anything down, I walked over to the stores again where I filled and trimmed the lamps.

Ron in the meantime had also been out on a hunting expedition and had found an oil bottle, a feeder and a gauge frame spanner.

'There's a decent slaking pipe on that one there,' he said, pointing to a '3F' standing two pits away.

I deposited my precious equipment on the footplate and, picking up the seven-eighths spanner, scampered over to the '3F', anxious in case anyone else should get there first. The slaking pipe was secured by a seven-eighths brass nut and a hefty heave with the spanner sufficed to free it. While still on the footplate, the thought suddenly struck me that fire irons might be concealed behind the heap of coal on the tender, and a quick ascent into the smoke clouds revealed that there was indeed a full set. I descended with my booty as quickly as possible and, after pausing for a brief coughing session, clattered back to our engine with the fire irons in tow. By now I was soaked with perspiration and I came to the firm conclusion that, if anything, preparation was even more energetic than disposal.

After depositing the fire irons on the back of the tender, I attached the slaking pipe and, still with the seven-eighths spanner in my hand, clambered round the framing to attend to the smokebox lugs. I pulled off the sandbox covers on my way and made the not entirely unexpected discovery that not one of them was more than half full. We were just about as far from either of the sand ovens as one could be at Saltley, so my heart didn't exactly pound with joy, although it was very soon pounding with exertion.

First I had to find the confounded buckets, which on this occasion were well hidden in a dark corner behind the tender of a '2P' in No 2 shed. Then came the strenuous work of hauling the sand across to the engine, which at two buckets per sandbox meant six trips. After only the second agonising journey my arms felt as though they were being torn out of their sockets, and I desperately wished that I could find a wheelbarrow. After the fourth trip, Ron declared that he had completed the oiling and he would bring the engine on to the table, since we were now falling behind schedule. He did this by himself while I staggered back with more sand.

The final trip found me at the engine in such an exhausted state that I had neither strength to lift the buckets up on the framing nor sufficient breath to call for help. Fortunately Ron, realising my predicament, came to my aid.

'OK, old son,' he said with a partially concealed smile, 'secure the table in No 3 shed and we'll get outside.'

I nodded in answer, being still short of breath, and just managed to forestall another preparation crew who were ready to bring out a Class '8F'.

The points were correctly set for the departure road, so as Ron trundled slowly over the turntable I hopped on the engine steps, and then climbed slowly up to the footplate.

'Getting a sweat on, mate?' said Ron with a broad grin.

'It was those blasted sandboxes,' I replied vehemently.

'Yes,' he said sympathetically, 'they can be real rough work at times, particularly with a high framed engine such as a "Black Five". By the way, we've got to drop her on the back departure road, so we'll top up the tank at the water column there.'

While the tank was filling, I went across to the arrival roads where a couple of engines were now standing, and managed to collect the two spanners, the bucket and the can of detonators, of which we were still deficient. Meanwhile Ron set about the task of tidying up the footplate. A lot of preparation crews never bothered to do this, but, as Ron said, while you were filling up the boiler it was no trouble to quickly hose the dust off the footboards, and this made things so much more pleasant for the men who were to work her. We moved up to the end of the departure road and, after screwing the hand brake hard on, dropping the damper, closing the firedoors, setting the reversing screw in mid-gear and opening the taps, we departed leaving her reasonably spick and span.

Our next engine was a Class '8F' in No 3 shed, and as we walked over Ron suggested that we remove everything from a Class '4F' that had just arrived, since it was unlikely that the stores had much to offer yet. Everything, that is, except the firing shovel which was a short-handled one, and the seven-eighths spanner which the disposal men would require to open the smokebox door with. We arrived at the '8F' and found it in a much better state than the previous engine. At least the cab wasn't covered in smuts, the water tank was just about full and there was a full complement of

fire irons lodged in the tender compartment. On the debit side, though, steam pressure was a little low at 80 lbs per sq in, so I felt that a good stir round with the rake was called for. Unfortunately there was insufficient fire under the doors to cover all the grate and, realising that I would have to do this in stages, I managed to spread what there was evenly over the rear half. Opening the back damper, I left this to burn up under the influence of the blower while I went off in search of a firing shovel and seven-eighths spanner. The stores were again able to supply a firing shovel of the correct size, albeit a somewhat battered specimen, but they were still short of spanners. However, while I was at the window filling the lamps, a full set arrived and I was able to extract the one required.

So far things were not quite such a mad dash as with the '4F', mainly because I had enjoyed better luck in acquiring the tools. No extra time was allowed for hunting around for equipment, and when the original study had been conducted to fix how long it should take to prepare the various classes of locomotives, it was assumed that all tools could be drawn without delay from the stores. Normally 45 minutes was scheduled for engines rated '4F', '3P' and under, while '4P' 'Compounds' and engines rated above '5MT' were allowed one hour. This was loosely based on the time it took to raise steam. On the whole, men accepted the additional burden of tool-hunting with commendable indifference, since it was largely in their own interests that the engines were ready to book off the shed at the correct time. If they had prepared their own engine, then any excessive delay could well result in a cancellation of their job, and they might be relegated to shed work. In the case of preparation crews, the sooner they finished their prescribed number of engines, the sooner they could go home.

I arrived back at the '8F' to find Ron still busy with the oiling, and I noticed that no black smoke was visible at the chimney. A look into the firebox showed that the fire I had spread around was now burning brightly, so I covered this with a dozen shovels of coal before climbing on to the framing to check the automatic lubricators and those benighted sandboxes. One cannot look directly into the sandbox of an '8F' since, unlike a '4F', they are filled via a cranked tube some 6 inches in diameter. The technique we used to determine the quantity contained therein was simple. If one could see sand at the bottom of the tube, then it was full enough. If it was not visible, then one filled it until it was. I breathed a very deep sigh of relief when I found that all were full, as indeed were the lubricators, and I mused on the irony of this engine being only a few paces from the sand oven and yet not requiring any sand. Such is life!

All effort could now be concentrated on raising steam and, with this prime consideration in view, I once more opened the firedoors to see how things were progressing. The fresh coal was burning well, so it was now possible to spread this to the front half of the grate, since until that area was covered no results would be registered on the pressure gauge. I achieved this by using the clinker shovel, experience having taught me that this was a most effective tool in these circumstances. By digging the blade into the fire under the door and by using a sort of seesaw action I was able to deposit pockets of bright fire all over the bare bars at the front end. Then, by filling in the gaps with a thin layer of well-chosen cobbles, it was only a matter of a few minutes before the whole bed was thoroughly ablaze. After that, by firing a small quantity of coal on to the brighter areas, and with both the blower and the front damper wide open, pressure soon began to build up.

'How's she looking now?' called Ron, who had just completed his oiling.

'Beginning to move - in fact, it's up to 90,' I answered.

'Right, I'll just nip over to the engine board and see what else is down for us,' he replied, and turning on his heel vanished through the entrance to No 1 shed. I was still tidying the footplate when a few minutes later Ron's head suddenly appeared in the gap between tender and cab. He craned his neck to see the pressure gauge, which by now was climbing past the 150 lbs per sq in mark.

'OK, mate, bring her forward,' he shouted.

'Me?' I replied, more than somewhat surprised.

'Yes, come on, I've got the table,' and with that, he walked back to the control position and leaned on the single retaining catch, waiting.

Things are looking up, I thought, for this was the first time Ron had asked me to move an engine. I quickly knocked over the steam brake handle, released the tender brake, and wound her into full forward gear. Leaving the taps open, I flicked across the small ejector valve and, as the

brakes came off, I gave a short hoot on the whistle before easing open the regulator. Steam hissed noisily from the cylinder cocks and she glided smoothly forwards. I gave another little heave on the regulator before snapping it shut and then, leaning out of the side window so as to judge my speed more accurately, I listened for the tell-tale clunks as the wheels passed over the gap between the pit and table. Five clunks for the engine, and one, two - hand poised on brake ready for the sudden application - three! I knocked over the handle and we eased to a halt just about in the correct position. Feeling mighty pleased with myself, I once more applied the hand brake, for we had to turn the engine through nearly 180 degrees and I knew Ron would use the vacuum motor.

'Blow up!' he bellowed when the hoses were connected.

I wound open the brass wheel of the large ejector and we started to rotate slowly so that the engine pointed westwards. This time we had to leave her on the departure road next to the one on which we had stabled the '4F', and Ron kindly allowed me to drive while he ran in front setting the points. Like many young drivers who until quite recently had been firing, he realised that, apart from being a necessary part of the training, allowing the fireman to move the engine about the yard helped to relieve the monotony of shed work. It also gave the driver a chance to assess his mate's potential capabilities so that if and when he decided to tackle quota work, he could do so with a higher degree of confidence.

After the '8F' we prepared a '3F' and a 'Compound', which Ron did not relish because of the difficulty and additional work involved in oiling the inside motion. We then allowed ourselves a short break for lunch, and I must admit that I was grateful for a chance to sit down for a while. Galloping around in search of tools and fetching sand was having a peculiar effect on my legs - they were beginning to feel as though they were made of lead.

All too soon this brief respite was over and we were soon hard at it, preparing another '4F'. This in turn was followed by a 'Black Five', and the day was finally rounded off with a 'Crab'. As the afternoon wore on, so the tool situation gradually improved, which in part compensated for my rapidly increasing fatigue, and I was actually able to draw all the equipment I required for the 'Five' and the 'Crab' direct from the stores. We eventually booked off with half an hour to spare and, as I once more pedalled slowly home, I concluded that in respect of the amount of energy expended, there was nothing much to choose between disposal and preparation. In the case of the former, it was the top half of the body that took all the stress, whereas with the latter the effort was biased towards the lower appendages.

This really set the pattern for the rest of the week. The jobs were always the same, though of course the engines were usually different, and after the first day Ron allowed me to drive alternate engines, irrespective of their class. When time permitted he showed me how and where to oil them, and how to set the motion so that it was in the most convenient position. Also he pointed out the most important parts to check and examine for possible causes of failure, and while I found this side of our work very interesting indeed, I soon discovered that oiling can be far dirtier than anything a fireman is supposed to do during preparation.

This particular week was somewhat outstanding in that shed work was enlivened by a spate of collisions and incidents of gradually increasing severity until at lunchtime on Friday an accident occurred that could well have resulted in tragic consequences. It all started when a senior driver nudged the shed wall when turning off a Class '5' in No 3 shed. He admitted to an error of judgment and, apart from putting a slight bulge in the aforesaid wall, which was the common one shared by No 1 and No 3 sheds, little harm was done. However, this minor incident seemed to open Pandora's box and release the jinx that reigned over Saltley for five days. Not wishing to be left out of things, one of the quota men effectively punched a hole clean through the canal-side wall of No 3 shed with an '8F', and deposited 2 tons of assorted masonry into a 12-ton open wagon which was conveniently parked on the track outside.

Looking somewhat tatty by 1955, the substantial walls of Saltley's No 3 shed had withstood many attempts to demolish them. The Luftwaffe came nearest to success, although numerous locomotives had over the years attempted to construct alternative entrances. Evidence of one such attempt can be seen to the left of No 43580's smokebox, where heavy timbers are shoring up the resultant aperture. On this occasion an empty 12-ton open wagon had been parked conveniently in just the correct position to receive the displaced masonry. *F. W. Shuttleworth*

The following day some marshalling men got carried away and a dead engine that they were manoeuvring for the fitters decided to run off on its own and constructed a neat third exit from No 1 shed. Getting thoroughly into the spirit of competition, a Passed Cleaner who had no business to be driving at the time demolished, with the aid of a Class '8F', another section of poor old No 3 shed's wall adjacent to the diesel oil storage tank.

Meanwhile the men out in the shed yard, intolerant of being outdone by their colleagues inside, tore the side out of a Class '5' tender that was standing foul on one of the disposal pits. The day's destruction was rounded off by a substantial head-on collision between a 'Black Five', which had been prepared for the Carlisle and which had been backed under the hopper to top up with coal, and a '4P' tank engine manned by an eager disposal crew who failed to realise that the 'Five' would be coming back up the arrival road. It buckled the latter's front framing and removed a buffer from the tank engine.

This campaign to deplete Saltley's locomotive stud was firmly re-established on the Thursday when a 'Super D' and a Class '3F', which were coupled together for the convenience of a disposal driver, ran away unmanned down to the stop block at the end of the ashpits. They clouted this formidable and ancient structure with sufficient violence to cause extensive damage to both engines' buffer beams and framings. For any two of these accidents to happen in any given month would be unusual; for all to happen within the space of less than a week was incredible.

Nothing more occurred until the climax of Friday lunchtime. One of the quota men had disposed of a 'Compound' and, while waiting to enter No 2 shed, had filled the boiler to a greater degree than was strictly wise. This also had the effect of reducing the steam pressure to little over 100 lbs per sq in. Now, the steam brake on a 'Compound' was notoriously ineffective, particularly when pressure is low; the designers in their wisdom envisaged their being used only on trains fitted with a continuous braking system. Another awkward thing about 'Compounds' was that they often tended not to respond to an initial opening of the regulator, and there was a considerable delay before the wheels started to rotate. Moreover, 24 turns of a very stiff reversing screw from full forward gear to full backward gear preclude any swift changes in direction, should the need arise to help out on the lack of braking power. All these factors could add up to a very lethal combination when trying to manoeuvre hastily in confined places.

Familiarity breeds contempt, and when one has executed an operation successfully many hundreds of times it is easy to relax one's concentration for a moment. Whatever the reasons, the 'Compound' was given a good handful of regulator when it seemed reluctant to move off the table. Then she did move - with a rush, the great 7-foot drivers slipping violently - and all that momentum could not be arrested by those feeble brakes in the few yards available. The result was inevitable. The 'Compound', still travelling at a fair speed, jumped the pit stops and crashed tender-first with terrific force into the shed wall that divided it from the main office. So great was the impact that a section of wall roughly the size of the tender exploded into the office, and some portions of the thick brickwork flew right across the room and through the windows opposite. Only a few minutes earlier members of the office staff were working in this area and, had they not just retired for lunch, would certainly not have lived to see another day.

The damage took several days to repair and, being right next to the enginemen's lobby, no member of the footplate staff could fail to see the extent of the devastation or realise the possible consequences. Fortunately it had a very sobering effect on all concerned and seemed to exorcise our jinx for, although incidents did occur from time to time in the future, they were infrequent and isolated affairs, quite within the bounds of reason for a motive power depot the size of Saltley.

6
CHARACTERS

As the weeks progressed, so my expertise developed under Ron's expert guidance, and his confidence in my driving abilities grew, even to the extent of allowing me to do much of the driving. We worked well together as a team and enjoyed each other's company, but then one Saturday he arrived with his normally happy face clouded with worry. He confided in me that his wife had been experiencing health problems for some while, and that cancer was now suspected. As a result she was going into hospital for tests, and since he needed to be at home with his children at night he had arranged to swop turns with another driver in the link, Doug Pinkerton. I knew that we were booked on nights the following week, and I had meant to question Ron on what this 10.18 pm Bromford job was all about, but having suffered such a bombshell, I forgot to do so. Understandably Ron was very quiet and detached that day, and I did not feel disposed to intrude on his thoughts. However, as we parted a hint of that old twinkle came into his eyes.

'You'll enjoy being with Doug for a week,' he said in a way that implied something, but what I could not be certain.

Doug Pinkerton, known as 'Pinky' to all his acquaintances, was a lean, powerfully built Brummie of just under 6 feet in height and the same age as Ron. Not even his mother would have called him handsome, but his chunky, square-cut features had a pleasant, alert expression, and he moved in a dynamic way, which unfortunately could be a little disconcerting for those more tranquil souls who might happen to be in close proximity. He was not as most men, for he seemed to attract those unknown forces that provided experiences few others shared, and he also possessed that strange ability to make things become

unstuck. Objects and structures that for years had withstood the tests of time seemed to suddenly give up the ghost when Pinky got near them. However, on the other hand his talents extended to having one of the most comprehensive route cards at Saltley, for he signed from Bristol in the south to Carlisle in the north, and on the many occasions I was to work with him in the future he proved himself to be a really first-class driver.

We first met in the enginemen's lobby at about 9.45 pm on the Monday evening, and after introducing ourselves he suggested that we went round to the cabin to mash some tea before joining the shed bus in the car park. Two Ford 26-seater utilities and one Bedford 12-seater were stationed at Saltley for the purpose of conveying engine crews to and from certain predetermined pick-up points in the locality. As we doubled round to the cabin (Doug, I duly found, did everything at the double), he explained that he always liked a drink of tea before starting work.

'What is this Bromford job, then?' I puffed as I trotted alongside in an effort to keep up with him.

'Garratts,' he shouted, for Doug always spoke loudly, rather like the first mate of a clipper ship calling to his men to reef the top gallants in the teeth of a raging nor'wester.

'Garratts?' I replied, non-plussed.

'Yes, Garratts. They're too big to dispose of on shed, so they coal them here and then take them down to Bromford where we dispose and prepare them, before they work the empties back to Toton. It can be quite cushy - sometimes you only get one all night, while on other occasions you can get three or four, and then you really earn your keep.'

So that was it then, same sort of work but a different location. Anyhow, it made a change and I

2-6-0+0-6-2 Garratt No 47998, one of the original three built with fixed 7-ton coal bunkers in 1927. Sister locomotive No 47997 was later equipped with the prototype 9-ton rotary bunker, but the other two remained as built. The later 1930 batch of 30 locomotives ultimately received 10-ton rotary bunkers. Waiting to return to Toton after servicing, this leviathan is shown on the departure road at Saltley on 30 January 1955. *F. W. Shuttleworth*

was very interested to have a close look at a Garratt. These monsters could be seen fairly frequently trundling around the area with great strings of wagons in tow, but so far I had never been on one, nor had I even managed to get near one during my weeks on the shed.

The old Midland Railway policy was to double-head two 0-6-0s on the heavy Toton to Brent coal trains, and after the Grouping this policy still persisted. Obviously such a situation was not economically viable, and many alternative forms of motive power that would conform to the rather severe loading restriction on that route were considered. The eventual outcome was that in 1927 the first three prototype 2-6-0+0-6-2 Garratts were delivered. These were supplemented in 1930 by a further 30 locomotives fitted eventually with 10-ton capacity rotating bunkers. With a tractive effort of 45,620 lbs they were well able to do the job intended, but unfortunately Derby design office interference resulted in them being equipped with short-travel valve gear and inadequate axlebox bearings, which proved to be a perpetual weakness. In later years traffic conditions changed so that Stanier '8Fs' could cope with the original work, thereby releasing the Garratts for more general duties. In the early 1950s they could be seen frequently on westbound freight trains, which is why we had a fair share coming to Saltley.

Sill at a half gallop we arrived at the cabin door and, flinging it open with great vigour, Doug leaped inside. A yell of anguish greeted this action for an unfortunate young fireman was at that moment making his exit.

'Oops, sorry, young man,' said Doug with genuine concern, while stooping to help the dazed lad to his feet.

Knowing that this particular duty would allow him time to cook a substantial supper, and Doug certainly liked his food, he had in his haversack a veritable banquet. Now, as he leaned over, this haversack inverted and the entire contents, commencing with a tin plate and ending with two eggs and a bottle of milk, poured forth. While the first part of his banquet was bouncing noisily off the stone floor, Doug realised with remarkable perception that the last three items would not. He therefore made a lightning grab for them while they were still in flight, a task made no easier by their following quite different trajectories.

Even a man a dynamic as Doug Pinkerton needed a minimum of three hands to achieve success in the time available, and of course he had but two. A frantic movement of his left hand only deflected the two eggs into a higher orbit, but he did do rather better with his right. A fleeting touch gave the milk bottle a bit more altitude so that he was able to get into position for a catch, but milk bottles are slippery things, particularly when shedding their contents in a whirling spray, and Doug was soon entertaining the onlookers with an unusual juggling display while he raced beneath it. A flying catch fully up to County Cricket standards was cushioned by the ample laps of three elderly drivers who up to that point had been enjoying a quiet read of their evening papers. At approximately the same instant the two eggs terminated their extended travels, one in the middle of a

Until 1956 staff facilities were rather basic, but then on this open space was erected a very pleasant Staff Amenity Block, much appreciated by all. Prior to its completion, train crews used the right-hand end of the building supporting Saltley's vast water tank. The checkers' hut, where the foreman's assistants also worked, can be seen adjacent to the two telephone poles, while the tracks on the extreme right lead to the entrance of No 2 shed.

dominoes school, the other splattering on the forehead of a bald driver who had just obligingly removed his cap.

I wasn't sure whether Doug was trying to apologise for or excuse his actions, because even his strong voice was drowned by the howls of derision from the offended parties. It's a strange thing, but when you know it would be considered inappropriate of impolite to laugh, the urge to do so increases tenfold. The tears were streaming down my face in an effort to fight this urge as I assisted Doug to clear up the mess and return the erstwhile

The interior of the mess room, known to all as The Cabin. On the left is the gigantic combustion stove capable of roasting all the room's inhabitants even on the coldest days. The three large zinc-covered dining tables also provided a surface for card and domino schools for those so inclined. Entering through the door on the right, the accident-prone Doug Pinkerton proceeded to wreak havoc on all and sundry!

contents of his bag to where they belonged.

Still muttering to himself as he wiped the remains of split milk from his clothing, he carefully made his way over to the large iron kettle. Normally this vital piece of equipment was kept filled to the brim with boiling water by Dusty the Mess Steward. Having been delayed that night, he had not been there to replenish the demands made upon it in his usual efficient manner, so when Doug opened the tap located at its base only a trickle ran out. No doubt still distracted by his recent exploits, he unthinkingly grasped the iron handle, which was just as hot as the body, and tilted it forward so that what remained of the contents would flow more quickly.

As the angle passed the point of no return, so the heat struck through the horny palm of Doug's right hand. The result was nearly as spectacular as his opening act. With a shout of pain he leaped backwards, the kettle crashed to the floor, whereupon it parted company with its spout, while his tea-can doused the front row of his audience with hot water and tea-leaves. Doug looked round for sympathy, which needless to say was not forthcoming.

'For Christ's sake, Pinky, buzz off before you wreck the rest of the place!' yelled the driver who had just received the egg-yolk beauty treatment. This sentiment was loudly echoed by all and sundry, and realising that further explanations were pointless, we beat a hasty retreat, leaving another urgent repair for the tinsmith.

Some of our composure had been regained by the time we had seated ourselves in the bus, where I tried to distract Doug from recounting his latest exploits to the other occupants. The ride to Bromford was the usual hectic mystery tour that the bus drivers always managed to give us through the ill-lit streets of east Birmingham. It appeared that they felt it incumbent upon them to bring a little excitement into our lives by driving at speed on only sidelights.

The men to be relieved were already waiting at the roadside when we alighted.

'You've only got one at the moment, Doug,' said the driver who was also in our link. 'She's at the end of the pit and well topped up,'

'Right,' replied Doug, now quite cheerful again, and he set off at a swift pace down the dark embankment with me in close pursuit.

The disposal area consisted of two roads, one with an ash pit. These converged into a single line leading to a turntable and a dead end just beyond. Between the two roads was a water column, and almost opposite this on the far side of the ash pit was a small, stoutly built wooden hut. As I approached I could see a dim outline of a Garratt standing at the rear end of the pit road, looking more massive than ever in the dark.

'We'd better check her first,' said Doug, hauling a rubber-cased torch out of his pocket. I followed him on to the footplate and viewed the acres of unfamiliar surroundings. As the relived driver had said, all was well, the boiler was full, the pressure gauge was showing 160 lbs per sq in, and when Doug pulled open the firedoors a healthy flicker of flame rolled up from the back corners. I had not realised just how large the Garratt firebox was, and I squatted for a moment peering in awe round that vast cavern. Doug must have read my thoughts.

'Yes, you can get a fair old bit of coal in there, my lad,' he said with a chuckle. 'In fact, you can shovel a ton and a half at one session and then not fill it.'

I could well believe that, for although the grate area was large by any standards, it was the depth that was so impressive. No wonder that most of them were fitted with rotating bunkers that rolled the coal forwards at the touch of a lever.

'Come on,' said Doug. 'She'll be alright for hours. Let's get settled in the cabin - I've got my supper to prepare.'

On opening the door a cheery glow greeted us from the old-fashioned cast iron stove that stood on one side of the hut, the warmth contrasting sharply with the now quite chilly night air outside. The wall opposite to the stove contained a window made up of numerous small panes of glass overlooking the ash pit, while under the window and projecting into the room was a zinc-topped deal table. On either side of this lay bench seats that looked, and were indeed to prove, very adequate for a comfortable nap should the opportunity present itself. The whole ensemble was illuminated by an electric light set high in the apex of the roof. I inspected our temporary home closely, decided that it was a very nice cosy little place, and settled myself contentedly on one of the benches to await developments. Doug, meanwhile, had emptied the contents of his bag on to the table and was sorting through the remains of his food. He started to lament the loss of his two eggs, but being at heart an optimist, announced

For sheer size the Garratts were in a class of their own, and for this reason they were often only coaled at Saltley, disposal and preparation being completed at nearby Bromford where they were less of an embarrassment. Filling the 10-ton rotary bunker was a time-consuming operation, while even watering seemed to take longer than usual. With so much engine to go at, Doug Pinkerton managed to perform some unusual antics when servicing them at Bromford!

that he didn't think their absence would spoil the rest of his mixed grill, for he still had bacon, sausages and tomatoes.

Doug had brought this fry-up being well familiar with the cooking facilities available in the form of that not too handsome but decidedly efficient Edwardian stove. He opened the dampers fully in order to raise the temperature of the cooking surface as much as possible and, having laid the rashers of bacon in his tin plate, removed the opening in the top of the stove so as to stir up the fire.

Exactly how he managed it I'm not quite sure. Out of the corner of my eye I had a fleeting glimpse of Doug armed with a stout poker attacking the fire with great determination. Suddenly a loud yell, quickly followed by an even greater crash, caused me to jump out of my seat and swivel round to see what had caused the commotion. I was just in time to be enthralled by another piece of slapstick. The stove was rocking back at an acute angle. Doug, still with poker in hand, was diving over it, while the 6-foot length of stovepipe that had been abruptly divorced from its rightful resting place was in the process of descending in two separate sections from the roof. As the various moving objects came to rest, the whole scene disappeared behind clouds of whirling black soot, and it was then that I leaped for the door. A split second later I was out in the fresh air, and looking back towards the cabin I could make out very little except for a dull red glow, rather like a miniature sun on a foggy winter's day, which turned out to be the electric light filament.

The first thing to emerge was a string of eloquent profanities, then a black shape groped its way over the threshold and tottered outside.

'Are you alright, Doug?' I called, fearing that he had done himself some serious mischief.

'No, I'm bloody well not,' he hissed, rubbing his right arm ruefully.

'Whatever did you do?' I asked, curious to know the cause.

'I slipped over that damned stove,' he said simply, for Doug had a habit of reducing the most complex matters to their basic terms. We waited for some minutes until the clouds of dust and soot had thinned somewhat, then entered to survey the wreckage. A Mills bomb could not have created much more havoc. It took us the best part of an hour to reposition the stovepipe and clean up the soot that had settled in a thick layer over every horizontal surface.

However, in Doug's eyes the accident was tantamount to a major disaster, for he kept repeating 'Just look at my flaming supper'. I once again could not help seeing the funny side of it, and every time he made this comment I just could not contain myself. We had nearly finished cleaning up when a Garratt arrived freshly coaled from the shed. It had rolled on to the pit completely unnoticed while we were so engrossed in our unscheduled labours.

The Toton driver, on opening the cabin door, was immediately confronted by Doug. He looked a little surprised, but quickly recovered himself and said quite pleasantly, 'Oh, hallo Sambo, where's your driver?'

Seeing that Doug wore the uniform of a footplateman, he had mistakenly supposed that Doug was a colonial gentleman employed as a fireman. This was not an altogether surprising error, since all that could be seen of Doug's now ebony features were the whites of his eyes and his gleaming teeth. Doug stood stock still for a few seconds, his mouth gaped open, his eyes bulged, while his large black hands clenched and unclenched menacingly. Quivering all over, he exclaimed in a hoarse shout 'Bloody Sambo, bloody Sambo!', then he let rip with a tirade of choice phrases, which among other things cast certain doubts on the parentage of the poor unfortunate Toton man.

I had just returned with a fresh bucket of water so that we could wash ourselves and had witnessed this encounter from outside the door. Hearing Doug called 'Sambo' was the last straw; the pent-up excitement of the evening's escapades was too much for me and once more I was helpless with laughter. The Toton driver, quite visibly shaken, grabbed his mate who had now joined him and literally ran from the scene, convinced in his mind that he had just had a very narrow escape from a couple of lunatics.

Back in the cabin Doug viewed himself in the mirror that was nailed to the wall opposite the door and shied in surprise like a startled foal, for he barely recognised the face that goggled back at him.

'Good Lord,' he gasped, because he really did look more like a member of the Black and White Minstrel Show than a driver on British Railways. 'Why didn't you tell me I looked like this?'

I bit my lip in an effort to keep control and said nothing.

'Anyway,' he continued, 'that Garratt can stay where it is for a while - we'll have something to eat first,'

He did in fact manage to first clean and then cook his food without further mishap, and feeling by now fairly peckish I too disposed of half my ample supply of sandwiches. Thus feasted, we felt better able to tackle the monster that had been patiently waiting outside.

Doug explained to my relief that cleaning the fire on a Garratt was not too bad really, since they were equipped with a section of grate in the left-hand front corner of the firebox that dropped in the form of a flap. This enabled the fire to be pushed straight through into the ashpan. Providing that one man cleared the pan while the other pushed out the fire, it was fairly straightforward. Everything about a Garratt on first acquaintance was outsized; the tank, for example, seemed to take ages to fill with its 4,500 gallons of water,

but Doug made good use of this time by clearing the fire from the area above the flap.

He was obviously having difficulty in keeping his feet, though, and when I queried this fact he proudly explained that he was wearing a new pair of shoes. They turned out to have thick crepe soles, which although very comfortable were quite unsuited for use on the footplate since the soles tended to absorb oil in liberal quantities. The co-efficient of friction between the oiled crepe and wet metal was practically zero, and the consequences were more than a little dangerous, even if highly amusing, particularly when the soles were placed underneath someone as accident-prone as Doug. He did, however, persist in wearing them for most of the week, but eventually his determination waned as a result of a series of spectacular acrobatics, which even he realised would inevitably end in some serious injury.

The fire-cleaning operation was therefore basically similar to that used when disposing a Class '8', and was only made difficult for Doug on this occasion by the fact that every time he pushed or pulled a fire iron he gave a pretty good imitation of a particularly energetic Egyptian sand-dancer. When eventually the tank was filled, we drew ahead across the table before dropping back on the pit road. Doug managed in his boisterous way to make the Garratt slip, and I noticed afterwards that eight exhaust beats emerged from the chimney for each revolution of the wheels instead of the previous four.

'This sometimes happens,' he explained when I questioned him on the point. 'Being in effect two separate engines, they can come out of synchronisation.'

When in position over the pit, Doug told me to clear the ashpan first, and when this was done he would start to drop the fire. Having dampers at both ends of the pan meant that I could both push and pull the contents out without the need for me to go underneath, although it did entail working from first one side and then the other. Although not particularly full of ash, it took quite some time because the pan, in keeping with the rest of the engine, was so large.

At last I was ready, and shouted to Doug. For what seemed hours, vast quantities of fire and clinker dropped into the ashpan, and I strove with all my might to keep pace with it. There was no chance of a rest, for to allow the clinker to build up would have resulted in a jam - it just had to be cleared as fast as it came through. This was as bad as anything I had yet tackled in disposal work, worse really, since you could at least have a short rest when on a normal engine, and I was soon soaked with perspiration, while my back and arms were numb with fatigue. When just about on my last gasp, Doug threw down the long rake that he had been using and called out that all was finished.

Never had I been so thankful to hear those words, and by the time I somewhat painfully regained the footplate, Doug had repositioned the flap and was topping up a feeder from the oil bottle.

'Just fill up the back of the box,' he said with a grin, 'while I nip round with the oil-can. Anything that will go through the hole is small enough,' he continued, indicating some huge lumps of coal laying on the shovelling plate, and with that he disappeared quickly down the steps.

I started to shovel steadily away, man-handling large lumps through the firehole in much the same manner as one might load a heavy Howitzer. After 15 minutes or so I was beginning to puff and blow more than somewhat, and by then still only one torpedo-shaped piece of coal was showing below the ring. I had just paused for a breather and was considering what an enormous appetite these Garratts had when Doug came charging up the engine steps and leaped on to the footplate.

I imagine that it had been his intention to stop in about the centre of the cab, but this was not to be. Garratts have a smooth steel plate running east to west across the rear of the cab, and during a recent struggle with a lump of coal approximately the size and shape of a small coffin, I had accidentally knocked over a bucket of soapy water that had been standing in a dark corner. Consequently this smooth plate was nicely wetted when Doug alighted on it with his new oil-soaked crepes.

His legs stopped but he did not. I had a fleeting vision of him still standing rigidly to attention, his arms outstretched, grasping an oil feeder in his right hand and a torch in his left, sliding rapidly across the footplate wearing a rather unusual surprised expression, only to vanish into the black void beyond the open door. He uttered no sound during this brief flight, but seconds after that distinctive thud of a body falling from a height on to hard ground, the air was blue.

I quickly thrust my head out of the side window and peered down into the darkness, concerned that he had really hurt himself this time. I could vaguely make out a dim shape crawling around between the tracks, and called out to ascertain his condition. Once again his guardian angel had done him proud, for the only reply I received was a string of oaths of which 'I've broken my blasted torch and lost the flaming feeder' is all that is printable.

Some minutes later he crept gingerly back on to the footplate, shaking his now dead torch - the bulb had not taken too kindly to being bounced off the top of a rail from a height of 10 feet.

'Christ, that plate is slippery,' he said, studying the floor assiduously.

Not wishing to labour the point, for I was still fighting to control myself, I merely replied, 'Yes, Doug - what do we do with her now?'

'Oh, we'll just drop her back to the other Garratt,' he murmured, still trying to make his torch work. 'I expect they'll be after that one first, but we'll shunt it out when they come for it.'

With this simple operation accomplished, we returned to the cabin once again, and with no more activity imminent, settled comfortably on the benches and soon succumbed to the soporific warmth of the stove that was now burning better than ever.

For three hours we slumbered peacefully, then were rudely awakened by the arrival of some more Toton men who were after the first Garratt. Still in a bit of a daze, we moved the second engine forward over the table so as to allow them access to the departure road, and just as we rolled past the cabin the Toton driver shouted something to Doug.

He immediately rammed his head through the side window in order to hear more clearly what was being said. As he did so there was a loud bang, followed by the tinkling of shattered glass. Doug staggered back with a surprised look on his face while he shook numerous shards from his cap.

'Blimey!' he gasped, 'that window was clean. I though the damn thing was open.'

'Well it is now,' I replied resignedly. 'Permanently.'

I could not help thinking that if these little episodes persisted, the Toton crews would be gaining rather a peculiar impression of us when they got round to chatting in their own mess room.

Doug, having suffered nothing worse than a slight cut on the bridge of his nose, cleaned out the remains of the glass from the window frame, while I shovelled more coal into the rear of the firebox; when this was done to our satisfaction, we returned the Garratt to its original position.

Back in the cabin I finished off the rest of my sandwiches and watched the first rosy tinge of dawn appear in the eastern sky. We had no more visitors, so after a brief tidy up we walked slowly towards the road bridge where our bus was due to collect us just after 6.00 am. Despite my three-hour snooze I still felt tired, but was able to enjoy the ride home through the quiet sunlit streets, reflecting that of all the shed jobs so far, this seemed to be the best.

The rest of the week was as variable as Doug had first indicated, with nights of what almost amounted to indolence alternating with nights of intense activity, and while Doug still managed to enliven our turns with the occasional accident, he did appear to get better as the week wore on. Perhaps I became used to his antics, for during the next few days the only incidents that stand out in my mind are the time he contrived to pull the chain off the water column arm, and the wheel off the column's control valve. On this latter occasion it was unfortunately fully open at the moment it came adrift, and we both got soaked before the thing could be persuaded back on to its spindle. It was, however, with some regret that I bade farewell to Doug on the Sunday morning. I had enjoyed the experience immensely in more ways than one, and I little knew at the time that I was to spend many more hours with him on a variety of turns in the years to come.

An indolent sun eased itself above the wraiths of mist that still lingered around the streets of Birmingham and bathed the damp, grey rooftops in a benevolent glow of golds and pinks. A particular young sunbeam, more adventuresome than most, struggled past the layers of grime on the ancient glass windows of the mess room at Saltley loco. After a momentary pause it hopped across an intervening gap and alighted on the two-day-old stubble that adorned the craggy chin of Dusty, the Mess Steward. Not finding this environment too much to its liking, it upped anchor and travelled a little further to the decidedly more handsome features of fireman Peter Brooks where, out of sheer devilment, it tickled his left nostril with great effect.

The dozing fireman yawned loudly, at the same time rubbing the offending organ with the back of his hand.

'Cor!' he exclaimed. 'I was having a lovely dream then! I dreamed that BR had decided to fit self-cleaning smokeboxes and rocker grates to all engines.'

I raised a quizzical eyebrow. 'That could indeed be a prophetic dream, or then again it may well portend something less pleasant,' was my studied reply, for I always liked to hedge my bets whenever possible. It was just as well that I had, because 10 seconds later the foreman's assistant laid a sympathetic hand on the shoulder of Peter's driver who was seated next to him enjoying a cup of tea.

'I'm afraid it's a "Super D" and a rough one at that. Leave a bit in and drop her in No 3 shed.'

Peter and his mate groaned resignedly, for 'Super Ds' blighted a disposal crew's day at Saltley. Not that many arrived really, but Midland men tended to regard them with a jaundiced eye since rumour had it that they were Webb's final revenge on footplatemen. Certainly they were a most awkward engine to dispose of, and it was generally conceded that you had to carry a number of congenital deformities in order to stand half a chance of firing them properly.

'That's what you get for dreaming on duty,' I said to Peter with a grin, hastily ducking a pair of leather gloves hurled in my direction.

When booking off at the end of the week with Doug Pinkerton I had been asked if I would work a Sunday night preparation turn. Despite the extra pay, Sunday night was not popular with firemen, for there always seemed to be a shortage. However, since I had nothing else arranged and could use the money, I acceded.

All week I had been wondering about Ron and his wife, but no news had filtered through, so having discovered he was due on at 9.00 am, which was only an hour after my booking off time, it seemed opportune to wait for him. Furthermore, Monday was my rest day, and I wasn't due on again until 8.00 am Tuesday.

Events had gone according to plan so, having prepared my quota of engines, I repaired to the cabin to pass the remaining hour until Ron arrived. I settled alongside Peter and his mate who were on disposal but not working the quota system.

The cabin stove was at full blast since the September mists had come early and the night had been damp and chilly. During a peaceful lull in activities Peter had succumbed to its warmth, and if I had not been engrossed in an interesting book I would have done likewise in the unusual calm. Following their departure to do battle with the 'Super D', I decided to walk round to the lobby, for despite a hard night's work I felt in quite high spirits. The sky was clearing nicely, and it had every appearance of being a very pleasant day, that is until I met Ron at the entrance.

A dramatic change had taken place during the past week, for he now looked strained and dejected, so it came as no surprise to learn that several tumours had been found and the prognosis for his wife was not too good. She was to remain in hospital pending further tests and treatment, which of course meant that Ron would have to continue swopping turns to remain on days. Once the Shed Foreman was aware of the situation, he arranged for Ron to be rostered permanently to the 2.00 pm disposal turn, which suited him admirably since, having opted for the quota system, he would be rarely on the premises after 5.00 pm. I only worked with Ron on one other occasion, which was when our booked 2.00 pm disposal turn came round again, and it proved quite enlightening in many ways.

The yard foreman and his assistants were extremely sympathetic to Ron's predicament and made every effort to allocate only the 'easy cops' to us. For example, every rocker grate engine that came on the shed was somehow reserved exclusively for ourselves. Nor did the other disposal crews object in the slightest degree; indeed, they went out of their way to smooth our path and render every assistance possible, which to my mind was a most generous display of camaraderie. Being constantly on the move it was of course hard work, and I found myself being entirely responsible for one engine while Ron handled another. He naturally performed his examinations on all engines and wherever possible we moved into the shed together, but working in this manner served to provide the right sort of experience to promote a great deal of self-confidence that I would not have acquired anything like so quickly in the normal way. I also enjoyed the unquestionable benefits of being back home again in time for tea; in fact, one memorable afternoon, when I had

received three rockers in succession, I found myself in the unique position of booking off in exactly one and half hours after booking on.

After that final week with Ron I once more found myself working with a great variety of drivers, which did much to broaden my outlook, but I found it somewhat unsettling in that I just became used to one man's methods when I had to spend a week with someone whose ways were entirely different. The advantage of this variety, though, was that I got to know intimately a large number of drivers, which stood me in very good stead in the following years.

One of the most interesting I was booked with during this period was Harold Busst, the strongman of Saltley. While he stood only about 5 ft 8 in high, his bone structure was that of a particularly robust gorilla, and everything about him was twice the size of a normal man. Being somewhat overweight only served to emphasise his colossal physique, but like many strong men his demeanour was quiet and he could never be persuaded to indulge in needless displays of strength. However, if one watched carefully, he might be observed while playing dominoes idly moulding a penny in the palm of his massive hand like so much plasticine. Out in the shed he could often be seen helping his mate by carrying two full sand buckets in each hand with less apparent effort than an average man would display when carrying empty ones.

While down in the ash pit he could bend a dart to the desired shape by simply placing it across his knee. Working with Harold therefore had its advantages, whether disposing or preparing, for he quietly took over any operation calling for brute force and made it look like child's play.

Another unusual character who always made his presence felt was a fireman named Kelly. He was a weird-looking young fellow sporting a mop of long, woolly blond hair, and usually wore the type of perpetual goggling grin normally associated with the village idiot. But idiot he certainly was not, for packed into that tall gangling frame was an athlete of no mean ability, and while he could rightly be labelled eccentric, the only idiotic thing about him was the dangerous escapades in which he indulged. He is the only person I have ever seen who would repeatedly jump from the top of a tender straight on to the track just for the fun of it.

Another of his more common tricks was, when having filled the tank and pushed the water column arm clear, to swing down to the ground by using the chain, Tarzan-fashion. He was completely fearless and could often be seen perched on the highest lamp standard impersonating a chimpanzee or performing a wild tap dance on top of the coaling plant. Many of his drivers could not put up with these antics, for his repertoire was as extensive as it was frightening, and after a few nerve-shattering weeks they invariably requested his transfer.

He was at that time booked in the Link Three group, and his present mate, George, who had a most phlegmatic nature, quite enjoyed his clowning, or probably more correctly, the effect it had on other people. The tales George told of Kelly's exploits kept most of us in stitches, although some of the older drivers just shook their heads in sheer disbelief.

Kelly had only lasted four weeks with his previous mate since friction, apparent right from the start, had quickly developed between the two and had reached a climax one night on that particularly dark stretch of track between Tamworth troughs and Whichnor Junction. Their job was a semi-fitted to Derby, their engine a 'Crab', and Kelly, having filled up both firebox and boiler, became bored. Unknown to his driver he contrived to wriggle his way through the fireman's front cab window and crawl right round the framing to his mate's side. Then, with a torch shining into his open mouth and pulling a fearsome expression, he suddenly reared up, pressing his face hard against the glass spectacle. On being confronted by this entirely unexpected and ghastly apparition, his poor driver nearly suffered a cardiac arrest. He could stand no more shocks of this nature, and a parting of the ways was quickly arranged.

Not all of Kelly's escapades had a detrimental outcome - in fact, on one occasion he apparently cured an over-indulgent goods guard of a condition approaching alcoholism. This time the turn was a westbound coal train that they worked as far as Gloucester. Their guard, who we shall call Bill Brown, habitually imbibed to some considerable degree in his local before booking on, and even then brought a substantial supply of ale to consume on the leisurely run west.

After descending the Lickey Incline Bill was able to relax, and he was in that pleasantly befud-dled state between consciousness and sleep when suddenly a ghostly voice began to emanate from his stove, or so he imagined.

'William Brown, William Brown,' it cooed, 'this is your conscience speaking. You must give up being a slave to drink for you are doomed to the downward path if you continue these excesses. See the light while you still have time and save your soul, for the only alternative is ruination and an early grave.'

Bill thought he was having a touch of the DTs and was fully sobered up by the time that ethereal voice had trailed away. The poor chap was so shaken by his experience that from that day onwards no alcohol passed his lips.

The voice, of course, had been Kelly's. In pitch blackness he had left the footplate, scrambled over the 40-odd wagons of the moving train, then, by laying flat on the brake-van roof, had called down the stovepipe. Kelly eventually left BR and went we know not where, but I suspect his real niche in life would have been that of a film stuntman, where his remarkable attributes could have been fully exploited.

Associating with these characters and listening to all manner of railway tales did much to relieve the undeniable tedium of the Washwood Heath link, and on the whole I found time passed relatively quickly. I celebrated my 17th birthday on 23 August by ordering a set of barbells with which I intended to settle down to some serious weight-training.

Towards the end of October I learned that Ron's wife had died, and although the news was not unexpected, it nevertheless came as a great shock. The strain of the last few months had proved considerable, and by then Ron was only a shadow of his former self. However, after the funeral I am happy to relate that he quickly recovered, but I was not able to witness this at first hand since a vacancy occurred in the Bank Pilot link, and as senior fireman I was promoted to fill it.

Although I had enjoyed some extremely happy moments and learned quite a lot in the Washwood Heath link, I was very glad at last to go once again beyond the shed limits and get down to the real job of firing. It was therefore with some considerable excitement that I looked forward to joining by new mate, Bill Smith, at the very civilised hour of 8.00 am on the following Monday morning.

7
THE BANK PILOTS

As previously described, the Bank Pilot link consisted of six Class '3F' 0-6-0 engines operated by 18 sets of men working three shifts of approximately eight hours duration. That they frequently enjoyed more than eight hours was no fault of the planners, who could not have possibly foreseen the severe congestion prevalent in 1950. In their wisdom they had arranged for the pilots to come off the shed at carefully spaced intervals so as to ensure that no two crews would require relief at the same time, which meant that five out of the six engines would always be immediately available for duties. However, since the drivers had their full share of human frailties, many of them spent a great deal of time cultivating the friendship of appropriate signalmen in order to try and be at some particular position on the bank when their relief booked on. In other words, if the driver in question desired overtime he would arrange, if at all possible, to be as far from the shed as this 4-mile stretch would allow. If for some reason he wanted to book off early, then relief right outside the loco was the ideal to aim for. We firemen were, of course, innocent of these machinations on first joining the link, but having no other option quickly fell in with our mates' inclinations. All the fretting, scheming and bickering that occurred amongst the drivers did seem rather petty, but it was generally treated with tolerant amusement.

Being in effect a small close-knit team performing a rather special function tended to develop in the crews a somewhat insular outlook and, because the job was as near routine as any job could ever be on the railways, a certain element of boredom inevitably crept in. The drivers, having experienced just about every possible contingency and knowing every sleeper of the track intimately,

could - and for that matter sometimes did - execute their duties with their eyes closed.

I found myself introduced to this select little group when I met Bill for the first time that Monday morning in late October. He was a stockily built individual of about my own height, sporting an amply filled waistcoat and an aggressive jaw. He wore a cloth cap in preference to a uniform one, and initially seemed reluctant to indulge in much conversation. However, after the formal introductions were completed, he did unbend to the extent of divulging the number of the engine we were to relieve and that we had better find out where it was. Although simply bursting with questions to ask about the job, I sensed his mood and decided to let him do most of the talking for the time being.

'We'll go and see the Controller at Duddeston Mill box,' he said gruffly after collecting some items from his locker, then, as we walked sedately the few yards to the signal box, he sniffed the air, glanced at the sky in a professional manner and pronounced, 'Wind's in the north-east. Hope they've got a sheet.'

'A sheet?' I enquired.

'Yes, a sheet for the cab. Otherwise we'll be starved all day, standing wrong way to the weather with the wind in this direction.'

I had already discovered that when running tender-first or merely just standing, if the wind was blowing directly into the back of the cab it could be most unpleasant, and decidedly wet if it was raining. Pilots were always brought out facing up-bank towards the west, and because the job necessitated a lot of standing around, and in any case 50 per cent of the running was tender-first, conditions in the cab could be rendered very uncomfortable in the teeth of a stiff nor'-easter.

Tarpaulins rigged between the tender and cab roof made a great difference, since they not only kept the wind and rain out, but also kept the heat trapped inside and, although inconvenient at times if coal had to be got down or fire irons used, they were generally considered very desirable in adverse conditions. Most of the sheets used were left over from the wartime days when they had been issued to all engines as a black-out precaution, and I later discovered that nearly all Bank Pilot and Trip link drivers owned one or more such sheets. In extremes of weather, the main screen could be supplemented with side curtains, then the cab could be made very snug indeed, but these, when fitted, generally restricted vision to such an extent that they had to be removed when in motion.

The Controller was housed in a small extension of Duddeston Road signal box and, having mounted the steps, Bill knocked politely on the door and entered.

'Morning Charles,' said Bill affably. 'Any idea where 3223 is?'

'Just a minute,' returned the Controller, hunting through a heap of papers lying on the top of his desk. 'Ah yes, she only went down about 20 minutes ago, so she should still be in the pilot sidings.'

'Righto,' said Bill and then, turning to me, continued, 'We had better have a gentle walk down there, mate. I don't suppose she'll be coming out just yet.'

This assumption proved in fact correct, but we walked along the path at the side of the intermediate line in case by chance 3223 had been called out again. I soon discovered that talking about his local working men's club was Bill's favourite topic of conversation. By the time we were passing Saltley station I already had a fair idea of the club's layout, decor, and the type of entertainment that it provided. Bill was just elaborating on the virtues possessed by a new brand of milk stout when I became aware of a powerful acrid stench that stung my eyes, pricked my nose and made me cough involuntarily. From my days in the school chemistry lab I instantly recognised it as sulphur dioxide.

'Good grief,' I choked, 'where the devil is that lot coming from?'

'Oh, that's Brothertons,' Bill replied, pointing to a chemical works some quarter of a mile away on the far side of the canal basin between Saltley Station and Saltley Carriage Sidings. 'Its usually like this when the winds in the north.'

I looked first at the dense brown fumes blowing from the high chimney and then at the corroded iron railings at the side of the track. Bill followed my glance and guessed my thoughts.

'They've only been up two years,' he said. 'If it does that to iron it makes you wonder what effect it has on us.'

I replied that I had a pretty good idea and could not imagine how people resident in the area tolerated it. During my career at Saltley I was only exposed to this pollution for short periods, but even so I detested it intensely and was always glad to move out of the effected area as quickly as possible.

At length the pilot sidings came into view. On my previous outings I had never taken much notice of them, but now I surveyed the scene with an interested eye. They consisted of two short roads (just sufficiently long to each hold three Class '3Fs'), which converged before leading out to the down goods and down main. The exit was controlled by two ground signals, one for the goods and one for the main, while the other branch of the points led to a short sand drag that terminated near the top of the steep banks of a small brook. Direct access to the sidings could only be gained from the up Camp Hill goods line. Between the sidings and lying under the shadow of the great brick viaduct carrying Western Division metals there was a drab but substantial-looking wooden hut.

Our engine stood behind another Class '3F' on the rear road, while a third one with a healthy column of black smoke erupting from its chimney stood on the front sidings. As we approached the points clanked over and the upper 'dummy' (the name by which we called ground signals) dropped. A cloud of steam, brilliantly reflecting the sunlight, enveloped the fore-end of this latter Class '3F' and, as the hiss grew to a crescendo, she shuddered into motion, slipped vigorously on the points then pounded past us on the down goods line in hot pursuit of the train it was to bank.

'Blimey,' exclaimed Bill. 'Walter's in a devil of a hurry. He must want to get past the shed before his relief books on.'

'Does he like overtime then?' I queried.

'Yes, he's a proper glutton for it,' replied Bill

Only at very busy periods would the pilot sidings at Washwood Heath be empty. They are the two roads leading between mounds of clinker to stop blocks in front of the bridge. Exit was controlled by the ground signals ('dummies') on the right of the picture. While waiting for trains, pilot drivers could relax in the cosy comfort of the cabin situated between the two sidings, but firemen were usually too busy with fire-cleaning, coal-trimming and other duties. In the distance under the arch on the extreme left of the picture can be seen a freight train waiting to be shunted over Hill 60.

with an air of disapproval. 'I don't mind a spot of overtime at night when nothing's spoiling, but I'm blowed if I'm keen at this time of day.'

I followed Bill into the cabin that, despite external appearances, was very clean and tidy. It

was also decidedly warm, since it contained another example of those good old cast iron stoves roaring away in the corner. A tall, thin, sallow-complexioned driver in his mid-50s stood, feet apart, warming his back against it, while another

Class '3F' 0-6-0 No 43223 after general repair at Derby Works in about 1951. The paintwork was not in this pristine condition when in 1950 I had it for a week on my first Bank Pilot duty. However, as related in chapter 8, I and my mate Bill Smith, with the aid of a generous supply of tallow, cleaning paste and plenty of elbow grease were able to make a very presentable job of the smokebox and cab interior. Despite their age, '3Fs' made ideal banking engines on the 4-mile climb from Saltley to Kings Heath. These banking duties were of course excellent training for young firemen before moving on to more arduous turns. *Pat Webb*

driver of about the same age, whose features resembled those of a humorous parrot, sat with a young fireman at the usual zinc-covered table. The tall driver regarded me keenly with bright black, intelligent eyes.

'Got your new mate then, Bill,' he observed with a slight West Country drawl.

Bill nodded, and at the same time introduced me to Alf, the other driver who was the one we were to relieve.

'She's not too bad,' said Alf, referring to No 3223. 'The left piston gland is blowing a bit and there are a few groans at the front end, but I've cleaned out the cylinder lubricator and it seems to be improving now. The brake wasn't very clever either; I've oiled it once, but I expect it will need some more. Oh, and I've rigged a sheet up, so you should be all right.'

'Well done,' said Bill, on hearing this piece of good news, and with that the three of us trooped outside and went across to our engine where Alan, the fireman, had just finished cleaning down the footplate. We had a quick exchange of information, then he joined Alf on the floor and they both departed towards the shed.

The general appearance of No 3223, from the absence of woodwork on the toolboxes to the sludge-encrusted boiler fittings, indicated that she had not been shopped very recently, but Alan had certainly made an effort with the slaking pipe. The well-worn floorboards, although not exactly white, were without doubt quite a light shade of grey, and not a single particle of coal besmirched the gleaming lap plate and tender front. Substantial planks had been acquired to serve as seats, which, with additional lengths to act as back-rests, looked adequately comfortable and would no doubt be much appreciated by the night shift. What I could see of the coal, with the sheet in place, was typical of the lower grades used on goods engines at that period; it burned quite well in the fierce draught of a Class '3' firebox, but produced an appreciable amount of ash and a soft porous type of clinker.

After depositing our belongings in the tender locker, Bill turned to me and said with a meaningful smile, 'By the way, that driver in there was Oliver Birchley. He's a black belt judo expert, trains the police in self-defence and all that, so don't ever tangle with him.'

Bill then announced that he was going to have a check round the engine and suggested that, since we had a few minutes, it would be a good idea if I took this opportunity to trim the coal and clean out the well at the back of the tender.

It seems that it was standard practice on bank pilots to remove spillage and old coal from the section behind the rear coal bulkhead around the tank filler, and also to trim the coal as low as possible on the driver's side to improve rearward vision when running tender-first. With the firing shovel grasped tightly in one hand, I wormed my way underneath the sheet and clambered over the coal to the back of the tender. There, true to form, I found there was indeed an appreciable amount of cobbles and slack, bleached to a bluish-black by prolonged exposure to light, virtually filling the well. I set to work with gusto in the crisp air, shovelling the mixture forwards, and at the same time cursing the rivet heads protruding from the steel plates forming the well, since these kept obstructing the shovel blade.

In a few minutes the task was completed, and I settled the fire irons - which I noted were nearly new - more securely before returning to the footplate. I was just in time to watch Bill oil the engine brake. This was accomplished by first opening the small ejector so as to ensure that the brake valve was properly closed, then by unscrewing a half-inch nut on the side of the small cup reservoir that was attached to the steam delivery pipe running to the brake cylinder. Black cylinder oil was dribbled into the cup, and when full the nut was retightened. I found at this juncture that it was not advisable to stand too close when the brake was first applied after filling, for any surplus oil laying in the cup tended to erupt violently into the air accompanied by a lot of fierce spitting and popping.

Bill had just returned his oil bottles to the locker when a Class '8F' with loose-sounding side rods clanked slowly past on the down goods line. By the tone of its exhaust beat it was hauling a fair load of what, as far as I could see, were all coal wagons and, as the rear of the engine drew just ahead of the sidings, a distinct single hoot came from its whistle.

'That's a Bordesley for Oliver,' commented Bill, who was also watching with interest.

'A Bordesley?' I enquired.

'A Bordesley tripper,' replied Bill a little impatiently. 'Haven't you worked one yet?'

'No,' I answered a trifle sheepishly. 'I have never been past Landor Street relief cabin.'

'Oh, well, Bordesley trippers work transfer traffic on to the Great Western at Bordesley Junction, which is only about three-quarters of a mile up the bank from Landor Street. There are dozens of 'em. In fact, I reckon there must be a Bordesley trip job in just about every bottom group road link. They're pretty cushy, not much work, and a lot of hanging around, a sort of rest between other turns; but they're usually coal trains, and heavy ones at that, which is why they are generally booked Class "8s". If unlucky, you can bank a couple of Bordesleys while one of the other blighters is lounging around up at Kings Heath.'

As the Bordesley' long train clunked slowly by, Oliver's fireman, Brian, who was one of the older hands in the link, leaped aboard his engine and started to prepare her for the work in hand. Oliver soon joined him and, as the dummy dropped, they surged gently forward out on to the goods line, with a fine pillar of black smoke climbing from their chimney as a result of a wide open blower. Seconds later two more pilots coupled together joined us in the sidings, and Bill departed to have a chat with the other drivers.

Left to my own devices I decided that, since we were next in line for duty, I had better liven up the fire, and therefore opened the damper a couple of notches. I was just preparing to place a few shovels of coal under the door when the two firemen from the other pilots scrambled on to the footplate. I knew them both from my cleaning days and they had preceded me into the pilots by some weeks, so I was glad of this opportunity to ply them with questions about the link.

It was soon apparent that they enjoyed piloting far more than shed work, although they felt that the attitude some of the drivers had towards each other and the job in general was a bit petty. Also, some of the drivers seemed to enjoy baiting firemen by asking all manner of questions intended to make them feel small and incompetent. Before the week had progressed very far, I too ran foul of one of the drivers most practised in this art. Fortunately, my educational background sufficed for me to more than hold my own on most general knowledge subjects, and indeed tie him in knots on many matters not pertaining to railways. This won great approval from Bill, who did not like the fellow and, of course, all the firemen present, and

thereafter I was treated with a new respect that I enjoyed for the duration of my stay in the link.

Our interesting discourse was suddenly interrupted in mid-flow by a Class '4F', bearing through freight headlamps, chugging vigorously past on the down goods.

'Get her hot!' yelled the fireman in a Gloucester dialect, giving at the same time a friendly wave indicating that they required a banker. A few seconds later, a shrill pop of the whistle officially confirmed the request.

'We'll leave you to it then,' said Mike, one of my guests, and they both departed to the cabin. I knocked the blower hard over, fully opened the damper and flashed a few shovels of coal evenly around the box before partially closing the firedoors, which were of the later sliding pattern.

'Everything all right?' said Bill as he hauled himself up between the uprights.

'Yes, I think so,' I replied, glancing reassuringly at the gauges, which showed 160 lbs per sq in and nearly a full glass of water.

'Take off the hand brake then,' he said affably, applying the steam brake and pushing the gear lever to the full forward position. 'And keep your eye on the dummy.'

It duly dropped and, with a hiss of steam from the open taps, we puffed out on to the goods line in pursuit of the retreating brake-van.

'There's no need to put too much on yet,' advised Bill as I bent to shovel more on to the grate. 'Just build it up under the door because, as like as not, we will stand for some time at Duddeston Road and we don't want to be blowing off all the time.'

We caught up our train as it came to a halt outside Saltley station and stood there for some 15 minutes before moving slowly to the intermediate line alongside the down Camp Hill goods. Oliver Birchley was still in position behind his Bordesley on that line, so obviously the GWR was not ready for them yet.

'I expect that we will go first,' said Bill, eyeing the Bordesley disapprovingly. 'They usually try and keep the intermediate clear if they can.'

This information only served to make me more fidgety than ever, for I was undecided whether to put more coal on at the risk of blowing off, and then drop the damper, which might cause the fire to set, or leave matters as they were and hope that I could build the fire up quickly enough to meet demands when we actually came to move. In the end I compromised by placing a few more shovels of coal in the back corners and leaving the damper open one notch. During the course of time, experience showed that when doubts existed, and they nearly always did exist regarding the actual timing when one was required to make the assault on the bank, it was prudent to keep a fair amount of fire in the back of the box. By leaving the damper open a small amount and the bars thinly covered at the front, the generation of steam while standing could be effectively controlled and consequent blowing off avoided. Even if the front of the grate went dead, and I often allowed it to at times, the situation could be quickly rectified by the simple expedient of digging the blade of the firing shovel into the mass under the doors and shooting it forwards. Generally speaking a '3F' warmed up so quickly and steamed so well that liberties like this could be readily undertaken without detriment to performance, even with low-grade fuels.

On this first trip I was playing safe, not knowing the engine's or my capabilities, nor for that matter knowing what demands would be made on the incline. As a result we were carrying too much fire at the front, so in a few minutes the safety valves lifted noisily. However, Bill would not permit me to quieten her by means of the injector since the water was already at the top of the glass and he did not want to risk the possibility of priming.

'Let her drop down a little,' he advised. 'Half a glass is quite safe on the section to Camp Hill'.

Another 10 minutes passed, during which time my eyes rarely left the signal controlling our line for more than a few seconds. Bill, on the other hand, was quite relaxed, sitting on his plank reading the morning paper. I stared ahead for the umpteenth time and then, as I watched, the signal came off.

'We're going now, Bill,' I shouted, and without further ado pulled up the damper and quickly flashed half a dozen shovels of coal round the box.

In contrast to my excitement, Bill methodically folded his newspaper, transferred his reading glasses to their protective case, slowly rose to his feet and gently eased open the regulator. We moved forwards a few yards before coming to a halt again, the train crew apparently not having yet noticed the signal. Suddenly the clank of couplings could be heard above the background hiss of our slightly blowing piston glands, and then we were off.

Bill made no effort to open the regulator any further, so that as we trundled steadily up the intermediate we were pushing no more than five or six wagons. However, as soon as we cleared the points and were firmly on the down goods, he pushed the regulator across a trifle more and our exhaust took on a more strident note.

Opposite the loco shed the gradient steepened to 1 in 105 and the bark from our chimney changed to that familiar raucous crash I liked so much. I saw that Bill had opened up to full first valve and, meeting my gaze with a broad grin, he nodded ahead.

'We've got the back 'un now, so you can get shovelling.'

A brief glance towards the Landor Street home signal indeed confirmed that the distant for St Andrews Junction was also off, so I rapidly plied more coal to the fire, which was already taking on that white furnace glow. At Landor Street Junction the track curves to the left then straightens before swinging right for the short but steepest section of the bank, where it passes under the main line to Euston at a gradient of 1 in 62. We were now accelerating quite briskly before hitting this stretch, the blast of our exhaust echoing back from the massive GEC works on our left, while up ahead a tall pillar of smoke and steam from the Class '4' stood out starkly against the bright blue sky, denoting that it was certainly getting stuck in to some effect. Our own engine was also in fine fettle, with the water just in sight at the top of the glass, the needle on the red line at 175 and a heavy pall of smoke keeping pace with us overhead, carried on the following north-east breeze.

Speed progressively slackened as we approached the Euston line bridge and, noting this, I glanced enquiringly at Bill. He read my thoughts accurately, for he came over and bellowed in my ear.

'The whole weight of the train is now on the steepest part. If we're going to stick, this is where it happens, but I reckon we shall be OK this time.'

His statement proved to be quite correct, for although our pace dropped to little more than a fast walk as we blasted under the blackened archway and past Brickyard Crossing, it picked up again on rounding the curve at St Andrews Junction, where the gradient eased slightly to 1 in 85.

On the straight section up to Bordesley Junction we pounded steadily away still in full forward gear, the exhaust amplified by the deep cutting, making a really glorious sound. This was great stuff, I thought, as I vigorously fired more fuel into that glaring white orifice. The injector had been on some time now and was just keeping the water level nicely in sight, while to my delight the needle had not dropped below the 170 mark. The distant for Camp Hill was off but our speed remained constant as we thundered explosively under the wide Coventry Road bridge and past Bordesley Junction signal box, where Bill came across and waved to the bobby who was looking out of an open window.

'That's Charlie Bunn. He's a pal of mine. We do well with Bordesleys on this shift.'

The significance of this remark did not register then, for Bill went on to point out the line leading into the Great Western system, and as we climbed still higher we passed over the massive viaduct which spanned the numerous GW tracks. The whole Bordesley complex was laid out before us like a huge model railway. We were now on top of a steep embankment, and a panoramic view of Birmingham was visible to either side in the clear autumn air. Old factories and warehouses lined a murky canal far below, while acres of slate-grey rooftops stretched in all directions. We then clattered over a steel bridge spanning what I recognised was the main Stratford road at Camp Hill, and I realised that on many occasions as a boy I

had enviously watched trains puffing laboriously over this very piece of track, never dreaming that one day I would be actually up here on my own engine.

Our pace began to quicken noticeably, but as I once more pounced on the shovel Bill laid a restraining hand on my shoulder.

'Let her go for now,' he yelled. 'We normally come off at Camp Hill box, which is just up ahead. If he wants us up to Kings Heath he will whistle and the bobby will wave us through with a green flag. Keep your eye on him and if he gives us the tip, then you can put some more on.'

I nodded to indicate that I understood, for the noise on the footplate now precluded normal speech, and after knocking off the injector I stared intently ahead at the rapidly approaching signal box. The bank had now flattened from 1 in 85 to 1 in 280 and, with no adjustment in the regulator position, our acceleration was progressive. Bill eased off a little, then I saw the green flag, but I was too late to advise him for he popped the whistle in acknowledgment, at the same time hauling back the gear lever to shorten the cut-off.

I rapidly fired another dozen shovels of coal and, as the safety valves began to lift, put on the injector again. At 35 per cent and just about full first regulator we fairly romped along the easy stretch from Camp Hill to Brighton Road, leaving

After the stiff climb up to Camp Hill, freight trains used this short easier stretch through Brighton Road to build up speed for a charge at the final gradient of 1 in 108 through Moseley Tunnel to Kings Heath. The high embankment here favoured a station of largely wooden construction. Seen here in Midland Railway days, it was demolished in 1941. All that remained of the site nine years later was the only modern semi-automatic colour light signal on the section. *T. J. Edgington*

an impressive trail of smoke and sound. Half sitting on the tender hand brake bracket I experienced a tremendous feeling of exhilaration as I swayed easily with this wildly bucking creature, which felt full of life and power and not at all mechanical.

Our pace began to slacken once more as the track curved to the right and the gradient increased to 1 in 108. This was the beginning of the second step of the climb up to Kings Heath. Moderately loaded trains usually managed the ascent through the Moseley Tunnel without too much trouble, provided that they had a clear road and were able to take a run at it after Camp Hill. Fully loaded trains, or those that for some reason were hauled by engines not functioning as well as they might, called for assistance right through to Kings Heath, for sticking in a tunnel is no joke for anyone. It was very noticeable in the course of time, however, that the majority of Class '4F'-hauled freights requested a pilot for the full distance, which was doubtless due to the fact that these engines in general seemed more short of breath on the bank than any other type.

From the embankment at Brighton Road we entered a cutting, the grassy banks of which gradually rose higher and higher on either side until finally the plain stone portals of the tunnel were visible. Since our speed had now fallen considerably and the distant for Kings Heath was off, Bill allowed the reversing lever to slam forward into full gear as we snorted vigorously into the black mouth, which was now belching clouds of smoke and steam left by the train engine. I later found that Moseley Tunnel always seemed clean and lacked that distinctive stale odour associated with many others with which I was to become familiar. This was probably due to its location in a roughly east-west cutting, allowing the prevailing winds to be channelled through at increased velocity, thereby quickly clearing any residual stench. Also, of course, it was not an over-long tunnel by any standards.

Bursting out into daylight once more, I found that we were still in a deep but wide cutting that gradually opened out on the right-hand side until it revealed an engineers' sidings located in what might have been an old clay quarry. A number of wagons and bolster flats containing permanent way materials stood on these rusty looking rails, while all around them towered precipitous red cliffs dotted with numerous rabbit warrens.

'Nearly there,' shouted Bill as I went over to his side to view this spectacle. 'I shall shut off at the next bridge.'

I looked ahead and noticed an overhead road bridge coming into sight as the track made a right-hand curve through Kings Heath station. The sharp blast of our exhaust gently subsided as we passed under this bridge and a prolonged application of the brake brought us to a grinding halt at the far end of the relatively short down platform. Although no longer in use, Kings Heath station showed no signs of neglect; on the contrary, it was extremely neat and tidy, sporting well-cultivated flower beds that must have been a blaze of colour earlier in the year, and very typical of many old Midland country stations. Even so, numerous roses, having survived the recent frosts, were still in full bloom, adding a splash of brightness to the autumn golds and browns of the tree-lined banks on the up side. Over to my left at the back of the

This view of Kings Heath station and the down platform in October 1964 presents a run-down and rather neglected appearance. When I paid my first visit some 14 years earlier the station boasted well-kept flower beds and not a weed was to be seen. However, the coal yard to the left of the picture seems to be as busy as ever.

station lay a small siding and coal wharf where a number of local merchants were busily engaged in transferring fuel to their respective motor lorries, while beyond the yard the rooftops of some houses and shops could be seen.

We had arrived with 160 lbs per sq in on the clock, half a glass of water and only a little more fire in the box than was strictly desirable, so I was well pleased with my first assault of the bank. Bill also seemed satisfied, for he chatted amiably while we waited to see what was going to happen to us.

'Syd Dean is the bobby on this shift,' he said, nodding towards the box. 'Funny chap. I don't get on too well with him, so I expect he'll shoot us back if there's half a chance.'

However, this was not to be. A few seconds later the dummy dropped and we found ourselves backing into the little slip road that lay parallel to the down line at the leading end of that platform. Once inside, Bill popped the whistle to indicate that we were clear and trundled up to the stop block, which was set in the embankment just below the stone pier of the overhead bridge. With plenty of boiler space I was able to reduce the steam pressure to 130 without overfilling it and, at the same time, swill away the accumulated dirt and debris with the slaking pipe.

As soon as I had completed this spot of housework, Bill, who had been fidgeting about on his platform, suddenly uttered 'By Jove, I could just murder a cup of tea right now. The trouble is, Syd doesn't exactly welcome visitors in the box, particularly to make tea, but with you being new he might this once. Its worth a try, anyhow'.

So saying, he handed me the teacan and a small oval tin divided into two compartments, both containing a mixture of tea and sugar, there being exactly the correct quantity in each compartment for one can of tea. With some trepidation I slowly strolled towards the box, which stood back on the near end of the platform, wondering what sort of reception I would receive, while at the same time noting subconsciously that our little siding would just about hold three pilots at a pinch. Nearing the box I braced myself, knocked on the door and entered.

Syd Dean was of medium height and chubby build, but his most distinguishing feature was an enormous RAF-type 'handlebar' moustache, which not only engulfed his upper lip but also spread round his face on either side to join up with his sideburns. Since he looked a touch eccentric, I felt that he might respond better to a different approach.

'Good morning,' I said politely, using my most refined accent in as steady a voice as I could muster. 'In your considered opinion are we likely to here long enough to make a can of tea, and if so would you be good enough to allow me the use of your facilities?'

This opening gambit must have struck the right chord for, cocking his head slightly to one side, he studied me intensely for a few seconds with keen grey eyes that gleamed brightly above the luxuriant foliage, then the severe expression relaxed slightly. Nodding towards the stove on which stood a simmering iron kettle, he said, 'Be my guest, it's nearly boiling'.

My initial gaze around the box had taken in a leather motor cycle coat hanging from a peg in one corner, and having already seen a nearly new Douglas Dragonfly machine outside, I quickly put two and two together and asked him what he thought of it. Well, that did the trick! Within minutes we were discussing bikes as if we had known each other all our lives - such is the fraternity of motor cycling enthusiasts. He had plenty of advice to offer on learning that I was contemplating the purchase of my first machine and, like Ronnie Jackson, strongly advocated obtaining the largest capacity I could afford.

Feeling full of the joys of life on discovering this new friend, I happened to hum a cheerful little ditty as I made the tea.

'Do you like *Don Pasquale?*' he asked with apparent interest.

'One of my favourites,' I replied enthusiastically, surprised that he recognised the opening theme of the overture from that particular Donizetti opera. It turned out that, like myself, Syd was an avid gramophile and opera fan with a strong preference for the Rossini school. We were on very firm common ground here and trains on both up and down lines came and went as we ran through our respective repertoires with little thought of passing time. We were engaged in our individual renderings, an aria from *The Barber of Seville* - with more exuberance than skill, I might add - when Bill walked through the door. His surprise was obvious, since his bushy eyebrows shot up with a force sufficient to lift his cloth cap well clear of his shiny bald pate.

'Good grief,' he uttered, rather indelicately. 'I thought someone was being murdered.'

'No, William' replied Syd stiffly, 'as a matter of fact, your mate and I have been indulging in a spot of cultural uplift.'

'Well you can indulge as much as you like,' growled Bill, 'but I've been dying of thirst for hours out there.'

This was a slight exaggeration, of course, but nearly an hour had passed since I had left the footplate, and while on the one hand Bill was quite content to be out of the way at Kings Heath, his thirst had now taken the upper hand.

'Sorry Bill,' I muttered apologetically, 'it's all made, anyhow - didn't realise I'd been so long.'

And so saying I handed him the can that had been stewing the while on the stove. He eagerly grasped it.

'Well, you can stay here all day if you like as long as I've got something to drink,' he said, managing a smile, and, backing through the door again, took his leave.

'How do you get on with him?' asked Syd.

'All right so far,' I said truthfully, 'but I've only been with him since 8.00 am so its early days yet.'

'I find their continual bickering gets on my nerves a trifle, so I'm afraid I tend to stir it up a bit when the opportunity arises,' said Syd with a sigh. 'At any rate it gives them something to talk about.'

I duly found that this was the case, Syd making out that he favoured first one driver and then another, which needless to say caused a certain amount of contention, but it was quite harmless really.

During my stay in the pilots Syd and I became very pally, which directly benefited Bill. Later Syd was promoted to the rank of Special Signalman, which meant that he was able to work a number of signal boxes in the area and consequently travelled round these in turn, standing in on rest days, holidays and in cases of sickness. I was always made very welcome by him, and if he could do us a favour by delaying or speeding our journey, whichever was appropriate, he would do so with pleasure; influential friends in the right places were always useful things to have.

Some 20 minutes later we were boisterously carolling our way through the livelier passages of Auber's *Bronze Horse* when another mixed freight clattered noisily through the station followed by a pilot, which halted abruptly just beyond the end of the platform.

'I'll drop Charlie [the newly arrived pilot's driver] back to you out of the way of the down fitted, then after the up fitted there's a Class A which you'll have to follow,' said Syd in a more serious tone now that he was talking business.

'Righto Syd,' I replied. 'I had better get back and make sure that everything's OK. Bill might have let the fire go out.'

We exchanged cheery farewells and I arrived at our engine just at the same moment that Charlie backed gently up to it. Peter, his fireman, was already in the 4-foot and I watched with interest how he coupled up, for this was a task of which I had little experience.

First he pulled off the vacuum hoses from both engines and left them dangling, so that neither could create a vacuum to release their brakes until he had finished. Then he heaved up the heavy shackle from our engine and, after dropping it securely in the hook of his own, screwed it tight enough to remove the slack. Grasping the ends of the hoses in each hand, he deftly clipped them together with a powerful twist of his wrists, finally locking the flanges with the safety pin provided.

'OK,' he said with a grin, handing up our headlamp. 'Been having a nice quiet rest?'

I answered in the affirmative, surprised to learn that our stay had not passed unnoticed by the other pilot crews.

As Syd had advised, we followed the Class A. Our release from the siding was simply effected by running forward on the down clear of the crossover, then proceeding back on to the up line. Being on a downward gradient of 1 in 356, only a few puffs were necessary to send the pair of us rolling easily towards the advance starter, which was still on, indicating that the Class A ahead of us had not yet cleared Camp Hill.

'That white diamond with a black "T" on it means that the signal is track-circuited,' said Bill, 'but we have to telephone the bobby if detained for more than a couple of minutes, then ring him at 5-minute intervals thereafter. Come on, I'll show you how it works, because it's your job really.'

We climbed down to the base of the signal, where a weathered wooden cabinet stood on two substantial posts. Access to the instrument was gained through a small counterweighted sliding panel not unlike a miniature window sash and, holding this down with one hand, with the other he lifted off its rest a single earpiece attached to a length of armoured cable. Prodding the call button with a podgy forefinger, he waited a few seconds before bellowing loudly into the mouthpiece inside the cabinet.

'That's all there is to it,' he said as we returned to the footplate. 'You only have to tell him who we are, and that should remind him not to send another train into the back of us - just a question of safety.'

I was about to use the telephone again when the whip and rustle of cables along their trackside rollers fractionally preceded the rising of the signal arm. Both engines accelerated impressively into the tunnel before being allowed to coast towards Brighton Road. I stayed mainly on Bill's side so as

to view the scenery I had missed on the way up, the keen air blowing in round the sheet and making my eyes water. The distant for Camp Hill was off as it came into sight and, since there was nothing to be gained in dawdling, Bill opened up again. As our speed rose, small particles of coal and dust from the tender were picked up in the airstream and peppered us unpleasantly at both face level and about the shins where they blew in from the shovelling plate. After this experience I always soaked the coal well before running tender-first, for to try it when already in motion was both futile and very wet. On this section from Camp Hill to Bordesley it became obvious how easily the Class '3s' coasted; they ran freely and steadily, with very little noise other than a distinctive double-three click of wheels over rail joints.

We were halted at Bordesley Junction, and while standing there an '8F' hauling a heavy coal train thumped explosively from under the Coventry Road bridge and pounded towards us. A towering mushroom of black smoke was being hurled skywards from the chimney at each tremendous beat and the volume of sound was absolutely deafening as it blasted slowly past. Because she seemed to be working so much harder than normal I peered intently to see where the regulator was set and, not surprisingly, noted that it was dead horizontal.

'That's the way to do it,' I shouted at Bill, pulses atingle at the sight of this demonstration of power.

'Wish they all would,' he agreed, apparently quite unmoved. 'Makes life easier for us.'

The banker was also well extended, its crisp exhaust note crackling to and fro in the brick-lined cutting as it emerged from the bridge, surrounded

Stop signals bearing a white diamond marked with a black letter 'T' indicated that they the line was track circuited (the presence of the train was indicated to the signalman by lights on the layout diagram in the signal box) and that they were provided with telephone communication to the box. These telephones were housed in a black-and-white-striped cabinet adjacent to the relevant signal post. When brought to a stop the driver blew the whistle and if, in clear weather, the signal was not cleared within 2 minutes, the fireman must use the telephone to advise the signalman of their position. In fog or falling snow this was to be done immediately. If after the first contact the train was still detained, further contact had to be made at not more than 5-minute intervals irrespective of weather conditions. I was first introduced to this equipment at the down advanced starter at Kings Heath.

by steam and smoke. I had been counting the heavy coal wagons as they thumped over the rail joints opposite and observed that the pilot was pushing 17 out of the total of 50. I often found myself doing this exercise, and it soon became apparent that a Class '3' on full first valve and in full gear averaged about this quantity on the bank. Bill came over to see who was on the pilot and exchanged a hasty greeting with Oliver Birchley, who was hanging his lanky form well out of the cab.

'I reckon he'll be going through to Kings Heath with that lot,' said Bill, 'so we won't see much of Oliver for a while - he's a pal of Syd Dean.'

Our signal came off and we rolled steadily down to St Andrews Junction, where we stood for some considerable while, so I was obliged to go to the signal box in order to carry out Rule 55. This simple but necessary regulation was a very frequent occurrence in the pilot link and, as a result, I came to know the various signalmen quite well, since I generally remained in the box after signing the log until it was time to move off. They were as interesting and as varied in character as any breed of men, and I spent many pleasant interludes in their company when the bank was 'on the block'.

The Class A preceding us had halted at Brickyard Crossing, which I found was not at all unusual, since many trains took on water at the column at Landor Street Junction, the next block ahead, this being also a relief point. Eventually it moved on and Bill stopped outside the box to allow me to join him once again.

'We had better get some water ourselves at Landor Street,' said Bill, nodding towards the tank gauge, which now showed less than 1,500 gallons. 'Charlie is OK, but we may not get another chance for a while.'

At Brickyard Crossing the canal runs beneath the track, one of those rare occurrences where three modes of transportation briefly meet. There was a lock a few yards beyond the up line, and watching the odd barge using this was always a point of interest when standing at the signal. Today quite a lot of excitement was going on for a barge horse had managed to fall into the lock, but fortunately the combined efforts of the fire brigade, the RSPCA and the bargee contrived to extract the poor old fellow with little harm done other than a ducking, and we arrived there just in time to witness this happy conclusion.

By the time we had watered our engine the Class A had disappeared, giving us a clear run down to Duddeston Road. Twenty minutes later I was uncoupling our engines in the pilot siding where, at Bill's suggestion, I tackled the job of getting some coal forward. Moving coal from the rear of the tender towards the front is an onerous operation until one digs down to the tank top; then, once one has found this flat platform to work from it is merely a case of some strenuous shovelling. It was an unwritten law in the pilots that the day shift did as much of this as possible, because the job was rendered much more difficult in the dark, and we tried to make life as easy as possible for our colleagues on nights.

Half an hour later a Class '8' struggled by and hooted for a pilot. It was our turn once more and, having by now heaped a good supply of fuel in the front half of the tender, I quickly descended to the footplate in order to set about livening up the fire. The first 30 wagons of the train were loaded with coal, while the remaining 20 appeared to be carrying pig iron, and a full complement at that, judging by the way the springs were flattened. Before the brake-van had gone past, Bill joined me.

'It's a Bordesley, I think,' he said, with a note of satisfaction in his voice. 'Charlie will draw ahead first and shunt on to the rear road,' he added, answering the question I was about to ask as to how we were going to get out.

The operation was accomplished as planned, and we duly caught our train opposite Saltley carriage sidings where, pushing little more than the brake-van, we chugged gently on without stopping until coming to a halt on the down Camp Hill goods line at Duddeston Road. Here we remained for some 40 minutes, during which time we took the opportunity to have our lunch while watching both Charlie and another pilot run past us on the intermediate, pushing their respective trains up the bank.

At last our signal came off and, with tissues fully restored after consuming my sandwiches, I briskly fired a dozen shovels of coal round the box. Right from the start Bill got stuck in with more purpose than on the previous train, since not only were we on a straight road with no facing points to cross, but we also had a much heavier load. However, our acceleration was lethargic, to say the least, while frequent surges and intermittent eruptions of smoke from our train engine indicated that it was slipping badly.

The distants were off for St Andrews, so Bill had no compunction about using full first regulator and full gear, but as we blasted past Landor Street signal box even I could sense that we were not going as well as we should, and I was not entirely surprised when he growled in my ear, 'If the chaps up front don't do better than this we will most certainly stick.'

I could see the smoke and steam from the Class '8' billowing up beyond Brickyard Crossing, indicating that it was now on the steepest section of the bank, and this could be felt on our own engine by a gradual falling off in speed. As the resistance increased, No 3223 began to perform little half slips, which Bill quickly checked by opening the sand valve.

We were just nearing the Euston line overbridge and our pace had dropped to nothing more than a crawl. The exhaust beats, having lost their sharp clear crackle, now became long-drawn-out muffled woofs. Bill pushed the regulator right across, but it was of no avail, and with a prolonged sigh of resignation we shuddered to a standstill.

'That's it, then,' said Bill in a tone just as resigned as the engines. 'Screw the hand brake on, mate.'

I did so, and as Bill released the steam brake we set back several wagon lengths under the weight of the train. The guard was already down on the ground shouting to us.

'I'll go and tell the bobby we want some more assistance,' he yelled.

'Righto,' replied Bill, then, turning to me, he said, 'We just sit tight now until another engine comes.'

Before assistance arrived in the form of Oliver Birchley, a full 10 minutes went by, during which we spent most of the time blowing off since I did not wish to overfill the boiler. Returning to the pilot sidings from Kings Heath, Oliver had been conveniently passing the loco at the right time and the Controller quickly arranged for him to be shunted across to the down goods, and up behind us. Oliver's mate coupled up while I removed our tail-lamp and placed his headlamp facing inwards on the framing.

'Short of steam?' he chided, with a good-natured grin.

'On the contrary, we've got too much,' I replied, as the valves lifted again with a roar, and then shouting so as to be heard above the din, 'I think the blighter up front is having a job to keep his feet, and there's a great load of pig iron down this end.'

He waved his hand in acknowledgment and we both returned to our respective footplates.

'OK, Bill,' I yelled, winding off the hand brake while he blew a couple of 'crow' whistles to indicate to the train engine that we were ready to start pushing. Unfortunately, a reply could not be heard, so Bill and Oliver opened up in unison, but it was like trying to move a mountain and both '3s' started slipping violently. These two drivers had obviously done this many times before, since they acted as one without any signals passing between them. With sanders running, we set back until all the slack was out of the train couplings, then, on full first valve, we charged into the wagons with no attempt at gentleness or concern for the guard's hide. To begin with we literally raced forwards, but as the train buffered up the weight of each wagon could be felt as a distinct check, rather like shunting, until after a few yards and still on the approach side of the bridge we came nearly to a standstill again. Once more Bill pushed the regulator right across, and judging by the bark from Oliver's chimney he had done likewise. Then, with a shudder of triumph, we surged ahead under the bridge and up to St Andrews.

With both pilots fully extended, the noise in the cutting was as shattering as it was exhilarating, and as the train passed on to the 1 in 85 stretch, our speed had risen sufficiently to allow Bill to come back on the first regulator. Although we had long since had a clear road right into Bordesley, we took things very cautiously once the train was on the curve leading to the Great Western. With such a weighty load, stopping at the signal there would be enough of a problem without any unwelcome pushing from us.

Despite Bill's alleged friendship with the bobby, we were quickly shunted across to the up goods for a speedy return to Landor Street. We concluded that they must be short of pilots and this was in fact borne out, for at Saltley Junction we were detached from Oliver and directed behind a through freight standing on the down Camp Hill line.

I had only just enough time to build up the fire a little when we were off again, but by way of a contrast this train was lightly loaded and we fairly romped over the stretch leading to St Andrews Junction. Having a good charge at the bank made a great deal of difference, and speed did not fall too significantly on the 1 in 62 section. However, it soon became apparent that No 3223 was not steaming as well as she had earlier in the day, and I was having to sacrifice the water level in the boiler after passing Bordesley Junction. Fortunately the train engine did not require us through to Kings Heath, for as we ground to a halt just beyond the old disused Camp Hill station platform we had no more than half a glass of water and 140 lbs per sq in showing on the clock.

'I reckon you've got some clinker in there, mate,' said Bill after we had backed inside the short slip road.

'I reckon you're right,' I replied, inspecting the offending fire. 'I'll clean it as soon as we get back to the pilot sidings.'

'When it's cooled down you can start right here if you wish,' went on Bill. 'In fact, the way things are moving at the moment it may be your only chance.'

'What if we have to go back when I'm right in the middle of cleaning it?' I stammered, somewhat surprised at this suggestion.

'That's all right,' replied Bill, quite unruffled. 'It's downhill, isn't it?'

Well, there was no argument to that, so after untying the ropes securing our sheet and rolling it over the roof I pulled the fire irons forward in readiness. There was rather more live coal in the box than was really desirable, but by the time the boiler had filled I was able to make a start.

It was not surprising that the old girl had been short of breath this last trip, for a large slab of thick clinker, topped with a layer of ashes, covered the rear half of the grate. What was surprising was that she had steamed at all in this condition; more proof, if any was needed, of the reserve capacity built into these engines.

As it happened, I had plenty of time to make quite a respectable job of the cleaning operation before we were required to depart in the company of two more pilots on their way back from Kings Heath. The red orb of the sun was now dropping towards the horizon and the wind had much more of a nip than a couple of hours previously, while distant objects tended to become merged in that watery haze typical of late autumn. After sweating profusely over my labours I found the return trip decidedly chilly, but this was one of the occupational hazards to which footplatemen were constantly exposed, and no doubt the cause of many of the bouts of muscular rheumatism, fibrositis, etc, that afflicted both young and old alike from time to time. As Bill aptly summed it up, 'What do you expect when you are standing all day on damp and draughty floorboards, roasted on one side and frozen on the other?'

We did manage to get to the pilot sidings this time, although one of the other engines accompanying us had to depart almost immediately. However, the brief respite there enabled me to complete the task of getting coal forward and make a thorough job of cleaning down the footplate.

At 3.15 we found ourselves behind another Bordesley, and Bill peering anxiously at his pocket watch.

'Our relief books on at 4.00,' he mumbled, half to himself. 'We don't want to be going past the shed at that time, or goodness knows when we'll be finished.'

Bill obviously did not want any overtime on this shift and would be glad to be relieved outside the shed. Ironically, half the other drivers would be only too pleased to sneak past and then have an hour 'inside' at Kings Heath. He need not have worried. It took the best part of an hour for the train engine to get to Duddeston Road, and we were still standing at the rear of it on the down Camp Hill goods when our relief climbed aboard at 4.25 pm. They were very happy, not having had a long walk, and Bill likewise was delighted, since he could not have been relieved sooner.

Mulling over the events of the day on my way home, I realised that I had developed an affection for No 3223, an affection that demanded that I did something for her. I had been very impressed by the glimpse of shining copper pipes on Oliver Birchley's engine and resolved to tackle Bill about bulling up our own first thing the following morning.

8
FOG

The idea of cleaning up the loco was still fresh in my mind as we walked towards Duddeston Road signal box with heads bent against the biting easterly that was blowing with considerably more vigour than the previous day, whipping surface grit from the car park into our faces with stinging force.

We were informed that Alf was on his way down the bank and were advised by the Controller to wander over to Landor Street relief cabin and wait for him there. When Bill was seated comfortably before the roaring fire with a freshly made cup of tea in one hand and a cigarette in the other, I felt the mood was right and tentatively broached the subject of brightening up our footplate. I was pleasantly surprised to find that he reacted enthusiastically.

'Do you really want to?' he said, looking me full in the face.

I replied in the affirmative, adding how attractive Oliver's bright pipework looked.

'That's nothing to what can be done,' he said confidently. 'As a matter of fact we shall have to go to the shed for stores today, so I'll get some materials and we'll make a start.'

Trains came and went during the next 45 minutes and then two pilots arrived coupled together, ours being the rearmost.

'By jingoes!' exclaimed Alf, who looked a trifle blue about the gills. 'It's been damned nippy during the night. She's OK though - my mate got a bit out of the fire-up at Kings Heath and we've only had one trip out of the tank.'

He meant of course that Alan had removed some clinker from the grate and that they had only done one trip since filling the tank.

We voiced our approval of these acts and bade them farewell after stopping briefly outside the loco. Another banker was already standing on the front road of the pilot sidings when we arrived, and since the points were correctly set, we came to a standstill on the vacant rear track. After uncoupling I climbed on top of the tender and inspected the coal, which was now more than somewhat depleted. Alan had obviously been busy up there also, for what remained was piled into the slope at the forward end and little could be seen elsewhere. I finished the job off with brush and slaking pipe, surprised to find how clean and bright the metal was underneath the coal. I calculated that we had only sufficient fuel left for about two trips to Kings Heath, and advised Bill accordingly. This fitted in with his plans quite well, since he liked to get on the shed about mid-shift so that the fire would still be clean and plenty of coal on the front of the tender when relieved.

As it turned out we did one trip to Camp Hill and another to Kings Heath before running on to the shed immediately after the latter. The procedure was similar to normal disposal except that we made rather more of a fuss over the coaling. By placing large lumps around the coal rails at the forward end we were able to pile it high there while leaving a bare shovelling space at the extreme rear.

Bill then departed with the oil bottle and left me to the now familiar but no less onerous task of cleaning the fire, ash pan and smokebox. I was conscious of him popping back at intervals with various bundles of unknown substances wrapped in paper, but I had little time to examine these since having been 30 hours in service, No 3223 was in quite a state.

Eventually I was finished and we ran on to an outside pit where Bill completed his oiling while I built up the fire once more and thoroughly cleaned down the footplate.

Bill had put on an old pair of overalls for the undeniably dirty job of oiling the motion, and he looked more like a labourer than a driver when he regained the footplate.

'While I'm still messed up, we'll have a go at bulling the boiler front,' he said, picking up a bottle of black oil from the drip tray. 'Stand aside,' he advised, and as I shrank back on the tender he reached up and poured the contents along the top of the boiler front.

It ran down in a thick torrent, spluttering and smoking on the hot metal, filling the cab with acrid fumes. Grabbing a lump of cotton waste from a small bale he had acquired, he spread the hot oil on every pipe, handle and accessory and into every nook and cranny. Then, putting on the injector he sprayed the whole area with the slaking pipe until all surplus oil had been emulsified and washed away. Within minutes the metamorphosis was complete. The rusty, stained and sludge-encrusted boiler face had taken on a perfect matt black sheen, and even some of the surface dirt had disappeared from the copper pipes.

'Right, that's the first stage,' said Bill with an obvious ring of satisfaction in his voice. 'Now you go and fill the lamps while I start on the brasswork.'

I returned to find him hard at work rubbing metal paste from a sizable lump, which had been wrapped in newspaper, on to the copper injector feed pipe on his side of the cab, while already both the blower and sander valve handles were gleaming brightly.

'You start on your injector pipes - just put plenty on and rub it well in,' he advised. 'The pipes will require several applications and lots of elbow grease before they come up bright, but the brass handles should soon take on a shine.'

I found that he was quite correct in this respect. The copper pipes had a hard surface layer of dirt and oxidation and were extensively pitted, but the paste quickly began to take effect and the copper started to show through the former black coating in a most rewarding way. The brass control wheels and handles being in continual use were already worn smooth, so only a brief wipe with a pasty cloth was necessary to make them really gleam. Within half an hour we transformed the drab interior of the cab to a condition I would not have thought possible, and certainly far better than I had seen on any engine to date outside a museum.

Even the metal cases of the steam pressure and vacuum gauges were shining brightly as we stood back proudly to admire our handiwork.

'We had better get cleaned up and ring off the shed,' said Bill. 'I normally reckon to have lunch while we're here, but we've used up our time doing this today.'

As we washed, Bill reminisced about bygone days when he was a fireman and crews had their own engines. Apparently they were kept so clean then that one could conduct a complete inspection holding a white cloth in one's hand and return to the footplate without it having collected a single smudge. Hardly credible when one looked around the shed these days and saw the filthy conditions even our top-line engines were in.

Munching our sandwiches while rolling down to the pilot sidings I enquired what was in the remaining brown paper parcel lying untouched on top of the tender locker.

'It's tallow for the smokebox,' explained Bill with an air of mystery. I turned round and viewed the dull and stained boiler while waiting for him to continue. 'We can't do all the boiler casing, of course, but we can bring up the paintwork on the smokebox. The only thing is that it must be hot, so we'll do it at the end of our next run.'

The next run was soon forthcoming in the form of a Class '4F' 0-6-0 on a heavy semi-fitted, but she was not in very good shape on the bank, being apparently short of steam. We struggled up to Camp Hill more like a mineral train, so it came as no great surprise when we were requested to go through to Kings Heath with it. Bill opened up to some purpose on the gradient through Moseley Tunnel, a fact no doubt much appreciated by the crew of the Class '4', who were left unaware of his true motive. By the time we backed into the slip road at the station platform, the smokebox, while not exactly glowing a cherry red, was certainly radiating a fair amount of heat.

'Right,' said Bill as we both stood on the front framing. 'Get a dollop on a piece of cotton waste and spread it around as quickly as possible.'

Bill took one side while I tackled the other, the thick yellow grease sizzling and smoking, giving off a foul stench but spreading evenly on the hot metal. We met at the front and covered the smokebox door together. Within minutes the transformation was complete, and again the results were quite astonishing, for No 3223's smokebox from even a close distance looked just as if it had been freshly painted.

'You know, its a funny thing,' said Bill after we had returned to the footplate and washed our hands. 'A clean engine always seems to perform better than a dirty one - it's just as if they appreciate the attention.'

Our bulling efforts seemed to inspire the other pilot crews, for as the week progressed their turn-out improved visibly day by day, so that when Saturday arrived Saltley must have sported six of the cleanest Class '3Fs' on the region.

During that week I had become familiar with the bank, its landmarks, its gradients, the various types of trains working on it, when and where the main effort was made as well as when and where to run the fire and boiler down. This knowledge, of course, was necessary if one was to work efficiently, and towards the end of the week I had gained sufficient confidence to experiment with my firing technique. Carrying too much fire around meant not only extra work firing, but the possibility of blowing off excessively, which in turn led to wasting water. The more coal fired, the more one had to shovel forward on the tender, and carrying a big fire meant that it got dirtier more quickly, particularly if the damper was being closed frequently. Therefore, in order to save my back as much as to save the company expense, I tried firing lighter and lighter until I reached the point where holes were being dragged in the firebed to the detriment of good steaming. However, this point was much lower than I originally supposed, and with No 3223 the ideal seemed to be having it just below the mouthpiece ring at the back, sloping evenly down to a thickness of only 2 or 3 inches at the front. She was very tolerant to different methods, though, and if one overdid things, either with too much firing or too little, the needle would quickly respond to corrective measures. It was in any case difficult to get into much trouble on that 4-mile stretch in the normal way, for if the train took a few minutes longer from point to point due to the pilot driver easing up, it was difficult to apportion blame.

The following week we booked on at 4.00 pm, and I was quite looking forward to my first taste of night work on the pilots. After a disturbed spell of wind and rain during the weekend, a high pressure system was settling over the country, and while this gave bright sunshine during the day, fog was beginning to form as I cycled to work on the Monday afternoon.

We went through the now familiar procedure of ascertaining the whereabouts of our engine, and found that it was conveniently standing behind a Class B on the down Camp Hill goods. Some 5 minutes later we relieved our colleagues, who were anxiously awaiting our arrival and obviously keen to set off home.

'She's OK, apart from the injector clack sticking sometimes,' said Syd, the driver, more to me than to Bill, and then as an afterthought as he climbed down the steps, 'We've got you some good seats.'

They had indeed, for there were enough planks on the toolbox lockers to build a small shed, and would be very much appreciated during the night if the chance came to have a quick snooze. I tried the offending injector, but it seemed to function perfectly well; however, as a precaution I kept a spanner handy just in case I had to persuade the clack valve to drop with a sharp tap to the top of the box. This was the unofficial method enginemen adopted should it stick, a method unpopular with the fitters since it distorted the access nut on the top of the clack box, but with an uncontrollable jet of steam blowing out of the injector overflow pipe one had no time for engineering finesse.

The light was now failing fast, and because fog was settling down on the scene one could barely see more than 150 yards.

'You'd better light the lamps while you've got the chance,' advised Bill, opening the tool locker and taking out the canister of detonators. 'Just making sure that we've got some - by the look of things, we may need them tonight.'

I climbed down and lit our head and tail-lamps, and as I returned to the footplate I noticed that Bill was stuffing a couple of potatoes behind the clack box of his injector. He then packed them well into place with a cloth and proceeded to do the same thing with a large onion on my injector.

'If you keep turning them every half-hour or so, they will be nicely done in time for supper,' he explained.

I must admit that I had not seen this form of cooking before, and the thoughts of some warm food on a winter's night prompted me to do likewise in the future. It was virtually dark by the time we set off up the bank and, although visibility was no worse than earlier, I was amazed how lost I felt.

Distinguishing landmarks could no longer be seen, and at the time I did not know the bank well enough to visualise every yard of it in my mind's eye. However, Bill seemed quite unaffected by the conditions, although he did come over to my side to check the distant for Camp Hill.

As is often the case with mist or fog, it tended to form in the hollows and on the low ground first, so that beyond Camp Hill we only had the dark to contend with. At first I found working on the footplate at night somewhat disturbing, inasmuch as the extremes of lighting were initially difficult to adjust to. From virtually complete blackness other than the small guttering flame of the gauge lamp, there was sudden transformation to blinding white light on opening the firedoors. Nor was this illumination diffused in any way, for the matt black surfaces inside the cab reflected very little light, so that it was rather like being in the beam of a searchlight. It took quite some time before I

adjusted to these conditions, but gradually the adaptation came about.

My other senses also played a much bigger part at night. I soon found how essential it was to keep everything in exactly the same place so that even in the pitch black of a tunnel one could immediately find the required spanner or coal pick or the all-important tea can.

We were detained for about 40 minutes at Kings Heath and here, although there was no trace of fog and little wind, the air was decidedly cold and the first traces of frost began to twinkle on the sleepers in the dim lighting. We had no cab sheet and I found that it soon became necessary to stand in front of the open firedoors at intervals to keep warm.

Descending the bank again coupled to another pilot, I was very glad of the thick, company-issue reefer jacket, for there was no shelter from the wind caused by our motion as we travelled tender-

Saltley (21A) had its 4-mile Camp Hill bank, but Bromsgrove (21C) enjoyed the glamour of the more famous Lickey Incline with its equally well-known 0-10-0 banking engine, frequently referred to as 'Big Bertha' or 'Big Emma'. With its powerful headlight, this unique locomotive was an unmistakeable feature of 'The Bank' between 1919 and 1956. Seen here behind the 8.10 Gloucester to Burton freight on 31 August 1955, No 58100 was rated equal to two Class '3F' 0-6-0T engines. *T. J. Edgington*

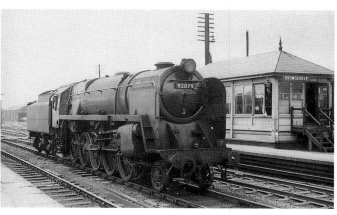

When 'Big Bertha' was finally retired in May 1956 with 838,856 miles to her credit, she was replaced by Standard Class '9F' No 92079. This was further proof of the amazing versatility of these '9s'. It is hard to imagine what other locomotive could be equally effective working specialised banking duties, express passenger, heavy mineral and fast long-distance fitted freights. The loco is shown here in August 1956 at Bromsgrove station carrying the headlight acquired from No 58100. *T. J. Edgington*

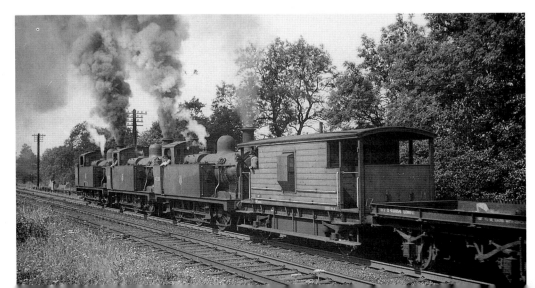

Opposite and above Although photographers sought out the more exotic specialised banking engines used on the Lickey Incline, the bulk of the work was carried out for many years by Class '3F' 0-6-0T locomotives. These mundane little engines performed in an effective if somewhat raucous manner on this daunting climb. They could work singly, in twos, threes or even fours, as seen here.

In the second photograph, at the far end of the down platform on the right, can be seen what was regarded as the best maintained facing points in the country. On many occasions I was diverted through the platform slow line at hair-raising speeds with runaway trains, but at no time did I experience more than a mild 'kick'. *All T. J. Edgington*

first. With tears streaming from my eyes, I found my gaze drawn to the lighted windows of lineside houses where the inhabitants were settling down for the night round cosy fires, but I felt no pangs of envy whatsoever - on the contrary, I would not have changed places for all the tea in China.

On the embankment between Camp Hill and Bordesley we once more looked out over the sea of fog that appeared to be at rooftop level and glowed eerily from the illumination of countless street lamps. Thrusting up into the clear air above could be seen the tops of the tall buildings and church spires that abound in that area. At Bordesley we plunged into the fog, but it was not thick enough to impede our progress unduly, although I found it just sufficiently dense to tax my memory and knowledge to the limit. Indeed, it was to prove a useful introduction to the old-fashioned pea-soupers that we were to experience later in the week.

The evening, while fairly busy, turned out to be quite routine, and weather conditions remained

more or less constant. Bill devoured his potatoes and onion during a lengthy wait at Camp Hill and pronounced them to be very toothsome indeed, a fact that had not escaped my notice. We were at Kings Heath when our relief booked on, and it was a further hour and a half before they eventually climbed aboard at Landor Street Junction, but as Bill exclaimed, 'Nothing was spoiling at that hour of the morning, and we were after all being paid time and a half.'

The following day, Tuesday, was fine and sunny and the evening quite clear although extremely cold for that time of the year, but on Wednesday morning, when I drew back the bedroom curtains I was confronted by a wall of fog. This had largely cleared by midday under the influence of bright sunshine, but at 3.00 pm great banks were beginning to roll in again, so I decided to set off to work somewhat earlier than usual. This was to prove a wise precaution, for although I was not over-exerting myself, very little traffic passed my trusty bicycle. A mile from the loco, visibility had closed down to between 15 and 20 yards, and the fog had taken on that yellow-grey colour that portends a real thick one. By the time I had parked my cycle in the racks I was relying entirely on memory as to where to find the shed entrance. Bill was already in the lobby when I entered, and from his expression he seemed relieved to see me.

'You've got here all right, then?' he queried.

'Yes,' I replied, wiping droplets of moisture from my hair and eyebrows, 'but it's getting a bit dodgy outside now.'

He nodded sombrely. 'Here, put these in your bag. I reckon we'll need a few extra tonight,' and he handed me a cardboard box containing 12 detonators.

We made our way outside again, where the fog clouds were rolling in thicker than ever and we could see no more than 10 or 15 yards. Sound travels rather better in fog, and because a strange eerie silence had also settled over the area, noises a long way off seemed quite close. We proceeded gingerly to the control box at Duddeston Road, relying more on our ears than our eyes to keep out of the way of traffic moving on and off the shed, while already we could hear the sharp crack of fog signals exploding from many different points.

'Yours is somewhere on the way up from the pilot sidings,' said the Controller, 'but I'm having a job to see the engine numbers in this blasted lot.'

We could readily appreciate that point, for even on the intermediate line just in front of the box engines were now appearing as only vague dark shapes. Keeping close to the gas works boundary fence, we cautiously headed towards the pilot sidings, listening intently for all signs of movement and at the same time peering continuously around our own little grey world that extended in a radius of no more than 10 yards or so.

The engine number on the banker at the rear of a train on the down Camp Hill could not be distinguished until we were virtually standing at the bottom of its steps, and then it was the driver's voice that first told us that it was not ours. A passenger train could be heard vigorously snorting away from the starter on the down main at Saltley Junction - a sure sign that things were getting bad, if expresses were being checked or their drivers were missing signals.

We eventually found our engine behind a west-bound mixed freight headed by a '4F', just beyond Saltley station. Although not yet quite dark, I noticed that the lamps had been lighted and both Syd, the driver, and Jack, the fireman, were obviously looking out for us.

'It's come down quick today,' said Syd gravely. 'Could get bad later in the night. I think we'll get off,' he continued. 'You are all right in the rear; there's a Class B standing behind the tender.'

He was, of course, referring to the chances of being run into from the rear while standing on a road where the permissive block system was operating, a not uncommon occurrence in foggy conditions.

After conducting the usual preliminary checks we settled down, placing our potatoes in suitable positions for a gentle baking, while speculating on what might be in store for us. A slight clank caused me to glance ahead and I was just in time to see the brake-van lights of our train receding into the limits of visibility that lay only a little way beyond the smokebox door. Bill was not caught napping and eased the regulator open instantly, but even so we travelled quite a few yards before making contact with the brake-van again. With just sufficient steam on to maintain position, we waited for the train engine to stop us, and when this eventually took place we found ourselves standing on the intermediate line.

'Go and drop a detonator on the track about 20 yards behind us,' said Bill. 'We don't want anyone spilling our tea.'

Listening intently and taking great care not to be run down, I placed the metal disc on top of the nearest rail, securing it in position with the lead strips provided for the purpose. I could hear what I took to be the Class B chugging towards me, so I scampered back to Bill to advise him what was happening. Seconds later a loud crash, seemingly right beneath the tender, made us both jump and we braced ourselves instinctively. There was no need, though, for the Class B shut off immediately and rolled up to our tender buffers with hardly a shudder.

'It gives the other fellow a chance and us some peace of mind,' explained Bill, well pleased with the outcome.

We waited some 10 minutes, during which time neither of us took our eyes off the brake ahead for more than a few seconds, before the familiar clank of couplings being drawn taut and a slight surge indicated that the train was on the move again.

Bill had just been explaining that had we been on the down Camp Hill and likely to be involved in a long wait, he would have got me to place a detonator under the brake-van wheel (having first advised the guard), so that constant vigilance would not have then been necessary.

He proceeded very cautiously with little more than a breath of steam on for, in the gathering darkness, the fog seemed denser than ever and we did not know for certain if we had the road. Keeping the firedoors tightly closed to prevent back glare, we both stood on my side of the footplate, straining to catch a glimpse of the signals at Duddeston Road. Not until we were almost directly beneath them did we just manage to see the double green of the home signal with the distant for Landor Street below it.

Bill now opened up more confidently while I added more fuel to the fire, trying hard not to become dazzled by the brilliant white light. He was soon over on my side again, intent on checking the distant under the Landor Street starter, for as long as we could see that the distants were off we could keep going. Miss one and we would have to be prepared to come to a stand at the next stop signal. Because of our leisurely start we had not worked up much speed, but as soon as Bill sighted the distant for Brickyard Crossing he pushed the regulator right across and our exhaust thundered out into the heavy atmosphere like so much gunfire. He could not possibly have seen me raise a quizzical eyebrow, but he answered my unspoken question nevertheless.

'We don't want to stick in this lot, and we're struggling a bit at the moment.'

With our engine, No 3507, doing more than its full share, we managed to keep going over the worst section between Brickyard Crossing and St Andrews without actually coming to a standstill, but one good slip and we would have done so. Unlike Monday night we did not run out of the fog at Bordesley Junction; in fact, it seemed to be getting thicker than ever, but I was able to sight the distant for Camp Hill on the approach side of the Coventry Road overbridge. The junction box was quite invisible and from there on I became completely lost over the lengthy stretch up to Camp Hill. Bill had reverted to the first valve once past St Andrews, and now he eased the regulator still further and took up position on my side of the cab again, straining his eyes into the murk ahead.

'We're coming up to the Camp Hill home signal,' he murmured without averting his gaze. 'I expect he'll want us through with this load, but we'll have a job to see the bobby.'

This distant was off, but Bill did not open up again. He was quite content just to maintain our slow and steady pace. I peered into the blanket of fog swirling round the engine, unable to discern a thing except for the faint glow of the brake-van tail-lamps, but Bill apparently knew exactly where he was because right on cue he leaned out between the uprights.

'Only a few yards now,' he said.

Seconds later we saw a diffused patch of light looking like a ghostly apparition come into view and there, leaning out of the open window, was the bobby waving a green lamp. Bill popped the whistle in acknowledgment, pulled the gear lever back a couple of notches and pushed the regulator on to full first valve. We gathered speed on the following easy grade, but once again I was hopelessly lost until the colour light signal at Brighton

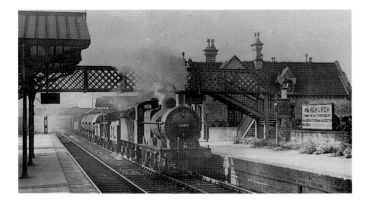

'3F' 0-6-0 No 3507 seen stretching her legs on a Class B through freight at Ashchurch where the lines from Evesham on one side and Tewkesbury on the other join the main Birmingham to Bristol artery some 23 miles south of Bromsgrove. The conditions here are very different from those when Bill Smith and I were groping our way down Camp Hill bank on this engine during the thickest fog for years.

Road flashed past. It was then that I realised how much more effective these powerful electric signals were in fog; not only did they emit a much brighter beam, but the lens was also closer to one's eye level.

We were into Moseley Tunnel before I realised it and, once through, Bill gradually eased off so that the train had already left us by the time we clattered under the Kings Heath overbridge and came to a standstill alongside the down platform.

'You'd better walk back to the box,' said Bill, 'and find out what he's going to do with us.'

I stepped blindly on to the platform and stumbled off in what I thought was the correct direction until, like a moth, I was able to home in on the dim light that served to illuminate it. Banging my shins on the short flight of steps, I entered.

'Gosh, it's black out there, Frank,' I exclaimed, ruefully rubbing the injured limb.

'Aye, lad,' replied Frank, who was nearing retirement and who hailed from northern parts. 'It's a real old-fashioned pea-souper, to be sure.' I signed the book while he continued. 'I've got a path for you right now, so you can tell your mate to set back as soon as he's ready. There's no sense in hanging about in this lot.'

'OK,' I replied and stepped once more into the wall of darkness outside the box. My brief exposure to even that dim lighting left me almost blind and I shuffled very slowly along the platform, guided purely by the gentle hiss of our engine. I did not spot the tail-lamp until only about five paces away and just remembered in time to remove its red shade and place it in what was formerly our headlight.

'Right, Bill,' I said as I groped my way back to the footplate. 'He's going to have us straight back down the bank again, and he's ready when you are.'

Bill popped the whistle and we chuffed gently over the crossover on to the up line, just spotting that both home and distant signals were off as we passed by. With the firedoors tightly closed I could not see a thing, and I certainly did not envy Bill his job of driving in these conditions, but as before he showed not the slightest concern, such was his knowledge of the road.

As we coasted down towards Brighton Road, I asked Bill how he knew so accurately where we were at any particular point, and he explained that it was quite simply done by observing certain lineside features such as bridges, and then count-

ing anything visible like telegraph poles or quarter-mile posts, etc. Needless to say, this required a vast amount of experience and a memory like an elephant. We were brought to a halt at the Camp Hill home signal, which could only just be seen when the tender buffers were level with the post. Conditions were definitely getting worse, for after 15 minutes we heard the clang of the signal coming off, but could not see it from the footplate, so I climbed on top of the tender to get a better view. The extra elevation was just sufficient for me to confirm that it was in fact safe to proceed.

Bill did not go forward to the starter, but stopped opposite the signal box - at least I had to take his word that we were opposite the box, because it was not remotely visible from the up line.

'Go and see the bobby and find out if the starter is off,' said Bill. 'It will be easier than trying to sight the damn thing in this.'

I did as requested, first listening intently in case anything was approaching on the down line, but under the heavy cloak of fog Camp Hill was as silent as the proverbial grave. Setting off at right angles to the track, I groped my way over rails and point rods until, after tripping over a cluster of signal wires, I came up against the base of the box. Once again Bill had been dead on target. Following the wall, I eventually found, and climbed, the long flight of steps which were slippery with moisture.

'Thought you might come up,' said the bobby cheerfully when I had announced myself. 'I could hear you stop, but I can't see a thing past the windows. The starter is off,' he continued, 'but be prepared to stop at Bordesley. There's a Class B in front of you.'

I thanked him for the information and, after nearly descending the steps in one, I conveyed the news to Bill.

We set off cautiously and I must admit that neither of us saw the starter light, only the post, for being quite a tall signal it was completely lost to view. I noticed after a short while that Bill was now leaning over the side all the time, striving to glimpse some point of recognition, and when I joined him on his side of the footplate he shook his head resignedly.

'Well, mate, I've never seen it worse than this. I can't even make out the sleepers.'

This was indeed so. One could hardly see across the cab, let alone what was outside. Because of this Bill, with the engine coasting at just a crawl, was relying entirely on the different sounds it made over the rails to pinpoint our position, an incredible feat of memory.

'Can't be far away now,' he murmured a trifle uncertainly.

'I'll climb up on to the back of the tender,' I volunteered, glad at last to be of some practical assistance.

Scrambling on all fours over the coal, I eventually found the well and stood upright peering out into a solid wall of fog like some ancient mariner.

'Nothing yet,' I called, glancing round, and then I had a shock, for I could not even see halfway along the tender.

We crept forwards for a few more yards, then Bill, realising the hopelessness of our situation, stopped and called me down.

'Take my torch and walk along the track,' he said. 'It's about the only way we are going to find it.'

By shining the beam directly down I could just see the ground and, after stumbling on for about ten paces without finding anything, I shouted for Bill to follow. I continued for another 30 yards in this manner before I suddenly blundered into the signal post.

'Stop, Bill, I've found it,' I called.

Bill halted, and joined me at the base of the signal. 'Is it off?' he asked optimistically.

'Blowed if I know,' I replied, shining the torch on the post and illuminating a small area only a few feet above our heads. 'Can you tell by the position of the counterweight?'

'I wouldn't like to guess,' replied Bill. 'No, there's only one thing for it, you'll have to climb up and have a look.'

I found the slender iron ladder used by the lamp men for servicing purposes and started to ascend. Until then I had never realised what rickety structures signal posts were, for it swayed alarmingly at every step, and when I gained the narrow slatted platform I was surprised how large the signal arms were at close range.

'It's on,' I called down to Bill.

'Well, you'd better stay up there for a while. I'll go back and put a detonator down. It will help the next chap, even though it's not strictly necessary here.'

His disembodied voice floated up out of the murk below, as I leaned back against the protective rail and took stock of the situation. Never in my wildest fantasies had I ever imagined myself

marooned on top of a signal post in the densest fog for years, and it was a caper I hoped would not be repeated too many times in the future. Suddenly violent shaking literally shook me out of my reverie and nearly off my precarious foothold. The signal came off with a totally unexpected force that left both the post and I swaying and shuddering, retained it seemed only by the securing guy ropes. I waited for the tremors to subside before slithering thankfully down the ladder and making my way back to the engine, where Bill was groping around with arms outstretched, trying to find the steps.

We rolled cautiously down to the starter where we carried out the same procedure, only on this occasion I found the signal already off. St Andrews home did not present quite such a problem since, because of the overhead bridges, the signals were set more or less at cab level and I was able to see them from the back of the tender. Finding the box in order to carry out Rule 55 was both difficult and hazardous, but the bobby did not allow Bill to proceed until the road was clear to Brickyard Crossing, so once again we could pass the starter with confidence.

Because of its close proximity the box at Brickyard was easier to find, and when we were finally allowed down to Landor Street, the glow from the relief cabin just warned us in time that we were near the signals. After filling the tank we had a long wait before the bobby advised Bill - who had joined him in the box - that the section to Duddeston Road was clear. Normally trains are allowed to follow each other down under the permissive system, but in these conditions no such risks were being taken. We had travelled no more than 50 yards when we were startled by the explosion of a detonator under our tender wheels. Bill instantly brought us nearly to a standstill.

'Probably left by the guard on the last train that was here,' he said, 'but keep your eyes skinned just in case.'

In fact, I could not see past the end of the tender, but at less than walking pace we were not likely to cause much damage. The fog signalmen were now out in force, and the friendly glow from their well-filled braziers did much to restore one's confidence. However, despite their efforts and the fact that very little traffic seemed to be moving, it took another 2 hours to reach the haven of our pilot sidings. Two other pilots were already standing on the back road and with the chaotic conditions prevailing, it was not entirely surprising that we were still there when our relief finally arrived at 12.45 am. Walking back to the loco, Bill pointed out that the sleepers were now white with hoar frost.

'That's a good sign' said Bill.

'Is it?' I replied, not too sure that he was right since I had just twisted my ankle rather painfully by slipping off one.

'Yes, it will freeze some of the fog out of the air,' he went on confidently, and sure enough by the time we reached the shed visibility was notably better, although still only about 5 yards.

The foggy conditions persisted for another two days but it was never as bad as on the Wednesday night, although severe enough to keep us on our toes and cause considerable delays to all forms of traffic movement. However, I welcomed the experience on the whole since it forced me to learn numerous little points of recognition used by drivers to establish their whereabouts, and I acquired more knowledge during that week than I would have in many months of good visibility.

As the winter nights became longer and more tedious, some of the firemen in the link showed signs of boredom and they tended to relieve this by indulging in a number of pranks that caused consternation to some of the drivers but amusement to others, particularly if the recipient of that prank was someone with whom they were not on good terms.

For example, one evening a driver had been entertaining himself at the expense of a few of the firemen in the cabin and afterwards, unknown to him, someone had placed a fog signal under each wheel of his engine and tender. When he set off after his train an almighty explosion nearly gave the poor old boy a heart attack, for 12 detonators going off simultaneously and unexpectedly at close range has a shattering effect on the most robust of nervous systems. Needless to say, he was rather more careful regarding the nature of his conversations in the future, and for weeks afterwards could be seen religiously inspecting the rails under his engine before making a movement of any kind.

Not all the escapades were intentional, however, and an incident that occurred one night just before Christmas served to show that on railways even a slight miscalculation can have far-reaching consequences. When conditions were extraordinarily busy, it was often difficult to find time to clean the fire should the need arise, since no sooner did one arrive at Camp Hill or Kings Heath

than one was returned down the bank again, not to the pilot sidings but straight behind a waiting train at Duddeston Road.

Although often there would then be sufficient time to do a fair job while standing in readiness to make the ascent, it was neither practical nor permitted, since one could not run the risk of being caught with one's pants down, so to speak. It was therefore common practice to tackle any fire-cleaning at the beginning of the descent so that all could be completed and the fire built up again by the time steam was needed once more at Landor Street Junction. Slabs of clinker thus removed, were piled in a corner of the tender in readiness for dumping overboard at the first convenient authorised place, usually Landor Street water column. On the night in question a fireman, whom we shall call Timothy, was having a rough time. Although the fire had been cleaned during the day shift, it was now showing all the signs of being choked with clinker, and having arrived at Camp Hill with no more than 120 lbs per sq in on the clock and the water just in sight, his driver instructed Timothy to pull some clinker out on the return trip in the prescribed manner.

Now, Timothy was a big, good-natured lad but a little slow in grasping the essence of anything new. In fact, most of his colleagues had long since come to the conclusion that in terms of sheer intellect, he was, as his driver put it, 'one gill short of a pint'. He had only just scraped through his passing-out test at the third attempt and unfortunately seemed somewhat lacking in the ability to foresee the consequences of even the simplest of actions. Modern psychologists would no doubt call him a late developer.

Timothy set to work with great gusto, pushing the fire forwards with the clinker shovel as soon as they departed from Camp Hill signal box. Having accomplished this, he swung the shovel back on to the tender so that he could dig out the offending material with a bent dart. Or at least this was his intention, but as he swung the heavy shovel outwards and upwards the tip caught the parapet of the Stratford Road bridge that they unfortunately happened to be traversing at the time. The resultant snatch pulled it out of his grasp and sent it spinning into the void.

The plummeting fire iron dropped towards the road like a javelin, and since it was the early hours of the morning they might, in normal circumstances, have got away with no more than a general complaint to BR for dumping unwanted rubbish on the Queen's Highway. However, a number 29A Corporation Night Service bus contrived to be passing on its sedate way at exactly the crucial moment. The blade of the shovel punctured the thin aluminium and plywood roof of the luckily deserted upper deck like so much tissue paper and ended up embedded in the fourth row of seats from the front. Naturally the Corporation frowned on such acts perpetrated against its buses, and with timings so accurately pin-pointed, Timothy and his driver had to face the consequences, which resulted in a week's suspension.

Early in January I was involved in an innocent little episode that received some minor publicity in the local press. It was a Saturday and I was working the day shift once more. We had experienced the first appreciable fall of snow of the winter during the early hours of that morning, and when I booked on, some 8 inches lay deep and crisp and even over the entire area. It seemed to me that it brought about a distinct improvement to Birmingham in general and Saltley in particular, for the acres of grimy industrial eyesores were all now discreetly covered by this pure white blanket.

I've always been fascinated by the pictorial transformation snow brings to any scene, and nowhere is this more apparent than in a railway view involving a steam locomotive at work. For one thing, all that can be seen of the track itself is two parallel black lines, while both engine and stock stand out from the white backcloth with a clarity of definition not normally observable in any other circumstances. However, it is the way that the exhaust of steam and smoke shows up so magnificently that impresses most. The cold air condenses every last molecule, so that even a single puff expands to enormous proportions and hangs in a glorious white cloud. Likewise every atom of carbon stands out in stark contrast and forms beautiful rolling patterns while entrapped in the steam.

Apart from the snow, which was not really deep enough to affect rail traffic, the Saturday in question was progressing more or less on routine lines until in the early afternoon, when we were requested by the bobby at Duddeston Road to run up behind a westbound mineral train that had stuck at Brickyard Crossing. The air was cold and damp and the sky heavily overcast giving the impression that more snow was imminent and not unnaturally the rails were wet and greasy. The mineral, hauled by a Class '8F', was exceptionally heavy, having literally slipped itself to a stand at the usual place. Bill, grumbling about doing an extra turn, shunted across to the down Camp Hill while I quickly set about the task of rallying both fire and boiler for the unexpected job ahead.

In those post-war austerity days, one could never guarantee what type or quality of coal would be delivered to the shed, and a couple of days previously a trainload of ovoids had arrived. We frequently had ovoids and briquettes, but usually these were mixed with normal coal. On this occasion no coal was available for mixing, however, and since the ovoids had to be used, every freight engine at Saltley was running on a pure diet of the things. As previously explained, there is nothing basically wrong with ovoids; being egg-size they burn fast and are ideal for firing over the bottom flap of the old Midland firedoors. They do produce, though, a lot of dust and a fantastic amount of smoke, and because of their shape they continually rolled out of the tender all over the footplate unless suitably constrained by a well-placed firebar or two.

By the time we buffered up to the pilot ahead I had baled in a fair quantity of them in an effort to build up the fire at the back of the box, and already a rich column of black smoke was billowing skywards, despite wide-open firedoors and the blower hard on. Len, the fireman on the other pilot, also got busy with the shovel and soon his smoke was matching my own. Bill opened the whistle to give the distinctive 'crow' indicating that we were ready this end and, after receiving an answering hoot from the train engine, allowed us to roll back a few wagon lengths before opening the regulator on to full first valve.

I whipped up the bottom flap of the firedoors and joined Bill on his side so that I could watch the spectacle of our three engines getting the heavy train under way. Both pilots slipped before the sanders took effect, while up ahead a gigantic pillar of jet black smoke confirmed that the '8F' was also on ovoids.

The slipping really livened up our fires, so that the smoke became denser than ever and, as I looked forwards, I could see Len's grinning face nodding at the triple columns of smoke and steam mushrooming up against the pure white background - a most impressive sight indeed. We clawed our way slowly past St Andrews Junction and, as we thumped up the cutting towards the Coventry Road overbridge, I realised that we could well be invited through to Kings Heath, so I started ladling ovoids in over the bottom flap as fast as I could shovel. When I looked out again we were just approaching the City football ground and, although no great enthusiast, I recalled that the Blues had an important home match on that day. A vast pall of dense black smoke and billowing clouds of steam had been left in the cutting by the Class '8' and, wafted by the faintest of breezes, it was now rolling gently over the boundary wall of the stadium.

A spasm of devilment caught me and I quickly closed the top firedoor flap, which until now I had left open in order to burn some of the smoke without admitting too much cold air. Len must have had the same idea, for there was naught to choose between the vast towering pillars of black oily smoke erupting from our chimneys. It was a fantastic sight, this tremendous volume of smoke held captive by the cold heavy atmosphere, following and reinforcing the smokescreen laid by the train engine. Of its effect we knew nothing, although even above the crash of the twin exhaust I thought I heard the roar of the crowd just before we passed under the Coventry Road bridge.

I had forgotten the incident until, when booking off that evening in the lobby, I happened to glance over the shoulder of a fireman reading the *Sports Argus*. There in bold print was the heading of the report on Birmingham's game.

'Mid-match black-out! The Blues gained a slender 1-0 victory today when they scored a controversial goal just after half-time when play was temporarily blotted out by smoke and steam drifting in from the nearby railway line. . .' I read no more and, pulling my collar well up, crept quickly away. . .

In February I purchased my first motor cycle, a BSA 500cc M33, which was delivered to my home and was waiting for me on my return from an early morning shift. Such is the innocence and foolhardiness of youth, that it never occurred to me to seek help or instruction of any kind before attempting to ride it. Over a hasty meal I read the instruction manual and, thus armed with a scanty knowledge of the controls, attached a couple of L-plates and, with a mixture of trepidation and great excitement, set off for my first spin.

Even wheeling the 360 lbs machine took a bit of getting used to, and kicking over the new and tight engine called for tremendous effort.

Eventually I managed to get the motor started and after ensuring that no other vehicle was in sight I slipped it into bottom gear and let out the clutch. With a series of kangaroo hops I got under way and steered it round a corner into a quiet side road where I was able to practice in reasonable safety. From the moment I felt the tremendous surge of response on tweaking open the throttle, I was hooked on motor cycling, and although for the first few rides I had to steel myself before setting out, once in the saddle I felt that I was in my natural element. After that I could not get back to my motor cycle quick enough, and I usually managed a ride either before or after work depending on what shift I happened to be on.

With the coming of spring my spirits soared to new heights - life was one long round of excitement and pleasure equally divided between motor cycling and firing. I had by now acquired a fair working knowledge of the bank and I could provide more than enough steam with a Class '3F' on that duty. Moreover, Bill was allowing me to drive the engine on return trips down the bank, and, when feeling in need of a little exercise, also occasionally handed over for the real business too. Even at 3.00 am in the morning when the human body is supposed to be at its lowest ebb, I could be heard singing at the top of my voice with sheer exuberance, inspired by the rhythm of the exhaust as we pounded along from Brighton Road up to Moseley Tunnel.

Just before Bill and I parted company he did in fact pay me a somewhat backhanded compliment as I was competing with the birds in their dawn chorus by saying, 'I've never known anyone so damned happy as you at this benighted hour of the day.'

Looking back, I had been extremely happy in the pilots. I had advanced my firing technique to a very considerable degree and had become thoroughly familiar with a Class '3F' from both sides of the footplate, even to the extent of oiling it from stem to stern. I had also gained a sound knowledge of that section of line between Washwood Heath and Kings Heath, apart from acquiring the countless little snippets of information that go towards making an engineman generally competent in discharging his duties. The training had been indeed most useful and an ideal stepping-stone for greater things to come, so that when the annual May reshuffle arrived I looked forward with eager anticipation to expending my horizons.

9
THE CONTROL LINK

The great advantage of the Control link was that one rarely knew what one was going to do from day to day. At least it was an advantage if you were a supreme optimist, and at 17 years of age I was very optimistic indeed. Every day I imagined that I would be required for some crack turn, but in reality things did not work out quite that way. As previously explained, there were no booked jobs, only booked times, and after signing on one just waited until something turned up. As often as not, this was no more inspiring a duty than walking across to Landor Street relief cabin and waiting an hour or two for some train that terminated at Washwood Heath up sidings. Or by way of a change one might go to Bromford and work the mile or so to the West End. Inevitably the engine was brought back to the shed and disposed of, and during an eight-hour shift this

tedious performance might be repeated three times.

Although a driver and fireman were booked together as in any other link, there was no guarantee that they would always work as a team. For example, if a driver was selected for a job because of his specialised route knowledge and his fireman had not arrived for some reason, the next available fireman would be borrowed. Absenteeism was not at all uncommon amongst the unmarried firemen, but because there was such an acute shortage of men the management was forced to be unusually tolerant.

Just to keep one's eye in and interest alive, so to speak, there were fortunately a few road jobs thrown in, which took one to such relatively faraway places as Bromsgrove or even Gloucester in the west, or Burton, Derby and Leicester in the

Much of the Control link's work was concerned with local relief, and crews would rarely venture more than a few miles from Saltley. These duties usually resulted in disposing of the engine on returning to the shed. While the fireman cleaned the fire, the driver inspected the engine for defects. Here the driver is seen checking brake block clearance by the well-tried method of pushing it with his foot.

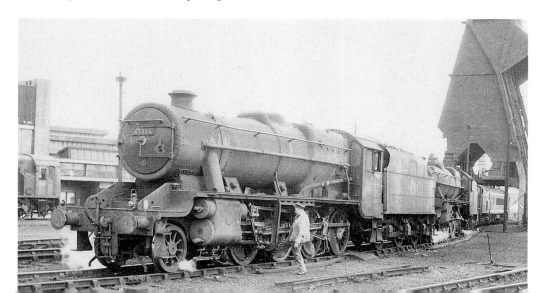

During the early 1950s congestion was so severe that Control link men were often sent to Castle Bromwich in order to relieve the crew of some freight train who were already on overtime. Nearly 4 miles north from Saltley, it involved almost an hour's walk unless a lift on a passing light engine could be obtained. However, sometimes progress was so slow that they themselves were on overtime before they had travelled the 2 miles to Washwood Heath.

This view, taken from the north end of the down platform at Castle Bromwich, shows ex-S&D Class '3F' 0-6-0 on the 1.40 pm Derby to Kings Norton freight. Despite their Victorian origin, '3Fs' were very popular with enginemen, and it was on one of these that I made my first descent of the Lickey Incline while in the Control link.

north and east. However, such was the volume of traffic in those days that even with local turns a fair amount of overtime could be had and one was always asked if one wished to work on Sunday if normal booked times allowed. My mate Harold, having three children, could never take home too much money, and as I now had a motorcycle to pay off I was also quite happy to earn a bit extra. We therefore always asked for any sort of work on a Sunday, for which we were, of course, paid double time. Frequently these Sunday jobs took the form of ballast trains, since track maintenance was carried out between midnight Saturday and midnight Sunday. They were not very exacting from the firing point of view, but like shunting duties demanded continual vigilance and attention when movements were being made. To relieve my boredom, Harold usually allowed me to occupy the driver's side, a privilege I gratefully accepted.

One Sunday, however, we were told to book on for a special coal train that was to be moved from Water Orton to the Corporation sidings at Washwood Heath, destined for the power station at Nechells, which we gathered was rather low on stocks. Things were more than usually chaotic that day, because a new crossover was being installed at Washwood Heath Junction and traffic was being kept to an absolute minimum - even passenger trains were being diverted where possible. We booked on at 6.00 am, prepared Class '8F' No 8669, rang off the shed at 7.15 and proceeded tender-first to Water Orton with our guard in attendance on the footplate.

Our passage to Water Orton was in itself unusual, since to avoid the work at Washwood Heath

Junction we were diverted over the up sidings and then allowed to run through an empty road, set aside there for the purpose, until we came out at Bromford. From there we travelled to our destination on the up main. At Water Orton we discovered just how special our train was to be. Apparently it consisted of two coal trains that had been left there overnight, and we were to couple these together and haul the combined load, which totalled no less than 105 wagons, equal to 116. This was in round figures something in excess of 1,500 tons.

My first question to Harold was, 'Will she do it?'

'Don't know,' he replied. 'I've never had that many on before, but we'll soon find out.'

We had, of course, to first draw half the train out, and then set back on the remainder before all was coupled up and we were ready to go. Our guard gave us the signal and started walking back to his distant brake, while Harold eased open the regulator.

We felt the pull of the heavy wagons as the couplings stretched out and, as we tended to be dragged to a standstill, Harold compensated by progressively opening the regulator. Despite a full head of steam and the gear lever at maximum cut-off, we were soon on full first valve as we wumphed majestically out on the down main. The rail was dry and No 8669 gave not the slightest hint of a slip as I watched the incredible line of wagons slowly worm out of the sidings.

However, such was its length that even my eagle eyesight was not up to being able to see that our guard had climbed safely aboard, over 700 yards back. We therefore assumed all was well and, winding the reversing screw back to 60 per cent cut-off, Harold heaved the regulator up to the horizontal. Gradually our blast took on a crisper note and No 8669 began to show her mettle by gradually accelerating that gargantuan load up the 1 in 975 gradient from Water Orton. Her task was made no easier by the fact that many of the wagons were equipped with the old greasebox-type axle bearings, which dragged heavily until warmed up.

As our speed increased, so the exhaust acquired that gunfire-like thump typical of 'Black Fives' and '8Fs' when working hard, and I revelled in the exhilaration of this unusual feat. I was carrying a medium-sized fire, but with this treatment I soon had to start shovelling in earnest. By now, however, I had gained sufficient experience with '8Fs' to be able to cope reasonably well and, having recently perfected the technique of bouncing the shovel blade on the mouthpiece ring, I could not only reach the front of the box, but could also place each shovelful in roughly the desired spot. I found that by building the fire up level with the mouthpiece, the rear half of the grate could be fired with the minimum of effort by more or less rolling the coal in to the required area. Using only the rear damper caused more rapid combustion in this section, which was easiest to reach, and, together with the natural tendency for the coal to shake forward, meant that one could normally fire two shovelsful to the rear half to only one at the front.

Harold did not allow our speed to build up too high, because stopping a 1,500-ton train with only the engine brake had to be considered; consequently, he came back to the first valve and further reduced the cut-off when we approached the distant for Castle Bromwich. We still had a clear road, though, and Harold opened out once more as the gradient stiffened to 1 in 486. Eventually we were brought to a halt at Bromford Bridge home signal, where we learned just how much energy is stored up in a 1,500-ton train, even running at only 15 mph. On drawing up to the signal box, the bobby informed us that a Traffic Inspector was waiting at Washwood Heath Junction to see us over the permanent way works and to supervise our rather complicated and unorthodox entry into the Corporation sidings.

Getting away again on the 1 in 326 gradient did

provoke a slip, but No 8669 kept her feet very well as we struggled slowly towards the junction, until we were stopped by a hand-signalman protecting the maintenance operations. Harold decided to walk the 200 yards to the box in order to ascertain just what procedures had been worked out for us, leaving me in charge with the instructions to bring her up when they were ready. Some minutes later he reappeared in the distance with a tall gentleman wearing a felt hat, who I concluded was the Traffic Inspector.

After some whistle-blowing and waving of arms, the hand-signalman indicated that it was all clear to proceed, so I gave a toot of acknowledgment and released the hand brake. Being still on a gradient of 1 in 326, the couplings were at full stretch, but despite the great weight dragging on the drawbar, No 8669 shuddered into motion as soon as I hauled the regulator up on full first valve. After a few yards, by way of experiment, I wound the reversing screw back to give 45 per cent cut-off, then quickly heaved the regulator wide open. At this setting she moved forward very smoothly, pulling her great load at a steady walking pace towards where Harold and the Inspector were standing engrossed in conversation. It was the one and only time I ever had the good fortune to handle a train of over 1,000 tons, albeit for just about 1 furlong, but it went down in my diary as a personal all-time record that is now not likely to be broken.

I dropped back to the first valve just before they climbed aboard and, with Harold once again at the controls, we chugged slowly over the unballasted crossover at the permitted 5 mph, giving the sweating workmen there quite a substantial breather. It was arranged that we draw ahead of Washwood Heath No 1 signal box, then back across the road to enter the Corporation sidings via Hill 60, but such was the length of our train that the Inspector alighted by Saltley station to relay the necessary signals to us. Eventually the operation was accomplished, but it is worth recording that it required full gear and a wide open regulator to push that huge load back over Hill 60's hump.

As the weeks passed by we did manage the odd job that took us further afield, and on two consecutive days we ran a Class A to Burton with a '4F' and a Class B to Bromsgrove with a faithful old '3F'. The former trip was interesting but uneventful, except that I had difficulty in maintaining steam, but the latter stands out in my mind because it was my first look at the formidable Lickey Incline. Our train was a mixed freight of 38 wagons, which, although a fair load for a '3F', did not prove too troublesome on the long haul of

mainly adverse gradients up from Duddeston Road to Barnt Green. From here we turned into the down loop at Blackwell, where we stood for an hour or so alongside the golf course.

I had heard many exciting tales of various exploits on the bank and was all agog to see what it was like. Now here it lay at last, just round the next bend while we were cooped up waiting for all the morning passenger trains to clear the line. Just when I felt that I could stand the waiting no longer, the signal came off, we eased out on to the main line and trundled slowly through the station.

A grey-haired rotund figure dressed in a shunter's uniform called a cheery good morning to us as he walked in a rolling gait along the platform, swinging in his right hand a rather battered brake-stick. A brake-stick, incidentally, is a piece of stout hardwood about the size of a baseball bat but, while the top half or handle is round, the bottom half is of square section. Its function is for gaining extra purchase when pinning down the brake handles of wagons by the simple expedient

of inserting the end of the stick between the brake handle and the solebar of the wagon, then using it as a lever. A hefty brakeman or guard, by swinging on the end of the brake-stick in this manner, can in fact even lock the wheels, providing that the brake mechanism is in good condition.

Just beyond the end of the platform I noticed an ancient black hut and a prominent signboard stating that all goods trains were to stop in order to pin down brakes, and here we ground to a halt. The brakeman walked back to the guard, with whom he consulted with regard to the load of the train. Having come to agreement as to the number of wagons to have their brakes applied, which might be, say, one in three, they then walked forwards towards the engine, dropping the brake handles from their resting places as appropriate but not pinning them down, the guard taking the up side while the brakeman attended to the down or platform side. On arrival back at the engine they would give us the tip to proceed, and we would draw slowly ahead on to the incline proper, while both men pinned down the brakes with the aid of their sticks as the wagons came by them.

This technique required a high degree of skill from the driver and a considerable amount of dexterity from both guard and brakeman, since if we went too fast they would not be able to pin down

No photograph can really do justice to the awe-inspiring view of the Lickey Incline as seen from Blackwell. It always seemed to me like a giant ski-jump and never failed to raise a tingle of excitement, particularly when I was in charge of a loose-coupled train.

With a predetermined number of wagon brakes pinned down, Class '4F' 0-6-0 No 43891 is now fully on the 1 in 37 Lickey Incline at Blackwell. At this early stage it was important to try and hold the train's speed below a certain critical factor, but even so there was no guarantee that this could be done over the ensuing 2 miles. Runaway loose-coupled trains were therefore a fairly common occurrence. *T. J. Edgington*

the brakes properly, and a runaway would be inevitable. On the other hand, if we went too slowly we might be dragged to a standstill, in which case some of the brakes would have to be picked up again, and as often as not this would again result in a runaway. The driver had to play it very much by feel and instinct, for every train and engine was different. It was, in fact, an open secret that every honest driver freely admitted that, once over the top, one could never guarantee being able to stop at the bottom.

While waiting for the guard to return, I was able to take a good long look at this famous Lickey Incline. Visibility was well-nigh perfect as I peered down that fantastic $2^1/_4$-mile stretch of perfectly straight track inclined at 1 in 37. It was almost like looking down from the top of an Alpine ski jump, and even the dimmest of intellects could well imagine the sort of speeds one might achieve if allowed to run free right to the bottom.

I had run the fire down quite considerably during our idle period in the loop and, being already on a falling gradient of 1 in 291, had not bothered to put any more on, so I was somewhat surprised when Harold, after a quick glance into the fire-box, advised me to spread a few shovels of coal around the grate.

'We often have to work quite hard to drag the train over the top when the brakes have been dropped,' he explained, 'and if we knock the steam pressure down too much we will be short of brake power.'

I had just finished when our guard shouted to us that all was ready and we could draw ahead. After releasing the hand brake, Harold gently opened the regulator in order to stretch out the couplings, then, as the drag of the dropped brakes was felt, he fed in more power to try and keep our speed at a steady walking pace. It was of course very difficult, because as more of the train got on to the 1 in 37 incline it tended to accelerate, and as we accelerated both guard and brakeman pinned the brakes down harder. Therefore a constant surging was at first noticeable and Harold had to make continual adjustments to the regulator.

With half the train on the incline we were virtually on full first valve and it was more like going up bank than down; then suddenly we began to run more easily and Harold shut back to just a breath of steam. The transition was quite remarkable, and I quickly realised that the force of gravity was now taking over. Closing the regulator, Harold immediately started to apply the steam brake while at the same time shouting for me to wind the hand brake on as hard as I could get it. We were now travelling at about 10 mph and it occurred to me that if we went much faster, the guard might be hard put to rejoin his brake-van. As if reading my thoughts, Harold called over his shoulder.

'See if you can spot the guard, mate - he should signal on your side.'

I leaned out of the uprights, staring intently towards the rear of the train, which now appeared to have passed the brakeman's hut. The background was dark but there, waving from the side of the van, was a piece of newspaper - attached, I assumed, to our guard via an unseen arm.

Harold was applying the brake intermittently, initially holding it on for 5 or 10 seconds, then releasing it for a similar period, so that our speed remained reasonably constant at some 15 mph. Then I noticed that the periods of application began to exceed those of release, while at the same time our pace, instead of being checked, was inexorably increasing. By now the distant signals for Bromsgrove could be clearly seen, and with the left one off we were to be diverted on to the slow line at Bromsgrove station.

A ten-coach express hauled by a 'Black Five', and pushed energetically by 'Big Emma', the 0-10-0 bank engine, blasted past on the up, adding a false impression of speed to our descent. Or was it false, because Harold now had the brake on continuously and without doubt we were going faster than before. Seeing my enquiring look, Harold smiled resignedly.

'Well, that's it, old son. The train's in charge now; we can't do much more except put the sanders on and pull her into reverse, but we are going to run well past now, so it's not worth straining the mechanism. In fact,' he continued while turning off the small ejector that was no longer of any use, 'if you haven't got control of the train by the time you reach the back 'uns for Bromsgrove, you can be sure of running away. I wish I had as many pounds as times I've run past the column,' he sighed pensively, 'but there's nothing to worry about, really. We'll get a bit of kick on the crossover, but it's the finest pair of facing points in the country, and we're bound to stop somewhere, so sit down and enjoy the ride.'

Enjoy it I did - my most exciting experience yet, and I relished every second, hopping from one side of the footplate to the other, first looking forward to judge how far we yet had to travel, then looking back at the trail of smoke and dust pouring up from the train wheels. Our own brake blocks were now getting pretty warm and the smell of hot metal and burning oil was strong in the cab. By leaning well out I could clearly see the Catherine-wheel-like showers of sparks splashing along the whole length of our underframes.

The base of the 1 in 37 ends at Bromsgrove station, where it eases for a short distance to 1 in 186 before dropping at 1 in 105 to the water column, relief cabin and signal box at Bromsgrove South. We were travelling at something like 40 mph when we passed with surprising smoothness through the crossover at the beginning of the station platform, and still being on a falling gradient, our speed did not noticeably diminish until we passed the water column at which we had intended to stop. Then with unexpected rapidity our pace fell when the whole train was on the 1 in 283 section between the South box and Stoke Works Junction, which was 3 miles farther on. Even so, when we eventually pulled up with a jerk amid the shriek of tortured brakes, we had run by several train lengths.

Harold explained that it was impossible to move until the pinned-down brakes had been lifted; even if one had only run past a couple of wagon lengths, the same procedure had to be adopted. He therefore took the coal pick and started walking back towards the guard, unpinning the wagon brakes. Not without some considerable

effort did we set back to the column, where we were relieved by a Worcester crew who seemed well pleased over the extra delay. Sadly, we were sent home in the brake-van of a northbound fitted, since there was not another train available for us to work back with, so I was therefore denied the experience of firing up the Lickey.

Although it was now the height of the summer season and special passenger trains were thick on the ground, they always seemed to elude us. This was in part due to the fact that Harold did not sign for places beyond Gloucester and Derby, and most of these specials required working to Bristol or Sheffield. However, one Saturday morning I walked into the lobby at 9.00 am to find that my arrival was greeted with a certain amount of relief by the foreman's clerk. It appeared that my old friend Doug Pinkerton was booked to relieve a special passenger train at Saltley station that had originated from Sheffield, and work it forward to Bath. Unfortunately his mate had been taken sick and I was the most eligible fireman to fill the vacancy.

'Do you feel fit enough to tackle it then?' hailed Doug in his usual hearty manner after the situation had been explained to me.

'You bet I do,' I replied enthusiastically as I hastily booked on. 'Tell me, though, why do we have to relieve it at Saltley station and not New Street?'

'Because it's booked through non-stop, so we're taking it up Camp Hill bank. In fact, the only stop we will have to make is for water at Gloucester station,' he replied, already moving towards the lobby doorway. 'Come on, we're due to relieve

My first descent of the Lickey with a loose-coupled train resulted in running past the intended stop at Bromsgrove South by half a mile or so. I was told that trains had been known to run away as far as Stoke Works Junction, 3 miles further on. In due course I experienced such hair-raising rides on more than one occasion, although in every case there were exceptional circumstances that created the conditions for this to take place. In this early view Stoke Works and its sidings are shown on the left, while the Worcester line can be seen curving right just beyond the signal box. *Basil Jeuda*

them at 9.28, so we haven't got much time.'

My head was in a bit of a whirl at the speed at which events were now happening, for I had had no time to prepare myself mentally for this situation. I learned from Doug, as he headed for Saltley station at his usual half gallop, that in summer passenger specials bound for the West were frequently routed via Camp Hill, thus avoiding the congestion of New Street. Likewise, empty stock specials working up from the west with their mammoth 20-coach trains also used this convenient avoiding line.

We arrived on the platform with a few minutes to spare, which was just as well, since the day was gloriously sunny and already getting very warm, causing more than a few beads of perspiration to be raised on our brows by sprinting from the shed. I then noticed that Doug had mashed a can of tea and I could not resist asking him if he'd left the kettle in one piece this time.

'Cheeky young blighter,' he shouted in mock anger as I nipped into the staff room to fill my own can with cold water, a wise precaution as it turned out.

9.28 am came and went without any sign of our train. In fact, the slow that should have followed on behind arrived first, but as soon as it had departed jauntily on its way to New Street, our special hove into view. It was moving quite slowly, and glided to a smooth halt at the end of the platform opposite where we were standing. It was exactly 9.42 am, 14 minutes late - not a good start to the trip - but Bath was a long way off, and a lot could happen in two hours or so.

The engine was one of our own Saltley 'Black Fives', No 4804, and although its appearance was drab and grimy it looked pretty good to me. The fact that people with their heads poking out of the windows were watching us made me feel pretty proud as I stepped on to the footplate, but my attention was concentrated on the Sheffield crew we were relieving. The fireman was a big lad, but he looked very hot and a trifle distressed.

'Coils good, but 'appen there's t'oil in t'fire,' he said in about the broadest Yorkshire dialect I had ever heard. 'She's not steaming well, but perhaps th'll manage. She's one o' thine.'

While I was trying to work out what he had said, I overheard the Sheffield driver advise Doug that we had on ten coaches, equal to about 320 tons. With that information imparted, they climbed on to the platform, and, having stowed my gear, I quickly conducted a check of the boiler pressure, water gauge and fire. She was only showing 200 lbs per sq in on the clock and the boiler was no more than two-thirds full, but she was carrying a big fire in the rear half of the box, although a ridge half way down indicated that it might he a little thin at the front end. Without further ado, I slammed about ten shovelsful in beyond the ridge while Doug set about the business of getting under way.

We only had the home signal off, so we eased gently out of the station towards Duddeston Road, where a train was crossing our path on the up Camp Hill. Taking advantage of this delay, I fired a further ten shovels of coal round the box and was pleased to see a uniform grey column of smoke coming from the chimney. I was also relieved to see that the needle was steadily moving towards the red line even with the injector on. As the Sheffield man had stated, the coal was good, although some of the lumps were more than king-size and would require breaking up. This may have contributed to the rather messy state of the footplate. Having already developed a fetish for tidiness, I hastened to clean up with handbrush and slaking pipe while I had the chance. I found the pipe was only half the normal length and, having no nozzle, delivered a widely divergent spluttering spray instead of the normal powerful jet. It was, however, to prove a distinct advantage later in the day.

Doug meanwhile had crept up to Duddeston Road, and I was leaning over the door behind him when I saw both home and distant signals for the down Camp Hill come off together. A shout from the first carriage caused me to turn round, and hanging out of the open window of the first compartment was a jovial looking bald-headed gentleman in shirt sleeves with a camera slung round his neck.

'Get a move on young man,' he called with a grin. 'Kids want to dip their feet today.'

I was just about to make a suitable reply when Doug opened up, rendering further conversation impossible. The boiler had rallied nicely during the last few minutes, the water was just in sight at the top of the glass and pressure was now up to 220 lbs per sq in - as good as I could have wished for.

Doug was in a determined mood, for as soon as

My first experience of passenger work was with Doug Pinkerton when we worked a Sheffield to Bath special with defective 'Black Five' No 44804 via Camp Hill. Pictured here is Caprotti '5' No 44745 heading a westbound special passing Duddeston Road signal box on the down passenger line. Just beyond this point the train will bear left on the Camp Hill diversionary line and commence its 4-mile haul up to Kings Heath. Off camera to the right is Saltley loco, and with gas works on both sides of eight parallel tracks, a chemical works and Metro Cammell in the near distance, it was a very busy area with its own distinctive 'atmosphere'!

we were safely over the crossing he pulled the regulator over to full first valve and only wound the reversing screw back a turn or so. We had a fair load to hump up this bank unassisted and Doug wanted to take a good run at it. Despite the adverse 1 in 105, acceleration was impressive and of a completely different order to that of any goods train. The exhaust soon acquired a delightfully vicious bark that caused a number of heads to be raised as we passed the loco, along with the odd wave from colleagues we knew.

With all the distants off as far as we could see, Doug heaved the regulator right across in preparation for the 1 in 62 section up to St Andrews, and at 55 per cent cut-off it was real stirring stuff as we thundered up through the cutting without slackening speed. I was, however, somewhat disconcerted by a violent knock coming right up through the floorboards at every revolution of the wheels; obviously No 4804 was not in mint condition.

After passing Bordesley Junction I started firing in earnest, although even prior to this I had not been idle, since a number of large lumps of coal required breaking up. With the firedoors open about 3 inches, the exhaust colour was about ideal, but even so I was a trifle disappointed to find that, despite having mortgaged the boiler level to the extent that it was now showing two-

thirds full, steam pressure had also fallen to 215. With the fire in such obviously good shape I had been led to suppose that a 'Black Five' should steam better than this.

As the gradient eased to 1 in 280 at Camp Hill and our pace quickened noticeably, Doug shortened the cut-off, for he was a great believer in expansive working, but the knocking became so bad that he quickly dropped it down a couple of turns and reverted to the first valve. Even so, acceleration continued as we passed Brighton Road, but now the cab was rattling and clanging in sympathy with the big-end knock, and she was developing a violent intermittent lateral shake that tended to throw me off balance, particularly when I was firing - which required one foot on the tender and one foot on the engine. I was getting a little worried by the marked fall in steam pressure, for the act of putting on the injector to maintain the two-thirds boiler level had caused it to drop back to under 200 lbs per sq in.

Despite this, we stormed through Moseley Tunnel in grand style and in seemingly no time at all we were clattering through Kings Heath station. Here the gradient eased considerably to 1 in 1547 and Doug was able to make further reductions in both regulator opening and cut-off, but with the water now showing only half a glass I was obliged to keep the injector on. This caused the

'Black Five' 4-6-0 No 44848 on a Sheffield to Kingswear special attacks the steepest part (1 in 62) of the Camp Hill line after emerging from the Euston line bridge at Brickyard Crossing. Taken on 19 June 1954, when summer specials proliferated, there was often a shortage of suitable motive power, which is presumably why '4F' 44259 is heading the 9.30 Coventry to Wolverhampton. Many specials were diverted over the Camp Hill loop when not required to stop at Birmingham, thus avoiding New Street's congestion. *T. J. Edgington*

needle to drop back to 190 lbs per sq in. However, we were now on the 1-mile level stretch through Hazelwell, and No 4804 was rattling along at a fair old pace. Through Lifford the gradient increased to 1 in 524, followed by a stretch of 1 in 301 up to Kings Norton Junction, but the severe curves here and the junction with the New Street line imposed a speed limit of 25 mph, so Doug was able to shut off while still some distance away. I was glad of the brief respite, but quite amazed by how quickly the boiler recovered when the regulator was closed, so that by the time Doug opened up again on the rise through Kings Norton station the water was up to two-thirds and steam pressure at 215 lbs per sq in.

For the next 3 miles I knew we would be going up a ruling gradient of 1 in 301 to just beyond Cofton, so I was shovelling in coal on the 'little and often' principle almost continuously while Doug seemed just as determined to remove it at approximately the same rate. Past Cofton the gradient was with us at 1 in 297 for half a mile before climbing once again up to the summit of Barnt Green. As our speed rose into the 60s at the bottom of this dip, the ferocious knocking, banging, swaying, rattling clamour on the footplate increased to unbearable proportions; even the cab itself was shaking like a jelly. Such was the vibration that the dampers would not stay open and I

was obliged to prop up the rear one with a spanner.

Doug was also suffering from vibration problems, or rather the regulator was, for being only partially open on the first valve the handle kept shaking itself shut. However, Doug had experienced this problem before and pulled from his pocket a small wedge-shaped block of wood that, when inserted against the quadrant stop, kept the regulator at something like three-quarters of the first valve. I later found that many drivers carried such wedges, since due to the differential action of the regulator when opening and closing, this same piece of wood could also retain it on a fair amount of second valve. This was achieved by fully opening the regulator and then slowly closing it against the wedge; the second valve was still open, and in this condition was said to be 'gagged'. If no wooden wedge was available, a small piece of coal served the same purpose, although of course this was inclined to break up in time.

To make life more intolerable for us, coal dust was swirling in from the tender, caught in the back-draught, and with the built-in sprayer inoperative and an inadequate slaking pipe I could do little about it. This coal dust storm was being ably supplemented by a veritable hurricane of ash, borne in a stream of hot air coming up the gap between the boiler front and the footboards.

Boasting four platforms, Kings Norton was quite a grandiose structure for a Birmingham suburban station. However, it was at the point where the New Street and Camp Hill lines merged, and each of these was served by separate platforms. Just beyond the bridge at the far end the Camp Hill tracks, seen in the foreground, diverge to the right. The main line to New Street follows a progressive curve to the left sufficiently severe as to warrant a 35 mph speed restriction. *T. J. Edgington*

Already I was soaked in perspiration and now the dust and grit was working its irritating way into every crevice of my clothing. If this was passenger work, I thought, as I staggered to regain my balance for the umpteenth time, you can stick it!

On the 5-mile haul up to Barnt Green I had been forced to mortgage the boiler once more, but, knowing that we would soon be descending at 1 in 37, I dare not let it drop below the half-way mark, so by the time Doug closed the regulator as we neared Blackwell pressure had fallen to no more than 165 lbs per sq in. Once over the top and hurtling down the incline proper, Doug came over and inspected the fire.

'What the devil's the matter with the old camel?' he bellowed, as I quaffed down mouthfuls of delicious cold water in an effort to quench the raging thirst I had acquired. 'Seems OK,' he remarked, a puzzled frown creasing his forehead, but, seeing that I was more than somewhat overheated, quickly fired a dozen shovels of coal round the box.

Determined to get some time back if possible, Doug allowed the train to coast unchecked for quite some distance and we descended like a plunging meteor. With steam off, she was much more smooth and quiet, and for the first time I was able to really enjoy our speed. As before with the regulator shut, recovery was remarkably quick, the needle fairly leaping round the clock in spite of the injector being on continuously. Nearing the bottom, Doug was concentrating on some pretty heavy brake applications, but at the same time he was fully aware of the state of the boiler.

'I reckon I know what's wrong with her,' he suddenly shouted. 'A pound to a penny some of the superheater elements are blowing. That would also account for us using so much water.'

I was insufficiently experienced to be able to offer an opinion, but from the high regard that everyone seemed to have of 'Black Fives' they must as a whole be an awful lot better than this one.

It was just as well that we ran through Bromsgrove station on the fast line, for our speed seemed rather higher than the permitted 40 mph, and with the gradient with us at 1 in 283 we were soon thrashing along again in a pandemonium of ear-shattering din. I had just staggered across to Doug in order to verify that we were passing Stoke Works Junction when, with a loud bang, my gauge glass burst. The cab was immediately filled with steam, but without thinking I grasped the combined shut-off cocks and tugged them down. I had often wondered in the past how I would react to such a situation, and I was pleased to find that I had acted on reflex without worrying about the possibility of being scalded - such was the trust I placed in wearing leather gloves.

I now had no knowledge at all of the road ahead, but Doug had previously advised me that the gradients in general were mainly in our favour - with the needle backsliding once more, however, I started firing in earnest. With our speed in the 70s I would dearly have liked to sit down and watch the scenery flash by, but since sitting was impossible - Doug had long since taken to standing - and with coal to be got forward and broken up between bouts of almost continual shovelling, quite apart from juggling with the injector, I was constantly occupied. It was also infernally hot in the cab, and I soon found myself staggering to the side window for a few seconds every minute or so to gasp in great gulps of air which, although warm, seemed delightfully cold by comparison. Were it not for this manmade gale, I would have expired long ago.

Despite my all-out efforts, which Doug kindly supplemented with bouts of firing when I was occupied in the tender with the coal pick, we rarely saw more than 180 lbs per sq in on the clock, and when the water level fell below half a glass, Doug would shut off for a short period to rally the boiler. That it did so with extreme rapidity certainly gave credence to his theory that the superheater elements were leaking, but for all her ails we certainly seemed to be eating up the miles at a crazy pace. The terrible racket and roughness made it seem faster, of course, but I had no time at all to count the seconds between mileposts. Occasionally when gasping at the side window I noted such meaningless names as Spetchley,

Pirton and Defford, and after the latter Doug yelled that from here down to Eckington was about the fastest section of the run. It felt like it, too, for we seemed to be making contact with the rails only every dozen yards or so.

It was just after we had thundered through Eckington and Doug was pointing out the beauty of the 961-foot-high Bredon Hill that we both noticed a peculiar small black cloud that was crossing our path and approaching at something like 80 mph. We only had a matter of seconds to work out what it might be, and although neither of us were entomologists, we quickly arrived at the conclusion that we were on a collision course with a swarm of bees. One irate bee can prove a nuisance - 15,000 of the little beggars is absolutely frightening.

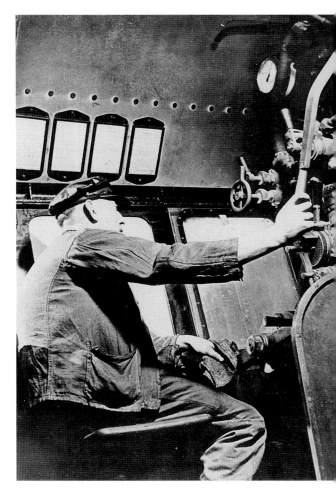

There were times when a driver could enjoy the luxury of being seated in this stance, but often he would travel for miles with his head thrust out in the slipstream, and with a rough-riding engine he would, like Doug on the Bath run, be obliged to stand while in motion.

Instinctively I dived back to my side of the cab and slammed the window shut, while Doug did likewise with his. The next second, the cab was filled with hundreds of little black and yellow buzzing bodies sucked in by the draught. Horrified, I shrank back into the corner against the front window, which was already plastered with their mangled remains, and grabbed the only weapon at my disposal, the 'sawn off' slaking pipe. Fortunately the injector was on, and as I fumbled to open the valve, I was vaguely conscious of Doug heaving the regulator up to the horizontal while at the same time kicking the firedoors wide open. As a great spluttering spray shot from the slaking pipe I heard a tremendous roar emanate from our chimney. I realised that Doug had wound down the reversing screw and was trying to suck them into the firebox by the action of the blast, and although against all good engineering practice, I pushed the damper shut with my foot so as to increase the effect. Swishing the slaking pipe round in all directions I was conscious of streams of bees, water and steam hurtling into the firehole. Even so, I could feel the little blighters whizzing round my face, and thinking that a powerful 80 mph blast of air might help matters along, released the catch on my front window. The maximum speed of the average honey bee in flight is some 35 mph, which meant that even if they were trying hard to get at me, they were still being blown backwards at a steady 45 mph.

They did not like it, nor for that matter did Doug, since the stream of air, liberally dotted with the by now homicidal bees, was deflected into a sort of U-turn by the tender whence it then travelled forwards along the other side of the cab, albeit at slightly reduced velocity. Even so the enraged insects were still doing rather better than 20 mph when they fetched up on Doug's desirable anatomy like so many machine gun bullets. I caught a glimpse of him through the steam and noted with interest that he was performing what appeared to be an exceptionally energetic type of Indian war dance while at the same time trying to swot half a dozen different places on his body at once.

I realised of course that he was in a spot of bother, and pondered the while whether Doug would prefer to be stung to death or scalded to death, but since he seemed in imminent danger of the former, I chose the latter option. I reckoned that with the slaking pipe at full stretch I could just about blanket his whole body in its cone of fire, so to speak. Taking careful aim I let him have it. Immediately his frantic cavorting speeded up, his mouth opened and his arms waved, but of his words I fortunately heard nothing, drowned by the fearful clamour on the footplate. Finally he turned round, pulled his jacket collar well up and crouched over the reversing screw.

Suddenly the air was free from flying bees, so I turned off the slaking pipe and forced my front window shut. It was then that I realised that things had gone relatively quiet and that we were now coasting, which was just as well for the boiler pressure had fallen to 160 lbs per sq in as a result of the terrific demands made on it. Doug was standing in the middle of a pool of water, soaked to the skin and looking very bedraggled. This could only happen to him.

'You've nearly drowned me, you bloody twit,' he exclaimed vehemently, and then as if suddenly remembering the cause of his discomfort, he asked 'Have they all gone now?'

I nodded an affirmative, waving a hand to indicate the heaps of soggy corpses laying strewn about the inside of the cab. I spent a busy few minutes sweeping and swilling away their remains just in case some of them were not quite dead.

As I returned to my labours of trying to satisfy the voracious appetite of No 4804, I felt quite sorry at having annihilated so many of these useful little creatures, but as in war it was either them or us. Once the immediate excitement had died down and Doug was able to take stock of the situation, he made the not unexpected statement that he had been stung. He dangled his right hand in front of me, which I examined sympathetically, and there on the knuckle of his second finger was an angry looking swelling.

'Christ, my neck is damned sore too,' he said, rubbing it tenderly, and sure enough this also bore the marks of a sting. It was the first time that I had seen his face for a few minutes, and although it may sound a little insensitive to say so, its appearance was most comical. He had been stung on both cheeks by bees that must have possessed a great sense of humour, for the stings were perfectly matched both for position and size. The crimson areas had now spread into perfect circles and looked for all the world like the make-up patches used by some circus clowns. I just managed to retain my composure long enough to advise him of this, before turning my back and grasping the shovel. Had I sufficient breath in my body, I would have burst out laughing, but as it was, all I could manage was a quiver or two of my diaphragm, which fortunately passed unnoticed.

By now we were through Ashchurch and thrashing on towards Cheltenham. The period of coasting after the bee episode had enabled me to fill the boiler, but our steam pressure was no more than 190 lbs per sq in. As can be imagined, it was getting harder than ever to fire due to the continual need to go into the tender and shovel coal forward, a task rendered difficult by the wild oscillations, and unpleasant by the blizzard of coal dust whirling round its interior. Contrary to enginemen's normal desires, I was very thankful indeed when we were severely checked by signals at Cheltenham. Once more the respite was just long enough to recover both steam pressure and water levels to a respectable amount, ready for the dash down to Gloucester. Doug consulted his watch as we approached the sharply curved platform.

'Bees or no bees,' he announced cheerfully, 'we've pulled back 5 minutes, mate,' and with the road now clear he heaved open the regulator to such effect that he caused many of the passengers waiting on the platform to scuttle quickly back from the edge. Having gained time despite our difficulties, Doug was inspired to even greater efforts over the 6-mile stretch to Gloucester, and since for the first time in miles we were showing 225 lbs per sq in on the clock, he felt justified in letting rip to some purpose.

As for myself, I realised that my blood sugar was beginning to run out and my limbs were beginning to shake with the sustained effort as we hurtled through Churchdown station in a leaping, clanging fury of sound and motion. I hated to admit it to myself, but I knew that I had just about shot my bolt.

Approaching Gloucester the Great Western tracks ran parallel to our own for a stretch and, forgetting our tiredness for a few moments, we were able to enjoy the boyish pleasure of steadily overhauling one of their expresses. Then, with the water level perilously low and pressure back to 170 lbs per sq in, we shut off to coast to a halt dead on target for the water column at the end of the platform. I climbed wearily on top of the tender and with my remaining strength pulled the heavy bag into position. We had cut it very fine indeed, for there was barely any in the bottom of the tank. While taking on water, I dragged myself back on to the footplate in order to make use of a static and stable platform to fire the front half of the grate, which had become sadly neglected over the last mile or two.

On commencing, a large bowler-hatted individual came up to Doug and I overheard him say, 'You are running 8 minutes late driver!'

I did not catch Doug's reply because of the noise of my shovelling, but I did see the red patches on his face turn to a brighter hue before he delivered his animated reply. Although his mouth was opening and shutting with great rapidity, there was really no need for words since his wildly gesticulating arms described most effectively every detail of our trip, the invasion of the bees being without doubt a masterpiece in the art of mime. Anyhow, it must have done the trick for the Inspector slunk off, at any rate as much as a BR Inspector can slink, looking very contrite indeed.

Gratefully I allowed Doug to take over the shovel while I pulled more of our now much depleted coal supply forward. He had just slammed the ninth shovelful in when he gave a sudden yell of anguish, dropped the implement with a clang and started hopping up and down in a most astonishing way, while at the same time trying to thump a spot somewhere between his shoulder blades. For a moment I thought that his kind-heartedness had got the better of him and that he had pulled a muscle, but the alacrity and suppleness he displayed in stripping off his overall jacket quickly disposed of this notion.

Now, even the most amiable of honey bees, if after being battered, scalded and half drowned, awakes from a daze to find herself imprisoned beneath a constantly moving coarse jacket and jammed tightly against a hot, sweaty, alien body she tends to cry out 'Enough is enough', lose her temper and sting that alien body as hard as she can. This is precisely what had happened. The bee, having been caught in the slaking pipe's field of fire, had become lodged beneath Doug's jacket, where she had remained until recovering sufficiently to let rip with all the pent-up emotion at her disposal.

'I've been stung again,' he howled in obvious distress, and it did indeed prove to be a real beauty.

The stings to his head, face and neck, although painful, were relatively superficial because the bees had been knocked off so quickly, but with the one on his back, plenty of time was available to really empty her poison bags. Understandably it must have unnerved Doug somewhat, because although he thoroughly inspected his overalls before leaving Gloucester, at intervals during the rest of the run he would suddenly jump up and pound some part of his body, thinking that another bee was about to seek revenge.

The remainder of the trip to Bath was nothing short of a nightmare for me; my whole body became numb with fatigue, and I was staggering about my tasks like a zombie. Were it not for Doug firing the front end we would never have made it. As it was, I realised that even six months ago I would not have had the strength and stamina to continue as far as this. I was driving myself beyond my normal physical limits by sheer willpower, spurred on partly by determination and partly by the fear that if I let Doug down now, I would not be taken on any good jobs again.

In my daze I was half-consciously aware of passing through Wickwar Tunnel, and of places like Yate, Westerleigh and Mangotsfield, praying all the time that my torment would soon be over. I dragged the firedoors open yet again wondering whether I could find the necessary strength to pick up the shovel, let alone use it, when Doug laid a restraining hand on my shoulder.

'Run it down now,' he bellowed in my ear. 'We're very nearly there and I'll be shutting off in a minute.'

Thank God for that, I thought, as I put my head in the slipstream for a moment in an effort to cool my superheated brow. Once more, however, pride overcame my exhaustion and I quickly scrambled around the shaking and bucking footplate, sweeping up coal spillage and dust before giving a final swill down with the slaking pipe. Doug had shut off before I had finished, but even so I was able to sit down for the first time in what seemed hours and enjoy the approach to Bath. In the brilliant sunshine it looked like heaven for more reasons than one, and I was most impressed by the wonderful cleanliness of the buildings, which contrasted very favourably with Saltley's unattractive grime.

We came to a halt in Bath station exactly 7 minutes late, a wonderful tribute to Doug's determination, superb enginemanship and his remarkably intimate knowledge of the road. To have accomplished the recovery of 7 minutes with a defective and rough engine plus a young and relatively inexperienced fireman, to say nothing of being attacked by malevolent bees en route, was a fine achievement. Quite a number of drivers I came to know in the future would have called it a day and failed the engine at Gloucester for any one of the above reasons.

I was already feeling a sight better when we were uncoupled by the station staff and sent off to Bath loco. On arrival there we were supposed to hand over to a Bath crew who had been detailed to clean the fire and get her ready again for our return working of a special relief train. This was due to depart at 2.40 pm, calling at Gloucester, Cheltenham and New Street, where we were to be relieved. They were waiting for us as we came to a halt, but when the driver saw our appearance and the virtually empty tender he cocked an enquiring eye at Doug and said, 'Had a rough trip, brother?'

'Like hell we have,' retorted Doug. 'Don't touch her yet,' he continued. 'I want the fitters to have a look at the elements. I reckon they're blowing badly.'

'Well, you've certainly used some coal,' mused the Bath driver, as if mentally calculating how many tubs would be required to fill it, for they had no mechanical plant here.

The fitters subsequently carried out their inspection while I was busily engaged in trying to drink the local reservoir dry. In a nutshell, it turned out that three superheater elements were blowing to such an extent that it was a wonder we got there at all. They could do nothing in the time available, and unless Doug was prepared to take her back as she was, another engine would have to be found. Suitable spare engines were hard to come by on a busy summer Saturday and I had the pleasant thought that we might get a Southern 'West Country' 'Pacific', since a number were standing in the shed yard.

At first the foreman said he had only a Class '4F' 0-6-0 available, but when Doug told him in no uncertain terms just what he could do with this, he went off to consult with Control. We were in the mess room, having just consumed a well-earned lunch, when he joined us with the news that we were to take No 5265, another Saltley 'Black Five' that had been prepared for a later job and for which another substitute had now been found. Doug seemed well pleased, for he turned to me with a grin and said, 'That's OK, mate. She's a good 'un. I had her only a few days ago on a job to Sheffield.'

While not in exactly pristine condition externally, there was certainly nothing wrong with No 5265 mechanically for, although we were some 4 minutes late departing from Bath, again with a ten-coach train, Doug had more than made this up by the time we arrived at Gloucester. With her there were no excessive knocks or rattles and, though admittedly I was kept very busy, every pound of steam generated was used in the cylinders, not wasted up the chimney. Pressure never dropped below 200, nor the water level below three-quarters of a glass; moreover, apart from not having to fire her so heavily, the coal was available right there on the shovelling plate, so I always had a few minutes to recover between bouts of firing.

Nevertheless, I was glad enough to hand over to my relief at New Street, and travelling back to Saltley by bus I suddenly felt strangely tired. The heat, noise and abnormal sustained effort had all contributed and, now that I had at last relaxed, I began to feel their combined effect. My ears were still full of the frantic clamour of the footplate and my head was still swimming with the fast-moving events of the day as I walked across to the cycle sheds. But then I should have known that a day out with Doug would be different. It was then that I realised that I had left my haversack in the lobby.

Resignedly I returned and pushed my way through the crowd of chaps who seemed to have arrived from nowhere. Doug had lingered there recounting to interested parties the details of how he had acquired his battle scars, and was talking in his usual loud voice to none other than Harold, my mate who had just walked in to book off.

'How did you get on with Terry then?' he asked of Doug.

My ears pricked up at this mention of my name, and although my conscience dictated that, having retrieved my haversack, I should walk away, I stayed and listened. Doug gave a quick resumé of the day's problems, much of which I missed in the general hubbub of many voices speaking at once, but I did hear him say 'Poor young devil had a hell of a time, very nearly killed him I think, but he's as game as they come and I'd take him anywhere with me.'

Coming from Doug this was praise indeed, and it made me feel that the torture of the down journey had, after all, been worth the effort. I quickly made my way out of the lobby before my head became too large to get through the doorway and cycled home, wet, tired and hungry, but well satisfied with my first taste of passenger work.

Once bitten by this passenger bug, I hankered for more, and whether it was a case of now being regarded as a safe risk or whether it was just the luck of the draw I do not know, but before the summer season drew to a close I managed to enjoy a few more such turns.

These included a Blackpool special, which I worked as far as Crewe, and a run to Gloucester with Harold that proved nearly as hectic as the one with No 4804. Again we had a 'Black Five', which, although the boiler was sound, was mechanically very rough, but the main problem this time stemmed from the fact that it had been coaled with about 80 per cent slack. Consequently I never stopped shovelling and rarely did we see more than 200 lbs per sq in on the gauge. All in all, though, I enjoyed the speed and excitement these jobs provided and the experience gained by having to fire up to two hours continuously. It was, therefore, something of a let-down when September arrived and we found ourselves back with the routine of local relief and few prospects of reasonable road jobs. Furthermore I was beginning to feel a little unsettled around this period, since I had been required to register for National Service after my 18th birthday in August, and consequently I expected my call-up papers to arrive with every post. At that age I found such uncertainties regarding my immediate future more than a little disturbing.

The Control link formed the only pool from which firemen could be readily drawn to cover any unforeseen emergency, and I therefore found myself with several different drivers on as many different jobs in the course of a single week. While this had the advantage of broadening my experience at a faster pace than normal, it also meant that I never had time to get to know the ways of my driver or the job concerned. On many occasions I was literally groping in the dark without sufficient general knowledge and skill to execute my work as competently as I would have desired.

The manpower shortage naturally caused an excessive amount of overtime to be worked, and it was not unusual to relieve a westbound train at Water Orton or Castle Bromwich, and be relieved 12 hours later still without having reached Washwood Heath.

As the autumn nights lengthened, life developed into a humdrum seven-day week of bed and work with often precious little of the former, and many weeks passed when I rarely saw the light of day. All this activity tended to produce fatigue and a dulling of the intellect in both drivers and fireman alike, so that when standing on a bleak and exposed section of track for interminable hours conversation lapsed, and the ability to snatch a quick 40 winks took top priority. Not that this was always possible, for with the exception of Class '3F' and '4F' 0-6-0s, most engines were not built for relaxation and, in any case, being soaked and frozen on one side while at the same time being roasted on the other is not exactly conducive to sleep.

Looking back on that winter of 1951-52, it would be fair to say that it was the least happy and exciting period of my railway career. Based on the philosophy that the human brain endeavours to forget unpleasant experiences, it must have been so, for I remember less clearly the details of the individual workings of the latter half of my stay in the Control link than any other time. However, a marathon turn, again with Doug Pinkerton, who was never one to shy at overtime, stands out in my mind.

One December night we worked a 'Maltese' (at least four fitted vehicles next to the engine) to Derby North. This in itself was a pleasant change from local relief work, but we had been badly delayed during the journey and had already completed seven hours by the time we relieved a Class B freight bound for Washwood Heath at Derby North cabin. Our trip home was the usual stop-and-go ritual until we were turned in at Elford, roughly halfway between Burton and our destination, in the early hours of the morning. Here we remained for no less than six hours without moving a wheel, and standing at that exposed spot, wrong way to the weather on a freezing night, was an agony best forgotten. When eventually we did get the road we had been on duty over 15 hours, and the need for food and drink, both of which had long since run out, was getting more than somewhat pressing.

Even then a clear path was not yet available and another two hours or more had elapsed by the time we were finally relieved at Washwood Heath Junction. Feeling a little the worse for wear, we walked to the shed and booked off exactly 19 hours after signing on, which was for me to stand as an all-time record.

With the coming of spring our spirits lifted, and I found myself looking forward once again to the prospect of being able to work the numerous passenger specials that I now felt more competent to handle. After all, I had another year's experience and physical development behind me, and it was logical to assume that this time I would get a rather thicker slice of the cake. Furthermore, it was now eight months since I had registered for National Service and, not having heard anything since, I was beginning to believe that they had forgotten all about me. The uncertainty of the past had consequently receded and I was fervently hoping to be booked with a driver who, like Doug Pinkerton, had a very extensive road card.

Alas, it was not to be, for when the May changeover lists were posted I found to my intense surprise that I had been promoted, not to another mate in the Control link or even to the next link, the Specials, but right up into the Trip link with driver J. Greatrex.

10
THE TRIP LINK

After the variations, the long hours, the uncertainties and general hurly-burly of the Control link, I unexpectedly found myself in the relatively well-ordered tranquillity of the Trip link in the company of an equally well-ordered and tranquil mate.

It was around this time I noted one of Nature's unexplained mysteries. Over the age of about 45, drivers tended to follow one of two courses with regard to their physical appearance. Either they seemed hell-bent on adopting the rotund hogshead model, or they took on the aspect of something resembling a bean pole. My new mate Jack Greatrex fell into this latter, generally longer-living, category. Jack, although only four years from retirement, was still blessed with finely chiselled features and undoubtedly must have been quite good-looking in his younger days. His temperament and demeanour was calm and quiet, but belonging as he did to the older school of ex-LNWR drivers, was set in his ways and quite a disciplinarian.

We first met in the lobby at 5.00 am on Monday morning prior to booking on for 28 Trip, a Bordesley job for which we prepared our own '8F' before setting out for the day's work. I soon discovered that everything had to be exactly right in every meticulous detail, and if only working a local tripper he would not take the engine off the shed if it showed the slightest defect. Had he been preparing a Carlisle, he could not have been more thorough. This, of course, meant that I too had to work to his high standard, which was, I must admit, a welcome change to the often slack attitudes found in the common working of my previous link.

For example, he insisted that the sanding gear was topped up and tested and that I spread a quantity of limestone over the grate before building up the fire. Furthermore, both injectors had to be proved satisfactory before moving on to the table, and although we would not be going within miles of the nearest water troughs, I had to operate the scoop while he inspected its action from beneath the tender. From the appearance of his somewhat faded but nevertheless well-pressed and immaculate overalls, I might have guessed that he was a stickler for cleanliness, so it was no surprise to find that all traces of coal and dirt had to be quickly banished from the footplate. Moreover, the tender had to be properly trimmed and the dust therein well and truly laid by a generous application of the slaking pipe, for he expected to finish up the week with overalls very little dirtier than when he started. However, since this fitted in very nicely with my own ideas on how a footplate should be kept, it proved no hardship, and in this respect we got on extremely well from the word go.

Bearing these aspects of his character in mind, it was therefore not unusual for us to book off the shed late, and on this first Monday we were something like 20 minutes awry when we finally departed. This delay was brought about by the need to obtain the services of a fitter and mate in order to attend to the sanding gear and a slight blow on the small ejector. When everything was in apple-pie order and we were trundling sedately, tender-first, along the up goods line heading for Washwood Heath Junction, I thought it was about time I got to know something about the job, and I questioned Jack accordingly.

'I've never worked a Bordesley tripper properly,' I said openly, since I wished to make this point quite clear. 'Just relieved one or two and brought the engine to the shed. What exactly do we do?'

'Oh, it's very straightforward,' replied Jack in

his quiet, precise manner. 'We pick up a train at the junction or sometimes the West End, and work it into Bordesley. Then we shunt it as required, run over to the down sidings, collect another train from there and work it back over Hill 60, and then start all over again. Nothing much to it, really, but it involves a lot of waiting around, particularly in Bordesley, where we have to have a good clear path before crossing their main lines. The Great Western get very upset if we stop one of their expresses and, of course, we cut right across their up and down fast and slow lines when drawing out of the down sidings.'

I was able to picture the scene fairly clearly in my mind's eye, for I had studied this expanse of tracks at Bordesley hundreds of times when crossing over them on the Bank Pilots.

At Washwood Heath No 1 signal box we whistled three short, two short for the junction and continued to clank easily down past the hump of Hill 60 to the left. Stopping at the ground signal just beyond the junction box we waited some minutes for a path, and I took the opportunity to ask Jack about the other jobs in the link. It seemed that we worked as far as Kingsbury to the north, to Rubery up the Halesowen branch in the west, and to Aldridge over the Walsall line, while at the same time covering most places on Midland metals enclosed in this triangle.

Not having yet visited any of the venues mentioned I was about to question him further when the signal dropped and we hastily crossed over to the down sidings. Here, under the guidance of a shunter, we backed on our train and waited for the appearance of our guard. Jack, meanwhile, instructed me to position our headlamps for trip working, which was one lamp over the left buffer, and having done this I packed some coal under the firedoors and into the back corners. When ignorant of a job's routine, it was always difficult to achieve the fine balance of just carrying the correct amount of fire; only experience could teach one that.

Shortly afterwards, Dennis, our guard, climbed somewhat laboriously on to the footplate in response to Jack's invitation to partake of a quick cup of tea. Holding the lid in one hand, he consulted a scrap of cardboard torn from a cigarette packet (guards, I found, universally seemed to prefer such pieces of cardboard to notebooks) and advised us that we had 48 wagons equal to 56 of mineral.

To clarify this remark, I should explain that for loading purposes a mineral wagon was calculated at 13 tons, but when a number of 16-ton wagons were in a train their extra weight had to be taken into consideration. In this instance we had 34 of the latter, which meant that another 104 tons was being carried. Dividing 104 by 13 gives the equivalent additional number of 13-ton wagons, which in this case was eight; therefore, although we only had 48 wagons behind the tender, they were equal in weight to 56 13-ton mineral wagons.

Having advised the yard staff that we were ready, Dennis duly returned to his brake-van, but a further 15 minutes elapsed before we were allowed to proceed. With a load of over 900 tons behind the tender we filtered out on to the down goods line and chugged sedately up the 1 in 326 gradient towards the West End. Being now somewhat familiar with the capabilities of an '8F', I decided to fire her lightly until we reached Duddeston Road. At this time I was just developing the technique of firing from the right-hand side of the footplate and, like most right-handed people, I found the action awkward and unnatural, but since all modern engines were built to be driven from the left-hand side I felt I must practice as much as possible until fully competent. Fortunately there is room on an '8F' to fire from either side, so initially I tended to ring the changes, using the driver's side to reach the front end only.

Passing the pilot sidings I had the pleasure of advising my old mate Bill that we required his assistance to Bordesley and that I thought his boiler front needed some attention, which needless to say brought forth a not unexpected rude gesture.

A long wait at Duddeston Road enabled Jack and me to relate some of our respective background history to one another, while at the same time it caused the usual difficulty of trying to strike the balance of keeping the fire reasonably lively without excessive blowing off. Fortunately, the thermal reserve of the full boiler of an '8F' was of great help, since one could virtually cover the run to Bordesley without resorting to use of the injectors, but it was on these jobs that I learned to leave a hole in the middle of the grate. By so doing the fire could be kept burning reasonably brightly with the back damper open a couple of notches, while the air entering via the hole prevented the firebox temperature from reaching too high a level.

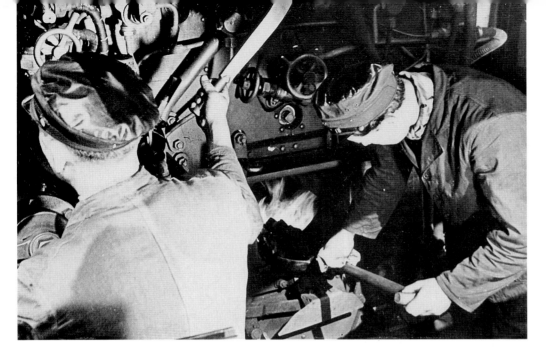

Although there was room to fire from either side in the roomy Stanier cabs, as depicted by this crew on an '8F', it was more convenient for the fireman to work from the right as shown. However, on long runs or during periods of prolonged heavy firing it was sometimes expedient to alternate sides in order to balance muscle fatigue.

This shows what a fireman should not do, coal spillage on the footboards forcing him to stand far to the left posterior-wise against the driver, while the anti-glare shield obstructs his swing.

When eventually we received the 'right away', all I had to do was dig the firing shovel blade into the live fire under the door and shoot it down into the hole, when normal firing could then be commenced immediately. This was the technique I used now, so that by the time Jack had finished calling attention to the fact that the signals were off by means of the whistle, I had already filled in the hole, had the firedoors closed and both rear damper and blower wide open.

Getting our heavy train moving from a dead standstill on the 1 in 105 gradient required full first regulator and maximum cut-off, but as Bill also opened up and our speed increased Jack was able to wind her up by degrees to around 55 per cent. Even so, this was making a pretty impressive volume of sound as we approached Brickyard Crossing, but despite the acceleration we had achieved at this point, our speed rapidly fell away as the gradient stiffened to 1 in 62. It was not Jack's nature to rely too heavily on the pilot and he quickly dropped her down to full gear once again for the stretch up to the Coventry Road overbridge. Just beyond we crossed over the facing points taking us on to the Great Western and, by the time we passed Bordesley Junction signal box, Jack had eased down to just a breath of steam.

'We have to be careful here,' he explained. 'From climbing at 1 in 85 it suddenly dips down to the stop signal at the entrance to the GW yard. If you come over too fast the train can push you past the signal and through the catch points.'

I soon realised what he meant, because Jack had to make two pretty hefty applications of the brake even though we were only travelling at a walking pace before we eventually shuddered to a halt at the signal. Some 10 yards beyond this lay the catch points he had referred to, and since the ground here bore no trace of weeds, I gathered that someone had been the victim of an embarrassing experience not too long ago.

We waited at the signal for some 20 minutes before the GW was ready for us. Bordesley is not a very salubrious part of Birmingham and although we had a fairly commanding view from the top of a 30-foot-high embankment there was little of interest to see, so we soon found ourselves talking shop. I quickly concluded that Jack was gently probing my knowledge of railway working, my understanding of engines and whether I was really interested in the job, without making it too obvi-

ous. Having once established that I was keen to learn more he adopted the role of tutor, and from then onwards for the duration of my stay with him we had at least one lesson per day on some aspect of railway life. This might take the form of a question-and-answer session about the function of locomotives or detailed explanations of the rules and regulations and why they were necessary.

Jack also supported the theory that firing was, or should be, a highly skilled art, and, like many other forms of physical endeavour, expertise more than made up for sheer brute strength. While he was no longer capable of practical demonstrations calling for great effort, his counsel was always much appreciated. However, I did consider his rather scornful regard of ex-Midland firemen a little unfair because I found good and bad firemen from all the pre-Grouping companies, but his attitude was quite typical of many ex-LNWR men who felt that even a navvy could fire the old Midland engines.

Our interesting conversation was abruptly terminated by a shrill blast on the GW head shunter's whistle calling attention to the fact that the signal was now off. We ran slowly into a lengthy siding, where for the next 20 minutes we were required to do some energetic shunting. Despite its bulk, an '8F' proved ideal for shunting a heavy train, for it had the power to accelerate smartly and, equally important, adequate weight and brake power to stop again. The only drawback was that it took a fair while and a lot of strenuous winding to move the reversing screw from full forward to full backward gear. Jack, never a hunky chap and now past his prime, was obviously happy when this unwelcomed exercise finally came to a conclusion.

Another period of waiting followed before a path was available for us to cross over to the down sidings, and I took this opportunity to observe the Western engines and their methods. Loyal as I was to the Midland Division, I had to admit that their locomotives in general were much better turned out than ours, while some of the 'Castles' and 'Kings' that roared by on the London expresses looked nothing short of magnificent in their gleaming Brunswick Green paintwork and polished copper and brass trimmings. Even the numerous Pannier tanks were impressively efficient as they went smartly about their shunting duties, while all around it was very apparent that the staff still considered themselves to be GWR men and a cut above the other divisions of British Railways.

Just before our signal dropped, I noticed one of our Saltley '8Fs', hauling a moderate coal train, come off the Bordesley Junction branch and without stopping head out on to the up slow line, where it accelerated with tremendous vigour in the direction of Small Heath. Puzzled by the sight of a Saltley engine working on the Western, I asked Jack what it was doing.

'Oh, that's the Long Marston,' he replied. 'One of the Group One jobs. They work a coal train up to Long Marston, which is the other side of Stratford-upon-Avon, then return with a load of empties. It must have been Percy Trotter. He's the only one in the link who works an engine like that.'

The name somehow rang a bell, then I remembered a very rough ride in a brake-van back from Water Orton one night when I had been working there on the shunter. When in the brake-van I had not appreciated his lack of finesse, but at least as a spectator I was forced to admire the determined way he handled that mineral.

Having run briskly across to the down sidings, we once more indulged in a period of shunting to make up our train, and when this was completed we settled down to wait for another path. I recalled what Bill had told me in the Bank Pilots about Bordesleys and it was undoubtedly true that, from the fireman's point of view, they were certainly not the most strenuous jobs at Saltley. As far as I could see the main object to aim for was to keep the fire as thin as possible and thereby use the minimum amount of fuel. This would then reduce the necessity to clean the fire and get coal forward during the 24 hours the engine was in service. A dozen shovelsful spread evenly round the box sufficed for the quick gallop back to Bordesley Junction, and thereafter it was merely a case of coasting down the bank to Hill 60. Here we followed the regular procedure of pushing the preceding train over the hump, and when this was done we shunted across the road to Washwood Heath Junction and started all over again.

On average about two round trips would be accomplished in an eight-hour shift but, as always, this could vary according to prevailing conditions. The main interest on these turns was the time available for discussion, and with a knowledgeable mate much could be learned.

Although the routine followed a general pattern, boredom was kept at bay by day-to-day variations, one of the welcome bonuses of railway work, and a new experience always seemed to turn up to add to one's store of knowledge. On the Thursday this took the form of sticking at St Andrews, an event that I had witnessed many times from the rear end when on the pilots but never from the train engine. After a prolonged dry spell, steady drizzle had made the rails very slippery indeed, and we unfortunately had an '8F' that was long overdue for a major shopping. She knocked and rattled in a most disconcerting manner even at low speed, and it was soon apparent that the wheels were badly in need of new tyres.

On arrival at Washwood Heath Junction we found that Dennis, our regular guard, had not turned up, and that his replacement was a pleasant young Pakistani whose lack of experience was only matched by his peerless enthusiasm. We later learned that he had not quite got the hang of what loading tables were all about, and he felt that it was his patriotic duty to couple just about everything in the siding to our tender hook. Under normal circumstances our all-up load would have been limited to manageable proportions by the number of vehicles we were allowed to take, but marshalled now to the rear end of our 50 mineral wagons were two special 'Weltags' carrying a couple of outsize steel ingots. These massive octagonal hunks of metal weighed over 80 tons each, but in his innocence our guard had regarded them as just two more mineral wagons. We therefore set out with a train equivalent to over 70 of mineral, a fact soon made apparent by the way we slipped and slithered up to the West End. Jack had to use a fair amount of regulator and full gear to move us up the 1 in 326 gradient and, because of the slipping, he was forced to use the sanding gear almost continuously.

'I'm sure our coloured friend has forgotten to take his brake off,' Jack muttered quietly in a puzzled way as he juggled with the regulator in an effort to keep us in motion. As far as we were concerned we only had 52 wagons in tow, but it felt as if we were still attached to the stop block.

Collecting our pilot en route we ultimately arrived at Duddeston Road, where during the usual wait I hunted around for a suitable bolt to insert between the upper edge of the baffle plate and the firehole mouth. Smoke baffles did not always fit too well and tended to drop down at the forward end, which in turn obstructed the free flight of coal from the shovel blade to the front of the grate. On the short steeply sloping grates of '3Fs' and '4Fs' this did not cause too much trouble, but on the longer, flatter grates of 'Black Fives', '8Fs', 'Crabs', etc, coal could be deflected downwards to form a ridge or hump halfway along the box. By reducing the gap between firebed and baffle, this ridge only compounded the problem until eventually the front end of the grate was starved of fuel. Therefore to correct this downward droop it was common practice to use a bolt or bolts of about half-inch diameter to act as a wedge, although care had to be taken of course so as not to foul the action of the firedoors, preventing their closure. Jack was the first driver to detail the importance of a sound and well fitting baffle, and in future I made it a matter of habit to never go off the shed with an unsatisfactory one. Many were so badly burned that they extended only a matter of inches inside the firebox, which because of incomplete combustion then produced a lot of smoke and inferior steaming.

Although somewhat out of context, it may be of interest to add that Bristol and Gloucester firemen often removed the baffles so as to get more coal into the firebox. They built fires up to a staggering amount, rising sometimes from the top of the firehole half way to the crown plate and burying the brick arch. So vast were these fires that I have relieved a through freight at Landor Street and worked it to Burton on Trent, doing no more than levelling the bed and filling the odd hole as it formed.

Having adjusted the baffle to my satisfaction, I built up the fire rather more than usual for a Bordesley, anticipating that we were going to have a struggle. Jack then climbed down and checked that the sanding gear was still functioning correctly by the time-honoured method of holding the back of his hand in front of the delivery pipe while I operated the valve.

At last our signal came off and Jack, having first given a prolonged 'crow' on the whistle, opened both sand valve and regulator. We eased slowly forward, gradually gathering speed, but any attempt at vigorous acceleration resulted in a slip, and Jack had to coax her along very gently indeed. The distants were off for St Andrews, but despite all his expertise with the regulator it was pretty obvious by the time we had passed Landor Street box that we were not going to build up sufficient momentum to stand even half a chance of getting up the bank.

'We're not going to make it,' observed Jack resignedly as we thumped slowly past Brickyard Crossing.

Having come to the same conclusion some little while ago, I had left the firedoors wide open so as to allow the steam pressure to fall back, for we had more than we could use and I wanted to avoid blowing off as much as possible. She would not keep her feet even on full first valve, and now that we were on the 1 in 62 section what speed we had rapidly fell away. It was frustrating not being able to transmit the power available to the drawbar, but with such poor adhesion we had no other choice, and after a final violent slip we came to a standstill some 50 yards short of St Andrews signal box.

'I'm sure we've got a dickens of a lot more on than 50,' said Jack, as I screwed the tender brake on as hard as possible. 'We should have come up better than that even though we were slipping,' he continued. I had not sufficient experience at that time to comment on the matter, but from my observations in the pilots we should have managed 30 wagons or so ourselves if the pilot was fully extended. After some 10 minutes we saw a column of black smoke move up behind the feather of white steam coming from our pilot's safety valves, and seconds later clearly heard the shrill, distinctive 'crow' whistle indicating that both were ready.

I quickly released the hand brake while Jack hooted our reply, then, after letting our engine roll back half a turn, he heaved open the regulator to the full first valve. There was a volcanic eruption from the chimney, the cab rattled and shook, and the wheels churned showers of sparks from the rails, but we did not move forward a single inch. Jack tried again as I leaned out of my window in an effort to see what the bankers were up to, but twin pillars of smoke and steam left no doubt that they were trying as hard as we were, and slipping just as badly. Jack made several attempts, but it was of no avail - the train might just as well have been welded to the track.

'I'm going to have a word with the bobby to see what's to be done,' said Jack, climbing down the steps after the final abortive effort.

Things must be bad if we can't get moving with two bankers, I thought. Having little to do but wait, I decided to see if I could improve our traction by the old method of applying grit to the rails. Leaving the steam brake on as a precaution, I descended shovel in hand to the ground and foraged around for some suitable material. I soon found what I was looking for in the form of a dark grey gravel lying at the side of the track. Although much coarser than sand, the chips were small enough for the purpose in mind and would crush under the wheels to form an abrasive layer. Scooping up a shovelful I quickly ran a trail along the surfaces of both rails for a distance of some 50 yards in front of our engine, and I had just completed this operation when Jack returned from the box.

'They're running a train up behind the bankers,' he said, 'which will then give us a nudge to get us started. Once on the move we should be OK with two pilots.'

I must admit that I had not seen this manoeuvre done before, but it seemed sound reasoning and would cause less delay than employing a third banking engine.

Once again the 'crow' whistle could be clearly heard from the rear and once again Jack heaved open the regulator. This time we moved forwards, did half a slip, then moved forwards again. After a couple of laboured revolutions Jack, taking heart from our new-found adhesion, pushed the regulator up to the horizontal and lo and behold we staggered on, gaining speed at every beat. My treatment of the rail surfaces proved very effective, for Jack was able to use both full gear and regulator until we were well and truly under way. Our exhaust crashed out in a deep-throated explosive roar that was absolutely deafening as I leaned out and regarded this unusual spectacle of an '8F' heading 50 wagons banked by two pilots, which were being pushed in turn by a '4F' hauling a train of some further 40 wagons assisted by yet another pilot.

Once off the gritted section we started to slip again, but our speed had built up sufficiently to enable Jack to come back to the first valve, which, with both pilots fully extended, enabled us to claw our way slowly up to Bordesley Junction. Jack took it very steadily indeed on entering the branch, but even so it required the combined efforts of the sanders and a bit of reverse gear to stop at the signal. It was only after we had shunted out the train that the true reason for our difficulties came to light, and

needless to say our guard was given a lengthy and pointed lecture on the subject of loadings.

The Bordesleys, therefore, had their moments of excitement, but in the main they were leisurely, mundane affairs involving more talking than shovelling.

The following week I found myself working on the Kingsbury branch, a place I had never been to before but, like all new jobs, it proved quite interesting. The line served the North Warwickshire collieries of Wood End and Baddesley and, in addition to being steeply graded, it was not in the best of condition. Spice was added to this by the fact that one of the local drivers had recently run away down the bank with a loaded coal train. With commendable devotion to duty he had ordered his mate to bale out while, remaining alone at the controls, he had managed to attract the signalman's attention with his frantic whistling. The runaway train was then duly turned into an empty siding where it would do least harm, but even so it ploughed into the stop block at a good rate of knots, reducing many of the wagons to matchwood.

With this rather daunting prospect in mind I keenly observed every section as we hauled our train of empties up to Baddesley with '4F' No 3912. The job itself was straightforward enough, involving a spot of shunting at Kingsbury sidings before departing with the empty wagons for the colliery. We worked tender-first up the bank to Baddesley, and this I found was a new experience, for I could not recall having worked a train in reverse up an incline before. Somehow the engine did not seem to steam quite as well, although no doubt this was mainly psychological, since the water level always showed a pessimistic reading and one could not afford to mortgage the boiler so much should the need arise.

At Baddesley we indulged in some more shunting in order to make up our coal train, which was destined for Washwood Heath Junction. However, before descending the bank we had to have a certain proportion of the wagon brakes pinned down in much the same manner as was practised at the top of the Lickey Incline, and whether one kept the train successfully under control depended largely on the guard's skill in assessing this requirement accurately.

My speculations of a hair-raising run were quickly dashed, for Jack had to literally drag the train fully on to the incline before being able to

No 3912, one of Saltley's old faithful Midland '4F' 0-6-0s, which took me on my first visit to the precipitous Kingsbury colliery branch, some 11 miles to the north of Saltley during 1952. The Trip link provided opportunities to learn some of the more remote backwaters around Birmingham rarely visited in other links. Behind No 3912 can be seen the skeleton of No 3 shed's roof, the result of wartime damage. Although No 1 shed's roof was replaced by a modern concrete structure, No 3 remained open to the elements.

shut off, then the hand brake alone was practically sufficient to keep us in check until we arrived at Kingsbury once again. Our journey to Washwood Heath was via the slow line that took in Whitacre and Coleshill, and I welcomed the opportunity to familiarise myself with this section, for there is no better way to learn a route than from the footplate of a coal train.

It was also just a sufficiently long trip to get to know the ways of a Class '4F' and experiment with firing techniques without the possibility of inviting too much trouble. I found in due course that they were basically similar to Class '3s' and responded in a more leisurely way to approximately the same treatment, but being superheated they always worked more efficiently when the elements had well and truly warmed up. This warming-up period of course took a certain amount of time, and if serious work was to be contemplated it paid to anticipate the event as much as possible and keep the fire bright, even at the expense of wasting steam through the safety valves.

Two weeks later I was introduced to another series of places I had never been to before. These were along the Walsall line from Castle Bromwich, and in summer it proved to be a delightfully pleasant run, since the route involved journeying through the very picturesque Sutton Park, where dense woods contrasted favourably with Birmingham's industrial areas.

At Castle Bromwich the track curves in a long sweep to the left on a low embankment where an excellent view could be had of the airfield on one side and the sludge treatment works on the other. At Park Lane signal box the line merged with the one leading down into Water Orton sidings, form-

ing a triangle that was useful when an engine required to be turned. From Park Lane the line climbed at 1 in 157 over a bridge at Kingsbury Road, through Walmley and past Wylde Green golf course up to Sutton Coldfield, where a small goods yard lay on the down side surrounded by trees - a very pleasant spot in which to spend a leisurely half hour knocking out and picking up the odd wagon or two.

From the goods yard the climb continued up through the woods of Sutton Park, where holiday-makers could be seen enjoying themselves boating on the well-known Bracebridge Pool. Just beyond the park was Streetly station and, after passing Roundabout Wood, the line crossed the Chester road on a high embankment before proceeding up to Aldridge sidings, the summit of the bank.

Our trip terminated at this point, and after more shunting we returned to Water Orton with usually a light train of freight, bound for northern parts. As might be imagined, the work was not very exacting and made no undue demands from either side of the footplate, but in keeping with the majority of Trip link jobs it afforded the opportunity to get to know thoroughly all aspects of railway operations over that section.

After a further interlude of local work including another Bordesley, we were booked on the Rubery trip, our farthest journey west, and again this was interesting for me since it entailed breaking fresh ground once more. Following the general pattern of most trip jobs, loadings were not excessively heavy nor timings severe, for after climbing the bank to Kings Heath we acted as a pick-up until reaching Longbridge. Here was the site of the well-known Austin Motor Works, and the

On a fine summer's day a pleasant hour or so could be spent leisurely shunting the yard and picking up an odd wagon from the goods shed in the tranquil surrounds of Sutton Park. In the Trip link most things were done at a leisurely pace whenever possible, which well suited the temperaments of the drivers, nearly all of whom were close to retirement. The generous platforms at Sutton were originally built to handle large numbers of visitors who came to the park by rail in bygone days. Beyond the goods shed on the left the tracks can be seen climbing beneath a distant road bridge, then up through the Park itself towards Streetly.

Halesowen branch made its way between the massive blocks of that extensive plant. The Austin works had its own sidings and, for that matter, its own motive power in the form of powerful 0-6-0 saddle tanks, painted in a distinctive bright green livery and invariably immaculately turned out. As may be imagined, a plant the size of Austin's daily required a great deal of material and also facilities for removing the unending flow from the assembly lines; the sidings were, therefore, very busy indeed.

On arrival, we quickly shunted out our train and, while this was in progress, I was able to take note of the intense activity all around. Longbridge sidings were really in two parts, the section nearest to the junction being devoted exclusively to works traffic, while 200 yards further along the line towards Rubery were some more tracks laid to serve the locality in general, in addition to Austin's overspill. Here also were the twin station platforms over which tramped the feet of countless workers brought in from not only the city but also the dormitory towns lying to the west.

Having done our duty at Longbridge, we proceeded the half-mile or so up a 1 in 96 gradient to Rubery, where after a further shunting session we took our lunch before returning to Lawley Street, picking up at intermediate sidings as required. It was an exceedingly pleasant little job, and terminating opposite the loco we were usually well placed for booking off at approximately the same time every day.

On Thursday a short-lived but nevertheless intense little heatwave had got well under way, and by the time we had completed our activities at Rubery and were settled to partake of our lunch, the early afternoon heat was oppressive. In fact, the trace of breeze that existed tended to draw heat from the boiler on to us so that conditions on the footplate were rendered almost unbearable.

Beyond the boundary fence, lush green meadows surrounded by shady trees looked more than a little inviting, so I decided to take my sandwiches and seek out a cooler spot. On the understanding that Jack would toot the whistle 5 minutes before

Halesowen Junction was located 10 miles west of Saltley on the main line to Bristol. Here the Halesowen branch led off to the right, passing en route through the extensive Austin Motor Works at Longbridge. Austin had their own sidings and stud of locomotives, since in 1952 much of the materials consumed was still moved by rail. Workers' trains brought multitudes of workers from Birmingham and the Black Country direct to Longbridge station, which lay in the heart of the complex. Here rival Divisions met, as can be seen in the photograph. In the foreground is 2-6-4T No 42337 with the 7.8 am Saltley-Longbridge, while across the platform stands the Old Hill-Longbridge headed by 0-6-0 Pannier tank No 7425. *T. J. Edgington*

we were due to depart, I took my leave. Finding an ancient and dilapidated stile I heaved my perspiring form over it and with a bottle of orange juice clutched in one hand and my sandwiches in the other, I headed through knee-high grass towards a fine specimen of a horse chestnut tree some 50 yards away. Relaxing on a bank of soft grass under its cool and ample shade I contently disposed of my lunch while reflecting on what a great life railway work could be.

On the far side of this green sea of meadow so brightly splashed with the yellows of buttercups and daisies was a herd of some 20 Friesians, their black and white bodies shimmering in the strong sunlight. As is the habit of bovine creatures, they were slowly moving en masse towards me, idly grazing as they came. Now, I've always been passionately fond of most of God's creation, from spiders to hippopotami, and possibly because of this I have frequently managed to hit up a pretty good relationship after only a brief acquaintance. Watching these gentle animals approach recalled

an article I had read some two weeks before in a popular nature magazine by one Latishia Spode.

This dear lady had described in detail how she had held long conversations with horses and cows, and that she had first gained their confidence and friendship by gently blowing up their nostrils. Miss Spode pointed out that these creatures always greeted each other and became acquainted in such a manner, and if one was to make any progress at all an exchange of breath was absolutely essential before any conversation could commence. I must admit that at the time I thought she must have, if not exactly loose, a screw or two that were only just finger tight. However, I've always been one to try anything new and felt that here was the ideal opportunity to put the Spode theory to a practical test.

The herd was now only 30 yards away and would probably have passed me by without a second thought, but I slowly sat upright and gave what I considered to be a very passable imitation of a virile young bull. As one, they stopped dead in their tracks and turned their heads towards me in that half sideways attitude peculiar to cattle. I mooed again, encouraged by the effect of my first effort. After cats, cows must surely rate a close second for their sheer curiosity, and these were no exception, for they all started ambling towards me with their necks outstretched, sniffing the air in order to catch my scent.

The largest animal, who was undoubtedly their leader, walked a few paces ahead of the rest. I rose slowly to my feet, giving at the same time another gentle moo. She stopped a yard away, thrusting her nose in the general direction of my face. Throwing caution to the wind, I leaned forwards and snorted into her dilated nostrils. She immediately responded and huffed right back at me. We repeated this performance some half a dozen times, and whether it was the smell of my recently eaten sandwiches or my own personal aroma that did the trick I do not know, but she suddenly gave a loud moo of what seemed to be approval and promptly nuzzled my chest, nearly knocking me over.

The ice was broken and, reaching down, I plucked a good handful of grass, offering it to her for appraisal. She gently took this from me and while munching contentedly I patted her neck and tickled her ears, quite delighted at the success of the experiment. It would seem that this Spode girl knew her onions after all. The rest of the herd had been standing back watching the ritual intently and now, having decided that it was quite safe to do so, wanted to enjoy a piece of the action.

While in all fairness their expressions could not be described as exactly smiling, their large brown eyes held a decidedly friendly gleam as they jostled around me for their handfuls of grass. After a hectic 5 minutes I was quite relieved to hear the pre-arranged whistle calling for my return. With the cows still in close company I grabbed my belongings and made my way back to the stile and, after bidding them a farewell moo, hopped over it to stroll leisurely across to the engine.

Jack was standing on the footplate between the uprights as I approached and when only a few yards away I noticed that he appeared to be looking beyond, rather than directly at me. His eyes widened and his jaw dropped.

'What the devil have you brought that lot for?' he gasped hoarsely.

'What lot?' I replied, glancing round, still unaware of the situation.

I staggered with surprise, for some 5 yards away was the herd leader plodding steadily after me, and strung out at precise intervals in a long line behind were her 19 sisters. They must have found a convenient gap in the hedge and decided to follow their new-found friend. Thinking that if I ignored them they might go away, I hastily climbed on to the footplate and set about putting some coal on, but no such luck, for when I looked over the side again a few minutes later I was greeted by the solemn gaze of 20 pairs of eyes, now arranged in a broad semi-circle around the engine.

Jock the shunter meanwhile hove into view round the end of a line of wagons, his cloth cap shooting into the air as he shied in amazement on taking in the scene. He seemed to be having difficulty in believing what he saw. His jaw was moving but no sound came from his lips and he was no doubt considering the wisdom of having had that last wee dram at lunchtime. With a great struggle he pulled himself together.

'Where ha' all these beasties come fe?' he asked thickly in his broad Scots dialect.

'My mate brought them,' replied Jack simply, in his usual calm manner.

I thought that this statement was a little unfair and needed qualifying somewhat, and was about to elaborate when Jock interjected.

'What the devil for?'

'Dunno,' replied Jack, now obviously amused at the way things were going.

Jock scratched his head in an effort to produce another pertinent question.

'What does he intend to do wi' 'em?'

The conversation was getting ludicrous, so I thought it high time I butted in.

'I'll get rid of them,' I said resignedly, but that in itself posed a problem. How do you remove 20 love-sick cows from a railway siding when they seem very intent on staying there?

I climbed down and tried shooing them away, but that had not the slightest effect. I then tried mooing at them, but this only brought forth a chorus of moos by way of a reply and they moved in closer than ever. In desperation I turned to Jack.

'Are we all ready to go now?' I asked.

'Just as soon as you feel disposed to clear these animals from the track,' he said drily.

'Well maybe they will follow me in to the field and then when the last one has disappeared you give me a toot on the whistle and I will come belting back and join you on the move?'

I phrased this plan as a question since being a junior fireman I was used to having my suggestions countermanded. However, on this occasion the scheme received a nodding consent. Feeling rather like the Pied Piper of Hamelin, I found the narrow gap in the hawthorn hedge through which they had come and led my string of charges in a wide semi-circle across the end of the meadow and back towards the stile. Ten yards from this the whistle sounded above the clank of couplings being drawn taught, and without looking back I sprinted for and leapt over the stile.

Jack had got the 17 wagons making up our train moving at a pace rather more than I had visualised when outlining my plot, and after having galloped halfway back to Austin West Works I managed to fling myself on to the bottom engine steps. It took quite some while before I regained my breath, and having had his little bit of fun also, Jack let the matter rest until we arrived at Rubery the following day. We were immediately greeted by Jock, whose manner could only be described as distraught.

'Fe gaud's sake, Jack, keep ya mate on the injun today,' he expostulated. 'We had they beasties roamin' down to the motor works all afternoon and the farmer accusin' us o' trying ta rustle his stock.'

I thought it was all very comical really, but everyone else took a dim view of the affair and I was confined to the footplate for the duration of my stay. I need hardly say that it was quite some time before I tried talking to animals again.

Three weeks after this episode a buff-coloured envelope bearing an 'Official Paid' stamp was waiting for me on the hall table when I returned home from work. With mixed feelings I hastily tore open the flap and read the contents. It contained a brief letter requesting me to report to Aldershot, a travel warrant to facilitate this, and some instructions regarding what to take, which incidentally was very little.

I felt relief that the long wait and uncertainties were now over, but on the other hand the inevitable butterflies of not knowing quite what was in store for me over the next two years. My brother had related details of life in the army, and I must admit that some of the restrictions and severe discipline, not to mention other aspects such as lack of home comforts and leisure, held little appeal. However, I was resolved to make the best of matters and try and gain as much as I could from the experience.

In August 1954, after my service in the RASC, principally in Germany - the long-awaited day of my demobilisation arrived. After two years to the day I re-entered civilian life. I had learned many new things during this time - to drive, to shoot, to receive and give orders, but most important perhaps the ability to live in harmony with my fellow men. The army also taught me to appreciate all the things we normally take for granted in this materialistic age - one's home, good food and freedom of choice, a diminishing commodity nowadays, but precious nevertheless.

Despite familiar faces and unchanged surrounds, I felt rather like a stranger when I visited the loco for the first time to advise them that I was once more available. Until a place could be found for me in the bottom road group to which my seniority now entitled me, I was placed in the Control link.

Things had changed only in a few details, with the exception of the proposed staff amenity block, the footings of which were now laid out in the area between the tank house and the checker's hut. I also saw for the first time one of the new BR Standard Class '5s', which on the whole appealed to me aesthetically from most angles, and ergonomically I thought the footplate layout was a vast improvement on anything yet built. I was still, of course, at this stage trying to re-adjust to civilian life, but it was remarkable how quickly I slipped into the swing of things again.

At the end of two weeks, involving a variety of local jobs, I felt almost as though I had never had a two-year break, and even my muscles had ceased to ache and my hands were regaining their former toughness. On the Saturday of the second week the foreman called my attention to the roster board, where he pointed out with a friendly smile that I was now booked with driver Syd Lloyd in Link Three, Section C.

'Syd Lloyd?' I queried. 'What's he like?'

'Oh, he's a great chap,' replied the foreman enthusiastically. 'A real character. You'll get on fine with him, without a doubt.'

Well, I would soon find out, for we were to work the 8.45 pm Gloucester from the West End, booking on at 7.16 to prepare our own engine. I went home that night feeling for the first time that I could now be considered an experienced fireman, and looking forward very much indeed to next week's work.

11
THE LITTLE GLOUCESTER LINK

When I walked into the lobby just after 7.00 pm I asked Peter the clerk for my card in the usual way, and was told that my new mate had withdrawn it a few minutes earlier and was now waiting in the far corner for me. Looking across, I perceived a broad back hunched over one of the writing benches studying notices. I laid a light hand on the nearest elbow, and as the body rotated, I enquired casually into a passing ear, 'Syd Lloyd?' Facing each other fair and square, our eyes followed roughly the same path, starting at the crown of our caps, running south until reaching our stoutly soled boots, whereupon they quickly returned north but this time scanning east to west also. Although all this took no more than a split second, I definitely liked what I saw.

Twinkling grey eyes regarded me keenly over horn-rimmed spectacles, perched on the end of a well-formed if somewhat pointed nose, while distinguished-looking iron grey hair could be seen under his uniform cap which was set at a jaunty angle. That his build could best be described as rotund may well be imagined by the fact that, although he stood only 5 ft 7 in high, he weighed the best part of 16 stone. As our gaze met once more, the laughter creases around his eyes and mouth wreathed with a smile of genuine delight.

'Welcome back to the fold, Terry,' he said in a soft, husky voice, grasping my hand and pumping it with a warmth I had never experienced before with any other driver. I was very much impressed by his charming manner - sadly lacking in the majority of army personnel - and I therefore responded to this show of friendliness like a long-lost son. From that very first meeting a bond of true affection sprang up between us.

'I'm very glad to be with you, Syd,' I replied, managing to free my right hand at last. 'I'm afraid that I'm still a bit rusty on certain details after two years absence, so perhaps you would fill me in as we go along?'

'By all means, old son' he said with a smile. 'Just ask away.'

'Well for starters, what do we do on this job?'

'Oh there is nothing much to it really,' he replied airily as I signed my card. We prepare a Class "4F", go down to the West End, collect a train destined for Gloucester and work it as far as Bromsgrove where we get relieved. Then after sitting around for an hour or two we work any train the Control cares to give us back here. Usually it's a "Maltese" terminating at Water Orton, but this of course depends on how it is running, so we can bring anything else that is travelling north. Occasionally, if traffic is light or there is an excess of relief men, we return as passengers in the brake-van of a suitable train, but that rarely happens these days.'

'Doesn't sound too strenuous,' I admitted as we walked round to the engine board where we picked out our engine, No 4165, which was standing nearby in No 2 shed.

I discovered that the tool situation had not improved too much since 1952, and I was therefore obliged to forage for some items of equipment, as in the old days. However, with plenty of motive power coming on the shed at that time of the evening, it proved no great hardship and we rang off with some minutes to spare. Our guard joined us, and we departed for the West End at a leisurely pace on the up Camp Hill goods line.

It was on this job that I really came to know our guard, Les Suffield, quite well. In future years I was to tow him around the countryside for literally thousands of miles with a variety of drivers, and never once found him any different. He was a tall,

In all classes of locomotives, some engines always seemed much better than others. '4Fs' were no exception, and No 44165 was one of Saltley's favourites. I enjoyed this locomotive when I worked my first turn firing with Syd Lloyd on the 8.45 pm Washwood Heath-Gloucester. No 44165 was built at Crewe in 1926 and, as can be seen, retained the Midland right-hand drive position. *J. Coltas*

thin, mild-mannered man, born and bred in the Hall Green district of Birmingham, and although only about 50 years of age, sported a head of almost white hair. His gentle disposition and serenity affected all he came in contact with, and listening to these two old friends chatting amiably reminded me - after army days - that such characters did still exist, so that by the time we reached the West End I was succumbing to their spell.

After backing on to the appropriate road, Les departed to check round the train, while I attached our headlamps in the Class A position, ie one on the smokebox and one over the left buffer. No 4165 seemed to be in pretty fair condition, but, not knowing her capabilities, the job, or Syd's methods of driving, I decided to play it safe and started building up a healthy fire in the rear of the grate with picked lumps. As I was manhandling a large piece over the mouthpiece ring, Syd passed the comment, 'Do you always wear gloves Terry?'

'Yes I do, as a matter of fact,' I replied, slightly on the defensive. 'I neither like getting burned nor any dirtier than I have to.'

'Don't blame you at all, I always did,' and then with a knowing wink added, 'The ladies are not very keen on dirty, calloused hands either.'

I returned his smile as the logic of the statement sank in, but before I could phrase a suitable reply he continued, 'That reminds me of the story about the Irish navvy and the shepherd girl. . .'

He then proceeded to relate this with a professionalism rarely seen off the stage. It was not so much the story itself but the way it was executed, with mime and expertly mimicked dialect thrown in, and to me it was extremely entertaining. This was the first inkling I had that Syd had quite a

sense of humour, but just what a comedian he turned out to be I did not discover until later. The tears were still rolling down my cheeks when Les returned to advise us that we had 42 wagons astern and that he was all ready to go if we were. The ritual lidful of tea was proffered to him and graciously accepted, and when this had been disposed of, Les lowered himself to the ground.

'I see that Syd's started on you all ready,' he said with a benign smile, eyeing my still wet face.

'Yes,' I replied, 'and any more like that and we won't get up the bank very easily.'

'Oh, that's nothing, you wait a while,' he called over his shoulder as he departed in search of the yard foreman.

The significance of his remark was lost as I concentrated once more on building up the fire, and when this was done to my satisfaction I sat down to take a breather, for the night was still quite warm.

The trip to Bromsgrove was relatively straightforward except that I found I had forgotten some of the details from Kings Heath onwards, and consequently was inclined to have either too much or too little steam at times. The descent of Lickey was a very well controlled one, rather too much so if anything, since we would have stopped half a dozen engine lengths short, had not Syd applied steam and dragged the train up to the column.

'I usually aim to stop slightly short if I can,' explained Syd as we filled the tank. 'You can always uncouple and run forward to get water while the brakes are being picked up, but you can't set back. Also it's our supper time that's being wasted then.'

I could see the sense of his argument, and mentally filed it away for the future.

We duly handed over to a set of Gloucester men and walked the few yards back to the relief cabin. Here I was not a little surprised and amused to find that Syd was greeted by, if not actual applause, certainly the nearest thing you can get to it without exactly clapping hands. Five sets of enginemen and two guards had previously been sprawled on the benches in differing attitudes of relaxation from snoring lightly to munching sandwiches. As one, they all sat up and began to take notice, and I suddenly became aware of an air of expectancy emanating from the gathering. This gradually heightened as Syd neared the end of his quite sizeable supper, a fact that he himself was not unconscious of, since he seemed to linger unnecessarily over the last few mouthfuls. I, meanwhile, relaxed in a corner enjoying a quiet cigarette while awaiting developments, feeling that something would soon happen.

Syd drained his second cup of tea, then, having replaced the lid on his can with exaggerated care, he looked up, beamed at his already attentive audience and said, 'Have you heard the one about the freshly ordained priest whose first appointment was to a remote country village in Wales?'

So this was it then, a free comedy show, and it must have been a regular affair because these other fellows had obviously known what was coming. Well I might have guessed, having already had a preview of Syd's story-telling ability at the West End, but even so I was flabbergasted at the marathon performance he gave that night. For two hours and ten minutes, story after story rolled from his tongue - each one had a religious background and each one was told with a skill worthy of a professional comedian.

Soon we were all writhing about in uncontrollable merriment. It was really a vicious circle - the more we laughed, the better Syd performed, which in turn made us more hysterical than ever. Always blessed with a vivid imagination, I frequently found my mind running ahead of the story, and consequently I was having convulsions long before the punch-line. Also, of course, the chain reaction effect was considerable in that confined hut, and we derived just as much amusement from seeing and hearing each other. One very fat old Gloucester driver in particular got me going. He had a most infectious deep guffaw and he heaved and shook like an enormous jelly, while the tears streamed in torrents down his face.

After about an hour he was gasping like a stranded fish and his booming belly-laugh was soon interspersed with a sizzling hiss as he fought for breath. Just when I thought he was about to expire for good, a Saltley crew arrived requiring relief and saved his day. Reluctantly he tottered off with his mate into the yard, still alternately rumbling and hissing with barely enough strength left to climb on to the footplate.

Bromsgrove South signal box. Note the concrete relief cabin alongside, the scene of Syd's comedy shows and near the point where he nearly lost his life. On the up main line, approaching the water column but not intending to stop there, is BR Standard Class '5' No 73046, heading the 5.10 pm Cadbury's trade special from Bournville to Salisbury on 11 May 1956.

Men came and went without interrupting the proceedings, for there was no stopping Syd once he was in his stride. Finally, when my sides ached so much that laughing was becoming more of a pain than a pleasure, the Controller popped in and advised us of the train we were to relieve and that it had now passed Stoke Works Junction. I dragged myself after Syd as he bade farewell to his erstwhile audience, and as we staggered off into the darkness I could still hear the racket caused by his last parting quip.

Making one's way from the South signal box to the water column on the up line where relief normally took place involved a walk of nearly 400 yards. Not an unduly great distance for a stroll along a well-made path in daylight, but taxing enough when one's course was strewn with slippery sleepers, wooden ramps, cunningly concealed point rods and signal wires cleverly arranged to trip up the unwary. Darkness of course rendered matters doubly difficult since such lights that existed only tended to dazzle, and left the ground in deep shadow; watering eyes and limp limbs certainly did not help either.

Crossing the four tracks south of the station could also be a hazardous business even when visibility was good, and although I am jumping ahead in time, it would be appropriate to mention that Syd and I nearly came to grief here one winter's night some five months later. It was in late January and on this very same job. The Controller had informed us that we were not required to work home and were to travel back to Saltley in the brake of a Water Orton-bound semi-fitted. The news was not at all unwelcome since the prospect of travelling home in a cosy brake-van, with the chance of an hour's sleep, was a pleasant alternative to the footplate on this raw, cold night.

Two or three falls of snow over the past few days had accumulated to a depth of some 8 inches, which over the route we were taking had become impacted and very slippery with alternate thawings and freezings. Syd, holding a torch in one hand and a freshly mashed can of tea in the other, picked his way cautiously through a veil of meandering snowflakes, prior to crossing the tracks. The signals at Bromsgrove station were not visible, so we had to rely on our ears to tell us when it was safe to make our move. We had not, of course, to walk as far as the water column, but aim for a point some 35 wagons back. However, before we could reach this point our train clattered past on what Syd took to be the up fast.

'Come on mate,' he called over his shoulder. 'He'll only stop for bankers. We'll miss it if we're not careful.'

At this stage I was a yard or so behind Syd and about to step over the down slow rails when out of the gloom hurtled a Class '3F' hauling, or rather being pushed by, a mixed freight, travelling with the speed of an express and the silence of a ghost train. With our feet a twinkling blur we managed to leap out of the way, traverse the down fast and pause momentarily in the relative safety of the space between up and down fast lines.

Somewhat shaken by this narrow shave, Syd glanced round to make sure that I was alright and then, with head lowered, he stepped on to the up fast. Out of sheer habit I peered to the left and as I did so my heart stopped beating. A pair of dim snow-encrusted headlamps surmounting the equally snow-encrusted buffer beam of a 'Jubilee' were only a few yards away and bearing down on us at a terrifying speed, the engine's sound completely masked by the runaway goods. With Syd already halfway over, his decapitation was inevitable, and time seemed to stand still.

Grabbing the only thing available, his coat tails, I hauled backwards with all my might. As we crashed to the ground together, every ounce of breath was knocked out of my body, but I was vaguely conscious of wheels and wind and snow spray whistling past my ears far too close for comfort. With 16 stone of driver and two pints of hot tea lying on top of me I wondered if I might have achieved the same end with a little more finesse, but fear had lent me strength and I had literally yanked Syd right off his feet.

Both of us were somewhat stunned as we scrambled up, and it wasn't until we'd been settled for a while in the safety and comfort of the brake-van that the shock wore off and the full impact of what had happened hit us.

'Thank you, Terry,' Syd said soberly. 'I reckon you saved my hide just then. Do you know, I was under the impression our train was on the up fast. That's why I never bothered to look.'

'That's quite all right, Syd,' I replied, still feeling a trifle sore around the ribcage. 'I could hardly let you go to the great railroad in the sky without hearing the end of that last story, could I?'

The moral of this tale is that no matter how

experienced one might be and how familiar one was with the job, walking across any number of tracks was fraught with danger and demanded the utmost vigilance at all times.

This first night, however, was a balmy one in late summer with good visibility, and I was quite content to follow Syd, being as yet unfamiliar with the area. When we were about 50 yards from the water column, a 'Crab' 2-6-0 bearing 'Maltese' lights clanked past us and, although it was too dark to make out the number, Syd assured me it was ours. I had not fired a freight up Lickey, and the fact that it was to be a 'Crab' added spice to the prospect because it was a class of engine I was not very conversant with.

The Gloucester men had already put the bag in when we arrived and were gathering their things together as we climbed on to the footplate. She was blowing off despite the injector being on, which made conversation a little difficult, but the fireman did bellow in my ear, 'She be alright brother, and I've put 'e a good fire on.'

I glanced in the firebox and nearly fell over backwards in surprise, for the smoke deflector plate had been removed and a great mass of fire rose from the top of the mouthpiece almost to the crown. It was impossible to guess if the front half of the grate was properly covered, but by a quick calculation of the depth of fire at the rear, the mere process of shaking down should ensure this for some time to come.

With the departure of the other crew, I climbed on the back of the tender, retrieved the rake from the well, and dropped its triangular handle over the securing peg ready for immediate use. While standing in this exposed position, waiting for the tank to fill, I looked back along our train. A brilliant light was closing on to the brake-van; for a moment I was puzzled as to what it might be, then realised that it was 'Big Emma's' searchlight - the first time I had seen this 0-10-0 banker in action at night.

Back on the footplate once more, I cleaned up and looked around the cab while I had the opportunity to do so, and the benefit of wide open firedoors in which to do it. The general layout seemed to be a cross between an '8F' and a '4F', the only peculiarities being the curious circular seats, which protruded like flat-topped mushrooms from the footboards, and the fact that the tender was much narrower than the engine left one with

a slightly insecure and exposed feeling, but gave excellent rearward vision.

Between the bouts of blowing off, Syd informed me that we had 46 vans in tow of which five were fitted, and he did not think that they would present much difficulty for No 2730. Within minutes the signals came off, and after giving the usual 'crow' whistle Syd opened the regulator and away we went.

From the starter to the end of the station platform the gradient is 1 in 186; even so, with 'Big Emma' weighing in at the rear, we bounded forward at a surprising pace until we were under the road bridge and on to the bank proper, where speed gradually fell away as more of the train got on it. We then settled down to a steady pounding beat on half the second valve and about 50 per cent cut-off.

I had initially closed the firedoors, an act usually referred to in the vernacular as 'boxing her up', but with the safety valves lifting I opened them some 3 inches and put on my injector, which at the present steaming rate just kept the water level steady at the top of the glass. I was also extremely pleased to see that, even with the doors parted and the injector on, steam pressure remained constant at 180 lbs per sq in.

With such an enormous fire in the box and things going so well, there seemed little point in doing anything other than enjoy the ride, so I poured myself a lid of tea and lit a cigarette. Trying to drink that tea made it obvious why these Horwich 2-6-0s were nicknamed 'Crabs'; with every thrust of the starboard piston the whole engine skewed literally to the right, while on the return stroke it gave a similar wiggle to the left, leaving one with the impression that if there had been no flanges on the wheels, she would have tried to climb the bank sideways. Apart from this the ride was smooth, while the crisp, deep-throated bark of the exhaust seemed to give an extraordinary incandescence to the fire.

Approaching the semi-automatic colour light signal halfway up the incline, I turned my back on these mundane matters and regarded the romantic glories of the night framed in my side window. A brilliant harvest moon, shining from a black velvet sky, bathed the gorgeous Worcestershire countryside in its soft mellow glow. General details could be seen for miles, but with no sharp edges or harsh shadows the view was given a beauty and serenity never to be observed in daylight.

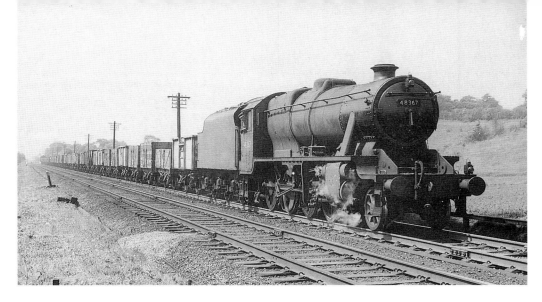

Class '8F' No 48367 working hard with a long train of empties approaching Blackwell towards the top of the Lickey Incline in July 1956. Assisting in the rear is Class '9F' No 92079. Because coal wagons were reserved for the conveyance of coal only, trains of empties were a common sight travelling back to the northern coalfields. Certainly it was not unusual for Syd and I to return with one rather than our booked 'Maltese' semi-fitted.

With Blackwell in sight, I made a quick inspection of the fire and decided that there was now sufficient room for me to replace the smoke deflector plate. Once more I proved the protection afforded by wearing gloves, but even so, my overalls were smoking after only a few seconds' exposure to that searing heat. However, I felt happier with the plate in position, although there was still no need to add more coal at this stage.

Once off the 1 in 37 gradient our speed increased rapidly as 'Big Emma', with a huge column of sparks erupting from her chimney, gave a final full-throttle burst before dropping astern. Although still climbing at 1 in 291, Syd made reductions in both regulator opening and cut-off until we were rattling along at a fair old pace with hardly a sound from the chimney. I was most impressed by the ease which No 2730 handled her not inconsiderable load, and I began to develop a healthy regard for a 'Crab's' suitability to work fitted freights. A regard, I might add, that was to be considerably enhanced in the future when I came to spend many pleasant hours actually driving them.

The Linthurst advanced colour light advised us that we would be turning on to the slow line at Barnt Green, and once over the summit Syd shut off. Coasting down the 1 in 290, we rolled steadily through the deserted platform, and when the whole train was safely on the slow line, Syd eased open the regulator once more. With only a breath of steam on we hardly noticed the short climb at 1

in 297 up to Cofton where, upon entering the cutting, we were able to drift down through Halesowen Junction to Northfield where we were halted by signals.

Here the slow line officially becomes the goods line where the permissive block system operates, and we eventually found ourselves standing behind another freight train at Kings Norton. When standing on the slow line at Kings Norton and wishing to proceed down the Camp Hill line, one is trapped, so to speak, by traffic travelling to and from New Street station, so it was the best part of an hour before we departed from here. This, however, suited us admirably since neither of us wanted to dispose of our engine, which we would have been obliged to do had we arrived on the shed with more than an hour to complete before booking off.

All this time excess steam escaping from our safety valves had been a source of nuisance and eventually I was forced to close the damper in order to allow the fire to cool.

'Hasn't that 'tater roaster burned down yet?' queried Syd on seeing my action.

'No,' I replied. 'There is still a fair bit left - I don't know how they manage to get so much in.'

'Ah,' said Syd, mimicking a broad West Country dialect, 'when oiv filled the firebox up to the crown, I opens the smokebox door and starts at t'other end, packing it down the tubes - be a lot easier loik that.'

It was all very well having a laugh about carrying so much fire, but it could have its embarrassing moments, for one might have a quick run to Lawley Street or even Washwood Heath up sidings, and arrive soon afterwards on the shed with a box full, which of course made cleaning both tedious and difficult. Travelling to Water Orton, as we did on this particular night, gave one a bit of a chance, especially if delays occurred, but it was very tricky explaining the subtle difference to these good-natured Gloucester lads, who thought they were doing us a favour, between having a good fire on and too much.

After leaving Kings Norton we enjoyed a straightforward run down the bank, travelling main line to Castle Bromwich, then completing our journey on the goods line. Even so, I never had to put any more coal on, although it was necessary to level the fire and spread it around by means of the rake.

Quite heavy thundery rain broke out when we returned light engine to the shed, and I then discovered that 'Crabs' could be very wet when running tender-first. The disparity in width between engine and tender was a distinct disadvantage in this respect, and the only reasonably dry area was immediately in front of the firedoors. Eventually we booked off with an hour's overtime to the good, and as we walked to the cycle racks I learned that Syd lived in Walsall. For the 15 miles journey home he used an ancient Francis Barnett two-stroke that somehow surprised me since I had never imagined Syd as a motor cyclist. He was however, quite keen, so this was another common interest we had, and we stayed chatting for another half-hour on the merits of various makes, since he was contemplating a replacement machine.

As the week progressed I found myself looking forward to going to work more and more, with the revelries in the relief cabin the highlight of the evening. Syd's story-telling capacity was prodigious - each night he would pick a different subject or theme and pack in as many hilarious tales as there was time available, never repeating himself once. In fact, during the nine months I was booked with him I can only recall hearing a previous joke on a few odd occasions, and then they were varied in subtle ways to make them equally interesting.

For me, Syd was the perfect tonic for post-National Service blues, and within a week or two I was back to my former exuberant self, philosophically accepting set-backs and shortcomings and once again seeing humour in every aspect of life. I quickly found that we had quite a variety of jobs in the link, working regularly to such places as the Kingsbury branch and Burton to the north, Walsall - familiar ground to Syd, being an old Bescot man - and Bromsgrove, with occasional runs through to Gloucester, Worcester and - most interesting of all - Ashchurch via Redditch in the west. Under Syd's able guidance I soon buckled down to start thoroughly learning the routes to these mainly unfamiliar places, and during the rest of my stay in the link I devoted most of my energies to this end.

Nearly everywhere we went Syd was known for his shows, and indeed it was expected that he entertained the local clientele in his usual manner. We were therefore often detained for longer than was strictly necessary at certain venues in order that full benefit could be derived from his rare talents. He also gained inspiration from local events for the writing of numerous amusing poems, which he scribbled down, usually on the backs of current train notices during odd moments of inactivity. I became his sort of unofficial critic since he would try them out on me before presenting the final work to a larger audience. For example, after two days on the Kingsbury trip job, while waiting at the Whitacre North starter, he suddenly looked up from his literary labours and announced that he had been meaning for some considerable time to write a poem about the exploits of the driver who got out of control there, and now had at last made a start. It was couched on the lines of 'There's a little yellow idol to the north of Katmandu' and was really very good indeed. I only regret that my memory does not enable me to reproduce the whole work, but it commenced:

'There's a funny little railway to the north of
   the River Thame,
The Kingsbury Branch to give the place a
   name.
Where they tell a thrilling story of a train
   that ran away,
On the night little Niggy sprang to fame.'

In its final form it was wildly applauded by all and sundry except driver Niggy, who did not seem to appreciate being reminded of the event.

Our next job of interest was a Landor Street to Derby mixed freight, which we generally worked with a Class '4F' 0-6-0 under Class B lights as far as Burton. I enjoyed this turn, not because it was particularly exciting as far as turns go, but it did afford me ample opportunity to study this important stretch of track at a nice leisurely pace.

From Water Orton we were diagrammed over the slow, then, after leaving virtually level track at Kingsbury Station Junction, we chugged steadily up the 1 in 460 rise to Kingsbury Branch Sidings. Gaining speed down the 1 in 460 past Cliff Sidings, we steadied on the 1 in 775 climb at Whatley Colliery Sidings and level run to Wilnecote where, as often as not, we were backed inside to allow the passage of faster traffic. Once a suitable path was available, the 1-mile fall of 1 in 837 to Kettlebrook enabled us to gain sufficient momentum to climb at 1 in 640 to Tamworth High Level and traverse the following undulations up to the 22^1/$_2$ milepost for Derby, without too much loss of speed.

Here the water troughs were situated, and once over these the fastest section of the route commenced. For over 2 miles the line descended at mainly 1 in 408 to Elford where, after a short rise of 1 in 366, it fell again, varying between 1 in 360 to 1 in 1509 right down to the level stretch approaching Branston Junction, where we were turned in on to the goods line. Almost outside the loco shed was the relief cabin and water column, and here a Burton crew took over to work the train forward.

After the usual hour or two wait, we would be advised by Control of the train we were to take back to Washwood Heath. Working home required a little more effort of course, since the gradients were mainly against us, but even with a '4F' it did not prove unduly difficult unless the fire was particularly dirty, in which case we would be turned inside at some convenient point if too much time was dropped.

It was in this link that I came to know, and to some extent appreciate, the qualities of the Class '4F' 0-6-0. They were essentially simple, robust engines, which, because they were not such ready steamers as the '3Fs', provided just that extra bit of challenge for a fireman, keeping his interest alive. They were quite a strong engine, too, and endowed with a surprising turn of speed when the

need arose, although at anything over about 50 mph they became distinctly uncomfortable. However, on freight work they performed reliably and effectively, even if not too efficiently in terms of water and fuel consumption. Unlike the '3F', they required much more time to warm up and were at their best when on long non-stop runs. Consequently they did not respond anything like as well to the stop-go type of operation so prevalent at that time around Birmingham, and this may have been the basic cause of the reputation they gained for being somewhat steam shy.

A week later, when on a Walsall turn over the Sutton line, Syd introduced me to a novel and convenient method of cleaning the tubes. With a light load of only some 16 wagons we were hitting up a good pace between Sutton Park and Streetly and, although we should have been eating the job, our '4F' was not steaming particularly well. Admittedly the coal could have been better, but I was having a job to maintain 160 lbs per sq in and two-thirds of a glass of water. Syd concluded that the tubes might well be dirty and instructed me to mortgage the boiler and close the firedoors so as to bring the pressure up to 175 lbs per sq in. At the same time he increased speed and, when going at a fair gallop with half a glass of water and the needle on the red line, he wound the reversing screw back to about 10 per cent and heaved the regulator fully open. He then quickly dropped her to very nearly full gear, left it there for a few seconds, then returned it to the 10 per cent position. The exhaust immediately exploded in a great tearing roar, the like of which I had never heard before from a Class '4'. It was a most exhilarating racket that left the pulses racing and the eardrums numb. We looked astern and saw with much satisfaction a great pall of black soot hanging in the air above our now fast-moving train. Syd repeated the treatment twice more, but since on the last occasion the exhaust was nearly clean, concluded that most of the offending carbon had been removed.

Whether it was due to this forcible evacuation of soot from the tubes, or whether the enormous blast had lifted residual clinker and ash from the firebed, the fact remains that she steamed much more freely afterwards. Quoting the effectiveness on this occasion, I frequently persuaded Syd to repeat 'the treatment' on other jobs in the future. I did so partly because the fire actually required livening up, but in all honesty the main attraction was the fearful cacophony created by the exhaust, and I suspect that Syd, being still a boy at heart, quite enjoyed it too, since he never failed to oblige.

My next mate, Freddy Galloway, in the Bottom Passenger link, also subscribed to this method of cleaning the tubes, but with the added refinement of spraying a bucketful of sand in through the fire-hole when the blast was at its greatest. The scour-ing effect of sand travelling along the tubes at high velocity can well be imagined, and since we frequently had the same engine on a job all week, it paid to ensure that she steamed as well as possi-ble.

From the moment I joined the Little Gloucester link I had been looking forward to working on the Redditch branch. This was the only lengthy sec-tion of single line over which Saltley crews regu-larly operated, and my brother had told me various tales of the problems that this entailed. Apart from the obvious one of picking up and dropping single-line tablets while on the move, Redditch Tunnel was quite the most formidable.

Although only 340 yards in length, it covered the best part of a short climb at 1 in 126 from Redditch South and, being single line, clearance around an engine was minimal. This meant that there was virtually no room for the exhaust to escape, and even under ideal conditions the atmosphere on the footplate was quickly rendered intolerable. To stick and then to 'blow off' was tantamount to disaster. Many men over the years had succumbed to heat and fumes, not to mention actual scalds and burns. I was, therefore, in a state of mild excitement when I arrived for work on that first Monday evening to work a freight to Evesham via the Redditch line.

We were allocated an '8F', although on occa-sions a '4F' 0-6-0 was substituted if the former were in short supply. However, on this particular evening we had No 8417, and providentially she turned out to be in quite good condition. Syd nor-mally allowed me to go about my duties without interference, but during the preparation he did ask me to ensure that the sandboxes were well topped up, and we thoroughly tested the apparatus before leaving No 3 shed.

'It's important that they are working properly on this job,' he said seriously. 'It's quite a drag up through Redditch Tunnel, and I like to give it some stick!'

We rang out on time and duly arrived at the West End, where we found our old friend Les Suffield waiting for us.

'We've got a good load tonight, chaps,' he called cheerily. 'Forty-six on altogether, 26 of mineral next to the engine.'

With the aid of a banker to Camp Hill, we ran fairly easily up to Barnt Green, No 8417 working well within her capacity and steaming like a kettle despite the mediocre mixture of fuel. The daylight had now faded as we trundled slowly from the down slow towards Barnt Green Single Line Junction box.

'I'll pick up the tablet to start with,' said Syd, 'just to show you how it's done. Then you can get some practise in as we proceed.'

The home signal was not lowered until we were almost at a standstill, then as it came off I noticed the bobby hurry out from the box and mount a small wooden stage that was dimly illuminated by a guttering oil lamp. With the engine checked by the hand brake, Syd pulled open the cab doors on my side, placed his right foot on the top step and holding on to the handrail with his left hand, leaned down with his other arm, crooked to receive the hoop containing the tablet. Hanging well out of my side window, I watched intently the whole procedure. At about 10 mph it seemed relatively simple and after a brief exchange of greetings, Syd hauled himself aboard, hung the hoop over the exhaust injector steam valve and remarked 'That's the easy part. It's a bit more tricky when you have to hand one over at the same time.'

In the light from the open firedoors I examined the tablet carefully, since I had never seen one before. The tablet, or token or key as it was some-times called, was a substantial brass disc about the size of a small saucer, notched in a special way on the periphery. It bore the name of the section to which it related, and was contained in a strong leather purse attached to a hide-bound wire hoop some 2 feet in diameter. I later found that these tokens could also take the form of a truncheon-like bar of brass, equipped with a number of cir-cumferential rings, in which case they were usual-ly referred to as a staff.

Whatever their shape, however, they all served the same purpose, that of authorising the engine to be on a specific section of single line. Until the token had been inserted into the appropriate instrument at the end of that block, another token could not be extracted from either end. This, in theory at any rate, precluded the chances of two trains being on the same section of line at any one time.

Down the 1 in 74 gradient to Alvechurch station Syd kept the train well in check, leaving the hand brake hard on until the short level section some 3 miles from Barnt Green. From here the track undulated for another mile before the short rise up to Redditch North. The sodium street lights of Redditch, reflecting on the low cloud cover, provided sufficient illumination for me to just make out the rolling hills surrounding the town.

I joined Syd on his side of the footplate where, having removed the tablet from its hook, he was preparing to hand it to the signalman. As before, he lowered himself to the top step and holding the hoop as low as possible, dropped it neatly over the bobby's awaiting arm as we rolled slowly past. Between Redditch North and Redditch South there is a short stretch of double line through the station, so we did not require a token here. The signal was on at the South box, but instead of drawing up to it, Syd stopped halfway along the platform.

'If the signal is on,' he explained, 'it pays to stop well back. Then when we get the road we can have a bit of a run at the tunnel.'

During the descent from Barnt Green I had allowed the fire to burn down somewhat, and Syd now advised me to spread a thin layer of coal over the grate and put the blower hard on so as to burn the smoke off. It was desirable to create as little smoke as possible through the tunnel, and in future I developed the habit of building up the fire towards the end of our descent, and running the boiler level down, so that I could arrive at Redditch South with a hot fire, a full head of steam but with no more than two-thirds of a glass of water. Not only did this preclude any chance of priming or blowing off in the tunnel, but it also meant that maximum power was instantly available with the minimum of noxious gases.

When I had done this little task, Syd said, 'Pop along to the box and collect the tablet when the bobby's ready. I'll wait for you here, then when we get cracking you won't have the bother of collecting it on the move.'

The bobby was just extracting the token from the machine when I arrived, so I was able to dash straight back to the engine where Syd was testing the sanders once again.

'Okay,' I yelled, leaping aboard and winding off the hand brake.

'Now, if you feel you're going to suffocate,' said Syd with a smile, 'hold your handkerchief over your nose and mouth and get down as low as possible.'

I grinned back at him, thinking that he was laying it on a bit thick, adjusted the firedoors to leave a 3-inch gap, checked that all was well with the gauges, closed my side window, and sat down.

The station lights had been turned off long since and it was pretty gloomy, but on my journey to obtain the tablet I had noticed the dark patch of the tunnel entrance in the towering hillside just

Redditch station down platform in 1955. Passenger work on the Redditch branch at this period was handled mainly by 2-6-4Ts and Ivatt '4MTs' with equal efficiency. Although loadings were light compared to freight trains, the choking climb through Redditch Tunnel was never a pleasant experience, and for this reason trains arrived in the station with a good body of well-burned-through fire. Saltley 'Doodlebug' No 43052 is pictured on this sunny morning on the 8.15 am New Street-Ashchurch train.
Pat Webb

beyond the South box. Now, as No 8417 pounded towards it on full first valve and full gear, that black circle just did not seem large enough to accommodate her, and I ducked instinctively as we entered. Immediately I was conscious of pressure building up on my eardrums, and I swallowed desperately to equalise it. At the same time dense clouds of steam swirled into the cab and, despite the brilliant shaft of white light streaming through the firedoors Syd, bending forwards over the reversing screw, disappeared from view. The steam was thicker and hotter than I had ever known it and, coupled with the strong, acrid taste of sulphur, made my breathing both difficult and laboured.

The noise in the narrow confines of the tunnel was tremendous and caused actual physical pain, due to the pressure waves from the exhaust beat. After what seemed like an age, but in reality could only have been a few seconds, an enormous weight seemed to settle on my chest, and for the first time in my life I had to concentrate hard on the normally involuntary act of inhaling. The smoke fumes burned my throat and stung my eyes, while I was surprised to find condensed steam trickling from my nostrils. The temperature in the cab was rocketing upwards and my clothing already felt decidedly soggy, since apart from the wetting effect of steam on the outside, streams of perspiration were running from every pore.

I suddenly remembered what Syd had advised regarding the use of a handkerchief. Fumbling in my trouser pocket, I pulled it out already damp and quickly wiped over my face to soak it completely. Folding the cloth into a suitable pad, I then clamped it over my nose and mouth. It did nothing to lessen the effort of breathing, but the air entering my lungs certainly tasted much sweeter and did much to reduce the compulsion to cough.

Just under a minute from entering the tunnel, we thundered out of the other end, but it was a few seconds before I realised that our ordeal was over, so thick was the steam trapped inside the cab. In fact, the easing of pressure from my ears and the change in the exhaust note were the only indications. I quickly slammed open my side window and, hanging my head well out, drank in pure, cool night air. After a few moments, I had recovered sufficiently to cross over to Syd, who was still likewise engaged in purifying his lungs.

'Crikey, Syd,' I shouted, 'I certainly didn't think it was going to be as hot as that.'

'Well, I did warn you,' he replied, panting like a husky in a heatwave, his face still a bright vermilion. 'And that was a pretty good trip too. Wait until we get a rough one. The trouble is that there is so little clearance in the tunnel that it's like sitting on top of the chimney. The heat just hasn't time to dissipate before it reaches us.'

Syd had shut the regulator almost immediately after leaving the tunnel exit and we were now rattling down a 1 in 127 gradient doing 'half an hour in twenty minutes' as he would say.

'It's downhill to Broom Junction, about 9 miles,' he shouted, 'so you can put the hand brake on and let the fire run down for a while.'

I settled to enjoy the ride, although there was little to be seen of the countryside under the heavy layers of cloud, but I pottered from one side of the footplate to the other in an effort to make out some landmarks.

On about my seventh perambulation Syd, having checked our speed down to some 15 mph, suddenly arose, announcing that he would now show me how to give up and collect a new tablet at the same time. We were approaching Studley where the exchange had to be made and, as before, Syd lowered himself to the top step, but this time, since both hands would be momentarily occupied, he braced his body firmly between the uprights. Holding the tablet as low as possible in his left hand, he simultaneously dropped it over the signalman's waiting arm while scooping up the new tablet with his right. It was very neatly performed considering that there was barely enough light from the oil lamp over the stage to see the bobby, let alone the tablet hoop.

'You can try your hand in a couple of miles at Coughton,' smiled Syd as he placed the hoop over the exhaust injector steam valve.

As can well be imagined, I could hardly wait for those 2 miles to pass, but as usual when attempting something new I had mixed emotions. Two basic fears existed; the one of actual physical danger was of course foremost, since there arose the very real possibility of being dragged head first off the engine, then the lesser one of muffing the exchange, which would only result in injury to one's pride.

I need not have worried, however, for Syd made things as easy as possible by reducing speed to a mere walking pace, and my confidence grew steadily when I found that I could wedge myself securely between engine and tender despite their constant independent movements. Although it was just as dark as the previous stage, I was able to sight the hoop in good time, and scoop it into the crook of my arm without any difficulty. After proudly displaying the new tablet to Syd, I ventured to suggest that he could go a bit quicker next time.

'OK,' was the reply, 'but like everything else it requires practice and there's no point in trying to run before you can walk.'

He did, in fact, speed up on the subsequent changes as we trundled down through Alcester, Broom Junction and Salford Priors to Harvington. Just beyond that station the track undulated for a mile or so before climbing at 1 in 171, then at 1 in 68 up to the approach to Evesham North, where it descended once more at 1 in 104.

Single-line working terminated at the North signal box, where the GW line from Oxford ran parallel to the Midland tracks. Although interconnected, each Division had its own goods yard, station and loco in the Evesham complex and, as usual where they both came into close proximity, a certain amount of rivalry existed.

We deposited our train in the Midland yard, then ran forward to the nearby loco where, having turned our engine to face north on the outside table, we left it in the capable hands of the Evesham shed crew.

The second half of our job involved working a passenger train from Evesham station to Birmingham New Street. It originated at Tewkesbury and was crewed by Gloucester men as far as Evesham, where we took over. From here we stopped at every station, picking up commuters to

Birmingham and arriving at 8.45 am. This gave them just sufficient time for a brisk walk to their respective offices and shops, and woe betide us if we were late, since a veritable avalanche of complaints descended upon our heads.

Syd explained all this while we were restoring our tissues in the loco cabin, adding that the Gloucester men were not always as punctual as they might be due to delays at Ashchurch Junction. However, we were generally booked a Fowler 2-6-4 tank and, with only four or five coaches in tow, these could generally be relied on to perform well if the need arose to give them a bit of a thumping.

I had never previously worked a 2-6-4, nor for that matter a stopping passenger train, and this, together with the prospect of having a look at the Redditch line in daylight, kept me in a perpetual ferment of excitement. For once time dragged heavily, but eventually Syd announced that we had better be making our way to the station, and I desperately tried to control my impatience as we strolled leisurely across the intervening goods yard.

The dawn had broken clear and bright as we walked up the platform, and right on time No 2326 with four coaches behind her bunker screeched to an abrupt halt right opposite us.

'She be alright,' exclaimed the Gloucester driver, who seemed to know Syd quite well.

'Right, George,' replied Syd. 'See you tomorrow.'

And with that brief exchange we climbed through the narrow uprights. I had only been on the footplate of one of these 2-6-4Ts for a brief moment when in the shed link, so I glanced

Evesham Midland station presents a delightfully timeless scene evocative of Victorian stability and permanence. Set in the centre of a prolific fruit-growing area, Evesham boasted its own fruit store, which was located to the right of the camera beyond the down platform. Double tracks only extended a little further round the curve to Evesham North signal box, where they merged into a single line for the 22 miles to Barnt Green. To the left behind the station lays the Great Western goods shed and station, through which ran that company's Worcester to Oxford line. Note the water column at the far end of the up platform; it was here that Syd Lloyd and I relieved Gloucester crews for our spirited romps to Birmingham with the excellent 2-6-4 tanks.

In contrast to the previous photograph, this view of Evesham, taken from the cattle dock looking south, presents a picture of great activity, that is except for the driver of 2-6-4 tank No 42326 taking water at the up column. While waiting for the tank to fill he is relaxing on a platform seat enjoying a cigarette. Beyond the large tree on the right can be seen the GW station and goods yard.

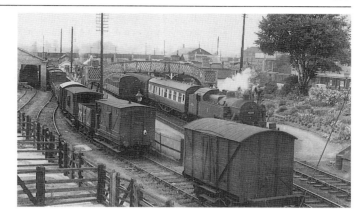

My first experience of passenger work on the Evesham to Birmingham line was with Syd Lloyd and No 42326. It was a challenging and interesting route, and No 42326 was in excellent form and typical of this Class of superb 2-6-4 tank engines. They were powerful and fast, steamed well and gave the crews a beautiful ride. There was little to choose between the Fowler, Stanier and Fairburn versions, since all mastered this type of duty with consummate ease. Built at Derby in 1929, No 42326 was shedded at Saltley during the 'fifties.

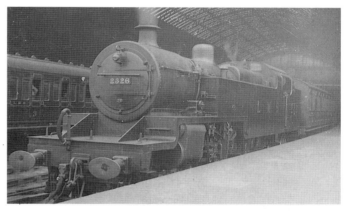

quickly around to familiarise myself with its alien surroundings. Tank engines, no matter how large, always appear to be confining on first acquaintance, and depending on whether it is summer or winter and how you view such matters, either claustrophobic or exceedingly cosy.

Being already quite a warm morning, the temperature in the cab felt a trifle on the hot side, but I was delighted to find an ample locker above extensive shelf space that formed part of the bunker. The footplate itself was restricted by two raised platforms on either side of the firing area, which elevated both driver and fireman when they were seated at their respective 'cut-outs', since no side windows existed on the pre-Stanier examples. It immediately struck me that this might make firing somewhat awkward for, having quickly inspected the firebox, I was surprised to find it as long as 8 feet. However, being steeply sloped after the fashion of a Class '4F' 0-6-0, provided that there was a good back on, coal tended

to roll towards the front.

The firing shovel provided was of the short variety, since there was insufficient room to swing a long one, and this I found entailed having to shuffle between the shovelling plate and the fire-hole if the coal supply was becoming depleted. Also, to fire the front half of the grate required a fair bit of thrust from the rear hand, for one had to employ a pushing motion rather than a swing. The engine, though, seemed in good shape with the needle just below the red line at 200 lbs per sq in, water half an inch from the top of the glass and a healthy fire blazing in the grate.

With little else to do, I joined Syd to see our passengers safely aboard, and when the last had embarked our guard, having studied his watch for the umpteenth time, blew a shrill blast on his whistle. Syd immediately responded with a brief toot of acknowledgement, eased open the regulator, and No 2326 flowed smoothly into motion. I say 'flowed' deliberately, for the response was immediate, with none of the clanks or jerks that accompany many tender engines when getting under way for, of course, there was no drawbar or moving fall plate beneath our feet.

It was normal practice to watch the train out of the platform in case any doors were not properly fastened, since it was frowned upon by the company to lose passengers in such a manner. This morning it was just as well because after a couple of revolutions, a portly gentleman dressed in pinstripes and bowler, clutching a briefcase and a tightly furled umbrella, suddenly appeared at the barrier and spurted across the platform with a surprising turn of speed. Syd snapped the regulator shut while the gentleman made a desperate leap through a door obligingly opened for him in the last carriage.

'That's Ponsonby-Smythe,' exclaimed Syd with mock affectation. 'The blighter does that trick nearly every morning - I'd almost forgotten him today.'

Our signal was off, but Syd kept the engine in check until I had scooped up the tablet at the North box, then he opened up to just about full first valve. A beautifully deep, crisp bark erupted from our chimney and we surged forward up the short 1 in 104 gradient in a most impressive way. I was amazed at the quality of the ride. Everything was so taut, with none of the jars, vibrations and clanks normally associated with footplate life.

As we surmounted an obvious hump in the track and descended the 1 in 68 gradient half a mile north of Evesham station, our speed rose rapidly, and Syd shortened the cut-off to about 20 per cent. Here the line runs through a continuous belt of smallholdings, and, despite the early hour, energetic market gardeners were out in the sunshine tending their crops. By the time we reached the 20 milepost from Barnt Green, we were hurtling along at an exhilarating pace with no more noise than a barely discernible exhaust beat and a subdued rumble from the wheels. Even at this speed I was able to leave the open can of tea on the drip tray without fear of spillage, while I quenched an ever-growing thirst from the lid.

'She rides well,' I bellowed in Syd's ear.

'Yes,' he replied. 'They're all the same, just like a 1st Class coach.'

I reflected briefly on the history of these fine engines. The design, originally drawn up at Derby in 1926-27 under the general direction of Fowler, benefited greatly from the Horwich influence of generously sized axleboxes, adequate piston valves and long-lap Walschaerts valve gear. Coupled with an efficient boiler derived from the Class '3P' 4-4-0s, a very lively engine resulted, which performed excellently right from the start. That the valve events and steam circuits were highly efficient was immediately obvious from the crisp exhaust beat, strong pulling capacity and effortless high-speed running. Although perhaps not as aesthetically pleasing as Stanier's taper-boilered 2-6-4Ts, I found myself biased slightly towards Fowler's design, mainly because of the quiet tautness of the ride, and their cosy warmth on a cold winter's day.

The coal was of good quality, but a number of large lumps had become wedged in the tunnel between the shovelling plate and the bunker, and I was obliged to open the enclosing doors to get at them. I then found that trying to swing a coal pick in those narrow spaces required a technique all of its own, and that if one was supplied with large coal it was better to leave the doors open so as to prevent a blockage occurring in the first place. This, however, did mean that extra care had to be taken to avoid barking one's knuckles on the open doors when actually shovelling.

I had just finished dropping the broken-up coal under the firehole mouthpiece when Syd shut off, and moments later we screeched to a halt at Harvington station. Once again, after collecting half a dozen passengers, we accelerated briskly away down the 1 in 291 incline before levelling out for the 2-mile run to Salford Priors. The engine was steaming like the proverbial old kettle and I was enjoying myself immensely on this bright autumn morning.

At Salford Priors there existed an old graveyard for retired steam-rollers and traction engines. Unique and beautiful pieces of machinery so much sought after today by avid enthusiasts, but looking, even on that glorious morning, rather pathetic and forlorn in their uniform coating of rust.

We blasted off once again in fine style up the 1 in 370 towards Broom Junction, after which it would be uphill all the way to Redditch Tunnel, some 10 miles distant. I found that I was tending to fire the engine after the initial hard acceleration and, by leaving about an inch of space at the top of the glass, I was able to prevent blowing off by judicious use of the injector when entering and

The island platform at Broom Junction where Syd Lloyd made his flying stop and the signalman came to grief during a tug-o'-war over a tablet. With stooks of corn ripening at one side and verdant parkland at the other, it was a delightful setting and, in summer at least, pleasant to work in Broom Junction North box, which can be seen to the left of the platform in the middle distance.

Another view of Broom Junction, this time facing south. Just under the road bridge can be glimpsed the South signal box, beyond which the Stratford line turned off to the left. Even in the 'fifties oil lamps were still in use, so on a dark winter's night 'spot the tablet' could be quite a game.

standing at the stations. This allowed me to give tablet swopping and the passengers my undivided attention when appropriate.

Broom station was unusual in that it sported an island platform in the centre of a loop of twin tracks. Apart from being the junction with the Stratford line, it was one of the few places where trains from opposite directions could pass. We were, in fact, booked to do that with a westbound freight. This normally arrived first and waited for us, in which case I would exchange the tablets at the south end of the platform. If, as sometimes happened, the freight was late, I would give up my tablet there, and we would linger in the platform until the signalman brought us the one for the next section. On this particular morning all was well and, having collected the fresh tablet and a fair crowd of passengers, we set off dead on time through the very pleasant stretch of countryside leading to Alcester.

Alcester station was sited on a 1 in 125 incline and Syd gave a most impressive display of fire-

works as we hammered away, with incredible vigour and surefootedness, to the accompaniment of a really cracking staccato blast produced from a full first valve and 50 per cent cut-off. Despite the last miles to Coughton station being at 1 in 107 we fairly romped up with no more than 20 per cent cut-off, the boiler producing so much steam that I was obliged to leave the firedoors wide open; as may be imagined, that did little to cool the already hot interior of the cab.

The departure from Coughton was slightly easier at 1 in 368, but this stiffened to 1 in 120 approaching Studley; even so No 2326 kept to time with consummate ease and, although I was having to do a fair amount of coal-cracking in addition to my other footplate duties, I was, all in all, having quite an easy time, and my opinion of these 2-6-4s rose to new heights.

We literally raced up the $2\frac{1}{2}$ miles to Redditch Tunnel, gaining time hand over fist with no trace of undue effort. As we coasted down through that black hole at speed, I was able fully to appreciate

Ivatt Class '4MT' No 43036 at Studley & Astwood Bank in April 1957 working the 5.10 pm New Street to Ashchurch. These 'Doodlebugs' were exceedingly lively and ideally suited to stopping passenger work.

just how little clearance there really was now that it was daylight. The following February, after a week of severe frost, I recall watching with great fascination our boiler and chimney ploughing through masses of enormous stalactite-like icicles that festooned the brick lining. It certainly paid to keep one's head well inside going through that tunnel, whatever the occasion.

It was Syd's practice to gain sufficient time from Studley so that the tank could be replenished from the column at the end of the up platform at Redditch without delaying our departure. This, of course, was not always possible if we were already running late, but the 2-6-4s had so much power in reserve that, provided we had the road, it was easily accomplished. I found that a tank engine had to be positioned very precisely when filling up from a water column, and if the hose was on the long side it was quite possible for it to foul a steel plate situated just below the filler cap, in which event a kink and an unwanted bath would result. However, Syd had it accurately marked and we experienced no difficulties on this particular morning.

Redditch was the largest town on our route, and from on top of the boiler I watched with considerable interest quite a large crowd of travellers

scramble aboard. Having taken our fill, I pushed the column arm clear and, as instructed by Syd, fastened the tank lid with its retaining clamp. This was most important with a tank engine, since under heavy braking, water will surge forward and erupt out of the filler like an outsize fountain, causing considerable wastage.

Right on time we eased out of the station, Syd keeping her on a light rein until I had collected the tablet from the North box. He then opened out on to the following gradient of 1 in 200, to take a run at the 4-mile climb up to Barnt Green, which terminated in a lengthy stretch at 1 in 74.

Syd pushed her on to the second valve for the first time, and at about 25 per cent cut-off we attacked the bank in a most impressive style, the exhaust ringing out sharp and clear across the surrounding hills. We were checked by signals at Barnt Green Single Line box, so handing over the tablet was no problem, although Syd had to give her some stick to lift the train up the final couple of hundred yards of 1 in 74 to Barnt Green station.

From here we had a mainly downhill run for $4\frac{1}{2}$ miles to Kings Norton station, and this section provided the only stretch where we could work up anything like express speed. I tried to take a rough timing from the quarter-mileposts at Halesowen Junction and was surprised to find that it appeared to be as high as 70 mph, for the ride was rock steady and the noise minimal.

I was unfamiliar with the main line from Kings Norton to New Street, so I spent as much time as possible observing this from both sides of the cab. With only 5 miles of mostly downhill work to go, I could afford to run the fire down, which of course left me more time than normal to take notes. Accelerating briskly out of Kings Norton station, we entered a sharp left-hand curve carrying a 35 mph speed limit, which, after straightening out, took us down past Bournville loco and on to Bournville station. Stopping at this picturesque wooden structure built on a high embankment gave me a fine bird's eye view of the well-known chocolate factory.

A series of sweeping left and right-hand curves, albeit on level ground, covered the next mile to Selly Oak station. We were not booked to stop there and, although the gradients were mainly level or in our favour, the nature of the track precluded any further high-speed running. At Church Road Junction, just over a mile from New Street, where a branch line runs down into the old Central Goods Depot we plunged into a deep brick-lined cutting, interspersed with five short tunnels. The gradient here was 1 in 80 and it was necessary to count the tunnels carefully in order to ascertain our exact position in the all-pervading gloom. It was useful to know that a water column was available at the end of one of the disused platforms at Five Ways since, if checked by signals, sufficient water could be taken on to get one to Saltley loco if things were getting desperate in that department.

From the last smoke-filled cavern we suddenly burst out into New Street station, clattered over the points outside No 5 signal box, and eased to a halt at the signals halfway along No 8 platform, 1 minute before time.

Almost immediately a small swarthy shunter made an agile leap into the 4-foot and started to uncouple us from our train. Meanwhile, having been previously briefed by Syd, I hopped on the platform, dropped the headlamp from the top of the smokebox to the centre of the buffer beam, and fitted the other one under our bunker. Ensuring that we were now free from our train, I rejoined Syd who was leaning over the uprights appraising the hordes of pretty young office girls rushing unheeding to the exit barriers.

However, not all the passengers were unappreciative of our efforts, for a couple of distinguished-looking middle-aged gentlemen came up to Syd and congratulated him on our prompt arrival.

'That's nice,' I remarked, as it was the first time I had heard such comments from the public.

'Oh, they are a pair of regular enthusiasts,' he replied. 'Stop-watches out on every section. Mind you, they are just as quick to tell me all about it if we are late.'

Our signal came off and we trundled slowly down to No 2 box, the sound of our motion being considerably amplified under the great grimy glass roof that spanned the Midland side of the station. We waited for the departure of the Bristol-Sheffield express standing in the adjacent No 7 platform headed by *Rooke*, resplendent in gleaming green paintwork, looking the very epitome of a real passenger engine. A deep-throated hoot on her whistle was followed by a powerful hiss of steam as she flowed into motion. Those great drivers gave a brief slip before they found a secure foothold and then she was gone, thundering down into New Street Tunnel, accelerating her 11 coaches as if on a roller-coaster.

Soon it was our turn, and we too snorted briskly into the hanging smoke clouds under Birmingham's well-known shopping area. It was quite apparent that all movements in and around this station area were conducted with an alacrity not to be found in any of the surrounding goods yards, where a more leisurely attitude seemed the order of the day.

Heading south from New Street was rather awe-inspiring on first acquaintance since, after hurtling out of the tunnel, one found oneself galloping down a 1 in 58 gradient that almost instantly reversed to uphill at 1 in 57 past Proof House signal box, giving the impression that somehow one had been suddenly shunted on to a switch-back. This of course accounted for the incredibly swift departure of the Sheffield express. Dipping into a stone-lined cutting, we descended once more, this time at 1 in 100 under the London line, and moments later we were passing Landor Street box, to be quickly shunted on the shed.

Leaving No 2326 on one of the arrival roads with a full boiler, plenty of pressure and a low fire,

I ended my first day of what I considered to be the most pleasant job in the link. Working with Syd, no matter what turn, was invariably an experience to look forward to, but somehow the Redditch line always seemed to produce that little extra in excitement that made all the difference. Maybe it was because of the passenger duty, the single-line operation or the dreaded Redditch Tunnel, but something always seemed to turn up.

I well recall the week's work some three months after my first trip. Continuous torrential rain for several days on end had caused the River Avon and its tributaries to burst their banks and produce heavy flooding in the area. It was so bad in some places that the water came right up to the tracks, and left us wondering if the line could possibly stay open if these monsoon-like conditions persisted. What upset Syd, though, was that he was unable to collect blue-legs, those mushroom like saprophytes with a kidney flavour, much coveted by the local country folk. He had, over the years, pin-pointed a number of prolific beds and it was his practice to stop the train whenever suitable and quickly harvest a pound or two. Regrettably the floods destroyed those beds and they, like many other wild mushrooms, seem to have departed permanently from our fields.

On the Thursday it was our misfortune to be given a Class '8' that was considerably below par, coupled with a load that was at top limit. The sand in our boxes would appear to have succumbed to the exceptional weather and, being wet and lumpy, it was not flowing as well as it might. This caused us a fair amount of trouble climbing the bank to Camp Hill, so we were anticipating another struggle up through Redditch Tunnel.

I was by now quite experienced in the procedures, and we had stopped well back from Redditch South with a good but well-burned-through fire, a full head of steam and three-quarters of a glass of water. I collected the tablet from the signal box, getting soaked in the process despite being huddled inside my heavy company-issue rubberised raincoat.

'OK, Syd,' I yelled as I scrambled aboard.

Syd, also dripping wet, since he had been out giving the sanding gear a poke and a tap, heaved open the regulator. We staggered forward, slowly accelerating the heavy train, our wheels finding sufficient grip to take full gear and full first valve, as we pounded up to that black hole. No sooner had we entered than we started to slip, the sanders no doubt having given up the unequal struggle. I had already taken the precaution of applying to my mouth a damp handkerchief formed into a pad and held in place by a wiper knotted at the back of my neck. Even so, the searing blast of hot steam and gasses that now came into the cab literally took my breath away.

Immediately, Syd - looking more like a train robber than a train driver, since he too was wearing an improvised gas mask - disappeared from view. From now on I felt very isolated and more than a little helpless, although of course I had to ensure that we had maximum pressure without actually blowing off. I soon felt the tremendous vibration cease and sensed by the regular pressure waves that once more our exhaust was beating out a steady if somewhat slower rhythm. Then we started slipping and this was again only controlled by constant juggling with the regulator. Every time we regained our feet our speed had fallen, until we seemed to be making hardly any headway. Indeed, we might well have been travelling backwards, for I had now lost all sense of time and movement, and could see nothing whatsoever more than 2 feet from my eyes. I was already squatting on the floorboards with my back against the cabside, and even here the heat was intolerable and the fumes choking, while rivers of hot water seemed to be flowing from every pore.

Must check the pressure, I thought, as I staggered to my feet, grasping the injector wheel for support while peering myopically at the gauge. Good lord, the needle was on the red line! I tottered over to drop the tender water feed, and as I did so we slipped yet again. A searing blast of scalding steam shot in through the uprights, catching me full in the face, and I reeled back, groping once more for the injector steam valve. Hanging on to it with my left hand, I beat desperately against the handle with the palm of my right hand, strength ebbing from my arm at every blow. If only I could have breathed it would have helped, but I was choking as I hung there in the hottest layer in the cab, burning up inside as well as out. Finally the valve spun open and I dropped to the footboards with senses swimming, holding my face as near to the floor as possible in order to gain some relief from the suffocating heat. Despite the general clamour and vibration, I could hear the injector singing and decided that at least one crisis was now over.

I was now conscious of a roaring in my ears, a thumping like a steam hammer right in the centre of my cranium and a body that felt like lead. It slowly dawned on me that I was being steadily asphyxiated, and the uppermost thought in my mind was how to get out of this inferno. If a healthy young fellow like myself was slowly going under, how the devil was poor old Syd, at more than twice my age, coping? Had he in fact succumbed already, and even now was I the only one still conscious on what was about to become a runaway train?

I crawled across the footplate and found he was, in fact, in the act of closing the regulator, and the resulting jerk would have sent me back to the footboards had I not managed to cling on to the conveniently sited anti-glare shield. Syd in one frantic movement disappeared out of view left, slammed open the side window and remained draped over the arm rest heaving like a stranded walrus. The dense clouds of steam seemed to be rushing out of the cab, and instinctively I rushed with them, collapsing over the side doors. We were out!

Tearing the handkerchief from my mouth I gulped in great lungsful of fresh air and, turning my face upwards, delighted in the luxury of feeling icy cold rain which was still coming down in torrents. Syd likewise, between fits of coughing, was enjoying the providential cold shower, but with one hand on the brake valve, was already controlling our descent. I wound on the tender brake, shut off the injector, then treated myself to some more fresh air. After a few minutes I felt sufficiently recovered to see how Syd was faring and crossed to his side. He was gulping down tea between the odd convulsion, but his breathing now seemed less laboured.

'Crikey, that was a bit rough,' I remarked hoarsely.

'Yes, you can say that again mate,' Syd croaked in a whisper. 'Just about as bad as I've ever experienced. To tell the truth, I'd have backed out if I thought we could have made it, but by the time I realised that I had had enough, I did not have sufficient strength left to wind the bloody screw into reverse, so I had to keep going.'

It was typical of Syd to make a joke about such a close call, for a close call it certainly was. He must have suffered more than I, since he had been obliged to remain at least semi-upright in order to operate the regulator. However, by the time we had reached Evesham and eaten our supper we were both pretty well back to normal and no permanent harm seemed to have been done, although it was an experience we had no desire to repeat too often.

With the same job the following February, after a week of icy weather, we were delayed on the Friday night outward trip by a tragedy again involving Redditch Tunnel. Six ponies had broken out of their field adjoining the tunnel and had entered it to enjoy the relative shelter and warmth therein. Regrettably an up freight train arrived soon afterwards and in those narrow confines there was no escape for the poor animals. The crew, who were completely unaware of their presence until their mangled remains began to be churned up on to the footplate, suffered severe shock, and the whole line was held up until the matter was investigated and cleaned up.

Being dark we fortunately saw nothing of the carnage, but we arrived so late at Evesham that we barely had time to get to the station before our passenger was due. As frequently is the case when things start going wrong, they continue to do so and our train was 18 minutes late on arrival, due, so we learned, to icing in the coaching stock brake system before setting out. This problem arose from time to time in extremely cold weather and was caused by condensed water freezing around valves and in brake pipes, preventing the brakes from releasing when a vacuum was created by the train engine. Indeed it was then a fairly common sight to see wads of oil-soaked cotton waste burning under such afflicted trains in an effort to thaw them out.

We quickly relieved the Gloucester crew and immediately appreciated the cosy warmth provided by the Fowler 2-6-4T. By the time I had done a check of fire and gauges including, on this occasion, the carriage warming system, which I always endeavoured to keep on the maximum of 50 lbs per sq in, we were ready to depart.

Syd was in a determined mood and had pushed the regulator right across as soon as the last coach was out of the platform. We had 2354 on this occasion and she was in beautiful condition, responding like a thoroughbred, her exhaust shattering the freezing air as we raced headlong for Harvington. This high-speed burst, together with a well-judged, full-brake-application stop, sliced 2 minutes off our deficit, and an equally energetic spurt did the same for us by the time we hammered away from Salford Priors. This thrashing meant, of course, that I was working harder than normal, but at least it kept me warm. Also I had now become expert in the art of exchanging tablets; in fact, it was a matter of some pride and I was constantly hinting to Syd that he might go a little faster so as to test the limits of my expertise.

In the low-lying area between Salford Priors and Broom where the river is in close proximity to the track, patches of freezing fog had reduced visibility considerably. Whether it was because of this, Syd's evident exuberance, or a combination of both, I do not know, but we made a very rapid approach to Broom station. Through years of practice Syd knew the points where a full application of the brake at a given speed would ensure stopping in the platform without recourse to easing off. This practice of single and late application of course saved valuable seconds when in a hurry. However, trains are not as consistent as cars in this respect and variables inevitably arise. No two sets of stock have exactly the same braking power, nor are the conditions always the same on any two consecutive days. As it happened, we had a good set, a fact discovered by Syd on our two previous stops, but unfortunately at Broom freezing fog had deposited a layer of ice on the rails, with the consequence that some of our wheels locked. What was intended to be a rapid stop two-thirds of the way along the platform resulted in a very frantic one, with the engine right at the extreme end of it.

It will be recalled that the signalman here stood on the approach end of the platform to exchange tablets, and this particular bobby was always rather nervous of the operation. He had been working the South box only a matter of some three months and from the start it was obvious that he did not enjoy the tablet-swopping part of his duties, for he would stand as far away from the track as possible, dithering first on one foot and then on the other as if undecided whether to go through with the business. As a result I found myself performing split-second acrobatics to accomplish the desired result. He was a podgy, Billy Bunterish young man, and on this morning as we flew into the platform I discerned a look of abject horror on his pallid features as I wedged myself tightly between the uprights in preparation for the fastest exchange I was ever called upon to make.

His previous dithering was not dithering at all compared to his antics now. Holding the old tablet low with my left hand, I aimed for the other gyrating hoop with my right and instantly felt a tremendous tug, which had I not been able to grab the handrail securely, would have pulled me from the footplate. Annoyed, I glanced back and was surprised in the extreme to see him gambolling head over heels up the platform in a most astonishing manner, half hidden by dust and grit. Seeing him suffer thus mollified my resentment somewhat, and having hung the tablet over the injector steam valve, briskly set about adding more coal to the fire.

Popping my head out to see how things were going a few seconds later produced a second surprise, for I was perplexed to see the bobby only a few yards away limping towards us. His fat features, even more pallid than usual, were contorted with pain, while he vigorously rubbed a limp right arm that seemed about 3 inches longer than when I last saw it.

'Why didn't you let go?' he wailed, wiping tears from his eyes with a coat sleeve. 'You nearly pulled my arm off, and anyway you've got the wrong tablet.'

'What do you mean, the wrong tablet?' I demanded, a strong feeling of irritation beginning to well within my breast.

Syd was by now taking an amused interest in the discussion, and collecting the tablet from its resting place, examined it studiously.

'Its certainly the Salford Priors to Broom one,' he exclaimed. 'How did that happen?'

I was absolutely flabbergasted and could not for the moment account for this conjuring trick. However, there was no time to debate the cause there and then for our guard was already trying hard to blow the pea out of his whistle. So, quickly collecting the correct tablet, we thundered out of the station leaving a disconsolate bobby trying to brush platform chippings out of his curly locks with his one useable arm.

Analysing this debacle I came to the conclusion that the signalman, whom Syd described as 'a bit of a fairy', had managed to strike the tablet I released with the one he was offering me. This had the effect of knocking it up so that my right arm collected it instead of the correct one, and since he also by now had his own right arm through the hoop but pointing in the opposite direction, a rather unequal tug of war occurred. Some 200 tons of train moving at 20 mph is a useful ally, and consequently the poor signalman had rather the worse end of the deal, but on reflection we were both lucky, for a serious accident might have resulted.

We attacked the relatively easy gradients up to Alcester with sufficient verve to cut another 2 minutes off our schedule, and during that time I was able to build up a really thick fire for the long climb to Redditch. Syd did not disappoint me and, using full regulator and never less than 40 per cent cut-off, we hammered up the 1 in 107 to Coughton at a scintillating speed, the exhaust ripping out from the chimney like an artillery barrage.

Getting away from Coughton produced another splendid display of pyrotechnics, and we were gaining time handsomely all the way to Studley. Although I was kept pretty busy with the shovel, we had as much steam as we could use; indeed, I was hard put at times to prevent her from blowing off. Halfway between Studley and Redditch Syd came over to examine the tank water gauge.

'We'll have to pick some up,' he bellowed. 'Thought we might save some time by not getting any, but it's far too low to risk it.'

So saying, he crossed to his own side and lengthened the cut-off another half turn. This was the price one had to pay for thrashing the engine. After all, one cannot obtain energy out of thin air, so consequently both fuel and water consumption increased enormously. Since we had to take on water, we might just as well work harder still, and gain a few more valuable seconds.

We approached the tunnel in an ear-splitting fury of sound, then all was suddenly quiet as we coasted at high speed into its black maw. Peering intently ahead through the spectacle glass, I was amazed to see clusters of large icicles hanging down from the roof at the far end. Instinctively I ducked my head as 2534's smokebox and chimney tore them off, causing a flurry of tinkling ice splinters to come bouncing back along the boiler. As we emerged, still going at a fair old pace, I was just able to lasso the lamp over the signalman's stage with the tablet since the bobby was still running down his steps as we flashed by.

Syd executed a brilliantly judged, if somewhat abrupt, halt on exactly the right mark for the column, and I had scampered along the platform and was opening the tank lid hardly before the screech of our brakes had died away. Syd likewise had moved with great alacrity and the water was flowing almost before I had the bag in place. From my elevated position I was able to take a breather and once again observe the crowds of passengers hustling aboard. Now, Worcestershire is well known for its beautiful girls, and none finer were to be found anywhere than at Redditch. It was generally considered that one of the perks on this particular turn was being able to appraise the merits of these lissome young souls.

I had just noted that the tank was three-quarters full when my attention was drawn to a vision of absolute loveliness gliding across the platform towards the first coach. I had seen some real beauties here before, but this one was incomparably the cat's whiskers. Syd too had seen her and turned round to feast his eyes on the spectacle. I goggled at the delightful creature as she drew near and received not a haughty stare but a most marvellous, radiant smile that seemed to pour sunshine and warmth into that gloomy February morning. The pulse quickened in response and the station seemed to swim before my eyes.

One hears of strange effects when men are thus smitten, but on this occasion the whole bally station was moving off stage left. The penny dropped. it was not the station that was moving, it was me, or rather the engine. The dashed thing was so eager to get going that it was taking off all on its own!

Many drivers of passenger and for that matter fitted trains evolved the technique of holding the engine brakes on while at the same time recreating a destroyed vacuum with the small ejector by wedging the retaining hook on the combination brake valve against the steam brake actuating arm. This allowed steam to enter the engine's brake cylinder while the brake handle was in the off position, and was a useful expedient when standing in a station for a short period to ensure that the train did not move when the necessary vacuum had been created. On BR engines separate steam brakes were fitted, but ex-LMS ones had no such useful facility available.

Syd had done just this, but in his haste he may not have positioned the hook quite correctly, and as the vacuum built up, pressure against the hook caused it to move away, releasing the steam brake. Being on a falling gradient, the train started to glide slowly forwards under the influence of gravity.

'Hey up, Syd, we're moving!' I yelled, alarm giving power to my voice as I shuffled along the moving tank top, undecided whether to try and throw the bag out or try and keep it in.

With a frantic leap Syd hurled himself on to the footplate and made a full brake application. He was, however, a split second too late. I had tried to pull the bag free, but the thick leather hose was rigid from the pressure of water running through it, and as the tank opening slid away the inevitable happened. The end of the hose kinked - forming a sort of U-bend - which caused the full flow of water to be directed vertically upwards like a huge gusher. I was bending directly over the opening, still wrestling away, when the violent eruption caught me amidships.

The powerful jet of icy water shot underneath my overall jacket, ballooning it out with such force that it nearly lifted me off my feet. For a second I stood there, a blown-up carnival effigy with water spraying out of both sleeves and around my neck like some unique animated fountain, then I staggered clear, soaked to the skin. The icy shock had taken my breath away, but there was no need to shout, for Syd came racing back and had already pounced on the shut-off valve.

Unfortunately for him the bag at last jumped free and the twitching hose, still disgorging umpteen gallons of water per second, swung back to position itself right over his bent form. It was now Syd's turn to receive a ducking, and my unspoken sympathy went out to him as he disappeared under that foaming, icy deluge.

A lesser man might have made a run for it, but Syd, with his now unshielded head hunched down between his shoulders (his cap was floating majestically down the platform on the crest of a small tidal wave), stuck to his post, and although he spun the control wheel faster that I've seen a control wheel spun before, he was quite as wet as me by the time the torrent ceased.

With teeth already chattering, I screwed down the lid and squelched back to the footplate to be joined seconds later by an equally squelching Syd whose face was even now turning a shade of light blue. We said nothing, partly because there was nothing much to say, partly because our dithering jaws rendered this difficult, and partly because the guard was already blowing his whistle and we had to get under way. My soaked clothing clung so tightly to my body that it was difficult to move, but I managed to collect the tablet from Redditch North box, although I found the act of firing impossible. As we pounded up the 1 in 91 gradient I removed my jacket, shirt and vest and draped these over the boiler front. I then put in a most energetic burst of firing in an effort to combat what

Redditch station in about 1910. With heavy Evesham-bound freight trains, drivers tended to stop well back in the station on the easier 1 in 283 gradient and sent their firemen forward on foot to collect the tablet. This enabled them to have a charge at the following 1 in 126 section up to the dreaded tunnel. Standing in the down platform is a Kirtley 0-6-0, while at the far end of the up platform can be seen the water column from which Syd Lloyd and I received an unwelcome bath! *T. J. Edgington collection*

felt like ice crystals forming in my blood stream.

Halfway up the bank I was down to only socks, boots, underpants and my uniform cap and leather gloves, while Syd had similarly divested himself of his saturated garments. It was then that we suddenly noticed ourselves, Syd in his long johns and me in my Y-fronts. Our eyes met and we simultaneously saw the comedy of the situation. Possibly it was reaction to the shock of being drenched, but we both doubled up in uncontrollable laughter.

'God' cackled Syd apoplectically, 'you look flamin' ridiculous.'

I could only gurgle and point vaguely at his long johns and cap - speech just would not come. Firing was murder without the protection of clothing ,and I lost most of my body hair in the searing heat. On the other hand, I had not until then realised how draughty a 2-6-4's cab could be, nor how cold the metal sides became in frosty weather. Modesty and a fear of getting my most precious parts frozen prevented me from opening the side door and lowering myself to hand over the tablet in the conventional way at Barnt Green Single Line. I did, however, score a bull's eye on the bobby's arm by tossing the tablet at him hoopla fashion. We both crouched low as we entered the station, for in those days 'streaking' had not become fashionable and we did not wish to alarm the female clientele.

It is amazing how the railway 'bush telegraph' works, though, and it was obvious by the time that we steamed into Northfield that a message had been passed down the line to the effect that the crew of the Ashchurch slow was doing a Lady Godiva on the footplate and up to no good. The bobby's face was pressed hard against the windows of the box as we passed beneath, and his goggling eyes goggled even more as he glimpsed our naked forms. Fortunately there can hardly be a more efficient dryer of wet clothes than the boiler front of a Fowler 2-6-4T, and although somewhat stiff, our garments were perfectly fit for wearing after leaving Kings Norton.

The luxury of getting dressed again was indescribable, and although there may be much to commend nudism in the right place and at the right time, I can definitely state that the footplate of a locomotive on a cold February morning does not fall into either category. The capers we got up to on that last dash into New Street were both hilarious and exciting, but we finally shuddered to a halt on platform 8 only 2 minutes adrift, which was a pretty good effort considering our preoccupation with other matters.

With the coming of spring the last couple of months with Syd seemed to speed by. However, as much as I disliked the idea of leaving him in May, it soon became apparent that instead of moving into another section of Group Three, I would be going into the Passenger Group, such was the pace of promotion then. This prospect was a powerful palliative and considerably softened the blow of our parting, since by now I had acquired a strong taste for this type of work.

When the fateful day at last arrived a quick glance at the new rosters confirmed that I had in fact gone into Link 2, Section C and was booked with a chap called Fred Galloway. Syd and I bade each other a fond farewell, but life is an endless flowing stream with new adventures around every bend, and to be perfectly honest I was really looking forward to that next bend in the Passenger Link.

On my way home I reflected on the events of the past nine months. Syd was not such a great railway enthusiast as some other drivers, but he was certainly one of the outstanding characters at Saltley. He had not pushed enginemanship and railway dogma down my throat, rather he had let me find my own way, demonstrating and explaining only when I wanted to learn. He no doubt realised that I needed to settle down slowly after the disruptive influence of military service, and being an expert in the psychology of human nature, considered this was the wisest method. It was most fortuitous that I had been booked with him after demobilisation, for his balanced and stable philosophy of life and wise council did wonders for me during this difficult period.

I had never driven an engine, except for shed movements, during the whole of the nine months, but then I never felt the need to. I had, however, developed both my firing technique and route knowledge considerably and was now as supremely fit as any 21-year-old should be. Furthermore, I was enjoying life immensely, work was sheer pleasure and I awoke every morning eager to live that day to the full. I will always be eternally grateful for the privilege of working with Syd Lloyd, and will forever benefit from the influence he had upon me during those formative years.

12
THE PASSENGER LINKS

In the past I had frequently felt overdressed when in the company of some of my colleagues, but when I was introduced to Freddie Galloway on that first afternoon with him, I was conscious of just the reverse. Although I had made an extra effort with my appearance that day, I could not match the dapper figure that now confronted me.

Fred stood only about 5 ft 2 in tall and, although in his early 50s, carried not an ounce of surplus flesh. In fact he looked positively fragile and could not have weighed more than 7 stone dripping wet. From his shining uniform cap down to his equally highly polished expensive shoes, he was the picture of sartorial elegance, and even his spotless overalls were neatly pressed. His face was sharp and alert, wearing that cheeky, slightly belligerent expression so common in many small men. However, from the purple capillaries tracing his complexion it was obvious that he was fond of alcoholic refreshment.

We were booked to work the 5.15 pm to Redditch, so after the usual formalities we got down to the business in hand and sought out our engine, 'Doodlebug' No 3013, which was standing already prepared in Woody's Sidings. It was in a bit of a mess, so while I set to work with brush and slaking pipe, Fred went off to make the tea.

I had not fired a 'Doodlebug' on any form of road job before, and this prospect, together with the fact that it was to be on a passenger turn, left me feeling as happy as a lark. With the rest of the cab now looking spick and span, I was just putting the final polish on Fred's windows when he returned. Instead of being delighted at the gleaming footplate his face clouded over.

'Damn, I meant to tell you not to wet the floorboards on my side.'

He went on to explain that he suffered from recurrent bouts of phlebitis in his left leg and he was quite convinced that standing about on a wet floor did nothing to help this painful condition. Notwithstanding this slight setback, I turned the conversation to our coming work and asked for details.

It appeared that we travelled down to Saltley Carriage Sidings, collected a train of four or five coaches, ran empty to New Street, then worked the 5.15 pm stopping train to Redditch. There we ran round our stock, shunting it into the carriage sidings adjacent to the old loco shed and waiting until about 9.15 pm when another shunt enabled us to back down into the station in readiness to work the 9.35 back to Birmingham. After that we returned our stock to Saltley, then ran on to the loco, leaving the engine to be stabled by the disposal crews. It was a straightforward job, and one of Fred's favourites, since during the long wait at Redditch he could retire to a convenient hostelry and indulge himself in the local brews.

'What do you think of these engines?' I enquired as we rolled towards the carriage sidings.

'Not a lot,' he retorted. 'They are cold and draughty things in winter. Mind you,' he continued, seeing that I was eager for further qualification, 'they run well enough, but they only steam when you haven't got the injector on.'

I was a trifle disappointed by these remarks since, as previously explained, I held these Ivatt 2-6-0s in high regard. This regard, however, was fostered purely from their ease of disposal, and I realised that now I had to view them from an entirely different angle.

As initially introduced with double chimneys they had gained, for good reasons, a reputation of being steam shy and, as with many other things, first impressions die hard. A considerable improve-

Right Ivatt Class '4MT' No 43013 with its original double chimney. In this form the class earned a reputation for being steam-shy, but later fitted with modified single chimneys they were capable of some very useful work.

Below right In this view No 43013's double chimney has been replaced by the decidedly more handsome single version, which also improved steaming. However, in this view No 43013 has more than her share of leaks, with a bad blow from what appears to be the steam supply pipe joint to an injector and another at the front of the boiler, which may be a delivery pipe defect on that same injector. While cold weather emphasises a steam locomotive's exhaust and makes for more spectacular photographs, it also shows up such blows, which could cause annoyance by restricting vision.

I found these locomotives lively performers, although because of their remarkable efficiency the injectors had to be used very circumspectly.

ment had been effected by fitting single chimneys, but even so the difference was not so great as to reverse immediately general opinion. I recalled reading that the brilliant engineer, S. O. Ell, had during the course of experiments at the Swindon Test Plant improved the continuous steaming rates of these 'Doodlebugs' quite dramatically. Minor modifications had brought about this miracle, since only a reduction in the chimney taper and that of its choke from 1 ft 2^1/$_4$ in to 1 ft 0^3/$_4$ in was necessary. No 3013 had a single chimney, but since she had obviously not been shopped for some considerable time, it was a pretty reasonable bet that she had not yet received Mr Ell's treatment. Apart from this, though, everything else seemed to be in splendid condition, and I decided to reserve my verdict until the end of the trip.

Having coupled up to our train and with empty stock lights on the buffer beam, I started to prepare the fire. At 23 square feet, the grate area was not over-large, and I thought it prudent to ask Fred's advice.

'What's the best method of firing these?' I enquired.

'Keep a good back on, but very thin at the front,' was his immediate reply. 'Much the same as a "4F", in fact.'

The answer seemed logical since the grate sloped down to the front in a similar manner, so I started manhandling some large lumps in the back corners. Being essentially mixed-traffic engines, they were not always coaled with the best grades, and today our fuel was a mixture of large lumps and slack. However, I was fairly confident that we would not get into too much trouble, working a stopping train to Redditch. As usual with passenger work, very little time was wasted and no sooner were we ready than the signal came off and away we went.

Immediately No 3013 showed that she could

handle her five-coach load with nonchalant ease by the brisk manner we accelerated up to Duddeston Road. There the distants also came off and we were able to take a run at the 1 in 90 section up to Grand Junction. Entering New Street station from the London end is even more exciting than from the western approach, since not only is there the thrill of the switchback beyond Proof House, but the Rugby and Bescot lines run in parallel to the Midland tracks and a short race often results.

We soon arrived on platform 10 where a crowd of passengers were already waiting for us.

'Make sure she doesn't blow off,' advised Fred as I leaped off to rearrange the headlamps.

Fortunately there was little fear of that just yet, for I had deliberately allowed the steam pressure to fall back to 180 lbs per sq in. Returning to the footplate I began building up the fire, keeping both blower and doors wide open so as not to create too much smoke, a heinous crime in New Street. Again I was amazed how quickly the injectors topped up the boiler, and reminded myself that they would only have to be used in short bursts.

Below Birmingham New Street station, Midland side, in September 1952. Both platforms 9 and 10 were departure platforms for westbound trains. Standing on the centre road, just simmering at the safety valves, is No 41025, one of the original Midland 'Compounds', stabled at Gloucester (22B). It was especially important not to blow off in New Street. The arched glass roof greatly amplified sounds and trapped smoke, and if loco crews transgressed in those aspects of engine management, they quickly drew wrath upon their heads. *F. W. Shuttleworth*

Below New Street in April 1959. 'Jubilee' *Kempenfelt* waits with a Bristol express at platform 10, while Standard 'Compound' No 41157 stands in the bay platform on the 12.57 pm to Ashchurch via Evesham. No 10 bay platform was regularly the starting point for passenger trains travelling over the picturesque single-line route I so much loved.

No 41157 was one of a batch of 25 engines built by the North British Locomotive Co in 1925. Thirty-two years on, it was still able to handle these secondary duties competently.

At 5.15 pm everything in my department was as it should be. The needle was on the red line, the water was just in sight at the top of the glass and the fire, well built up, was burning brightly. Unfortunately something was blocking our path because, although our guard had given us the 'right away' whistle, the signal remained stubbornly in the on position. I was now on the horns of a dilemma, whether to let her to blow off, or inject more water into the boiler, which was already as full as it ought to be. Deciding that she could probably take a little more, I chose the latter option and knocked the steam pressure back 5 lbs per sq in. In the future I found this annoying problem arose fairly frequently, and I adjusted my departure preparations so that we often set off slightly low on water, rather than be a noisy nuisance while in the station.

With the valves just lifting, the signal came off at 5.18 and Fred, who had been impatiently hopping from one foot to the other, yanked back the regulator. A couple of sharp barks erupted from our chimney as the wheels gave a half-slip, then, finding her feet, she blasted off into the series of tunnels leading up to Five Ways. The benefit of our little 5 ft 3 in driving wheels was most noticeable as we stormed up through those smoke-filled catacombs, the exhaust ringing out sharp and clear and at a much faster rate than normal. Some of the impression was no doubt psychological, but even so there was no doubt at all that these Ivatt '4s' got off the mark, and climbed banks surprisingly well.

We stopped at every station along the route, so there was no problem with steaming; in fact I was unable to decide at the time just what No 3013's limitations might be. Certainly the lively acceleration proved ideal for a stopping passenger train, and even better than that of the 2-6-4 tank engines, although the ride was nothing like as stable and the noise level definitely higher.

On the final stretch from Barnt Green to Redditch, Fred introduced me to a young couple who had recently moved into an old but picturesque lineside cottage. I do not know just how the relationship came about, but he made it a practice to arrange for a large lump of coal to fall from the tender as we were passing by. In the past I had engineered such accidents for the benefit of signalmen and platelayers, but never before for anyone not working on the railway. From the cottage it was only a matter of minutes before we gave up our tablet at Redditch North and rattled into the station, where we disgorged our remaining passengers.

While they were streaming by I hopped down in the 4-foot and uncoupled our engine, when a simple shunting operation enabled us to run round our train. We then dragged the stock forward on to the up line and finally backed into the siding alongside the loco where we would have to wait until 9.15 pm.

Having well filled the boiler and dropped some lumps of coal under the door we both washed, and as I prepared to eat my supper Fred announced

The westbound exit from New Street. 'Compound' No 41123 piloting 'Jubilee' No 45626 on the 8.15 am Newcastle-Cardiff wait to depart on the stiff climb up through the tunnels to Five Ways.

that he was going to slip off for a pint. Not harbouring any such inclinations I preferred to remain with the engine, although I did find it rather lonely, particularly when the dark winter nights arrived, and in future I always made a point of carrying an interesting book with me.

Later on, as Fred's confidence in my capabilities improved, he would save himself a walk by taking his leave at the station, allowing me to stable the train, and for that matter bring it back again, single-handed. Needless to say I enjoyed this spot of driving, coupled with the responsibility involved, and considered it more than adequate compensation for being left alone.

Fred always returned in excellent spirits after his little binge, and was usually very talkative. Although initially I had doubts as to whether his ability to drive was impaired in any degree, I found that I had no cause to worry. Despite his lack of inches, Fred could hold his drink as well as anyone.

On this first occasion he was back in good time, and advised me when to start building up the fire again. He also recommended opening the tender doors and thoroughly wetting the coal, since travelling tender-first with a 'Doodlebug' at speed caused a blizzard of coal dust to swirl around the cab.

This wetting of coal could be overdone on occasions, particularly if there was a high slack content that absorbed large quantities of water before it was well and truly laid. In this event one would tend to find oneself firing a heavy black slurry, which was hardly conducive to promoting a bright, hot firebed. However, it was in freezing weather that one really had to take care, as I discovered on this very same turn the following winter during a severe cold snap. After backing into the siding I had liberally hosed the mixture of dust and slack in our tender in the usual way, and then settled to read a book that I had just bought. We were halfway up the bank from Redditch on the return journey when I found that coal was no longer falling down on to the shovelling plate. Thinking that some large lumps must have become jammed I opened the tender doors to investigate and thereupon found a vertical wall of slack, frozen as hard as concrete. I was forced to literally hack out every shovelful for the remainder of the trip, and while this effectively combatted the intense cold, it kept me very busy, to say the least.

In the merry month of May there was no such problem, although the night was chilly enough for me to agree with Fred's verdict that these Ivatt '4s' were cold and draughty when running tender-first. In all other respects, however, they were well designed for this purpose and vision was as good as on any tank locomotive. The return run was uneventful and No 3013 mastered the job effortlessly; not many people patronised this train, so the stations were largely deserted, but even then departure times were strictly adhered to.

Later in the week with the same engine I came to curse the fact that they were fitted with twin regulator handles. It was often debated as to the logic of retaining this unique arrangement on 'Doodlebugs' because, although the regulator could be operated from either side of the cab, the brake and reversing screw were located on the driver's side. A theory was offered that Ivatt, realising that these engines did not steam too well, sympathised with the firemen and gave them the facility of being able to surreptitiously close the regulator when in times of difficulty. Whatever the reason, this extra handle could be positively lethal at times.

There was a permanent way restriction of 15 mph at the 3 milepost from Barnt Green and, after traversing this, Fred opened up for a quick burst on the following level stretch. Anticipating his final shut off accurately, I bent down and started to close the rear damper, which, on a 'Doodlebug', took some little while since it was effected by means of a wheel operating on a screw. I had half completed this when the world suddenly exploded in a myriad of stars, and I found myself dazed and not a little puzzled, sitting on the floor. As the pain and confusion in my head eased slightly I slowly realised what had happened.

During our sprint away from the slack, Fred had opened the regulator on to the second valve for a short while and it had become 'gagged'. To free it he had yanked it fully open just as I was bending forward, and that hefty bar of steel had caught me right on top of my head. Fortunately, being pretty nearly solid bone, no real harm was done, although I sported a lump the size of a golf ball for a day or two. Needless to say, afterwards I always experienced a slight pang in the cranium when operating dampers on 'Doodlebugs'.

Two weeks later we were booked on the 5.5 pm Birmingham to Leicester and, not having been there before, I was looking forward to it even more than the Redditch job. A 'Compound' was allocated for this duty, so at last I was able to try my hand with one of these famous Midland engines. The 4-4-0 wheel arrangement deceives the eye, so that at a distance they do not appear particularly large, but when in close proximity their true size becomes obvious. I was surprised at the length of the firebox when I first glanced through the doors on boarding No 1109 in No 2 shed. The engine had been prepared, but we had to take her outside and, since moving a 'Compound' was always an exacting operation, I concentrated on raising maximum pressure as soon as possible. She was in a filthy state and Fred left me to clean up while he went and made some tea.

I had already secured the turntable when he returned, and warned the crew preparing an engine on the pit opposite that we were about to make a move. Fred eased gently on to the table without any problem, but I noticed that he seemed a long time backing out after I had called him from the shed entrance. I climbed on to the engine steps for the short ride down to the next set of points.

'The bloody reversing screw is as stiff as hell,' yelled Fred, looking rather red about the gills.

Casting my mind back to the good old shed link days, I recalled that 'Compounds' were inclined to be a bit heavy in this respect, which is possibly why they required 24 turns on their low-geared screw from full forward to full reverse.

I dropped off and, setting the points for the departure road, called Fred forward. I had already walked up to the water column and No 1109 still had not moved; I rightly concluded that Fred was having another struggle. Eventually he arrived, sweat glistening on his forehead and cursing profusely.

'Never had one as stiff as that,' he grumbled as we filled the tank. At the time I did not attach much importance to his comments since my thoughts were more on how I would fare with my own duties.

With some minutes to spare, we booked off the shed and ran over the points on the up Camp Hill line prior to crossing on to the down main. It was here that Fred first asked me to try the gear. Normally, reversing screws can be wound quite easily with one hand, but with this one I had to use both hands and a fair bit of effort to obtain the desired result.

'Wouldn't like to do a day's shunting with her,' I replied to his inquiring look, for Fred had a habit of cocking his head on one side like a bird when asking a question.

Muttering under his breath, he climbed back on his platform and opened the regulator. It was then that I noticed that, due to his lack of inches, this was also a bit of a struggle for him. Fortunately, 'Compound' regulators were equipped with twin handles in the form of a V, so that they could be pushed and pulled at the same time.

The action of the 'Compound' regulator was unique in that opening it to the halfway position allowed high-pressure steam to be admitted to the two outside cylinders only, and in this condition she operated as a simple engine. When speed had built up to a sufficient degree, opening the regulator further allowed 'compounding' to take place by admitting high-pressure steam to the inside cylinder, which in turn exhausted in to the two outside cylinders. The regulator could be then eased back in the normal way until on final closure the sequence of events would be repeated.

Ascending the bank up to Grand Junction I first noticed how swiftly No 1109 covered the ground. The exhaust beats were deceptively slow, but her large driving wheels had an enormous stride, and it was only when one studied the trackside that the pace became apparent.

After arriving in New Street we had to wait some 10 minutes before backing on to our train of six coaches, and then a further 5 minutes before receiving the whistle to start. During that time I was able to build up the fire and get everything else shipshape, although I left plenty of room in the boiler because our first stop was Saltley station only 2 miles away and all downhill at that.

We were both watching when the guard gave us the tip and, answering with a toot on our flute-like whistle, Fred clasped both handles of the regulator and heaved it open. There was a loud hiss at the front end but nothing else happened. A string of curses came from Fred's lips as he opened the taps and laboriously wound the screw back to full reverse. With the taps closed again, he quickly opened and shut the regulator, which this time caused us to nudge back on our stock.

Another long hard wind into full forward gear was followed by a generous opening of the regulator. Immediately a shattering explosion of sound erupted from our chimney as the wheels spun violently, and then we were off, pounding down into the tunnel with a much louder and sharper exhaust than I would have thought possible from a 'Compound'. In virtually no time at all we were coasting past Saltley loco and braking for the station. Here, amongst a dozen or so passengers, were three sets of enginemen I did not recognise, and concluded that they must be Leicester crews on their way home. Since the platform was on my side, I was obliged to keep a look out for the guard, and this time when he waved us away No 1109 blasted off with no hesitation whatsoever, much to Fred's relief.

By the time we had passed Washwood Heath Junction, he had the regulator right over so that she was then on 'compound'. Much to my surprise, the blast did not subside to the customary hiss, but continued as a peculiar, loud, syncopated beat which seemed to indicate that the valve events were somewhat unusual to say the least. Just what was wrong we never found out, but we fairly hurtled through Castle Bromwich station, and I was then able to assess the ride at speed.

There were no knocks in the motion, but there was a certain amount of lateral movement in the axleboxes that seemed to accentuate a natural rolling tendency. However, on the whole the ride was good by any standards and we were certainly covering the ground very quickly indeed.

Once more we accelerated out of Water Orton station without any problems, at least not on Fred's side, although I was having the unusual one of her steaming too well. I ought to qualify this statement because an engine cannot really steam *too* well; No 1109 was steaming better than I had allowed for, mainly I think due to the unusually fierce blast burning fuel at twice the normal rate.

Up the bank from Whitacre Junction was real stirring stuff working on simple engine, but by Shustoke we were compounding again with little diminution of exhaust volume. By the time we breasted the summit I was sweating profusely from my efforts, but I was able to take it slightly easier on our dash down to Nuneaton. Here we struck trouble again and Fred had to mangle away at the reversing screw before she could be persuaded to go forwards.

From now on the line was unfamiliar to me and this always makes firing just that little more difficult, since one has to rely on the driver's advice, and he is not always cognisant with all the facts. Fred recommended that I kept a good fire on because Hinckley, our next stop, was approached up a 2-mile bank mainly at 1 in 160, and after that we were 'right away' to Leicester.

We were dead on time arriving at Hinckley, but when we came to depart No 1109 would not budge an inch. Resignedly Fred wound it into reverse, and still she would not move. At this stage he was just about all in, so I pounced on the screw and, when in full forward gear, heaved open the regulator. There was a slight shudder, but

Freddie Galloway found Standard 'Compound' No 41109 very reluctant to move in either direction; it was obvious that the valve events were a trifle odd, since the exhaust roared in a most un-'Compound'-like manner. She pulled exceptionally well up banks and ran like the wind, but had a voracious appetite for coal. She was built at Derby in 1925 when 'Compounds' were very much in favour.

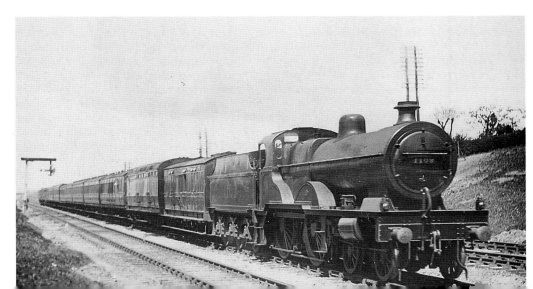

nothing more. The guard was whistling frantically all this time thinking that we had both dropped off to sleep, and the Station Master was walking up to investigate the matter. Fred tried to indicate our difficulties by sign language without much success while I wound the confounded screw back through all its 24 turns. I could now appreciate Fred's distress for, although I was probably twice as strong as he, I was now beginning to puff and pant. Desperately heaving up the regulator I breathed a sigh of relief as the wheels revolved, unfortunately giving the passengers a hefty jolt as they did so.

Then came the long wind forward until we could again move in the correct direction, but I finally accomplished this, happy to do so because I was sort of driving, and Fred was quite happy to let me expend my energy. With another jerk we set off some 4 minutes late, and I stepped down from the driver's stand to allow Fred to regain his rightful position. That 4 minutes had to be regained and here was the ideal place to do it, for, after an initial fall of 1 in 320, the next 2 miles dropped at 1 in 162. With the regulator wide open we fairly bounded down that bank, our exhaust beating back at us in a great tearing un-'Compound'-like roar.

We hurtled through Elmsthorpe station at the bottom of the incline at a speed that left no doubt why 'Compounds' were labelled 'greyhounds' in their heyday. In fact, to use one of Syd Lloyd's expressions, 'telegraph poles were going past like palings'. The short rise of 1 in 351 up to Stoney Stanton Sidings was barely noticed and we continued our headlong flight over the falling gradients past Croft Sidings, Narborough and on to

Blaby where, despite another slight climb, Fred was obliged to ease up for Glen Parva Junction. Here the Rugby and Bedford lines merged from the right, and frequently we were checked on this complex. However, today we had the road and, after observing the 25 mph speed restriction, we were able to sprint into Leicester right on time.

After refurbishing our engine on the nearby loco, we were required to work the 9.00 pm back to Birmingham. This was again a stopping train, but it involved rather greater effort since we had more uphill work. However, No 1109 was well up to the task and she steamed as well as ever, providing I kept baling in a plentiful ration of coal. Her reluctance to start unfortunately still persisted, and Fred was very glad when we finally left her for the disposal men on Saltley shed. His term for 'Compounds' - 'one-arm bandits' - seemed most appropriate in her particular case.

I very much liked the Leicester runs and we fortunately had a number of them in the link. The 11.15 am was interesting in that we were booked a Class '4P' 2-6-4T, and I was at last able to make a direct comparison between the Stanier and Fowler varieties. We always ran bunker-first to Leicester, and to be quite truthful there was little to choose between the two types. They both pulled well and ran like deer, riding beautifully at high speed. Because of their side windows the Staniers were perhaps a little less draughty, but on the other hand their cabs and fittings tended to rattle rather more, so we never really cared which type was allocated.

Possibly one of the easiest jobs was working the 12.50 am parcels to Leicester. We were relieved in the station there and, after walking across to the

The Leicester stopping passenger trains provided an excellent opportunity for crews to make comparisons between various locomotives. The 40 miles of undulations supplied the right mix of gradients and fast stretches while plenty of intermediate halts gave ample scope to test acceleration with various loads. The three designs of 2-6-4 tank engines were one such exercise - all were superb, and there was little to choose between the Fowler, Stanier and Fairburn versions. I only regret that I never had the opportunity to try a BR Standard.

Pictured here at Crewe is Fairburn No 42054, one of two allocated to Saltley. Built at Derby in 1951, it had a shorter coupled wheelbase and was some 2½ tons lighter than the Stanier design.

loco, we collected a 2-6-4T and backed on to four or five coaches standing in the bay. We were booked to heat the stock before working it forward as the 5.50 am early morning workmen's train to Birmingham. Needless to say no effort was spared to couple up as soon as possible, and while we ate our supper I gave the steam heating apparatus full pressure. Then, after filling the boiler to capacity and putting a good charge on under the door, we retired to the first coach to slumber peacefully in comfort for some three hours or so. When vitality is at its lowest ebb it is surprising how alert three hours' sleep can make one, but then it was just as well, because sometimes we miscalculated and awoke to find passengers already boarding the train and the engine low on fire and water.

There were also a couple of regular Derby turns in the link and an occasional run to Gloucester, which kept our hand in on these sections. It was on a return working from Derby on a very wet and grey autumn Saturday afternoon that I first got my hands on a BR Standard Class '5'. I had been eagerly awaiting such an opportunity since entering the link, and now at last we were able to sample a brand new engine straight out of the works.

We only had this job on Saturdays and, being a through express stopping but once at Burton, it was worked all week by the top link men. Conservative by nature, Fred was not too pleased with the prospect of having to drive this unknown type for the first time on what was just about our most exacting job, in foul weather conditions. Initially he protested about taking her, but the Derby men were both enthusiastic and persuasive and, while the tank was filling, quickly showed us the unfamiliar controls. The driver lightly dismissed Fred's objections.

'Just like a "Black Five" only better,' was the parting verdict, and the fireman was just as positive about her steaming capabilities.

On receiving the 'right away', Fred tugged open the regulator and off we set. As might be expected with a brand new engine, everything felt delightfully taut, with no knocks or rattles, giving an immediate sense of confidence and well-being. The exhaust was sharp and clear, but pitched somewhat higher than that of a 'Black Five'; as we thundered out of the station with ten coaches behind the tender she seemed very determined to show us what she could do.

Unfortunately we soon caught up with a fitted that was making slower progress than Control had anticipated, but at least the delay gave us an opportunity to have a closer look at our charge. The back of the boiler, compared with other LM engines, was particularly neat and free from the plumber's nightmare of pipes that cluttered even Stanier's latest designs. The general layout seemed ergonomically ideal, with all the driver's controls positioned around him, while likewise the fireman's controls - including both injectors - were within easy reach of his seat. These seats were excellent, being of the fixed variety, comfortably padded, and an immense improvement on anything I had yet seen.

The cab, attached directly to the boiler, was not subjected to the stresses and different movements as on previous types, and was particularly free from noise, although it did give rise to a unique drumming sound as the wheels passed over rail joints. Furthermore, since the footplate extended right back to the tender in a continuous area, the fireman had a more stable platform on which to work. My only reservation was the design of the shovelling plate, which was formed into a hump along the leading edge. While this tended to prevent small coal from rolling on to the footplate, it did require a different angle of attack when shovelling, but I found in due course that this was only a question of adaptation.

Another desirable feature was the provision of twin whistle handles mounted so that they could be operated from either side of the cab, and I have already described the glorious chime whistles originally fitted to these standard Class '5s'. Even Fred, on this first trip, used it far more often than was strictly necessary. The GWR-type gauge glasses and protectors were also very neat and easy to read, but what really held my interest was the provision of two other instruments, namely a steam chest pressure gauge and a speedometer. Here for the first time I was able to note the actual pressure achieved from the various regulator settings, and an instant read-out of the effect it was having in terms of mph.

Fred did complain of the strangeness of the brake handle and the reversing screw, the former being horizontal instead of vertical, and the latter lying longitudinally instead of the usual transverse position. However, he did concede that the seat was comfortable, although because of his short stature he had to bob around a good deal more than the designers had no doubt intended.

Strange or not, after leaving Burton we had a clear road and, although the steam chest pressure gauge showed no more than 160 lbs per sq in on full first valve, the speedometer needle was hovering in the upper 60s all the way up the bank to Tamworth, where I tried out the water scoop. It was lower geared than that of a 'Black Five', and while it operated quite freely, I was a little slow in extracting the blade, so that a couple of hundred gallons of water sloshed back over the leading coaches. Had it been a hot, dry day, complaints would soon have been forthcoming - as it was, the deluge passed unnoticed in the torrential rain.

Beyond Tamworth our pace gradually increased and, although Fred notched her back to 15 per cent cut-off, the needle crept into the lower 70s, at which speed she was commendably smooth and quiet. Further checks approaching Birmingham caused us to arrive in New Street some 3 minutes in arrears, but by that time I was thoroughly converted and an out-and-out enthusiast for BR Standard locomotives. Fred, like many other drivers, regarded them with a somewhat cooler eye. He and his kind required more than one trip to pass any balanced judgment, and in fact a year or two passed before the majority of drivers accepted them as competent, reliable engines.

Being human, Fred at times had his moments of fun, and one particularly amusing incident happened whilst working the West Pilot turn on Christmas Eve that year. The West Pilot was regarded in the link as a sort of rest job, since it never involved much work. A '2P' 4-4-0 was allocated to perform this duty, which consisted of spending most of the night standing by in New Street station in case any westbound train required assistance. Only once in the whole 12 months were we called upon to pilot a train through to Gloucester, and this was because part of the engine's brick arch had fallen down. Therefore only a few short bouts of shunting broke our nightly relaxation, which on a '2P' could be very comfortable indeed for the fireman.

The tool box on the fireman's side was just about the largest on any engine and formed a very adequate bed. Not unnaturally, the drivers tended to allow firemen to drive on this job, under the pretext that it was good training for learning the intricate moves in New Street station. Be that as it may, I suspect the true reason was that they

could make full use of the very inviting tool box during the lengthy quiet periods.

Christmas Eve was cold and frosty and New Street station, normally busy, had been a veritable hive of activity all evening. At 11.00 pm it was still crowded with cold and hungry passengers from end to end, awaiting the innumerable specials that, regrettably, were not always running to time. In those days the restaurants and snack bars, such as they were, closed down around 10.30 pm, which was neither enterprising nor considerate.

We were standing in the bay on No 10 platform when the manageress of the restaurant approached us with a sack of onions that were decidedly on the turn and causing her establishment some considerable embarrassment. Here I must point out that it was a fairly common practice for such garbage to be disposed of in the firebox of the nearest loco, since one would be lucky to find a more efficient incinerator anywhere. I was therefore not surprised by the request, and after bidding her a Merry Christmas, heaved the odorous sack on to the footplate and prepared to dump the contents into the fire.

Fred, whose sense of devilment was no doubt heightened by the extra tot or two of hard stuff he had taken with his nightly pint, stopped me.

'Don't put 'em on the fire,' he said with an air of mystery. 'Throw them on top of the brick arch instead.'

'What for?' said I, puzzled by this unusual instruction.

'You'll see,' he replied with a twinkle in his eye now evident. 'They'll roast slowly on there, and then you just watch their mouths water.'

He waved a hand indicating the mass of humanity stamping their feet and flapping their arms on No 9 platform. Perhaps this was a little unkind, but my curiosity was now aroused and I readily admit to having felt a few pangs of envy since we were to 'see Christmas in' working on the footplate while everyone else was seemingly enjoying this festive occasion.

Removing the deflector plate, I quickly 'fired' the onions on to the top of the brick arch, spreading them over the whole area as evenly as possible, where they started to sizzle away in a most satisfying manner. Within 2 minutes of completing this task, we were asked by the shunter to take a van down to the north end of the station and stand on the centre road, prior to backing it on to a westbound mail train due shortly.

As anyone knows, even a single pound of onions produces a considerable aroma when frying in a pan, so one can well imagine the effect of half a hundredweight cooking merrily away. As we puffed gently through the whole length of the station, this most appetising smell was trapped under the great glass roof and percolated into every corner, while 400 or so heads turned this way and that, trying to detect in vain the source of their torment. . .

The year with Fred passed very quickly and, although I did no real driving, I received a thorough grounding in passenger work, which incidentally required a whole new range of techniques. It was a really enjoyable year, but during the second half a longing for faster, harder, more exciting jobs grew, and neither the link nor Fred was able to fulfil this.

He was a very competent and careful driver who had the happy knack of being able to run punctually from point to point without constantly consulting his watch. He would, wherever possible, try and regain the odd few minutes lost, no matter by what cause, but he would not flog any engine or run at exceptional speeds for the sheer fun of it, and in my youthful enthusiasm I yearned for a driver who would do both these things and also explore the limits of the engines and my capabilities.

At the annual link change my prayers were well and truly answered when destiny brought Tommy Charles and me together.

He was the very epitome of what I then considered a driver to be, and while I needed him so he, as it turned out, also needed me. It may sound a trifle arrogant, but by enthusiastic encouragement and an untiring willingness and ability to fire at exceptionally high rates, I enabled him to drive with an unrestrained abandon that produced performances that would have made the designers themselves shake their heads with disbelief. Every day we both delighted in proving that a steam locomotive, enthusiastically even if uneconomically handled, was capable of just about double what was normally expected of it.

Tom and I were both on the same wavelength in as much as we considered that the crew's attitude was the main limiting factor to a steam locomotive's performance. Most drivers were kind, mature men at heart who had arrived at their positions only after many long, hard years with the shovel. It was therefore not unreasonable that they should be sensitive to their mate's labours, and cause them no unnecessary work since, after all, the company only required them to run to schedule. To the majority of firemen, footplate life was only a job, a job that was demanding enough even when working to the minimum requirements, so that an excess of physical effort was to be avoided if at all possible. Furthermore, not all crews were aware, or capable, of exploiting the tremendous reserve of energy that could be stored in the boiler and firebed. Thorough route knowledge and keen anticipation could tap this reservoir and exploit it to produce short-term efforts way

Class '2P' locomotives were booked to Station Pilot duties at New Street. If all went well no greater effort than a few minutes light shunting was called for during a shift. The fireman's seat was long enough to lay full length on, which is possibly why drivers frequently decided that it was a good opportunity for firemen to learn 'station movements' while practising their driving. Occasionally, however, a passenger train required assistance, then the old '2P' had to hitch up her skirts and travel at a quite indecent pace at the head of an express to Gloucester or even Bristol.

It was on the West Pilot that Freddie Galloway tantalised cold and hungry passengers with the smell of roasting onions one Christmas Eve. *F. W. Shuttleworth* above the considered norm, which is why some startling performances appear on record.

Everyone in the passenger links seemed to know of Tommy Charles, and when the new rosters were posted they were quick to tell me just what I was in for. With this prior knowledge of Tom's methods in mind, I lost no time in airing my own theories and attitudes, telling him that as far as I was concerned he could not drive an engine too hard or too fast, and that I was fully prepared to bale coal in as fast as he could knock it out as long as I could still stand up. Having this 'carte blanche' invitation did wonders for Tom's outlook since I later learned that several firemen had refused to work with him on the grounds that he worked them too hard, and he had not unnaturally been a trifle hurt by this criticism. It took a few days before he realised that I meant exactly what I had said, and during this period I made a point of deliberately standing by his side spurring him on to even greater efforts when occasions arose. After that we fully understood each other and it was then that the sparks really began to fly.

Tom had joined the LNWR in 1919 after having served in the Royal Navy as a torpedo-man during The First World War. It is now well known that LNWR men drove their engines harder than just about any other railwaymen, and Tom, well schooled in this method, liked to hear the exhaust beat, no matter what the type, load or conditions. Moreover, the fact that he was slightly deaf only meant that an engine had to be opened up just that bit more to achieve the effect!

In his mid-50s, Tom resembled an amiable rhinoceros - tough, thick set and utterly dependable. Nothing seemed to upset or disturb him, even when near disaster loomed ahead, and during my stay with him I heard no complaints about anyone or anything, although he had to endure a painful open ulcer on his left shin, a legacy from the war. Tom took life as it came, obstacles and difficulties were part of that life and it was no use whining about them - they were there to be surmounted and surmount then he did, for he was by nature one of those strong, silent men of action.

After only the first week I discovered that he was susceptible to a little encouragement, provided that it was subtly presented. We were working the 1.55 pm slow to Leicester, which was in itself a bit of a misnomer since timings were quite keen and the train ultimately ran through to Great

Yarmouth. Usually a 'Black Five' was allocated along with eight corridor coaches, although this could be made up to ten at the height of the holiday season. I was already enjoying myself very much on this turn because the loadings, the frequent stopping and starting and the gradients combined to necessitate giving the engine a fair bit of stick, and Tom was prosecuting this in a manner I had not previously experienced.

On the Thursday I was delighted to find that we had a BR Standard Class '5' and looked forward to see just how she would perform. Tom, as usual, showed no particular emotion and hammered on in his normal enterprising way, until we reached Hinckley. This, as previously mentioned, was the start of the fastest stretch, but unfortunately we were booked to stop at Elmsthorpe only 3 miles further on. I felt that this stop was a cruel quirk of fate for, had we been able to run straight through to Leicester, Tom would doubtless have worked up some exceptionally high speeds by the bottom of the bank.

As it was, we set off vigorously enough using full first valve and, after half a mile or so, 25 per cent cut-off. With help from the gradient our speed rose steadily and, as it did so, I stepped over to Tom's side of the cab to see what the speedometer was reading. Without any alteration to the controls the needle gradually crept past 70, and steadied on 74 mph.

'Do you think she would reach 80?' I enquired. Tom looked up at the speedo as if noticing it for the first time.

'Should do,' he replied in the manner of a schoolboy seeing a new game.

He brought the regulator back to the fully open position, and immediately the steam chest pressure gauge indicated 220 lbs per sq in instead of its former 170. I noticed a slight sharpening of the already rapid exhaust beat, and the speedometer needle started to creep upwards again - 75, 76, 77 mph. Elmsthorpe was now getting perilously near, but having been set a target, Tom seemed determined to achieve it at all costs. I suppose that had we sufficient time, 25 per cent cut-off would have taken us well over 80 mph, but we were now rapidly running out of road, therefore Tom dropped down to 35 per cent forcing the engine along above her normal effort.

It was amazing what a difference that extra 10 per cent made; the exhaust increased to a ferocious staccato roar, while at this speed the individual beats were barely discernible.

The effect on the speedometer was equally dramatic, for the needle started to move quickly towards the 80 mark. It had just touched 82 mph when Tom slammed shut the regulator and made a full brake application. As usual with trains, there was initially little apparent effect and, looking ahead to see just where we were, I was horrified to see Elmsthorpe station looming towards us at a tremendous speed. Then, as the brakes overcame the momentum, our pace slackened noticeably, but even so it was quite apparent that we were not going to make a controlled stop in the orthodox manner, and I stood behind Tom fascinated by the spectacle.

The leading edge of the platform hurtled past and then all too quickly the trailing end swept by at a pace greater than I would care to have alighted at. Four coach lengths beyond this we jerked to an abrupt halt with the vacuum gauge still registering zero.

'Didn't think that we were that near,' murmured Tom, as cool as if this happened every day of the week. 'Still there are four coaches in the platform - only holds five anyway,' and with that he watched the few alighting passengers sorting themselves out with plenty of time to spare because, as usual, he was running well ahead of schedule. On arrival at Leicester I had time to reflect that if Tom was willing to put up this sort of performance on a stopping train, I could look forward to an exciting year ahead on some of the other turns.

It was on this 1.55 Leicester that I discovered his eyesight was nearing the minimum acceptable standard. All enginemen, of course, had to pass periodic eyesight tests, and although this presented no problem at his last one, he admitted that a number of signals under certain conditions were proving difficult to sight.

Most of the passenger and top link drivers were in their 50s and 60s, and for their age a better-sighted group of men would be hard to find, but there is no doubt that their vision was not as keen as it had been 20 years earlier. Fortunately experience and constant practice largely compensated for this, but passenger drivers discovered any problems of this nature first because of the higher speeds that their jobs demanded, and Tom travelled at a higher speed than most.

With this problem frankly exposed, I soon learned the whereabouts of those difficult signals, and also the ones that were sighted first from my side of the cab, so that like many other experienced firemen I was able to act as a sort of advanced warning system for the driver.

Gradually I became used to Tom's exceptional everyday driving methods and these were then the norm by which I judged other performances. Like

The Birmingham-Yarmouth headed by BR Standard '5' No 73003 waiting to depart from New Street's platform 7. When Tommy Charles and I had such a locomotive for the first time on the 1.55 pm to Leicester, we were distracted by the speedometer during a spirited sprint from Hinckley and nearly overshot the platform at Elmsthorpe. Although based on the 'Black Five', these Standard engines were superior in most aspects, particularly convenience and comfort, and, if given the choice, I would select one every time.

every other driver, Tom occasionally, by dint of circumstance, or merely through joie de vivre, produced an extraordinary effort out of the blue, and these episodes are indelibly printed on my memory.

For example, after only a few weeks together we were booked to work the 4.00 pm Bristol Parcels from Birmingham New Street to Gloucester. After perusing the engine board we found that our engine, No 4744, was already prepared and waiting in the shed yard. This was a Caprotti 'Black Five', and although I had never worked a Caprotti before, I was well aware that they were not held in high regard by the majority of drivers. This stemmed from a reputation of not being able to pull very well on banks and of being indifferent steamers into the bargain. On the other hand, all drivers readily admitted that on the level or downhill they ran like greyhounds and could be linked up to almost mid-gear.

Naturally I was very keen to see what Tom would do with one and broached the subject as we walked over to her.

'What do you think of them, Tom? I've heard that they are not too clever on uphill work.'

'Never had any problems,' was the studied reply. 'Think the trouble lays in the fact that they've got a louder bark than the Walschaerts "5s", and most drivers wind them up too much.'

I then remembered what Doug Pinkerton had told me once. He had been working an express one night with a Caprotti and found to his amazement that on the easy gradients down to Gloucester he had been running for many miles at 7.5 per cent cut-off in back gear! It was therefore logical to assume that there was a good deal of truth in Tommy's theory.

Climbing aboard No 4744 I was more than somewhat surprised and a little annoyed to find that she had been coaled from end to end with ovoids, and the footplate was 6 inches deep in these little synthetic 'eggs'. We had a little time to spare, so after a quick check around Tom went off to make the tea, while I set about the task of cleaning up. First I sought out an old firebar from the disposal pit, which I wedged between the bottom of the tender doors and the shovelling plate. This was the usual method of reducing the flow of small coal or ovoids, which tended to flood on to the footplate with the movement of the engine. Also shovelling off the floor was much harder work than off the shovelling plate, apart from the annoyance of walking on the things and the dust they produced when crushed underfoot. I then cleared all traces from the footplate, packing the ovoids under the firedoor and around the sides of the firebox, swilling the remaining dust away with the slaking pipe. This was just completed to my satisfaction when Tom returned saying that he had rung out and as soon as the signal came off we could go.

From the first shudder as we moved out of the yard, to when we came to a halt in New Street, a steady stream of ovoids rolled on to the footplate, so that once more we were wading knee deep in the things. There was still some 20 minutes or so before we were due to depart, so I decided to deposit this lot in the firebox as well. By the time I had finished, a very thick bed of ovoids was lying on the firebars except for a hole some 3 feet from the mouthpiece. This was of course necessary to prevent the generation of too much steam and help reduce the production of smoke, which even then was belching from the chimney in greater volumes than was strictly desirable.

No 4744 had been out in service for some considerable time, and as was common with many engines fitted with rocking grates and hopper ashpans, she had been subjected to a certain amount of misuse. At some period in her life a fire had been dropped into the ashpan before first opening the doors, and the resultant excess of heat had distorted these doors, preventing their proper closure and admitting a considerable quantity of air. I therefore could not control the draught to the firebed as well as I would have liked; however, on the other hand the fire was burning through evenly over the whole grate area.

The needle was on the red line by the time we backed on to our train, but since I had deliberately arrived with only half a glass of water I was able to prevent blowing off by use of the injector. Our guard, whom I deduced knew Tom quite well, came up to us while we were being coupled on and, with tongue in cheek and an apologetic smile, announced that we had a gross load of 364 tons.

'I'm afraid there isn't a pilot available, Tom - 320 tons is your limit unassisted, so it's up to you. Will you take 'em?'

Without any hesitation Tom nodded his consent. I'm quite sure that he would have done so if asked to take double this load, for it was his philosophy to give his engine the lot and see what happened.

The guard disappeared, but it was already 4.10 pm before our signal dropped, and knowing that an express was shortly due to follow us, Tom was in no mood to hang about. Everything was in good order from my point of view. In full gear, which was 85 per cent cut-off on a Caprotti, Tom opened the regulator; No 4744 took a pace forward, checked, and then almost immediately the regulator was heaved right across. An almighty explosion of sound shattered the air, reverberating under that great arched roof like an artillery barrage as the wheels spun in a gigantic slip, and the area round New Street station was transformed from brilliant sunshine to a darkish midnight within a matter of seconds. The enormous draught produced by that slip had well and truly stirred up the fire, and although the blower was hard on and we were once more moving with a wide open regulator, a great towering column of jet black, oily smoke was erupting from our chimney.

I had left the firedoors wide open in an effort to burn the smoke, but so much was now being produced by that thick bed of ovoids that it was beyond the capacity of the firebox to consume it with the draught available at our present speed. As we pounded into the first tunnel a blow-back between each beat occurred in the form of a great red cone of flame that flattened itself menacingly against the tender doors; I shrank back in my corner, fascinated at this spectacle. I had never experienced anything quite like it before and, apart from thoughts of becoming singed, I was fearful that my shovel, which was in the line of fire, might lose its handle.

Through the thick smoke and steam now streaming into the cab I could see Tom's bulk, as unconcerned as ever, leaning forwards over the screw with one hand poised on the horizontal regulator handle, taking little or no notice whatsoever of these footplate pyrotechnics. After all, this was the fireman's business and he was quite confident that I would cope with it.

Up through the tunnels to Five Ways the cacophony was deafening, for under full gear and regulator we were accelerating our train up the 1

Caprotti 'Black Five' No 44757 leaving New Street on the Sheffield-Gloucester on 8 June 1953. It would seem to be coaled with the very smoky 'eggs' so prevalent at this period, but the smoke seen here is a mere trifle compared to the 'blackout' that Tommy Charles and I produced at the same place with No 44744 when working the 4.00 pm New Street to Bristol parcels.

in 80 in a manner that totally belied the load we hauled; I was left wondering how Caprottis could possibly have acquired their reputation for not pulling well on banks if they were all like this one. When we finally broke out into daylight I was delighted to note that the needle was still glued to the red line, although the water level had fallen to half a glass, so it was necessary to put on the injector and start ladling in ovoids with great gusto. Under the incredibly fierce draught generated by a wide open regulator and 50 per cent cut-off, they burned at a demoralising speed; fortunately it was only necessary to scoop them up and let fly in the general direction of the mouthpiece since the blast then took over and distributed the ovoids in much the same way as a mechanical stoker would.

Over the level stretch beyond Church Road Junction our pace increased rapidly, and as we roared through Selly Oak station the exhaust had risen to an absolutely earsplitting staccato bark that had my pulses racing, for not even Tom had previously hammered an engine like this. In seemingly no time at all we were through Bournville and shutting off for the 35 mph restriction round Kings Norton station junction, and I used this opportunity to turn on the live steam injector in an effort to top up the boiler because the exhaust injector had only managed to maintain the half glass level from Five Ways. The firebed was also now only a third as thick as when we had started and I frantically fired all round the box as fast as I could shovel before Tom opened up again.

This he did as soon as we were on the straight and, after shutting off the live steam injector, I paused on his side of the cab, taking a quick breather while blinking through rivers of sweat across at the carriage sidings. To my delight I saw Freddie Galloway gesticulating wildly from the footplate of a Class '5'. He was trying to convey in mime that Tom ought to give her some more. That was hardly possible, for with the boiler at 225 lbs per sq in, the regulator horizontal, and the cut-off at no less than 60 per cent, the cylinders were handling just about as much as they could take. The exhaust, as it thundered off the brick-lined embankment rising above us on the up side was nothing short of shattering.

Some days later I saw Fred in the engineman's lobby when booking off, and he remarked jocularly that I looked about 2 stone lighter than when I was booked with him.

'No kidding,' he went on, 'we could hear you all the way up to Barnt Green!'

This may have been something of an exaggeration, but with the wind in the right direction they no doubt heard us for some considerable way because we stormed through Cofton cutting at 45 per cent, and even on the down grade of 1 in 297 approaching Barnt Green Tom did not condescend to shorten the cut-off beyond 30 per cent. Here, with our speed well into the 70s, the impression of sheer power was indescribable. Never before had I witnessed such a sustained effort with a steam locomotive.

Despite these tremendous demands made on the boiler, the steam pressure gauge was still showing 220 when Tom finally shut off for the descent of Lickey. However, the water was again down to half a glass since the exhaust injector had not kept pace with usage, and I quickly brought the live steam injector into action as we started down that notable incline. As previously mentioned, the fireman can usually depend on a few minutes' respite while coasting to just beyond Bromsgrove South, but not so on this occasion, for the firebars were now only covered by a very thin incandescent layer. I was therefore obliged to pack in more fuel with undiminished vigour, knowing full well that this would be my last opportunity to build up an appreciable bed before reaching Gloucester.

Being now truly warmed up and having had all the cobwebs blown out of her, No 4744 showed us that she was as fleet of foot as any 'Black Five' in the region. Past Stoke Works, Tom, with wide open regulator, gradually pulled her up to 15 per cent cut-off, and over the following easy gradients our speed rapidly built up, certainly the fastest I had yet travelled on a steam engine, and I only wish that she had been fitted with a speedometer so that I could have recorded the peak reached at the bottom of the 1 in 385 drop to Eckington. I also wished that I had had a coke shovel available, since I could hardly bale in ovoids quick enough with the standard implement to keep pace with the excessive rate of combustion. Despite our tremendous speed, she rode very well indeed and, although the footplate was one frantic seething mass of motion, there were no excessive bangs or rattles, while the furious tearing roar of the exhaust could be clearly heard above everything else.

Approaching Cheltenham it became obvious that not only had we wiped out our 10-minute late

Caprotti 'Black Five' No 44744, one of a batch built at Crewe in 1948 with plain axlebox bearings. These loco-motives initially gained a reputation for being weak on banks, although all agreed that they were very fast and very free-running. Tommy Charles soon disposed of these notions when working the 4.00 pm New Street-Bristol parcels with this same locomotive. Despite having 364 tons behind the tender (44 tons over-load) he made a non-sense of the loading tables, giving a scintillating performance on the rising gradients up to Blackwell, and indeed gaining time hand over fist all the way along the route.

start, but had begun to catch up the preceding train, for we ran into a series of signal checks. In a way I was glad of the opportunity to build up the fire again for the final spurt to Gloucester, although I had no complaints with the way No 4744 steamed. Admittedly it had required a great deal of physical effort, for I had been firing almost continuously all the way, but the needle had bare-ly left the red line and although I was a bath of perspiration, I was still feeling in fine fettle.

With a clear road once more, we thundered away from the station, accelerating with a most impressive display of power using full regulator and 30 per cent cut-off and consuming ovoids at such a rate that I was now obliged to open the tender doors. With Gloucester almost in sight we literally hurtled past a Western express running parallel to us. This caused black looks from its crew, but gave us a great deal of boyish satisfac-tion. Despite a further check just north of Gloucester station, we glided to a halt at the end of the platform 4 minutes to the good and, having put the bag into a now virtually empty tank, handed over to the relieving Bristol men.

They were pleased by our early arrival, but not at all happy about the depleted fuel supply nor the fact that it was composed entirely of ovoids. However, you can't have everything in life, so we left them to it and wandered off to a small pub Tom knew of just outside the station. Standing at

the bar I suddenly realised how thirsty I was, and within minutes sank three pints of ice cold cider shandy. Adequately satisfied, we returned to the messroom for a well-earned bite, happy in the knowledge that as a team we had performed well above the required standard - Tom confident that I was both willing and able to supply just about as much steam as he could use, and I now confident that I could meet his demands, no matter how excessive they might prove to be.

From then onwards Tom's driving became even more dynamic, but I had no regrets, for despite the extra physical effort this involved I constantly exhorted him to break new records. Strangely enough we were never once short of steam. On the contrary, we even made engines that were sup-posedly steam-shy perform as never before, as this next incident will illustrate.

The 5.00 pm Derby slow was crewed on week-days by men from that Mecca of the old Midland Railway. An Ivatt Class '2P' was allocated, and they worked this down on the 1.30 pm slow from Derby. After terminating at New Street station the engine was brought on to Saltley loco and refurbished by our shed men while the train crew restored their tissues in the canteen. However, on Saturdays the 5.00 pm became the 5.15 pm, and its return working was entrusted to ourselves in Link 2, the Derby men travelling home on the train as passengers.

While in the shed link I had at times been involved in refettling the Ivatt Class '2Ps' and thought them grand little engines, since, being fitted with self-cleaning smokeboxes and rocker grates, they were very easy to work on. I was therefore looking forward to actually firing one, particularly since it was to be for the first occasion.

On climbing aboard No 6446 I was a trifle disconcerted to find that she was coaled with what appeared to be a tender full of slack, the surface of which was broken by the odd large lump of dull, poor-grade coal. Following previous exploits with Tom, my confidence was running at an unprecedented high, but this was rather dispelled when, after just having cleaned down, two sets of Derby men clambered on to the footplate.

'God!' exclaimed the leading driver, 'have you got to take this camel back?' Before either of us could ask the obvious 'Why?', he continued.

'We worked her down this afternoon and lost 9 minutes - 9 minutes on a slow!' At this juncture, he spread out his hands and, looking up, appealed to the cab ventilator for sympathy. 'I booked her for not steaming, didn't think they would have the cheek to turn her out again, and Christ, we had a lot better coal on than that rubbish you've got there. You'll be in trouble with that lot. I say, you'll be in right trouble with that lot, won't they, mate?'

I glanced across at his fireman who was nodding his head in vigorous confirmation. He was a tough looking fellow, several years older than myself and obviously no novice. If he had had problems with a familiar engine and reasonable coal, then how would I make out? I quickly transferred my gaze to Tom and received all the assurance the trace of a shrug can give one. Tom's face betrayed no alarm, but then it never did, so I decided to play safe and build the fire up some more.

But here was a problem, for there were already six of us on the not over-spacious footplate, and now three guards, seeking a ride up to New Street, came scurrying on board and mingled with the crowd. I found myself jammed hard against the open side window, barely able to lift an arm, let alone find sufficient room to swing a shovel. I was therefore obliged to adopt a passive role during our protracted journey to New Street, and by the time we arrived there, no more than 160 lbs per sq in was showing on the clock, while the boiler level was down to half a glass.

The delays incurred outside the station left me little time to put matters right, although when our passengers finally left the footplate I was able to quickly drag out a few of the exposed lumps of coal and drop them under the door. One advantage of a grate area of only 17 sq ft was that even a few lumps covered a fair percentage of the bars. Leaving the blower hard on, I hared round to the front of the engine, for the shunters had already coupled up, and positioned one headlamp on the smokebox. I hated having to dash around like this when the engine was not in a condition to my liking, but we were due away at 5.15 pm, and even now it was 5.18.

I was able to get in another half dozen shovelsful before we received the tip to depart, 4 minutes awry, but steam pressure was still 10 lbs per sq in light at 190, and the water level was showing only half a glass. With six well-filled coaches behind the tender, and a late start into the bargain, Tom didn't pussyfoot about and immediately yanked the regulator well across the quadrant. If any read-

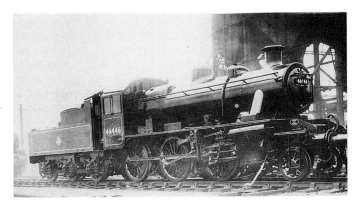

Ivatt Class '2MT' 2-6-0 No 46446 just out of the paint shops at Crewe. When extended to the limit, these engines could perform surprisingly well. In fact, the harder they were worked the better they steamed, as Tommy Charles proved on his boisterous 'demonstration run' with the 5.15 pm Derby slow. Being the first modern LMS locomotives designed to handle light duties, these '2MTs' were generally well received by crews, who particularly appreciated their ease of servicing.

er has never heard the wonderfully crisp, sharp exhaust of an Ivatt Class '2P', I can strongly recommend a visit to the Severn Valley Railway at Bridgnorth, Shropshire, where they operate a beautifully preserved example in the form of 46443. Even on the modest requirements of this line they sound more impressive than just about any other type and, when opened up, have a bark closely akin to that of a Bofors gun.

We executed a typical Tommy Charles New Street getaway, the little 5-foot driving wheels spinning viciously on a perfectly dry rail, touching the equivalent of 70 mph without moving an inch, while the exhaust rose to a shattering crescendo. Then with barely a pause to obtain adhesion we were off, thundering down through the tunnel, into the switchback at Proof House and on to Grand Junction, all the time accelerating furiously under full gear and regulator. I had witnessed some pretty vigorous getaways since being with Tom, but from a cold start this certainly took the biscuit, and the rapidity with which our wheels revolved only accentuated the fact. How so much steam could pass through cylinders measuring only $16\frac{1}{2}$ in x 24 in to make such a racket was truly remarkable, but pass through it did and the sound as we dived into the cutting leading down to Landor Street Junction was splendidly exhilarating.

Our first stop was Saltley, and as Tom shut off I quickly knocked on my injector and glanced at the pressure gauge, expecting the worst. However, I was pleasantly surprised to see that it was on the 190 mark, although having mortgaged the boiler somewhat, the water very nearly disappeared from sight under heavy braking for our brief halt.

There was just sufficient time to flash a few shovelsful of coal round the box before we were on our way once more. Tom was absolutely ruthless in his working of the engine, for with the regulator wide open we were past the West End before he deigned to touch the reversing screw, and even going through Bromford like a bat out of hell, the cut-off was no less than 40 per cent.

With only half a glass of water in this very small boiler, the reserves were slender indeed, and while using steam at this rate I decided that it would be tantamount to folly not to leave the injector on continuously, no matter what effect it had on the steam pressure. Furthermore, this fearsome blast was consuming fuel much too fast to use the fir-

ing-after-shut-off method I had employed on previous stopping passengers. I therefore opened the firedoors, flipped up the small bottom flap and sprayed slack and fines over this as fast as I could shovel. Judging by the trail of rich, black smoke we left billowing in the air far behind us, a certain amount must have passed through the tubes unburned, but most of it was obviously doing some good, for the pressure fell no lower than 175 prior to shutting off for Castle Bromwich.

Here I found and broke up some large lumps of coal that had become exposed, and with these I was able for the first time to build up a respectable back on the fire. The short sections between Water Orton, Coleshill, Whitacre and Kingsbury provided just the necessary amount of respite to allow both the water level and steam pressure to gradually attain their optimum readings. The blast generated by Tom's merciless hammering kept the fire at a really fierce white heat, so that by the time we left Kingsbury station she was ready for just about anything. This was just as well because with the perception of years of ingrained experience, Tom sensed that all was now as it should be and properly set about showing the world what an Ivatt Class '2' 'Mogul' could really do.

We departed from Tamworth dead on time for the longest non-stop stretch of our journey. Had one not known Tommy Charles, it might have been imagined that, having pulled back the lost 4 minutes, we could have taken things a little easier over the generally falling gradients to Burton-on-Trent. However, with water to be picked up over the troughs, our departure from Tamworth was as aggressive as anything Tom had achieved to date, and we thrashed away in a devastating blaze of smoke and sparks and sound. With the tank topped up, we started the descent down to Elford, first at 1 in 484 and then beyond Wiggington at 1 in 408, while all the time I was working like a madman, spraying in fuel over the bottom flap mechanical-stoker-fashion.

As our speed rapidly built up, Tom, sitting as phlegmatically as ever, gradually linked her up, keeping the game little engine at the absolute limit of her front-end capability, until at Wiggington he finally settled for rather more than 30 per cent. We had the benefit of a stiffish tail wind in addition to the favourable gradient, and from the lively, cavorting footplate it became obvious that No 6446 was now travelling a good deal quicker than her designers had envisaged. Approaching Elford the crisp, clear exhaust beats began to merge until they became one long, incredible, continuous harmonic roar. Never before had I heard an engine worked in such a manner, and indeed only once more in my life was I to experience the indescribable exhilaration that this ultimate effort produced.

Our headlong dash from Tamworth had lowered the boiler level to the halfway mark despite one injector being in continual use, but just before Tom closed the regulator for the inevitable signal checks at Branston Junction, I could not resist showing off by dispensing with that injector for a few moments. This allowed the needle to come right up to the red line, so the instant Tom shut down our safety valves lifted, indicating to the world in general, and the Derby men in particular, that we still had plenty of steam.

Not unexpectedly, we had gained so much time that we were held for several minutes in Burton station, but I welcomed this delay since it enabled me to fill the boiler, build up the fire and drag some coal forward, for I was now obliged to work with the tender doors open.

When our guard finally blew his whistle, Tom did not let up one little bit; on the contrary, he hammered up to Repton & Willington just as vigorously as on any previous section and knocked another couple of minutes off our schedule in the process. From here, which was our last stop before terminating at Derby, Tom really went mad. The adverse gradients, varying from 1 in 387 to 1 in 1861, did not allow the extraordinary high speeds

we attained at Elford to be repeated, but in terms of horsepower generated in the cylinders there could not have been much in it.

Being on top of the job and now able to run the fire down, I was well placed to observe cut-off settings, and with a wide open regulator and 200 lbs per sq in on the clock, never once did Tom link up beyond 40 per cent. I realised later that he was demonstrating just what could be done with the engine, and he could not have done so more effectively than over this last stretch for, with the benefit of a clear run, we screeched to a halt in Derby station exactly 3 minutes in front of time. Admittedly the schedule was not particularly exacting, but with a load of six coaches and an engine that was reputedly a poor steamer, it was no mean feat.

The climax to this tale occurred while we were still standing in the platform waiting to be detached. During the final run in I had been able to swill down the footplate and have a wash myself, so that on arrival everything was spick and span with a full head of steam and the water an inch from the top of the glass. Voices raised in argument caused me to look over the side, and I then found myself confronted by the two sets of Derby men we had taken up to New Street as passengers and who had, of course, travelled home on our train.

'There you are,' said one of the drivers, 'I told you it was the same engine.'

The other driver who had worked her down to Birmingham just goggled and, thrusting his head between the uprights, stared round the cab in stark disbelief.

For over a century Derby had a profound influence on railway practice both on the Midland Railway and the LMS. Modernised in the 'fifties, this view of platform 1 taken at 4.05 pm on 24 September 1957 presents an almost deserted picture. However, 1¹/₂ hours later it was invariably crowded with passengers when the Carlisle and Glasgow fitted freights from Water Orton sped boisterously through on their long journey north. Being 40 miles from Birmingham it was a convenient point to change crews, particularly on freight duties, where a round trip from Birmingham could represent more than eight hours' work in those days of severe congestion. However, it provided just sufficient distance for Tommy Charles to demonstrate how to work the 5.15 Derby slow on his epic run with the Ivatt '2MT' No 46446. *BR*

'Well they must have done something to her at Saltley,' he mumbled as he turned away, and off they all went, still arguing.

'What do you think they did to her at the shed?' I asked of Tom.

'Don't suppose they did anything,' he replied, with a sort of smirk. 'The trouble is, these chaps probably charge the firebox, and then when she doesn't steam too well, work her lighter and lighter until it's all choked up, instead of putting a bit of blast on the fire. I've always found that these "2s" like a good thrashing. Never did harm any engine.'

There comes a moment in every being's life when he or she hits an all-time high, achieving the ultimate peak performance that is never again exceeded. This applies to just about every form of human endeavour from playing golf to composing grand opera. So too, is it true of machines, particularly machines as full of human characteristics as steam locomotives, and when all the good variables come to work together for a while, then that is the time when records are broken. Should, by some strange chance, the appropriate human and

mechanical peaks be achieved at one and the same time, then wonders can occur. Such a wonder was brought about on the last occasion Tom and I worked the Bristol to Sheffield Night Mail together from Gloucester to Birmingham. That night belonged to Tommy Charles and *Galatea*, one of the 'Jubilee' 4-6-0s. This was their supreme effort, and I am forever grateful for the privilege of having witnessed it and indeed for having played some part in making it possible. My own peak in terms of sustained physical effort was yet to come, but without doubt this run with Tom was the most enthralling, fantastic performance I was ever to enjoy during my railway career, and it stands head and shoulders above all others, to be remembered and relived for the rest of my days.

The Mail was normally worked weekdays by Bristol men as far as Birmingham, where they were relieved by a Sheffield crew. However, on Sunday mornings it was routed the hard way, via Worcester, and this one turn fell into our own Link 2, Section B. Tom and I had taken a late-night passenger train down to Gloucester and, having completed a relaxed supper in the station

'Jubilee' *Galatea* seen here at York on 3 September 1957 apparently still in good condition two years after her magnificent effort with the Night Mail on the Lickey Incline. When first introduced in 1934 with a GWR-style low-degree superheater, 'Jubilees' gave poor performances. Urgent attention was given to rectifying this, and when *Galatea* was built at Crewe in 1936, changes to superheating, draughting, boiler and firebox had been incorporated, which then proved very successful.

messroom, were all ready for our coming exertions. We were due to relieve the Bristol crew at 2.50 am, but it was something like 3.05 when No 5699 *Galatea* trundled in with no fewer than 14 coaches behind her tender.

Even in the dim platform lights I could not fail to notice the gleaming green paintwork of a recent shopping, and my heart gave a little skip of joy, for nothing raised my spirits more quickly than having a 'new' engine.

'She's a beauty. Steams like a kettle even with the dampers shut,' were the only words spoken by the Bristol fireman as we scrambled aboard.

Having dumped my kit into the locker, I hastily climbed on to the back of the tender and thrust the water column bag into the tank. As the water flowed in I was able to take stock, and was delighted to find a tender full of best-quality hard coal, real black diamonds that had a ring when struck with a pick and could be split with absolute precision by a single blow. Moreover, it was already well broken and neatly trimmed, and since this required no further attention I descended to the footplate.

Unbesmirched paintwork, shining brass handles, polished copper pipes and white unscarred footboards heightened the impression of newness as I glanced at the gauges, which showed the water level an inch from the top and steam at 220 lbs per sq in. A short inspection of the long firebox revealed a perfect fire, well burned through and in the classical shape; everything was too faultless to be true.

Here then, was a freshly shopped '5X' in superb condition, with a perfect fire burning in her box, backed by a tender full of Grade 1 coal, hauling a heavy load over a demanding route containing one of the steepest banks in the country. The control of this juggernaut was in the competent hands of just about the most determined and fearless driver on British Railways, aided and abetted by a fireman whose enthusiasm for speed and power was only exceeded by his ability and willingness to work. With the added incentive of a late start and a desire to get home to bed as soon as possible, we had all the ingredients for an extraordinary run. Just how extraordinary it was to be I could not of course imagine at that stage, for although I was by

This view of the curve between Holmes and Rotherham was taken in 1951 from the footplate of No 45699 *Galatea* when hauling the 9.04 am Derby-York. Although the background is different and, in this instance, in daylight, the view reminds me of departing from Gloucester with this locomotive on the Bristol-Sheffield Night Mail when Tommy Charles really made the sparks fly. As with Gloucester, the relevant signals are first sighted from the fireman's side. *Pat Webb*

now well used to Tom's methods, we had not worked a '5X' together and I was very much looking forward to see what he would do with her.

After filling the tank I had sufficient time to fire ten quick shovelsful round the box before we received the 'right away' - 15 minutes late. Tom eased her out of the platform while I busied myself with sighting the signals that were first visible on my side.

'OK, Tom!' I yelled. 'We've got the back 'un.'

The blast sharpened and that beautiful double-three beat that the '5X' played with such virtuosity sounded like music in my ears as I bent to flash another quick ten round the box. The run to Cheltenham was not spectacular due to the numerous permanent way restrictions in operation on that section. However, it did serve to prove what a magnificent piece of machinery *Galatea* was. It also enabled me to get used to the longer firebox of the '5X', build up the fire and experiment with injector settings.

Having to draw up at Cheltenham because of our inordinately long train caused a further delay, but finally the whistle blew and we were off at last. A brief half slip and *Galatea* quickly accelerated the 420-odd tons out of the platform and down the favourable 1 in 196, her piercing blast crashing out into the still night air. Tom, as always, was determined to pull a bit back, but it was not to be - just yet. Down the 1 in 306 bank to Cleeve, *Galatea* started to get into her stride. Everything had that superbly taut feeling of new machinery, her 6 ft 9 in driving wheels turning so smoothly that one might have been in a 1st Class dining car. With no knocks, no rattles and no violent lurching, speed was deceptive and only the rapidity of our exhaust beat, giving six pulses to one revolution of the wheels, indicated our true pace. If only all locomotives were like this!

I was really enjoying the ride when I noticed that the distant for Cleeve was on and shouted across to Tom. A quiet oath indicated that he too had seen the signal at caution, and correctly guessed the cause. Since we were running 20 minutes late, a fitted freight had been turned out in front of us and we had caught it up. Needless to say, we were obliged to follow at a sedate pace until Abbotts Wood Junction, where we turned left to Worcester while the fitted carried straight on to Stoke Works Junction.

At last, with a clear road, Tom opened up to some purpose, attacking the rise to Norton Junction with great vigour, and then fairly rattling down the 2-mile descent of 1 in 363 to Wylds Lane. Slick work by the GPO at Worcester saved a few minutes, but knowing Tom this was where the real effort would commence, to try and haul back the massive deficit that had now accrued. I therefore strove to prepare for the coming onslaught, filling both firebox and boiler to their practical limit.

Without so much as a shudder No 5699 surged forward, and before our last coach had cleared the platform we were on full first valve and still in full gear. Out of Worcester Tunnel she stormed, the very epitome of power, blasting up the short incline before dipping down to Blackpole Sidings where, as our pace quickened, the double-three beat took on an even crisper note. Over the easy gradients to Droitwich Tom linked up to about 30 per cent and, although the distants were off, he kept her on a tight rein until past the Kidderminster line junction, and then he really let rip.

Over went the regulator, right across, at the same time dropping the screw to 40 per cent. Out through that sleepy little spa we thundered, making enough noise to wake the dead, accelerating hard before the 2-mile climb of 1 in 158 up to Stoke Works Junction. The fury of the exhaust had now risen to incredible proportions, and, taking a quick breather from what was by necessity almost continuous firing, I suddenly became aware of what appeared to be a miniature volcano erupting on top of the smokebox.

Despite the thickness of fire I had managed to maintain, a continual stream of blazing coal and cinders was being hurled high into the air by this enormous blast, and sparks could be clearly seen bouncing off even the last of our 14 coaches. '5Xs' had a reputation for throwing fire out, but here the whole countryside was illuminated by this firework display. *Galatea* certainly had the bit between her teeth now, and it was a wonderful sight to behold. So great was the evaporation rate due to this unmerciful hammering that the exhaust injector could not maintain the water level and I was obliged to supplement it with bursts from the live steam injector, but even so the needle never left the red line.

Since the tender doors had been open for some time now, I was having to drag coal forward, apart from breaking up numerous large lumps, so that I was never still for a second, but this was a small price to pay to witness such a fantastic spectacle. However, I was very thankful indeed of the brief respite afforded by our halt for bankers at Bromsgrove. This was my last chance to make sure everything was in perfect order before our assault on the 1 in 37.

With both injectors singing away, topping up the boiler and just keeping the safety valves closed, I was able to make my final preparations to the fire. A dozen accurately placed shovels brought the bed back to a perfect shape, preventing any tendency for holes to be dragged in that great incandescent mass.

The two Class '3FT' pilots had by now rolled into position and I leaned well out of the side window to listen for their distinctive 'crow' whistle while at the same time trying to regain some breath. The shrill call came clear and bell-like in the still night air. Before the echoes had died away, *Galatea* bellowed her reply and Tom heaved open the regulator.

Turning both injectors off, I took a quick look astern to see that all was well and noted a tall column of sparks indicating that at least one of the pilots was trying hard.

Acceleration over the first few yards through the station before we reached the base of the bank was impressive, but as we started the steep climb, No 5699 settled to a steady ponderous beat. Almost immediately I was obliged to put the exhaust injector on again and take up the shovel, for the regulator was now wide open, and although pressure showed a full 225, I had every intention of keeping it there.

Halfway up the bank *Galatea* was incredibly smooth at 50 per cent cut-off, showing as before no signs of shortness of breath. Then suddenly, without any warning, she checked in her stride, as if some giant hand was dragging her back. Somewhat baffled, I glanced enquiringly across at Tom who, as calm as ever, merely muttered a few oaths of vaguely nautical origin. Loosely translated, these meant that he did not think that the bankers were contributing much to the overall effort as of now. He was quite correct in this assumption; they were not contributing one iota, although of course we were quite unaware of the details at that time. It took a couple of weeks before the full story of what had occurred filtered along the grapevine.

Apparently the fireman of the leading banker, while commendably enthusiastic, was still very inexperienced and had filled the boiler to such a degree as to cause excessive priming. This, apart from forcing his driver to close the regulator, also led to a simultaneous failure of the ejectors and consequential, if only temporary, application of the brakes. Despite rapid action by the driver, our 14-coach train actually left the bankers (this was the snatch we felt) and it is to his lasting credit that he was able under such difficult circumstances to once again take up position at the rear of the train without so much as a shudder being transmitted to the occupants. Unfortunately the priming was so severe that we had almost reached Blackwell before he was again able to do any useful work.

A lesser driver than Tom would not have taken up the unfair challenge and would have shut down while waiting for the pilots to recover. A lesser locomotive than *Galatea* would probably have given him no other option, but by now Tom knew his engine and without further ado he wound the gear down to the full forward position of 75 per cent cut-off! Fortunately, all this happened in less time than it takes to tell, and our speed had only diminished slightly. With a wide open regulator and 225 lbs per sq in on the clock, the 'Jubilee' responded like the magnificent thoroughbred she was. The exhaust crashed out in an unbelievable volume of sound, reverberating across the hills like a gigantic, unending thunderclap. *Galatea* had the lot!

Imperceptibly at first, but increasing all the time, the exhaust beats gradually quickened. The impossible was happening; *Galatea* was actually accelerating this huge load of 420 tons up Lickey with practically no aid from the banking engines! The sight and sound of this wonderful locomotive in full song inspired me to redouble my own efforts, and I was already working like mad, but the reward was on the pressure gauge and the boiler was as full as it should be. With Blackwell in sight, she seemed to gallop forward in a triumphant blast of energy, while twin columns of sparks at the rear showed that the pilots were trying desperately to make up for their midbank lapse. We caught a fleeting glimpse of unlit platforms and a through freight waiting to descend and then we were away and heading for Barnt Green with the bankers already left far behind.

On the falling gradient of 1 in 290, Tom wound back the reversing screw, for our speed had by now increased to the point where, once again, single exhaust beats were barely discernible and an ever-increasing column of fire was rocketing from our chimney. Fascinated, I went over to Tom and glanced at the gear indicator, which was showing, as near as I could determine in the reflected glare of the fire, 45 per cent. Seeing me do this, he looked up enquiringly.

'She OK at that?' he shouted above the uproar, genuinely seeking my opinion, since after all I was responsible for generating the steam being consumed at such a colossal rate.

I bellowed my consent, adding in what I thought was a jocular manner, 'In fact, Tom, I should drop her down another half turn.'

Knowing him as I did, I should not have been surprised when he promptly complied with my suggestion, but I was surprised nevertheless, for not even Tom had thrashed an engine like this before.

Beyond Barnt Green and still on a favourable gradient, acceleration was truly fantastic. The continuous jet of fire now erupting from our chimney was bouncing and rattling along the full length of the train, lighting our progress with a glare that gave it the appearance of some phantom from the underworld.

I had built up an immense fire while climbing the bank and had continued firing heavily until Barnt Green. Provided that they enjoyed an uninterrupted run from Blackwell, the majority of express drivers shut off at the road bridge just beyond Halesowen Junction signal box. From here, since the track is still falling at 1 in 301, they coast down through Northfield and along to the severe curve at Kings Norton Station Junction some 2 miles distant, where speed has to be reduced to 35 mph. I calculated that even consuming fuel at this terrific rate, Galatea had more than enough in the box to last until Tom's own shut-off point, which was likely to be somewhat beyond that of the majority.

As we thundered down through the cutting towards Halesowen Junction I made no attempt to fire the engine. The mere act of opening the doors would have now admitted too much cold air, and although the water level was down to little more than half a glass, the pressure gauge was showing a full 225 lbs per sq in. We were living off our fat, so to speak, calling up the vast reserves of energy stored in the firebed and boiler, because Galatea's prodigious effort was far beyond normal continuous steaming rates. This was the wonder of steam locomotives; skilfully handled, they could perform at twice their accepted output for short-lived but crucial periods, and thereby work a miracle.

Tom did not even have his hand on the regulator as the road bridge flashed overhead, and he still made no movement to close it when the distant for Northfield loomed up. I had never seen anyone hold on past this point, so I decided to dispense with the exhaust injector for a few moments since I wanted to maintain full pressure right up until the end, for surely he must shut off soon.

Galatea's exhaust had by now risen to a terrible, shattering ferocity, a continual thunderous roar. Never in my life had I experienced such a vast cacophony of sound. She seemed to be tearing out her very heart and soul for us, and the emotion of this caused a lump to rise in my throat, particularly when I saw that the needle was still immovably fixed to that red line. How could she possibly stand up to this murderous treatment and continue to steam? It was incredible to think that '5XPs' were temperamental in that respect when first introduced, and quite amazing what a few years development could produce.

I caught a fleeting glimpse of the bobby's goggle-eyed face pressed hard against the windows of Northfield signal box and as I looked back along our train, as far as the eye could see a veritable blizzard of fire and flame swirled and danced around the coaches; I recall wondering if the firebars themselves would be the next to go. Never before or since had I travelled through Northfield at such a speed; in fact, this moment represented the ultimate I was to experience in terms of sheer speed and power while on the footplate.

Then, with a final tremendous volcanic blast, we roared under the road bridge beyond the station where the distants for Kings Norton could be sighted. Three seconds later, Tom slammed shut the regulator while at the same instant making a full brake application. This time the sparks and flames came from the wheels!

Quickly knocking on both injectors, I was now able to have a peep at the fire, or rather what was left of it. I had expected to find it somewhat run down, but I was frankly amazed to discover only a thin layer of white hot cinders with some firebars

'Jubilee' No 45676 *Codrington* having an easy time with the 4.40 pm New Street-Gloucester stopping train, seen here passing Bournville on the down line in October 1963. When travelling in the other direction, only 4 miles of mainly falling gradients separated New Street from Bournville, and when working passenger trains firemen were usually able to tidy the footplate ready for the relief crew. Eight years before, Tommy Charles still had the regulator wide open when *Galatea* thundered through here with 14 bogies, so it was a case of heavy firing all the way. T. J. Edgington

even showing through in places. Still, at least it was clean! It was a case of back to the shovel, and from Kings Norton I had the rare experience of firing in earnest as far as Five Ways.

As previously explained, a fireman can normally devote the last few minutes to dragging forward coal, cleaning down the footplate and making sure that everything is in apple-pie order for the relief crew on arrival at New Street. On this occasion it was a very hard fight indeed to keep enough fire in the box to get us to Five Ways, for we still had nearly 5 miles to travel and Tom meant to exploit every inch of it. As the brake blocks released from the wheels on the last coach rounding Kings Norton curve, so Tom heaved up the regulator to the horizontal again and *Galatea* once more shattered the calm with her explosive roar, swaying majestically through those numerous bends from Bournville to Selly Oak, and then on to Five Ways. Here at last she was allowed to coast down through the tunnels into New Street.

I could not help wondering as we finally rolled to a halt at the end of platform 7 just what Tom

might have achieved with a 'Scot' or a Stanier 4-6-2! However, the relief fireman's adverse comments regarding the amount of coal we had consumed quickly brought me back to reality. The poor chap would have to spend most of his time in the tender, so perhaps it was just as well that the 'Lizzies' were not allocated to our area.

I joined Tom as he made his way to the exit intent on catching our shed bus, which always contrived to meet the Mail. The faintest of smiles playing around his mouth was the only indication that he was well pleased at regaining so much time from Worcester, for we had arrived only 2 minutes adrift. On the other hand I was still all of a tremble with the excitement and exertions of the past hour or so. Out in the station yard our guard caught us up, and from his manner seemed to be somewhat agitated. We knew him well as a conscientious railwayman who enjoyed a great sense of achievement when his train made up lost time.

'Hey, chaps!' he cried, 'I've had the very dickens of a job with a young soldier who caused an almighty panic running up and down the train shouting that it was on fire and wanting to pull the cord. Took me all the way from Barnt Green to convince him that it was only sparks from the engine. Mind you,' he added in an aside to me, 'I rather thought that you were chucking out more than usual even for Tom.'

Two sets of our colleagues had also travelled home as passengers in the train, and one of the drivers who was in Link 2, Section 1 overheard this last remark.

'Chucking out more than usual!' he exclaimed. 'I've never heard such an infernal racket in all my life. We couldn't sleep a wink this side of Worcester. Thought it must be Tom, though - no one else drives like that. Whatever did you do for him to give you a rollicking like that - have a row at Gloucester?'

I dismissed the question with a light laugh, for he was obviously impressed but did not want to admit it. To have made a hard-bitten top passenger driver sit up and take notice when he dearly wanted to sleep was proof enough that Tom had produced an exceptional performance. What a pity a dynamometer car had not been attached, or even a skilled observer to take timings, because I am pretty sure that some interesting figures would have been recorded. As it is, I have only got my memories, which fortunately are still as vivid as on the day it happened.

Some while before Tom and I parted company it became obvious from the roster sheets that promotion was going ahead at such a rate that I would miss the Top Passenger Link and go straight into Group 1. This was in many ways a disappointment, for I had been looking forward to working the Birmingham-Bristol and Birmingham-Sheffield expresses, particularly since most of these were allocated '5XPs'. On the other hand, to become a top link fireman had for many years past been my main ambition, and to be perfectly honest, after the scintillating performances Tom achieved almost daily, I felt that even the Top Passenger Link would prove something of an anti-climax. After all, I knew of no other driver who would consistently hammer engines in the Tommy Charles manner, and I preferred to leave my memories of passenger work unsullied by lesser feats.

Furthermore, in November 1955 I had been married, and could well use the fatter pay packets that went hand in glove with the greater percentage of night work and overtime to be found on freight duties. In addition, I had purchased a powerful new sports motor cycle, which provided all the speed and excitement one could wish for. I was never happier than when riding this as far and as fast as possible, and did so at every opportunity. With this alternative expression of power and speed so freely available, I began to realise that there was more to being an engine driver than merely thrashing a locomotive to its limit just to see what it could do. Moreover joining the elite in Group 1 only served to strengthen this realisation and bring home the fact that in the not too distant future I would be required to pass out as a driver myself.

Bearing this sobering thought in mind, I decided that I should now cease to treat work as an exciting game and buckle down to the task of acquiring the vast amount of knowledge and technique necessary to be successful in that very exacting role. I could not possibly have been more fortunate in this respect, for when in May I fervently scanned the rosters, every bit as nervous and excited as when I was a Passed Cleaner, I discovered that destiny had placed me in Section D, the Long Marston link, with none other than Percy ('Piggy') Trotter.

2
THE LONG MARSTON LINK

When it became generally known that I was to be matched with Percy Trotter, just about every driver and at least half the firemen of Saltley offered their commiserations at my misfortune.

The picture painted was not a rosy one - indeed, it was downright daunting if even half the descriptions of his character were to be believed. He was supposedly a self-opinionated, garrulous tyrant who spent most of his time arguing with everyone about everything, and amused himself in between sessions by telling his fireman in plain language just how incompetent his every action proved him to be.

To be forewarned is to be forearmed, and having taken much of this well-intentioned advice with a pinch of salt, I resolved to be the essence of happy geniality, which I had found in the past proved effective in deflecting even the most vicious verbal lashes, and to follow his wishes whenever possible, for after all Percy was to be my chief for a full 12 months. Obviously I would now have to be most punctilious in my work, and the week prior to our first meeting I spent many hours with Rule Book and *Questions for Enginemen* in my hand, brushing up on matters I had neglected during the last hectic year.

My confidence was running pretty high when I booked on for our first turn together. Providentially it was the lowliest job in the link, being no more exacting than a Kingsbury tripper, slipped in to provide a rest week from the hurly-burly of the other 11. Despite the fact that I had arrived a quarter of an hour before time, Percy had booked on some 15 minutes previously and was already hard at work preparing our engine, Class '4F' No 4209 stabled in No 2 shed. I soon discovered that it was his practice to arrive anything up to an hour before he was booked. That he did so was partly out of necessity, since the Corporation bus service did not always obligingly key in with our train times, but mainly because the official preparation time allowed was insufficient for his purposes. His oiling was the most comprehensive of any driver I have ever known, and his inspection so meticulous that only a portable X-ray unit might have revealed more.

It was therefore in the hot, smoky interior of No 2 shed, under the shadow of No 4209, that I first confronted 'Piggy' Trotter. There was no need for me to ask his name, for apart from obviously being engaged in oiling the engine, his descriptive nickname fitted perfectly. He was a biggish man, some 5 ft 11 in tall and about two-thirds of that measurement around the waist. Come to think of it, most of his 16-odd stone seemed to be distributed around those swollen equatorial regions, since his body ballooned progressively outwards, then tapered down to inordinately slim ankles, accentuated by the wearing of bicycle clips. These lower limbs were terminated by small feet that appeared too tiny to support the vast bulk above. As a matter of fact, his ankles were rather on the weak side and caused Percy to hobble about in a most ungainly manner at times.

His fleshy face was an unhealthy purplish hue, indicating high blood pressure and a liking for a pint, and this colour spread down over double chins sporting a two-day grey stubble to the top of his chest, which was revealed by an old-fashioned, open necked collarless shirt worn summer and winter irrespective of prevailing weather conditions. I later found that Percy rarely felt the cold and his one and only concession to a freezing day was the donning of an old silk scarf knotted loosely around his ample throat.

A thin-lipped slit of a mouth, permanently pulled down at the corners, gave him an unfortunate sneering expression, even when he was not actually sneering, and small light blue eyes set rather deep and close together did nothing to improve matters. Short, sparse grey hair combed into a divided fringe, Oliver Hardy fashion, completed one of nature's less aesthetic pieces of handiwork. I could see at a glance how he might have come by his nickname, for there was no denying the strong resemblance to an overfed porker, but from what I had been told, the obdurate stubbornness of his character had also considerably influenced the choice of phrase.

As I rounded the front of our engine, Percy had just topped up the feeder he was holding in his right hand and he acknowledged my cheery greeting with an abrupt nod. Depositing the feeder on the framing, he wiped his sweating forehead with the back of his hand, adding another grease smudge to the half-dozen already there, then with over-elaborate movements he pulled out a large pocket watch that he held at arm's length, perusing it by squinting down his nose. I had never seen a chap lean so far back from the hips as Percy. It was an ingrained habit of his, derived no doubt from the necessity of adjusting his centre of gravity to counterbalance the weight of his paunch; since this also tilted his head back, it only served to emphasise the built-in sneer. This study of the time was, I fancy, engineered to make me feel guilty for arriving late, and I did, until I realised that I was still 15 minutes early.

'I've drawn the tools for you, but we are low on fire and steam, and the sandboxes need filling,' he said evenly enough, then, picking up the feeder, turned to carry on with the oiling.

'Dash it,' I thought, for I had wanted to investigate these things for myself, and mentally made a note to book on even earlier tomorrow.

Nothing more was said, and by working at the double I managed to complete all my tasks, even to the extent of adding limestone to the fire, in good time. We tested everything that could be tested before moving on to the table, and working strictly to the book I preceded him out of the shed and walked in the prescribed manner to the water column. Here, Percy left me to clean up while he went over to the amenity block to mash the tea before ringing off.

I thought that I had made a pretty good job of it, trimming the coal and neatly stowing our fire irons, apart from removing every trace of dust and soot from the footplate. However, when Percy returned, we still had to wait a further 5 minutes before departing, and during this time he was able to conduct a quick inspection that revealed an omission on my part. He did not say it in so many words, merely observing that he could not understand how enginemen could work with dirty cab windows and spectacle glasses. Ours were slightly smutty! I should not have allowed this to bother me, since it was generally understood that drivers cleaned their own, but in future I felt obliged to clean all glasses at the first opportunity.

Having collected our guard we duly arrived at Bromford after a trip that was notable for the higher than normal speeds that were usually attained by a light engine on the goods line.

The reader may recall that a Kingsbury trip involved nothing more than taking a train of empties from Bromford to Kingsbury Colliery and returning to Washwood Heath with a loaded coal train. However, Percy managed to make it look like the most important job at Saltley, and took off from Bromford as if he was driving the up express, setting the couplings clanking and the rust flying with all the delicacy and finesse of a medieval battering ram.

Not that this bothered me much, for had I not just completed a year with the most energetic passenger driver on the Region? But driving loose-coupled trains with 30 feet of slack between the engine and the brake-van requires an entirely different approach, and my sensitive soul felt every snatch and bump transmitted to that poor, long-suffering guard. Moreover, I rightly deduced that pointing this out to a man of Percy's character would only have incited him to go the opposite way and be more violent than ever. In fact, I soon learned that he was an ideal subject upon which to apply reversed psychology, and with practice found that he could be made quite pliant within certain limits - but all this took time, of course.

In common with most trip jobs we had a lot of free time on our hands and Percy, never an idle man, lost no time in plumbing the extent of my railway knowledge both practical and theoretical and, needless to say, soon exposed some extensive gaps. There was no question that he knew his stuff, for I never did meet his equal in terms of engine matters, but it was the manner in which he delivered his lectures that left so much to be desired, and I could readily appreciate why so many of his firemen took umbrage and promptly requested a transfer. It was common knowledge that he went through more firemen in the course of a year than any other driver at Saltley, but I was determined to retain my sangfroid no matter what malediction was hurled at me.

Nevertheless, my self-control was sorely tried on numerous occasions in those early days, and more than once I came very near to beaning him with the coalpick in thought, even if not in action. And so commenced a most memorable year, which, despite starting out on a somewhat shaky and strained footing, developed to become not only one in which I learned more about engines than in the previous six, but one that proved both exciting and enjoyable.

Once I had become used to Percy's congenital peculiarities, and learned to deal with them, I found I was not only able to live with him, but actually derived pleasure from his company. It may possibly be cruel to laugh at other people's weaknesses, but Percy's fiery temper, the arguments he inevitably became embroiled in, and the histrionic attitudes he struck while so doing, provided me with endless hours of entertainment, and after all, who could fail to be amused at the sight of a 57-year-old, 16-stone driver, purple in the face and frothing at the mouth, hopping up and down in a temper tantrum like a brat in a kindergarten.

I might well be accused at this point of only describing Percy Trotter's worst features, but this was the side of his character one noticed on first acquaintance. His more endearing qualities and, let there be no mistake, he possessed a great many, were deeper beneath the surface and only came to light after a longer and more intimate association. Over the course of the next few months he proved not only to be a vast fund of knowledge, but a meticulous if somewhat brutal teacher, and a loyal and good friend who would toil tirelessly for you if he found you to be worth your salt.

From that very first week he laid his cards firmly on the table, asking point-blank whether I intended to become a driver and, if so, was I willing to take instruction from him? Since my answer was in the affirmative my education was in his hands, and when he found that I was an attentive pupil, his enthusiasm to teach increased so that in a very

short space of time the whole thing snowballed. No day passed without some aspect of engine management or section of the Rule Book being laid bare, and on frequent occasions my head swam with the effort of trying to grasp this enormous input of information.

Gradually Percy's attitude changed and a bond of mutual trust developed to the point where I felt he sometimes regarded me as a slightly wayward son, and I for my part looked upon him as a sort of father figure, at least as far as railway affairs were concerned. In keeping with most human relationships we had our ups and downs. For one thing he would never praise me to my face, no matter how well I had accomplished a task. On the contrary, he seemed to find faults everywhere, even in matters outside railway work. For example, he continually derided my love of motor cycling and the fact that I possessed such a powerful machine.

'You'll break your silly neck on that contraption,' he would say, and I sincerely believed that he meant it until one day I overheard him boasting to a crowd of chaps in the messroom. 'My mate has the fastest motor cycle there is, and he must be a marvellous rider to handle it at over 100 mph.' (Actually this rose to 120 mph before the ensuing argument finished.)

I could barely believe my ears, but I later discovered that this was Percy! He would spend all day being as provocatively uncomplimentary as possible to you, then the moment your back was turned he would praise you to the hilt, usually throwing in a few imagined and embarrassing extras for good measure, the exact opposite of how the majority of human beings behave, but in many ways, may I venture to presume, more preferable.

My sense of humour was the main problem on my side for he had no sense of humour at all. He took everything said at face value, a fact that I kept forgetting, and the worst instance of this caused quite a scene one night in the shed. On the whole, though, we worked far better as a team than I had at first imagined possible, and even then there were some very pleasant surprises in store for me.

In general, Group 1 jobs not unnaturally contained the cream of the work at Saltley. Each link within the group seemed to concentrate on a particular area, and in the case of Section D we mainly covered all points west as far as Gloucester. However, so that drivers could retain a fairly comprehensive route card, we also had two jobs to Derby and one to Burton, but the most interesting turn was the one that gave the link its name - 'The Long Marston'. This was unique at Saltley since it involved working over Great Western metals, and, of course, here Midland Region's pride was at stake, so that every effort was made not only to run to time, but to show the Western just what a clever lot of fellows we were.

As with all other links, it required 12 weeks to cover all the jobs, and it was when we came round to the Kingsbury trip turn again that I received a pleasant surprise. By now I had fallen into the habit of arriving just about as early as Percy, and on Monday morning I was more than a little staggered when he suddenly announced that we would swop places.

'You are the driver this week,' he said, 'so get oiling. I'll look after the fireman's work.'

I must admit that until then I had considered him to be the last person at Saltley willing to take up a shovel, but there it was, and the opportunity was too good to miss. Right from the start he made it quite clear that I was not to do any of the fireman's jobs, and unless a crisis developed he did not expect to have to do any of mine. Fortunately, being more slender and agile than he, I was able to get through the oiling in good time, even though I lubricated every moving part in sight. Of course, that wasn't quite good enough for Percy, for I had put too much on here and not enough there, but all in all he wasn't hypercritical, being far too occupied with the, for him, strenuous firing duties. These he performed well enough for me to compliment him on his expertise, and I confirmed that I was prepared to take him anywhere with me!

It was grand to feel the response of an engine beneath my hands again, and although I had hardly touched a regulator for a year, by the time we had reached Bromford driving had become instinctive once more. Stan Jones, our little cockney guard, came up and advised Percy of our load just before we departed.

'Tell him,' said Percy, airily waving a hand in my direction. 'He's the driver.'

Stan, who closely resembled a cheeky budgerigar, and who tolerated the violence of Percy's driving with resigned good humour, stared incredulously for a moment, uttered the single word 'Strewth!', then hopped away. His expression left me with the impression that while he did not

exactly approve, at least he thought that I could not possibly be much worse than Percy.

On receiving the 'right away', I eased gently out of the siding. The memories of hours of shunting at Water Orton came flooding back, and I was pleased to find that I was able to get the brake moving with hardly a judder.

'You don't have to be as gentle as that,' cried Percy derisively. 'They're not made of glass'.

At first my driving came in for a lot of criticism; I was always going either too slow or too fast, or shutting off too early, but gradually as the week wore on things improved to the point where only my starts were at fault. These, I am afraid, remained a bone of contention between us for as long as we were together, for my principal aim when driving was to give the guard as smooth a ride as possible. The more he tried to make me liven these up, the more gentle I became, and the guards highlighted this difference in our styles on jobs when we drove on alternate days. Most of them, out of sheer devilment, liked to rile Percy on every conceivable occasion, and a typical ploy would be to ask who was driving that day.

'He is,' he would say, as gullible as ever.

'Oh in that case,' replied the guard, 'it will be safe to make my tea now.'

This brought forth the desired reaction from Percy, who would invariably swell up, turn purple, spit profanities at them until out of earshot, then give them a hell of a ride the next day. However, they must have thought it well worthwhile, although for my part I dearly wished they would desist, because as may well be imagined, he vented his temper on the only person close at hand - yours truly.

As my confidence grew I was allowed to drive for longer distances on the less demanding road jobs such as the Class B freight to Burton, and the pick-up to Droitwich. However, fitted freights, particularly the westbound ones, were more than Percy could physically cope with, although he did on occasions let me take over for a short stretch while he indulged his appetite. Life therefore became very pleasantly interesting despite his being such an exacting task-master, and my all-round knowledge and skill developed apace under his guidance.

After a few weeks two unusual features of his character became very apparent. One was that he could not tolerate overtime at any price, and his

As Percy was no doubt well aware, on joining an engine a fireman's prime task was to build up the firebed. In the interests of safety and cleanliness it was policy to use the inevitable spillage on the footplate first. The experienced fireman, though, would first close the cab doors, since when folded as shown they were a constant danger to his knuckles while swinging the shovel.

whole time while on duty was dedicated to finishing as early as possible. He would do battle with both the yard staff and the Control to achieve this end, and drive like the wind to obtain and keep in an earlier path if at all feasible. Fortunately for him, the Control staff knew that he would not delay a more important following train, and frequently agreed to an unofficial rearrangement of the working timetable.

The other feature was that he was never happier than when he had a spanner in his hand, and I often wondered if his true vocation was really that of a fitter. He simply loved to take things apart and repair them, and rarely a day passed without some item on the engine not functioning to his satisfaction was stripped down. Not that he always effected an improvement; on the contrary, occasionally he made matters a good deal worse, because no matter how many times one takes down and reassembles a defective part, it still remains defective. However, I never failed to be amazed at the magnitude of some of the jobs he

tackled, armed with no more equipment than the four regulation spanners, a coalpick, a few odd pieces of wire and his own pair of pliers. During the year I was with him, he accomplished while on the road just about every repair imaginable short of a major refit, but sometimes his enthusiasm had its embarrassing consequences.

I well recall one instance when working a Class B to Burton. I was driving that day and as was often the case we were backed into the loop at Wilncote out of the way of some faster traffic. We had a '4F' and the regulator handle was a very loose fit on its spindle, making delicate control difficult because of the excessive amount of free play.

'Right,' said Percy as we came to a standstill in the loop, 'we won't move until after the two fitteds and the slow, so that gives me half an hour to fix that dratted thing. I'll take the regulator off and make up a shim. Just sit there and watch.'

Perched up on the narrow driver's seat over the reversing screw, I watched him struggle with the securing nut, which over the years had lost its original hexagonal shape and was now virtually round. Eventually he succeeded, after much sweating and cursing, and he was hammering a large washer, procured from the vast collection of junk carried in his jacket pockets for just such an event, into a suitable shape for the shim, when the first fitted rattled past.

I had just wistfully watched it recede into the distance when I suddenly heard the familiar clunk of points being pulled over, followed by the clang of a signal arm. Looking out, I saw that we had indeed got the road and, by way of reflex, automatically kicked the taps shut, opened the small ejector and groped for the regulator handle. Not finding it in its usual place caused me to search around, then realisation dawned as I took in the boiler front bereft of that most important fitting; Percy of course, had only just removed it. With the distants now off as well, I regarded the regulator handle reposing peacefully across the fireman's seat.

'Percy, we've got to go now,' I called as gently as possible, since I did not wish to startle him too much.

'Eh?' he replied, not bothering to look round for he was enjoyingly engrossed in belting the daylights out of that inoffensive washer with the coalpick, using the handbrake handle as an anvil.

'We've got to go now,' I repeated, more insistently this time. 'Can I have the regulator back please?'

He stared first at me, then at the signal, then back to me, his jowls wobbling, and visibly turning bright vermilion as he strove to find suitable words.

'We can't,' he stuttered. 'Only one fitted has gone. What does that bloody idiot think he's playing at?'

Crossing over to my side he hopped up and down, shaking his fist in the direction of the signal box as if by so doing he could reverse the course of events. In the meantime the bobby, obviously thinking that we had gone to sleep, started rattling the signal arm violently. Percy, finally realising that we now had no choice,

Because the Long Marston Class A freight was run on Great Western metals it carried a prestige out of all proportion to the actual importance of the train. Usually the best available '8F' was allocated just to ensure that the Midland flag was kept flying high. Percy Trotter's boisterous driving was so well known to the Western Control that he was often allowed a path in front of their vacuum-braked trains. Class '8F' No 48414 is seen here at Hatton with a Class A mixed freight. *T. J. Edgington*

slammed the regulator handle back on to its spindle, and as soon as it was in place I tried to open the valve. Unfortunately it was now so sloppy that at first I could gain no purchase, but with Percy's penknife acting as a temporary shim I managed to make a start that, unfortunately for the guard, was far from gentle. Some frantic spanner work over the next few hundred yards was called for, but with a clear road the crisis passed without further mishap. Needless to say, Percy never had a regulator handle off again while I was with him.

The real highlight of the link, though, was without doubt the Long Marston job. This was a Class A mixed freight turn which, because it was run over foreign metals, carried a prestige out of all proportion to the actual importance of the train. We were allocated a Class '8F', usually the best available, and ran from Washwood Heath Junction on to the Western via Bordesley Junction and through to Long Marston, the massive Ministry of Defence establishment, some 5 miles south-west of Stratford-upon-Avon. The route was a picturesque but precipitous one and, since we were mixed in with the Great Western vacuum trains, we had to really go, for there was hell to pay if one should happen to be delayed. As it happened, Percy had made his mark on the Western in much the same way as he had on his own native Region, and frequently we were turned out in front of their fitteds, since it was generally recognised that they were more likely to stop us than we would stop them. The Western men called him 'Peggy', which of course was a corruption of 'Piggy', but all the signalmen knew when he was driving, and had no hesitation in providing a path, no matter how slim the timings. From my own point of view, further interest was added because the route passed right by the house in which I was born, and travelling over the very rails upon which I had seen my first locomotive provided an enormous thrill.

In deference to my lack of knowledge of the road and also because we had only been together for four weeks, Percy did not drive with his customary enterprise the first time we worked the job, but on the second occasion he really cut loose. On the Friday of that week it was quite a memorable trip. We had No 8669, and although she had just about lost her post-shopping sheen, that crisp, taut feeling of newness was still there. The engine had been prepared for us, but as usual we booked on early enough to give it a thorough check and clean before leaving the shed. Our initial favourable impression was confirmed during the quick romp down to Washwood Heath, and when we backed on to our train the guard advised us that we had 20 load of coal next to the engine, and a further 28 wagons and vans behind that.

Everything else waited until the Long Marston had been got away, and within minutes we were being called out of the siding. As the week had progressed Percy's driving had become more inspired, and on this particular day, as if sensing the quality and eagerness of our steed, he set off in his best 'Scotch Express' style. I suppose on the engine we were already doing something like 10 or 15 mph when the brake-van jerked into motion, and with a clear road we were soon snorting past the pilot sidings, whistling for a banker as we did so. Although only travelling under Class A lights, the Long Marston was treated like a crack fitted, and Percy took full advantage of the situation as the distants came off in front of us.

I felt sorry for the poor pilot, though; he had to go like a dingbat to even catch up at Duddeston Road, and with 50 per cent cut-off at full first valve, we went past the loco making enough racket to cause a good many of our colleagues to stand and stare. Percy had meant to take a charge at the bank, and charge it he did. At Landor Street Junction the regulator was right across and we simply galloped up the section from St Andrews, barely noticing the 1 in 62. Shutting off at the Coventry Road overbridge, he allowed our impetus to carry us into Bordesley, where fortuitously the signal was off, for I am quite certain we would never have stopped had it not been.

A quick clanking snake through the sidings, then out on to the slow, where, with distants off, he opened up again. I always found this stretch a little tricky because, with six parallel roads, sidings at either side, and criss-crossed by numerous tracks, the signalling system on first acquaintance seemed rather complex and confusing. However, I always enjoyed passing under the Golden Hillock Road bridge at Small Heath, since it brought back nostalgic memories of spending many happy, if somewhat windswept, hours standing on that very bridge watching the pride of the Western go by.

From here we had to take things fairly gently, for after progressive signal checks we were brought to a halt at Tyseley South Junction, but I normally used this stretch to build up the fire for the 7-mile haul up to Earlswood Lakes, and today was no exception. A local passenger train was the culprit, but as soon as this had cleared we had the 'back 'uns' (distants) and Percy, begrudging the 3 minutes lost time, attacked the ensuing 1 in 200 with more than customary vigour. Full first valve and 60 per cent cut-off sufficed to get us nicely on the move, then, as the gradient eased to 1 in 502, so he wound back the screw to 45 per cent. Keeping her at this we fairly hammered up through Hall Green station, then on to the level stretch of line that ran near to the house where I was born. Here I always made a practice of crossing over to Percy's side to see the old homestead and wave to a small group of boys who inevitably gathered at the lineside fence there. It was hard to believe that some twenty years earlier our positions had been reversed and it was then I who was waving to the engine crews.

Over this short level section our speed built up impressively, but almost immediately the bank rose again at 1 in 500, steepening to 1 in 159 at Yardley Wood station, and this not unnaturally checked our pace. However, Percy was in no mood to allow No 8669 to find her own speed, and promptly compensated by lengthening the cut-off. Following a short level stretch approaching Shirley the gradient is less severe at 1 in 264, but still sufficient to keep me very busy indeed with the shovel.

Having now left Birmingham's suburbs behind, the scenery progressively improved and, as we climbed higher, opened out to give some really splendid views of extensive verdant woods, highlighted by the strong summer sunshine. At Whitlocks End Halt, which consisted only of a few well-weathered planks standing on rather rickety looking piles at the side of the track, I was able to take things a little easier, for with only 2 miles to the Lake's summit, I could now gradually run down the fire in anticipation of the 10-mile-long descent to Bearley West Junction.

The Long Marston link also enjoyed a number of freight turns to Gloucester, but because Percy never liked over-time he tended to run loose-coupled trains at rather higher speeds than the timetable compilers had envisaged. With most '4Fs' this often resulted in both me and the engine being a little short of breath at times. Built at Horwich in 1928, No 44466 is seen passing through Ashchurch station on a Washwood Heath to Barnwood Class B freight in 1957. *Pat Webb*

No 8669 was steaming so well that despite a very spirited attack on the final 1 in 230 section, we rolled over the top with rather more steam and water in the boiler than I had intended, but now I was able to enjoy a lengthy rest with a well-earned lid of tea and a cigarette. The descent commences at 1 in 281, soon increasing to 1 in 181, then from the short (176 yards) Wood End Tunnel there follows an uninterrupted 4½-mile drop of 1 in 150. Obviously with a loose-coupled train of this size a good deal of heavy braking was called for, and it was customary to apply the brakes on both the tender and brake-van and leave them thus for most of the way. With well-nigh perfect visibility, Percy let them run somewhat more than usual and we were soon rattling along as fast as any fitted. This had me a little worried at times, since apart from the fact that I considered we were sailing a bit close to the wind if ever we were required to stop, the wildly cavorting footplate kept spilling my tea.

Looking along the train during that hectic descent was fascinating - and for the guard I would have thought a frightening spectacle. A great fog of dust streamed aft from the rapidly moving vehicles, completely obscuring the brake-van at times. Had there been a hot axlebox, and this was a not infrequent occurrence when Percy was at the helm, neither I nor the guard would ever have known, while the wagons themselves were swaying and bucking so much that half the train appeared to be using the up line.

The distant for Henley-in-Arden being on, a full application of the steam brake was needed for the best part of a mile, and indicated that we had caught something up. We were in fact checked over the next 4 miles to Bearley West Junction, where once more the road cleared. Aggrieved at being delayed, Percy blasted No 8669 up the short bank to Wilmcote station where he was obliged to shut off for the sharp 1 in 75 drop down towards Stratford-upon-Avon East. Care had to be taken on the approach here over the switchback-like curved humps, but then, with the distants off, he absolutely ripped down the 1 in 92 descent into Stratford station at a higher speed than ever before.

The station is built on quite a severe right-hand curve, and taking 20 well-filled coal wagons through at that pace caused the inevitable to happen. Centrifugal force momentarily overcame gravity, and about 2 tons of best cobbles were suddenly strewn in an untidy trail along the full length of the platform. We were often called upon to supply unofficially our much-prized hard coal to Western stations and signal boxes, since their own native Welsh coal was difficult to burn in ordinary fires, but this unintended display of generosity was quite ludicrous.

Completely unaware of the commotion we had caused, Percy tore on over the Evesham Road Crossing, past the racecourse and out to our destination, now only some 5 miles distant. Just beyond the racecourse and right alongside the up track there was a platelayers hut, and as we roared by half a dozen of those 'stalwarts of the length' gave us a friendly wave and indicated by simple sign-language that they would be much obliged if we dropped then some coal. However, such was our speed then that it was quite impossible, but Percy, by dint of equally simple sign-language, made it clear that we would do so on our return trip.

'It pays to keep in with the natives,' he declared. 'Might want a favour some time.'

No wonder he had plenty of friends on the Western, for he went out of his way to 'butter up' signalmen with these gifts of black manna every day.

Once our train was safely deposited at Long Marston, we had to turn our '8F', and this was effected by running down to the triangle at Honeybourne, a round trip of about 8 miles. On occasions this operation took an inordinately long time, but Percy never seemed to mind too much, providing that we departed with our train of empty wagons on schedule. Today we were fortunate and accomplished the exercise quickly enough to enjoy a relaxing hour over our lunch, but all too soon it was time to prepare for the much tougher ordeal of the return trip. Although it involved considerably more physical effort on my part, I enjoyed this latter half of the turn better than the outward run, mainly, I think, because of the challenge presented by 16 miles of virtually continuous uphill slogging. It paid handsomely to ensure that everything was in good order before leaving, and I always made a practice of going into the tender to break up coal and drag it forward if necessary.

We had quite a lot of slack and fines in that day's mixture and I wanted to extricate as many lumps as possible so as to first build up a hand-picked firebed. I had nearly completed this task to my satisfaction when I discovered an enormous lump as big as a medium-sized coffin and weighing fully 2 hundredweights. With some difficulty I dragged it down on to the footplate with the intention of breaking it up and using the fragments to complete my preparations. With the coalpick poised above my head, Percy stopped the downward swing in the nick of time.

'Don't smash it up mate, that's just the thing for those platelayers by the racecourse.'

It was of course logical and practical to deposit our gift in one large piece rather than a shower of small ones, which bounced and ran all over the place and took a devil of a job to find.

'OK, Percy,' I replied, 'but you will have to tell me when - it's as much as I can do to move the bally thing, let alone see the platelayers hut from the middle of the cab.'

With more optimism than I felt was appropriate Percy continued, 'We'll drop it 15 yards from the hut on the approach side - there's a clear patch there. The other side is too grassy, and in any case the embankment is steeper.'

With the details thus arranged, I finished off building up the fire, then gave the footplate a good clean down, working over and around that great ebony monster.

Shortly afterwards we departed and over the easy gradients from Long Marston we soon had our train of 50 empty wagons rattling along at a good pace with only a whiff of steam and 25 per cent cut-off. I used this 5-mile stretch of light working to allow the fire to burn through thoroughly and get everything warmed up before the real hard slog started the other side of Stratford.

I suppose we were doing something between 30 and 40 mph when the racecourse came into view, and I decided it was high time that I moved the huge lump of coal into position for a quick heave over the side. It was far too heavy to slide on its side out between the uprights, and I therefore poised it on one end so that merely a light push at the top would suffice to send it toppling into space. In good time I checked clearances and found that it would just pass between the handrails with about a quarter of an inch to spare. With the hut just in sight I heaved the great lump upright and by a wiggling action manoeuvred it right up to the edge of the gyrating fallplate where with a struggle I just managed to balance it.

'Are you ready?' shouted Percy when the rapidly approaching hut was about 100 yards away.

'When you say the word,' I bellowed in reply, trying to keep my eye on the target over his shoulder and at the same time inching the lump even nearer the edge. As the point of release came up I experimentally pushed the 'coffin' between the uprights to make sure that it would fall cleanly when the time arrived. To my horror it stuck solid when halfway through - the left-hand curve we were now on had caused the tender and engine handrails to close just that fraction of an inch, trapping the lump firmly between them. Desperately I pushed and heaved, but to no avail - the thing was absolutely immovable. With all the aplomb of an RAF bomb-aimer, Percy began his countdown.

'Stand by.'

I pushed and heaved harder than ever, the coal groaning and chaffing in its grip of steel.

'Ready. . . go!'

It was all very well Percy doing his 'bombs away' routine, but the damned thing gave all the appearance of becoming a permanent fixture on No 8669. Percy sensed that something was amiss and looked round.

'Go on then, push it off!' he shrieked, his voice rising a couple of octaves as he absorbed my predicament. Whether it was Percy's excitement or just my normal mental processes eliminating other possibilities, but inspiration suddenly struck and, holding on to the waterscoop handle for balance, I delivered a flying kick to the top of the lump Kung Fu-fashion. With a loud crack of splintering coal, the massive chunk disappeared over the side with me very nearly following it.

Anxious to see what happened to the missile, I leaped to the side and was just in time to observe its leading end strike a patch of gravel 5 yards in front of the hut. In a cloud of flying debris, it took off again, and following a low parabolic trajectory very reminiscent of one of Dr Barnes Wallis's bouncing bombs of 'Dam Busters' fame, its torpedo-like end struck the front wall of the shack about 3 feet above ground level.

A solid 2-hundredweight lump of coal travelling at some 50 feet per second has a fair bit of energy, and it penetrated those stout timbers with the ease of a cannon ball and a resounding crash that could be clearly heard above the rumpus on the footplate. Fifty years of accumulated soot and dirt were suddenly shaken free from that aged building and its outline became momentarily obscured by a black haze. By now we had travelled to the far end of the building and were therefore nicely positioned to witness the door, torn from its hinges, burst outwards and go cartwheeling down the embankment. This was quickly followed by the still intact lump of coal, wearing the mangled remains of what a few seconds before must have been a smart, deal mess table.

There was a stunned silence on the footplate for a moment, then Percy threw an apoplectic fit, already feeling the hangman's noose tightening around his throat. Luckily 200 yards further on we spotted the gang of platelayers, and Percy, now somewhat red in the face, indicated to them that we had dropped off the coal as requested.

With grateful waves they disappeared into the distance, but whether they would be quite so happy when they revisited the scene of demolition was a matter of some conjecture. Funnily enough, although we expected to be called upon to answer for our sins, we never heard any more of the incident nor, for that matter, of the deposition of coal on Stratford station's down platform. Perhaps the Western men were too grateful for the fuel thus supplied, or maybe they just put it down to the peculiar ways of the mad Midlanders.

At Stratford, with this little piece of excitement now behind us, we concentrated on the task ahead, but having built up an immense fire, and with No 8669 steaming so well, I was confident that we would put up a good showing. Fifty empty wagons take a surprising amount of effort to hump up a bank of 1 in 75, particularly in the strong cross-wind that was now blowing. The wind gets into the wagons and causes a lot of drag, but full first valve and 50 per cent cut-off had us thumping up to Wilmcote in grand style at a speed more appropriate to a fully fitted. Unfortunately we were unable to take advantage of the momentum imparted on the descent to Bearley, for once again we were checked by signals at the junction.

However, this caused little hardship, since speed was quickly restored over the 2 miles of falling gradients to the point where the bank up to Earlswood Lakes commenced some three-quarters of a mile from Wootton Wawen. This was where Percy liked to demonstrate just what we could do, and we thundered through the station with a wide open regulator and 40 per cent, but as the distant for Henley-in-Arden came into sight we noticed that it was at caution.

'Damn their eyes!' he yelled, showing his displeasure by giving the brake valve handle a swift clout with the palm of his hand. 'We've caught up one of their blasted trains!'

He eased back the regulator and the gradient rapidly reduced our speed, but as this fell to around 10 mph so both the home and starter signals came off. He immediately slammed the regulator up to the horizontal and dropped the gear pretty well right down the rack. No 8669's exhaust exploded like a thunderclap, shooting up a great column of black smoke and, despite being on a 1 in 150 incline, started to accelerate most impressively. Leaving her blasting away in this ferocious manner, he came over to my side of the cab, then spotted what he was looking for. There, parked on the down line, was a Western fitted hauled by one of their 'Grange' Class. Its blower was wide open and the fireman hard at work with the pricker. Obviously it was short of steam and had been shunted across the road out of our way for a blow-up.

Being thus distracted for the moment, our own safety valve lifted, but before I could put the injector on Percy stopped me.

'Let it blow off for a bit, mate!' he cried jubilantly. 'That'll show 'em we've got plenty of steam to spare.'

He was as pleased as a dog with two tails, and waved derisively at the Western crew, who by their hang-dog looks seemed to appreciate that having to shunt a prize vacuum train out of the way of a Midland empty wagon Class B was rather letting the side down.

This little piece of one-upmanship seemed to put Percy into excellent spirits and inspire him to achieve one of the most sparkling performances I have ever seen with a Class '8F'. For the next 7 miles he thrashed her up that 1 in 150 bank in a manner closely following the traditions of Tommy Charles, keeping the regulator wide open and the cut-off at around 40 per cent. Our little 4 ft 8½ in driving wheels were turning so rapidly that we sounded more like an express than a nondescript freight, and for that matter it felt like it, because at that speed the cab was heaving about like a rowing boat on a rough sea. Despite this merciless treatment and low-grade fuel she steamed beautifully, although of course I was forced to fire almost continuously all the way, and towards the top the needle did fall back slightly.

Past Earlswood Lakes and starting to rattle down the falling gradients that now faced us for the next 6 miles, a still exuberant Percy suddenly got up and came over to me.

'See if you can take her down to Tyseley without losing any time, mate,' he said, with a facial expression that was the nearest thing he could manage to a broad smile. This offer took me aback somewhat, for he had never before allowed me to handle the Long Marston, but I gratefully accepted and enjoyed the added pleasure of actually driving past my old home for the first time. Instead of losing time I fell into the spirit of our exceptional run, and nearly overdid things when I had to stop at the junction. I had a few worrying moments, but Percy seemed to think it was just good judgement and said nothing when he took over for the rest of the trip.

We were over an hour early at Landor Street, but were nevertheless relieved by a spare Control crew. The men scheduled for this turn had not even booked on by the time we were off the premises, but then Percy liked it this way.

We had our moments of excitement, we had our ups and downs, but as a team we generally worked well and, if I may say so, efficiently together, each trusting in the other's competence. He still had his daily arguments, his tantrums, and hourly rages. This was the nature of the man and I learned to take no notice. However, one night towards the end of our spell together, when we really should have known each other's ways too well for it to have happened, Percy flew into just about the most violent rage of his life, and I was the target.

We were working a through freight to Gloucester, which departed from the West End at 11.20 pm, and because we were booked to travel home by passenger train the following morning, we prepared our own engine. This was a '4F' and, as was our habit, we always arrived in good time to make a thorough job of it.

Percy had not forgiven me for a little prank I played on him the previous night, when he got a trifle confused over engine numbers and prepared 44404 instead of 44004, which was lying on the opposite side of the shed. It was a pardonable error that many enginemen had made in the past and, when having gone to the correct engine, and then spotted him oiling the other, I at first thought that

it was I who had made the mistake. However, after checking the train board again and confirming this with the shed foreman, a little spark of devilment urged me to say nothing at this juncture. After all, I had plenty of time to do both jobs and no harm would be done provided that we rang off at the right time. So, taking great care not to be seen by Percy, I set to work on 44004.

He meanwhile, not only oiled the other engine but loyally did my work as well, thinking that for some reason I had been delayed. We finished our work at roughly the same moment, and timing it to a nicety, I confronted him just outside the oil stores, holding an empty oil bottle in my hand as if about to go through the motions of drawing more lubrication.

'Good heavens, Percy,' said I in a tone of mock censure, 'wherever have you been? We're due out in ten minutes!'

I waited for the explosion, which true to form came right on time.

'Where have I been? Where have I been?' he screeched, eyes popping and wobbling jowls turning bright purple. 'Where have you been, more likely? I've only prepared the engine all by myself, and done your bloody job as well! I was just going to the lobby to see about getting another fireman.'

As he paused for breath I seized my chance.

'Don't quite see how you could have done that, Percy, because I've just prepared our engine and I've oiled it as well,' I replied with deliberately exaggerated serenity. 'As a matter of fact, I was just going to get the table.'

He visibly dilated to even greater proportions so that I thought his eyes were going to pop out of his head, then, when almost at the point of detonation, his expression suddenly relaxed into a sarcastic grin.

'What's the number of the engine you've prepared then?' he asked, the apparent explanation germinating in his mind.

'44004, the one on the board,' I replied as calmly as before.

'Ha!' he smirked, 'you've prepared the wrong one. 44404 is ours. Come and look.'

As was usually the case when Percy was having an argument, a small crowd of interested enginemen had gathered around and, with the promise of further good entertainment, they followed us to the engine board just like spectators do in Laurel & Hardy films.

'There you are,' he said, then stopped dead as the awful realisation dawned that it was he who had made the mistake. 'Somebody must have altered it since I first looked,' he exploded, trying to seek some excuse for his error. This tantrum would probably have continued for another half an hour, but fortunately Mr Evans, the Senior Foreman, arrived on the scene and quickly absorbed the gist of what had happened.

'Go on, Percy,' he chided 'it's been that number for hours. What you need is some new glasses.'

The happy band of spectators had had their money's worth and, to the sound of their laughter, I and a deflated Percy went about our business. He did not, however, speak to me for the first part of the shift, and gave the engine and myself the very devil of a rollicking all the way to Gloucester.

Although 24 hours had elapsed since that episode, the embarrassment still rankled and, while we now conversed again, I sensed that the mere act of preparing our engine brought back unpleasant memories that pained and worried his very being, like the exposed nerve of a bad tooth. I, for my part, had practically forgotten the incident, and was doing my level best to be the essence of good-natured geniality. Things were going very well indeed, and I was quite advanced with my side of the business, when I decided to check the sandboxes and tighten up the smokebox door en route.

He, meanwhile, was endeavouring to oil the big-ends. Unfortunately the engine was not set in quite the ideal position, but since it was on a short pit and hard up against the stop plates, there was little he could do about it. Now the reader may have deduced from my original description that he possessed a body that fell far short of the ideal shape to go climbing up the narrow gap between

Nos 44004 and 44404, the two '4Fs' that Percy confused and which inevitably led to quite a rumpus. Sunday afternoon was always a most profitable time to spend an hour or two engine-spotting at any loco depot, and Saltley, as these photographs show, was no exception, with nearly every available foot of track occupied.

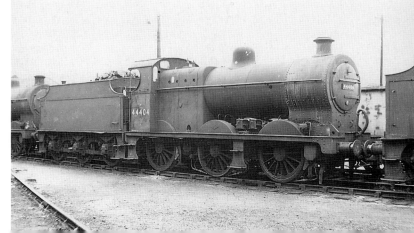

big-ends and firebox throat-plate. He could, under normal circumstances, just about make it, but with one big-end set back slightly further than desirable, he met trouble. With much heaving and struggling, he had managed to wiggle his ample and wobbly corporation up past the offending hunk of metal, but now that he wanted to slide down again, that self-same hunk of metal squashed the resilient flesh up to form a ring around his equator like a spare tyre, thus effectively plugging the gap.

Percy was, therefore, firmly and uncomfortably supported by nothing other than his paunch, and to compound the problem his overall jacket on its downward slither had become rucked up and was now inextricably entangled with oil cups, set pins and strap nuts that had been cleverly distributed in that area to ensnare the unwary. In my usual manner, I had departed from the port side of the cab, trotted round the framing, tightened the smokebox door, and having made the pleasant discovery that all sandboxes were full, was just about to re-enter via the starboard side when I heard his voice, albeit somewhat muffled and distorted.

'Hey, mate! I'm stuck!' he gasped. 'Give me a hand, will you?'

Now, ever since I had first joined the railway, the time-worn joke of portly drivers being stuck in the motion had been bandied about, and the stock answer to such a situation was, 'Hang on mate, I'll move her back a bit.'

Everyone knew it, for it was as old as steam engines themselves. My honest intention was to climb underneath and assess the situation with a view to releasing him from his predicament, but, without thinking, that old stock answer slipped off my tongue: 'Hang on, I'll move her back a bit.'

Any other driver would have laughed wryly and retorted, 'Come on mate, stop mucking about and get me out of this.'

But not Percy, who, devoid of any sense of humour, took everything said as Gospel. To make matters worse, as I entered the cab the heavy spanner I had been holding slipped from my grasp and fell with a loud clatter to the footboards. This was the last straw: he evidently thought that I was about to put intention into practice, for a loud, hysterical scream rent the air, followed by the sound of tearing cloth and a thud.

Seconds later a hideous and terrible form emerged from the dark depths of the pit trembling with fright and rage. Holding a feeder in one hand and an oil torch in the other, it glared balefully around seeking its tormentor. Slowly it moved into the light and I could now see the extent of the disaster.

His overall jacket had suffered considerably, for the left half had been completely ripped away and was now trailing by a thread behind its erstwhile owner, that is to say except for the sleeve which was still incongruously in its original position. The right sleeve, together with the sleeve of the shirt beneath, were conspicuous by their absence, while the area from midriff to matted hair was plastered with streaks of black oil and grease.

On numerous occasions over the past months I had managed successfully to control my mirth over the escapades and incidents Percy became involved in, but the sight of this caricature was too much for me this time. I let out a howl of laughter that could be heard all over No 2 shed; I then realised that it was the worst thing I could possibly do, but the more I tried to desist, the more I laughed, and the more I laughed the more that malevolent red glow that had begun to emanate from Percy grew in intensity.

'You bloody young lunatic!' he shrieked. 'You could have crushed me!'

I was unable to speak for laughing and tears rolled down my face.

'So you think it's funny?' he roared. 'I'll - I'll bloody well show you how funny it is. I'll bloody murder you!'

So saying, he let out a howl and, waving both oil feeder and torch about his head in a menacing fashion, charged straight for me. I took the only option now left open, and diving round the back of our tender set off NNW as fast as my legs could carry me. That was the problem, though - the dashed things would not carry me very fast at all. I imagine that everyone at some time in their life has dreamed of being chased by a monster or demon or some such equally terrifying apparition, and although one desperately wants to leg it as fast as possible out of the immediate vicinity, one's feet appear to be transformed into lead and will barely move. Well, that was the situation I now found myself in. Nothing saps one's strength more than being convulsed with uncontrollable laughter, and I was convulsed, so instead of achieving the desired sprint, all I could do was to stumble along at a very indifferent pace.

On the other hand, rage and a determination to get his hands on what he now looked upon as the cause of his near assassination fired Percy with a speed and energy hitherto quite unimaginable. This, then, was the equaliser, for an 11-stone 23-year-old in prime condition should have had no trouble whatsoever in getting away from a 16-stone, overweight 57-year-old driver with weak ankles.

After about two laps round the inside of No 2 shed it was all too evident that Percy was slowly gaining on me, and had he not been expending so much energy on shrieking profanities at the top of his voice, I would have been by now doubtless nursing a sore head. By lap three I could almost feel his hot breath breathing down my neck, and unfortunately for me every time I glanced over my shoulder the sight of a blackened and tattered Percy frothing at the mouth and galloping along with all the grace and elegance of a hammer-toed rhinoceros with advanced footrot was just too much, and a renewed outburst of laughter impaired my performance even more.

Two circuits later age began to tell, and Percy started to fall inexorably further behind despite quite a crowd of enginemen cheering encouragement from just outside the lobby. This sizeable mob had grown lap by lap from a small knot of chaps initially fascinated by the unusual spectacle of an hysterical top link fireman being hotly pursued by a ragged, demented driver waving a feeder and a flaming torch about his head, screaming blue murder. I do not know whether anyone actually made a book on it, but both Percy and I had our respective band of supporters going wild with excitement.

By lap eight, the penultimate one, the scene was reminiscent of the Grand National on race day, all quite happy to stay and witness the conclusion despite the distinct possibility of a late start. Percy was now puffing like a grampus, and realising that he was losing the race, made one last desperate effort with his remaining strength and hurled both feeder and torch at my rapidly retreating figure.

The former, spraying its slippery contents over all and sundry, went very much wide of its intended target and caught the portly figure of Mr Evans right on the tummy button just as he stepped from the lobby to see what all the rumpus was about, leaving a mark on his impeccable cow gown that never did wash out. The latter, whirling and weaving a fiery trail like a tracer shell, missed my left ear by only a whisker and plunged spluttering into a nearby pit beneath the bowels of a Class '2P' 4-4-0.

Mr Evans, always the soul of reason and toleration, quietly called us together.

'You two really seem to have it in for each other this week, don't you? I would have thought,' he said, turning to me with an imperious gesture like a headmaster lecturing a naughty schoolboy, 'that you would have had more respect for your driver than to go playing silly pranks on him. As for you, Percy, I am surprised to see a man of your age behaving like a young hooligan. Now put a stop to this skylarking and get on with your work. You're late!'

Neither of us had breath left to argue and we meekly returned to our engine under this imposed truce. Eventually when I was able to explain things and apologise, Percy took it in surprisingly good part, although his wife nagged him for months over the amount of sewing he had created for her that night.

The following few weeks sufficed to heal the rift, and when May came along once more, we parted as good friends, both of us having benefited from the partnership. There was no doubt that I had learned more of the practical side of being an engine driver from him than from the rest of my mates put together. He had insisted on perfection in all things right from the beginning, and both my firing and driving techniques had benefited enormously. I was also grateful for the amount of driving he had allowed me to do, despite the strictness of his tuition, and although I did not know it at the time, this practice was to prove most fortuitous, bearing in mind the attitude of my driver in the next link. Percy had also sparked off a growing interest in the theory of railway operations and the rules and regulations necessary to put this into practice, and again, in view of the exacting and responsible work over the next two years, it could not have come at a better time.

14
THE LITTLE SHEFFIELD LINK

My year in this link turned out to be the happiest and most carefree of my railway career, and this was due partly to the fact that I spent nearly half of the time driving, and partly to my daily contact with that delightful gentleman who brought this about.

Although I knew Freddie Burrows by sight, I knew nothing of his ways, but right from the start we took an instant liking to each other, a liking which grew as the year progressed. Fred was the exact opposite of my previous mate in every respect. At 56 he was still a handsome man, standing some 5 ft 10 in tall, of medium build, lean and active, and carried his years so lightly that at first sight he might well have been still in his 40s. The expression worn on his well-chiselled features was that of good-natured tranquillity, while his blue-grey eyes regarded the world with honesty and humour. The only thing belying his age was a thick crop of almost white hair, which even then only lent a certain reverent dignity to his overall countenance.

While physically Percy and Fred were poles apart, the difference in their respective dispositions was equally well defined. Fred was affability itself, for a more even-tempered person was hard to imagine, and during the 12 months I was with him never a cross word passed his lips. His easygoing, calm outlook on life rubbed off on all he came in contact with, and he never became embroiled in arguments no matter how provocative the situation.

Fred's only vice, if indeed it could be called a vice, was a liking for a daily flutter on the horses, but since this involved only a few pence it was done mainly for entertainment value rather than any monetary gain. Admittedly he enjoyed the odd cigarette, but seemed far happier with a cup of tea than a pint of ale, and even then only indulged on a hot and thirsty day when nothing else was available. This tranquil mode of living thus protected him from many of the everyday stresses of life and, coupled with a generous helping of exercise derived from firing on alternate days, did much to preserve his youthful appearance.

Unlike Percy he was happy to work as much overtime as providence meted out, and consequently he never flogged an engine in an effort to avoid excessive hours. On the contrary, in keeping with most other top link drivers, Fred used the minimum of steam necessary to run to time and, because starting and stopping were the great wasters of energy, he aimed at keeping the train in motion for as long as possible. There was little sense in dashing up to a signal, then waiting for 5 minutes for it to clear, when by shutting off early and coasting gently along a complete halt could be avoided. The miles of running we achieved with the regulator closed were a real revelation after my previous two mates, and much appreciated on the longer freight runs when the going was frequently far from easy.

Our first job together turned out to be one of my favourites in the link. This was the 8.00 pm Lawley Street to Leeds semi-fitted, which we worked as far as Derby. On arrival there, we walked up to Derby North relief cabin and waited for the fish train from Hull, then worked this semi-fitted back to Washwood Heath. Although we were due to take over at around 11.30 pm, delays were not infrequent and many happy hours were spent with congenial company in that cosy little cabin. Even when running to schedule we made a little overtime, which of course pleased Fred, and on occasions we were hard put to catch our job for the following day.

During that first week we had plenty of opportunity to explore each other's working methods, knowledge, capabilities and general characteristics, and I was also able to discover what turns our link encompassed. We principally covered the northern runs, going as far afield as Sheffield, which in itself was a unique experience for me since not only was it to be the first time I had worked a freight job to that famous steel centre, but it also involved lodging there, and so far I had never been on a lodging turn. Apart from the seemingly inevitable Bordesley tripper, we also had a couple of westbound jobs that occasionally took us to Gloucester, although we were officially booked relief at Bromsgrove. By Saturday I was already quite convinced that I was going to enjoy working with Fred, but at that stage I still had no inkling of the joys to come.

The following week we booked on at the very pleasant hour of 8.30 am - made even more pleasant by the fact that our engine was already prepared - in order to work the 9.20 am Class B to Gloucester. Because of the considerable amount of passenger and fitted freight traffic at that time of day, we rarely got past Bromsgrove, but on about four occasions during the ensuing year we did manage to run to time and made Gloucester.

On Monday we were allocated Class '4F' 0-6-0

No 4108 and, after the usual check and clean-up session, we tootled gently down to Washwood Heath Junction to collect our train. This proved to be a fairly substantial one of some 40 wagons, equal in weight to 44 of mineral, with approximately two-thirds of those loaded coal wagons. However, No 4108 was a strong and efficient engine and, dispensing with the pilot at Camp Hill, we ultimately arrived at Blackwell far too late to entertain any ideas of working through.

I always took a great interest in drivers' techniques when descending Lickey and, after receiving the signal to draw ahead, I carefully watched Fred's every move. Both our guard and the brakesman must have been feeling full of beans, for initially they were rather over-zealous in pinning down the brakes and nearly dragged us to a standstill. This always boded ill, since they then had to desist for a while until the train had picked up sufficient speed to keep it in motion. The pre-calculated distribution of braking effort was therefore upset, thus leaving it very much more to chance whether a runaway would occur.

No doubt something of this nature happened, for although Fred initially appeared to have the train under control, by the time we were halfway down the bank the engine was being given a full brake application, and there it remained. We ran

'Jubilee' No 45589 *Gwalior* on the down 'Devonian' running past Bromsgrove South signal box having just descended the 2 miles of Lickey Incline in September 1951. *Gwalior* was an outstanding performer during the early 'fifties, and was often seen on the more demanding duties.

Freight trains aimed to stop at the water column in front of the signal box, no easy task for non-fitted trains relying on only the engine brake and a number of pinned-down wagon brakes over which the driver had no control whatever.

past the column with some 20 wagons before finally juddering to a standstill, and Fred observed, like so many other drivers I had worked with, that one could never really be sure of stopping at the other side of the column, let alone in the correct position for filling the tank.

After the brakes had been picked up and we had set back, I casually mentioned that I thought we would run past soon after commencing the descent.

'Have you ever driven one down?' asked Fred.

'Not yet,' I replied a trifle wistfully.

'Well I think it's about time you had a bit of practice,' said he. 'In fact, you can take her tomorrow!'

I was both surprised and delighted to say the least, because I had no foreknowledge that Fred was prepared to indulge in firing turns and of course no idea at all that he would carry this to the length of firing on alternate days over the routes I knew on just about every job in the link. As it turned out, even when I didn't know the road he soon made sure that I did, so that in time the only duties I did not drive on were the Sheffield lodging turn, which was routed over the Erewash Valley, and our one Sunday night express passenger job to Derby. In both instances the work was too rigorous for Fred to cope with, and in any case I never did fully learn the Erewash Valley in the time available. Even so, 11 weeks out of 12 at the regulator was beyond my wildest dreams, particularly when half of those were semi- or fully-fitted.

Needless to say, with the prospect of my first drive down Lickey in the offing I found it difficult to sleep soundly, and just could not get to work soon enough. Consequently I arrived a good half-hour early and was delighted to discover that we had been allocated a Class '8F'. This I found was not an infrequent practice when the Traffic Department notified the Motive Power that a heavier than normal train was waiting.

By the time Fred arrived I had thoroughly checked No 8420, added a few extra spots of oil to places Percy would not have neglected, and had virtually filled the firebox with hand-picked lumps of surprisingly good-quality coal.

Unlike Percy, Fred never regarded any assistance I offered in the way of firing as interference, nor looked upon it as a doubt aimed at his firing ability. On the contrary, we cleared up this point

very early in our association. Feeling extremely grateful for the chance to drive, I told Fred quite bluntly that I would enjoy a greater peace of mind if he would allow me at least to build up the fire before the start of a run, thus saving him some of the hardest work. Fred with equal frankness retorted that while he quite liked a spot of exercise, he was not that addicted as to want to have it all to himself and that I should feel free to pick up the shovel any time I so desired provided that it did not detract from my driving duties. I therefore made a habit of filling the box for him whenever possible, and also firing in safe situations such as when slowly climbing a bank, since at that time I could bale in 20 hundredweights of coal in half that number of minutes without raising more than the odd bead of perspiration.

Fred I think was quietly amused at my eagerness to get going, for I even volunteered to mash the tea, but in fact I was trying to cover up my emotions with activity, for I readily admit to having felt more than a few butterflies fluttering around in my stomach.

Backing on to the train at Washwood Heath, we found that we had the expected full load of 50 wagons, which added a little more spice to the great occasion. No 8420 was in good condition and, since the braking power of a Class '8' matched its hauling capacity, it had a distinct advantage over a '4F' despite the heavier train. I was therefore a trifle more confident as we slowly drew out of the sidings than I would have been had we been equipped with one of those ubiquitous 0-6-0s.

The haul up to Duddeston Road was the usual protracted affair, involving the use of only a partially opened first valve, and just about full gear, but I did have the added pleasure of exchanging a few words with my former mate in the Pilots as we chugged past. We had to wait some 20 minutes before being allowed to tackle the bank, and while Fred sorted out his winners for the day I prepared a magnificent fire for him. At last the signals came off and, after giving a prolonged 'crow' whistle, during which time Fred released the hand brake, I eased open the regulator.

In near ideal conditions No 8420 was able to transmit her full torque to the wheels without fear of slipping, and as soon as we were nicely on the move I opened up to full first regulator. By Landor Street box I linked up to 60 per cent cut-off and, since our safety valves were lifting, decided not to waste the steam being generated and promptly heaved the regulator wide open.

It is a tremendously exhilarating sensation to feel the vibrant power of a large locomotive working hard, and as we hammered under the bridge at Brickyard Crossing I would not have exchanged places with anyone in the world. Once off the 1 in 62 section I eased back on to the first valve again, and still at 60 per cent cut-off we pounded steadily up to Camp Hill where, after consulting with Fred, we dispensed with the pilot. Over the 1 in 280 stretch to Brighton Road I reduced the cut-off by small increments to 40 per cent, which sufficed to build up enough momentum to give us a good run at the 1 in 100 climb through Moseley Tunnel. However, the distant at Kings Heath was at caution and we rightly concluded that a tripper was still performing at Hazelwell.

Following Fred's example I shut off early and kept the train in motion without actually coming to a standstill, then, as the signals cleared, I was able to open up gently and continue to Kings Norton. Here, as expected, we were turned up the goods line, receiving a green flag at the box to indicate that at least one train was preceding us.

We clanked steadily along to Halesowen Junction without actually sighting the other train's brake-van, before waiting a further 30 minutes for the road to clear. At Halesowen Junction the permissive section ends and the goods line is thereafter officially designated the slow. There then follows a block of some 2½ miles up to Barnt Green, involving a steady pull at 1 in 301 for most of the way but, with little need to hurry, No 8420 was allowed to amble along on a breath of steam and 45 per cent cut-off.

This time we were halted for no more than 5 minutes, and since the fast and slow lines converged to but one track from there until Bromsgrove, we were obliged to move a trifle more briskly, but not for long. As anticipated, our train was turned into the loop at Blackwell where we enjoyed our lunch amid those verdant surroundings, while a number of passengers and fitteds hurtled by.

At last the signal came off and with it realisation that my moment of trial was close at hand. Easing out on to the main line I experienced a momentary twinge of apprehension, but this soon disappeared as I became immersed in my work,

and keeping the train well under control, rolled gently down the 1 in 291 gradient to come to a standstill just in advance of the brakeman's hut.

Over the last few years I had viewed the incline from this self-same spot on many occasions and in all sorts of conditions, but never had it appeared quite so long and so steep as it now did on this bright sunny afternoon. Despite a slight heat shimmer from the track, one could see quite clearly right to the bottom, and during that seemingly interminable wait for the brakesman and guard, it resembled a gigantic ski-jump more than ever.

Eventually they arrived, advising me of their readiness, and since the signal was already off I applied the steam brake so that Fred could release his hand brake. Trying to act as unconcerned as if I was merely moving an engine in the shed, I closed the taps and eased open the regulator.

Having watched many different drivers start off on innumerable occasions, I had already evolved my own theories on how it should be done, and consequently realised the importance of keeping the train moving at a steady pace while the brakes were being pinned down. Many factors were of course involved, since as more of the train ran on to the 1 in 37 gradient there was a tendency to accelerate, while, on the other hand, as each wagon brake was applied, so the resistance and drag increased. It was therefore very necessary to be extremely sensitive to these varying forces, and quickly compensate by small changes of the regulator opening in order to keep the train taut and moving steadily at about 4 mph.

As a matter of fact, I found this relatively easy, although it did demand a high degree of concentration and continual juggling with the regulator. At last I spotted the guard's waving arm indicating that he was now in his van and, after giving an answering hoot on the whistle, turned round to view the 2-mile descent ahead. There is a certain critical speed with any train in this situation, which must not be exceeded if one is to retain control, and, since it is a complicated formula full of variables, the driver has to rely ultimately on experience and a sort of sixth sense of what is actually happening at any given moment. I had no previous driving experience of the Lickey Incline to fall back on, but I had carefully studied cause and effect as a fireman. This had developed my sensitivity to a considerable degree so that the feeling of what was right or wrong now came very naturally.

After an initial application of the steam brake had enabled Fred to wind the hand brake hard on, I found that the train was already quite well under control, the guard and brakesman having done an excellent job in this respect. Even short applications had an instant effect in reducing speed, and I considered myself very lucky to have so much in reserve. I was therefore able to experiment and gradually allow our speed to increase, for if one ran off the 1 in 37 section on to the 1 in 186 too slowly, the uncontrolled braking effect of the wagons would bring the train to a standstill far short of the water column at Bromsgrove South. Momentum had to be judged very finely indeed on the latter part of the descent to achieve this desired result.

Halfway down the bank we could clearly see the distant signal was off, showing that we were being routed over the fast line, and once again I thanked my lucky stars, for this meant that the column would be on my side and that I could keep it in view all the time during the final approach.

As the roadbridge at Bromsgrove station loomed ahead I permitted our pace to build up by letting the train run free and, as we thundered through the platforms, I waited for the inevitable rapid deceleration that would occur as all the wagons came on to the less severe gradient. Anticipating this by a split second, I gave a gentle touch on the brake to eliminate the possibility of a snatch, then made a series of applications to get the feel of the train again.

The column was now only 100 yards ahead and, although I sensed that I had more than an even chance of stopping in about the right position, I realised that every single yard would demand my full concentration. I had originally intended to play it safe and try and stop just short of the column, but with only 20 yards to go and everything seemingly fine, I decided to attempt to stop exactly right for water. That would be an achievement to write home about if it came off.

Ten yards, 5 yards, 3 yards, and with a final light rub of the brake we came to a halt right opposite the marker. I made a great effort to retain my outward calm, and with the air of someone who pulls off such a feat every day of his life, I climbed on to the back of the tender and put the bag in.

Whether Fred considered this a shining example of beautifully judged driving, or merely a fluke stemming from beginner's luck, I do no know, for he passed no comment, nor had he done so during the entire descent of the bank, and for that I was extremely grateful. Only the man holding the brake handle has the real feel of the train, and unless an obvious error is being made any advice or interference can only make matters worse.

The following day we had another '8F' on a similarly loaded train, and to my delighted surprise Fred once more gave me the engine. I was this time somewhat more confident, and right from the start aimed to reproduce the previous day's performance. This, I am happy to relate, I managed to do, at any rate within a foot of the exact spot, which was near enough for watering purposes, and I was led to conclude that descending Lickey was easier than I had supposed.

On Thursday we were allocated a '4F' and by the time we reached Blackwell I realised that I was faced with a somewhat tougher proposition, for in terms of brake power to weight ratio the '4F' was

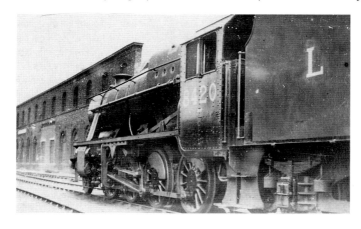

'8F' No 8420, later 48420, in LMS days. One of the 14 '8Fs' stabled at Saltley during the mid-'fifties, she was in fine fettle when I drove her for the first time down Lickey, and even obliged in stopping perfectly positioned at the water column at Bromsgrove South.

noticeably inferior to the Class '8s'. We set off from the top well enough, but by the halfway mark I was having to make prolonged brake applications in order to keep below the critical runaway speed, and for the last part of the descent the brake was on continuously. Moreover, it was raining fairly steadily and this threw in another variable to contend with. When passing through the station I was quite certain that we would over-run, but then we decelerated so suddenly that with some 50 yards to go it became apparent that we would stop short. I therefore eased open the regulator, intending to drag the train right up to the column, for I wanted to make it a hat-trick if at all possible. Shutting off at what I judged to be the correct point, everything seemed nicely under control over the last couple of yards as I made the final brake application.

I was just about to congratulate myself on another perfect stop when a powerful surge from behind suddenly pushed us past the column, locked wheels and all, by some three wagon lengths or so. Despite a vigorous attempt to set back, I was still a wagon length away when we had to call it a day. Whether the guard had noticed us dragging the train forward and released his brake I do not know, but the surge was so unexpected that it took me completely by surprise and I could have kicked myself for not settling for a stop on the correct side of the column. The disappointment must have shown in my face, for Fred, with a sympathetic grin, remarked, 'We all try to be just a little bit too precise to start with. If you can stop a few yards short you've done well enough.'

I remembered that Syd Lloyd had said more or less the same thing a few years ago, and decided in future to err on the short side.

The next day we again had a '4F', and bearing in mind the embarrassment of the previous trip I came down a little too cautiously and ground to a halt 10 yards from the column; however, it was then but an easy matter to uncouple and run forward for water, so no harm was done.

We finished the week with a Class '8', and since the train was somewhat lighter and very well braked, I found it relatively simple to stop right on the marker. With only one failure, I had come through the baptism much better than expected and, although Fred still passed no comment, he must have considered that I showed some promise, for from now on he allowed me to drive on alternate days over the routes with which I was familiar.

After my first week of handling trains down the Lickey Incline I became even more convinced that whether one stopped or not at the water column depended to a considerable degree on just how well one started from Blackwell. Maximum concentration over those first vital yards gave both the guard and brakeman a chance to exercise the skills upon which so much depended, and any lapse on the driver's part preventing the proper implementation of those skills was usually paid for at Bromsgrove South.

Our next turn also proved to be a great favourite of mine once I had learned the road. This was the 7.5 pm Water Orton to Toton, which ran under Class A lights. Outward-bound it was a very cushy number - the loadings were normally so minimal that I concluded that the principal reason for running the job was to return the Toton engine to its native depot. The most we ever had on was 18 vans, and on one occasion as few as six. The return trip, however, more than made up for this, being always a fully laden coal train destined for Washwood Heath.

The first time round Fred drove all week, for while I knew the road to Derby reasonably well, I had never been over the section from Stenson Junction to Toton and, of course, I had to learn this before being allowed to handle the regulator. We were generally allocated an '8F' for the job in both directions, and usually a pretty rattly, run-down one at that, but on the Thursday to my great delight we found on the engine board none other than No 92018, one of the new BR Standard Class '9Fs'.

I had been most impressed on first seeing one of these magnificent locomotives at Saltley shed the previous year. It gave the appearance of tremendous power, and looked the very essence of what a heavy freight engine should be. Percy Trotter, always conservative at heart, was with me at the time and, after we had given it a perfunctory examination, passed the comment, 'Bloody great thing, all boiler and wheels.' Although intended as derisory, it was nevertheless an accurate description.

Ever since that day I had been dying to get my hands on one, but although with every passing week they became a more familiar sight, until now no opportunity had arisen. Other than Garratts,

When Percy Trotter first saw a BR Standard Class '9F' at Saltley his remarks were somewhat deriso- ry - 'Bloody great thing, all boiler and wheels'. What he later said about the original Franco-Crosti versions with a side chimney is quite unprintable.

No 92025 was one of ten Crostis built at Crewe in 1955. The experiment was not success- ful, so that by 1960 the preheater drums had been removed and the engines converted to normal draughting. It is depicted here on the down slow line at Water Orton station after conversion. *Pat Webb*

neither Fred nor I had fired a wide firebox before, so this initial acquaintance was to become a pro- tracted experiment for both of us. The general cab layout was very similar to that of a BR Class '5' except that the boiler was noticeably more mas- sive and the firebox sloped outwards at its base. Looking through the oval firehole at the wide grate made me wonder how difficult it would be to keep the back corners filled, but as with so many other things experience and practice soon showed the way.

While still on the shed I manhandled a quanti- ty of large lumps into the firebox and poked these across to the rear corners so as to form a bed on which to build. Over the rest of the 40.2 sq ft of grate area I spread a fairly thin saucer-shaped layer of coal, somewhat thicker in the corners and under the door. In the course of time I found that Class '9s' were not at all sensitive to the manner in which they were fired. The shallow firebox pre- cluded an unduly thick firebed but, this apart, they did not seem to mind if they were fired heav- ily or lightly, haycock or saucer-shaped, and such was their vast steaming ability that they were the only engine I have ever known to perform normal work with actual holes or dead areas in the fire.

Our old friend Les Suffield was the guard and, having given him my armchair to repose on, we tootled off light engine to Water Orton. None of us had been on the footplate of a '9' in motion before, and those next 6 miles, mostly on the main line, served as a real revelation. Judging by the dirt and grime ingrained on her broad boiler, No 92018 had travelled a fair mileage since leaving

the paint shops, but she felt just like a new engine. The ride was uncannily stable, with no rolling or pitching, no lateral oscillations and very little ver- tical movement.

Admittedly Fred was only using a breath of steam, but the complete absence of any bangs, rat- tles and knocks was nothing short of staggering, considering that our speed rose to something approaching 50 mph through Castle Bromwich, and even here the most obtrusive sound was an intermittent buzz from the open cab ventilator as we passed over some of the less well-aligned rail joints. Until then I had considered these engines as purely for heavy freight, sort of super Class '8s', suitable only for slow-speed work, but now this impression of very free running plus a rock-steady ride made me consider far wider possibilities. I was not on my own by any means in this thinking, for it is now past history that these 2-10-0s soon found themselves working crack fitteds and even- tually express passenger trains, when they caused some embarrassment to the hierarchy by running at speeds of up to 90 mph.

It would be fair to say that no one at that time fully appreciated just what a wonderful machine had been created in the '9F'. With an axle loading of only $15\frac{1}{2}$ tons on each of its driving wheels (the BR Standard Class '3' 2-6-0 was $16\frac{1}{2}$ tons), route availability was as wide as engines of half their power, and what other locomotive was equally happy and efficient on either heavy miner- als or express passenger trains? The other point that became obvious on our brief run to Water Orton was the colossal reserve capacity of the boiler even when compared to '8Fs'. On arrival the water level seemed hardly lower than when we had departed from the shed, and although the fire was by no means properly burned through and the firedoors left wide open, pressure had remained constant at 245 lbs per sq in.

After backing on to our train, it was only a matter of minutes before Les returned and stated that we had but 16 vans, and since the five next to our engine were fitted, would we like them piped up? Fred immediately agreed to this because any additional brake power was always welcome, and with nearly a third of the total under direct control we would in this respect be equivalent to a semi-fitted.

Although designated Class A we were timed quite briskly, but with only 16 vans behind the tender, No 92018 hardly noticed them. With just a whiff of steam on, Fred quickly had her linked up to 15 per cent cut-off, and at this she travelled so swiftly that we soon caught up the preceding train. I had a very easy time of it since we ran for miles without requiring either coal or water and, because I was so unoccupied with firing, I was able to concentrate my attention on just how the fire burned over the whole grate area, damper settings and injector delivery rates.

The favourable gradients from Tamworth to Burton of course assisted our effortless progress, but even the rise of 1 in 454 to Repton & Willington station passed unnoticed and soon we were at Stenson Junction. I did not know the road from here on, but one advantage of changing links in May is that the lengthening days permit a much more detailed study to be made of any new route, which in turn is naturally conducive to its rapid learning. When only viewed at night it takes considerably longer to acquire the necessary knowledge, particularly of gradients and scenic landmarks.

From Stenson Junction the road falls at 1 in 226 for a mile then travels through flat, uninteresting country for the following 2 miles, when there are some small undulations up to Chellaston Junction. Fred pointed out that from Stenson there were seven overbridges before sighting the distant signal at Chellaston, and these should be noted to determine one's position on a dark night.

There is a slight rise of 1 in 440 up to Weston-on-Trent station, then the road drops for the next mile at 1 in 220. This is the fastest stretch on the

section, since the gradients continue to be favourable through Castle Donnington right down to the approach of Lock Lane Crossing some 4 miles distant. Here a short rise of 1 in 330 is useful in checking one's pace if so desired, before dropping again at the same inclination to the Crossing itself, which is but three-quarters of a mile from Sheet Stores Junction. We were usually brought to a halt before joining the Derby line, which then took us down to the complex of Trent, and after running round the back of this island station we were generally held until relieved by a Toton crew.

Having no other means of transport, we stayed on the footplate for the short 2-mile run through Long Eaton to Toton itself, where we left our colleagues and walked over to the loco sheds for a spot of supper before collecting our engine for the return working. Obviously it was not in our interest to be late since it ate into our rest period, but on the run back to Washwood Heath with the coal train there was no such sense of urgency, and Fred never complained of the resultant overtime as long as we were not too late to catch our job for the following day. I soon learned the stretch from Stenson Junction to Toton and, 12 weeks later, after an initial refresher run, Fred let me take over.

From then on I drove on alternate days and, since a Class '9' was usually provided, enjoyed myself enormously, particularly outward-bound when I was able to let rip. Fred generally gave me full freedom to drive in my own style, although with such a lightly loaded Class '9' it was so easy to travel rather too swiftly, and on these occasions he did restrain my over-exuberance.

As the year progressed so did Fred's confidence in my ability increase, and I well recall a magnificent run to Toton that stands head and shoulders above all the others and serves to illustrate one aspect of Class '9' capabilities. It occurred in November, when after six months of driving with Fred I was really beginning to get the feel of things. We were now having Class '9s' every trip and, although darkness prevailed over the whole distance, by the end of the week I had fully acclimatised to the change in conditions.

Examining the engine board on Saturday evening I saw that we had a high-numbered Class '9', so it was no great surprise to find that No 92137 was in mint condition; not so much as a single stain blemished her gleaming paintwork when we climbed aboard. She had obviously just been run in, and this was probably her first true road job, for even the leather seat coverings had that distinctive smell of newness.

After the usual checks had been accomplished, I built up the fire and swilled down the footplate while Fred went off to make our first can of tea prior to ringing out. He returned with our guard, Les Suffield, who, after bidding me good evening in his usual courteous manner, remarked on the weather.

'Chilly tonight, chaps. Almost cold enough for snow I would say.'

We both agreed, since it was one of those raw, damp nights that despite heavy cloud cover gave one the feeling that the temperature could very quickly get down to freezing point.

'You'll soon be all right Les, when you get in that cosy little caboose of yours,' chided Fred.

'Well, you're not too bad on these, are you?' the latter replied, indicating the wide oval firehole that even now was radiating a comforting warmth to our three posteriors as we stood in front of it.

'Not as long as you can keep the doors open,' admitted Fred, 'but then when you're firing it's too damned hot.'

This latter statement was only too true, for I had soon discovered that the large oval firehole permitted a far greater amount of heat to be radiated out into the cab than on engines equipped with the standard circular hole. When the fire was white hot under normal working conditions even a brief exposure at close proximity caused one's overalls to smoke in a most disconcerting fashion, and any flesh coming into contact with the hot

material suffered accordingly. With 40 sq ft of grate area to cover, the fireman generally applied more coal at any one session and spent that much longer doing it, so the problem was compounded. Furthermore, to reach the back corners the shovel had to be virtually thrust inside the furnace, bringing one's hands very close to the flames. Substantial gloves were to my mind a necessity when firing a Class '9', and this was another reason why I built up as large a fire as was practical for Fred's benefit when he was firing.

Later I discovered a little dodge that greatly helped to reduce this emission of unwelcome heat. Before starting a round of firing I always dropped two or three shovelsful just inside the firehole so that a small hump of dead coal was formed. This not only blanketed off much of the radiation, but also acted as a deflector, since by bouncing the shovel blade against this hump at the correct angle, coal could be shot into the back corners with the minimum of effort and without the need to get too near.

Having thus briefly debated the relative comforts provided by our respective charges, the shed signal came off and the yard foreman shouted across to us that we could go. Leaving the taps open to blow out the condensation that would have accumulated in such a cold atmosphere, I eased open the regulator and, amid much hissing and great clouds of steam, we rolled smoothly off the shed and over Duddeston Road bridge. We were turned out on to the main line and by the time we were passing Bromford it was obvious that even for a '9', No 92137 was exceptional. I have already extolled the virtues of the class, but this

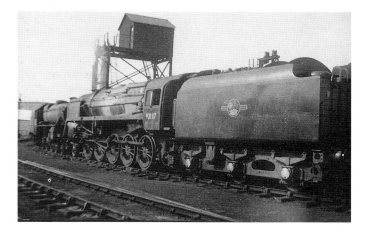

Although designed as a heavy freight locomotive, '9Fs' proved to be possibly the finest mixed traffic engines ever to grace British metals. They were masters of any job allocated to them, and No 92137 was by far the best I experienced. *J. Coltas*

one was truly remarkable, for with no more than 40 lbs per sq in showing on the steam chest pressure gauge and 15 per cent cut-off, we were already going like a racehorse. Furthermore, there was not the slightest whimper of steam, trace of vibration nor rattle coming from anywhere; in fact, the only noticeable sound was the click of passing rail joints, and had it not been for this one might have easily imagined that we were not running on wheels at all but merely floating just above the tracks. All the controls were incredibly smooth and light to operate, giving one the immediate impression of being in full command, and I particularly relished the tautness of the regulator, since this allowed for adjustments as fine as 5 lbs per sq in to be made on the steam chest pressure gauge.

In a remarkably short space of time we arrived at Water Orton, neither Fred nor Les having conceived the slightest notion of how swiftly we had travelled, since they had been deep in conversation while toasting themselves in front of the now bright fire.

After backing on to our train, I dropped down to change the headlamps and have a quick feel at the wheel bearings to make sure that all was well, for new engines sometimes ran warm until a certain mileage had been logged. I had just completed this inspection when I was surprised to meet Les at the end of the tender.

'Shouldn't give you much trouble tonight, Terry,' he said brightly. 'We've only got six. They're all fitted and so is the brake. Shall we pipe them up?'

'Might as well,' I replied with a tingle of excitement beginning to form within me. 'It will give you a better ride and me a bit more stopping power if I get the chance to run 'em.'

So with Les illuminating the scene with his handlamp, I ducked under the buffers and wrestled with icy couplings and stiff hoses until all were screwed up as tight as I could manage. When the brake-van was finally connected I joined Les in the 6-foot, and for the first time noticed that the van also appeared to be just out of the shops.

'Oh, so you've got a new one too,' I remarked, indicating the spotless tail-end appendage, the stovepipe of which was already topped with a healthy red glow from the roaring fire beneath.

'Yes,' smiled Les, 'it's a North Eastern one, so I should be all right, and some kind soul lit the fire for me as well.'

I had often discussed the riding qualities of different types of brake-vans with Les and other guards in the past, for this too had to be borne in mind if the occupants were to be treated with consideration, and, as previously mentioned, when driving I made a particular point of giving them as good a ride as possible. It was generally agreed that for fast travel a North Eastern brake could not be bettered. Next to these came the standard BR variety that were closely styled on the Eastern pattern, followed by the LMS, SR and GWR brakes, in that order. I personally liked travelling in Great Western brakes, but this was only because they were more commodious, and the full-length lockers enabled tired passengers to lie upon them in comfort while catching up on their lost sleep.

Returning to the engine, since we still had time to spare I set about building up a really massive fire for Fred. With this engine and such a light load I calculated that if I filled the firebox to its practical limit we should make Stenson Junction without need of much further attention.

At last we were called out and, with the signal set for the fast, we left Water Orton in our correct path. With only six vans No 92137 required very little more steam than when moving as a light engine, and by the time we reached Kingsbury Junction we were fairly romping along at less than 15 per cent cut-off and 50 lbs per sq in steam chest pressure. By Wilnecote the distants were beginning to appear at caution and, since there was no point in coming to a standstill, I reduced the regulator opening even more. With the firedoors wide open and the rear damper just cracked off its face, she was steaming so well that Fred had filled the boiler up out of sight in an effort to prevent blowing off, but with working so lightly there was little possibility of priming. This was about the only effort Fred was put to, though, for with his feet resting on the damper control wheels, reclining comfortably on his padded seat and listening to the soporific clickety-click of wheels over rail joints, while all the time bathed with the warm radiance from the fire, he was having a job to keep his eyes open.

Despite being brought to a halt in Burton station, we were slightly ahead of schedule at Stenson Junction, thanks to the rapid and effortless acceleration at my disposal, and possibly because of this we had a clear run across on to the Trent line. While standing at Burton I had quickly fired a dozen shovelsful, filling in the odd spots where it was a trifle thin and generally levelling the firebed, so again there was no need for Fred to disturb his repose.

Once clear of the junction we normally enjoyed an uninterrupted run, and banking on the probability of having nothing ahead to block our way, I gradually eased open the regulator. With 60 lbs per sq in now showing on the steam chest pressure gauge, and the cut-off at 15 per cent, our pace began to quicken. At night this stretch of line is as black as the ace of spades since there are no towns nearby to cause a glow in the sky, and being overcast not even the stars were present to help one distinguish between ground and sky. Peering out of my open side window I could see nothing of the cutting nor the leafless trees that I knew grew in abundance atop its banks, and save for the fleeting glimpse of a passing telegraph pole as it was briefly illuminated by a shaft of light from the fire, the whole world seemed to be enveloped in inky blackness.

How fortuitous was the existence of those seven bridges, for without them acting as regular markers I would not have had a clue as to where we were. By the sixth bridge it was obvious from the click of the rail joints that we were travelling faster now than we had at any previous point of our run, but otherwise there was nothing at all to signify this. Still the same silent, turbine-like smoothness prevailed, while the ride was so steady that not even the lid of tea I was resting on the brake pedestal showed more than a ripple or two on its surface. That a 140-ton locomotive could travel in excess of 50 mph with no more commotion than a well-oiled sewing machine was surely a wonderful tribute to the near perfect engineering attained in this Class '9F'. Suddenly remembering Les, I glanced back towards the brake and was reassured to see his side light still there, although I must admit it was bucking about more than somewhat, then, with the approach of the last bridge, I concentrated my attention on seeking the distant for Chellaston Junction.

Our speed was by now higher than it should have been, but with all wheels except our pony truck braked, I decided to keep her going, for although the night was dark, I should be able to pick out the signal in good time. Fred had been literally nodding off up to this point, which I thought was a considerable show of confidence in my driving prowess, but I was surprised to see him

rouse up at the seventh bridge, stare ahead until satisfied that the distant was clear, then drop off again. He was so familiar with the road that he must have been subconsciously counting the bridges. The expression 'he could do it with his eyes closed' had more than a ring of truth in this instance.

With the short rising gradient of 1 in 440 up to Weston-on-Trent just ahead and Fred once more with his eyes closed, I gently inched open the regulator so that 70 lbs per sq in appeared on the gauge. Even on the incline a slight increase in pace was perceptible, but having surmounted the hump and falling at 1 in 220 we really started to go. I could still see nothing of the trackside, but the click of the wheels - one pause, five pause, three pause - rang out more rapidly than ever.

Feeling that this was now an ideal moment to experiment with gear settings, I reduced the cut-off to just under 10 per cent and increased the steam chest pressure to 80 lbs per sq in. No 92137 was as smooth and as quiet as ever as we hurtled over the falling gradients down to Castle Donnington, where the red aircraft warning lights on the power station chimneys and cooling towers stood out clearly against the jet black backcloth.

Goodness knows at what speed we were travelling when we reached our peak about 2 miles from Sheet Stores Junction but, the click from the last tender wheel was followed almost immediately by that of the pony truck striking the next joint. Even so, not a sway or a tremor disturbed Fred's peaceful slumbers, and I can honestly say that no other class of tender engine I ever worked on approached this '9' in terms of riding quality. Unfortunately this incredibly smooth, silent, effortless progression was extremely deceptive, particularly when no landmarks were visible, and no sooner had I shut off on spotting the distant for Sheet Stores than I became aware that it was swimming towards me at an alarming rate. In keeping with other BR Standard types, the Class '9' was equipped with an independent steam brake and, not wishing to alarm Fred by making a heavy and noisy application of the vacuum brake, I grasped the handle, yanking it back to the limit of its ratchet.

Very little appeared to happen at first and I became conscious of a slight pang of anxiety as the yellow light continued to approach at a seemingly undiminished pace. I still did not want to disturb

Fred, but quickly concluded that he would be infinitely more disturbed if I over-ran the home signal, so as the distant loomed up I started making gentle applications with the vacuum brake.

The distinctive hiss of this soon roused Fred, who stared out in an effort to orientate himself. Meanwhile the lights at Sheet Stores and beyond were now visible, as was indeed the home signal, and I was now able to calculate stopping distances with a useful amount of visual aid. The answer came out in about two-fifths of a second that I would have to kill our speed pretty quickly if we were to stop at all, so instead of taking out some 10 inches of vacuum, I started knocking the needle down to zero for quite a lengthy period. I sensed Fred's tension as he stared ahead, also working out speeds and distances, and I smiled wryly to myself when I thought of how much more he would have tensioned had he known that the steam brake had been hard on for the last half-mile or so. However, his only observation was, 'It's on, you know!'

'OK, I've got it, Fred,' I replied more calmly than I felt, at the same time making another prolonged full application. Suddenly our speed fell away in that unaccountable manner so typical of vacuum-braked trains, and for the last hundred yards I barely had to check our pace, even though I had by now released the steam brake. Before we actually came to a standstill the signal dropped and I chuffed gently down to Trent station, where we were brought to a halt.

Presuming that we were being detained pending the arrival of our relief crew, I crossed over to Fred's side and joined him at the bucket for a quick swill. Moments later voices raised in earnest discussion could be heard approaching, then the dazzling beam of an electric torch flashed across the cab side from down below. Voice A, a deep bass, suddenly exclaimed in astonishment 'Bloody hellfire!' You're right mate, it is her!'

To this forthright statement voice B, a light tenor, made the reply, 'I thought she looked a new 'un as she passed the end of the platform.'

The bass, now directed his voice at us and endeavoured to attract our attention.

'Ay up! We're after you.'

I pulled open the cab door and, after a bit of puffing and blowing, voice A materialised through it in the form of a portly Toton driver who was obviously a trifle short of steam.

'Christ Almighty,' he continued, pulling out a pocket watch. 'What have you done, come over the fields? Do you know, you were supposed to be passing Stenson 15 minutes ago? Bloody Control, don't know what they're doing half the time; haven't even had time to mash our flaming tea yet!'

This old driver was not in a very good mood, thinking that the Control was to blame for him having to dash around, and it would have been

Trent Station South Junction signal box, looking north-west towards Toton. The main lines from Derby and Castle Donnington (left foreground) merge with the London main line alongside Trent's island platform. The line on the extreme left loops round the station, and it was here that the 7.5 pm Water Orton-Toton was usually relieved. *BR*

imprudent of me to say otherwise. Fred, who was only just beginning to realise how early we were, also said nothing except to remark how inclement the weather was for this time of the year.

Ten minutes later Fred and I bade them farewell outside the loco as we made our way over the numerous tracks towards the ancient but nevertheless cosy messroom, feeling just as sprightly as when we had started out. With the possible exception of a diesel or an electric, I do not think any other locomotive could have brought us there with so little effort or fatigue as did that Class '9'.

We had just finished our sandwiches and Fred had joined in a game of dominoes while I was enjoying a quiet smoke when Les bowled in. As usual he had had to stay with the train until it was stabled, but now he was free to relax for an hour or so with us. With his customary friendly smile he seated himself next to me and got out his supper. As he did so I asked my inevitable question.

'How was the ride, Les? Hope I didn't rattle you around too much, only we seemed to be getting quite a lick on through Donnington.'

'Ah!' he replied, looking a trifle uncomfortable. 'I hope no one looks at my journal too closely. I've had to book 15 minutes from Stenson to Sheet Stores, and that was stretching it a bit. They'll think I was drunk unless they check with the bobby's, then Fred will be asked some embarrassing questions.'

I fervently hoped that a check would not be made, but I was on tenterhooks for the next two weeks. Fortunately nothing came of the matter, and Fred never did know that we had covered 12$\frac{1}{2}$ miles in 15 minutes, rather faster than a Class A is permitted to travel. Les did admit, though, that the Eastern brake-van had given him an impeccable ride, although at times he thought that some of our six vans had spent as much of their time on the down line as they did on the up.

'Mind you, I have been faster than that once,' he said, 'working the "Pines Express" down through Eckington!'

Our lodging job to Sheffield also followed this same route through Toton and up the Erewash Valley, rather than the more direct one via Derby, and even in summer we always traversed this section in darkness. The 21 miles from Toton to Clay Cross was a difficult road in many respects, and I found it the very devil of a job to learn during the time available. By the end of the year I had only managed to

grasp essentials from the firing point of view, and would have required a much longer acquaintanceship to drive competently over it at night.

On the Sheffield we were booked a Class '4F' 0-6-0 and usually hauled a full load under 'Maltese' lights. By the time we arrived at Toton the fire was already past its prime, and from here on there is a steady 18-mile pull right up to Morton Sidings, with the gradient as steep as 1 in 150 over the section between Pye Bridge Junction and Coats Park North. The stretch contained no fewer than 28 blocks, which meant of course an almost unbroken chain of signals, and this was made twice as complicated because there were four tracks. Furthermore, numerous sidings lay strewn on either side and, since much of the area was subject to severe mining subsidence, speed restrictions, both permanent and temporary, abounded. To make matters worse there was a pronounced tendency for mist to develop along the course of the valley, and when this became well mixed with the heavy smoke pall coming from the many collieries and industrial plants that were dotted along the line, real old-fashioned peasoupers occasionally blanketed the scene for days at a time.

Bearing in mind the above facts, and with the whole of my attention concentrated on providing enough steam to run efficiently, I had little time available for road learning. When I did look out of the cab and my eyes had adjusted to the darkness, I found that one lot of signals appeared very much the same as the next. Only by constantly asking Fred and making continual references to a route card that I had previously made out, was I able to pin-point our position and gradually learn the correct block sequence. However, it was all very interesting and instructive and the knowledge came in extremely useful a year later when I was working the Carlisles, which on Saturdays followed this route.

From Morton Sidings it was far easier, since we were able to coast for 7 miles right down to Tapton Junction, where the roads to Sheffield and Masboro parted company. I always made use of this downhill stretch and built up the fire for the 5-mile slog at 1 in 100 up to Bradway Tunnel. It was quite a drag and with combustion efficiency deteriorating we were very hard put to maintain time. I was therefore always well pleased to see those grimy stone portals loom up because they signified the end of my ordeal. At slow speed, though, it did seem to take a dickens of a long time to pass through those 2,027 yards of dripping, noxious brickwork, but at least outward-bound we were coasting. In fact, the road fell at 1 in 100 for the 6 miles to our destination, Queens Road Depot, so apart from cleaning both the footplate and myself, I was able to sit down and watch the view.

After depositing our train we ran the 3 miles or so down to Grimesthorpe where we left our engine for the shed staff to deal with. Grimesthorpe shed was well named, for Saltley seemed by comparison like a luxury hotel. On the other hand nearby Brightside, where the Company Lodge was situated, appeared to be a bit of a misnomer, since it was just as filthy as the rest of the area. However, the lodge itself was quite presentable on the inside, with adequate if unappetising food, clean and reasonably comfortable beds, and just sufficient warmth if the weather did not happen to be too inclement. Unfortunately, a shunting spur ran just beneath the bedrooms and the local Sheffield lads seemed to spend half the day with the noisiest Class '3F' on the system trying to knock the buffers off a rake of rusty wagons with their brakes pinned down. With this fearful racket going on outside, sleep, after the first couple of hours became rather fitful; indeed, it was sometimes a profound relief when the call came to get up.

The return journey was somewhat easier since most of the hard work was done during the earlier stages when both I and the fire were fresh, although the 8-mile haul from Grimesthorpe to Bradway Tunnel could prove something of a problem with a cold engine. Six miles of unrelieved 1 in 100 had those old '4Fs' extended to the limit, and it required all one's skill, together with a little bit of luck, to maintain sufficient pressure. Needless to say the tunnel itself seemed twice as long when pounding up through it, but once out into clean air again one could practically coast the next 5 miles all the way to Tapton Junction. From there it was admittedly a fair pull up to Morton

Sidings, but on as far as Trent it was easy running over favourable gradients, and I did much better at learning the route from its northern end than from the other direction. This lodging turn came round every six weeks, since it required two crews to cover one week's work, and it provided a pleasant introduction into such duties and was to prove an excellent grounding for the Carlisles later.

As mentioned at the beginning of this chapter, one of my favourite turns was the 8.00 pm Lawley Street to Leeds, returning with the Hull semi-fitted. On this job I discovered a method to eliminate the snatch problem over one tricky little section of the run. Quite early on in the year, when our fish train was cancelled, we had to travel home from Derby as passengers in the brake-van of another semi-fitted. Approaching Burton station I decided to help myself to a lid of tea, and since we had so far enjoyed a smooth ride I was very surprised when a sudden snatch slopped half of it down my shirt. After I had uttered a derogatory comment about the driver, Les Suffield, who was also travelling with us, explained that on all loose-coupled trains, including semi-fitteds, one invariably experienced a snatch at that point.

Intrigued, I asked him why, and from the ensuing discussion it appeared that there was a slight

Sheffield Grimesthorpe MPD. Coaling plants came in all shapes and sizes, but invariably they were noisy and dirty structures. When I visited this depot on my first lodging turn, I felt that it was aptly named. Certainly the coaling plant did not look out of place, for the surrounding area matched it perfectly. Note the electrically powered capstan and rope (left foreground) by means of which wagons were positioned on the lift for loading into the hopper.

hump in the track there. Because of the speed limit through Burton station, and also because the signals were difficult to sight, drivers shut off somewhere around Wetmore Sidings, then coasted down to the station. However, the hump caused the train to buffer up quite tightly, but once over it the forward part ran away, making the couplings feel taught to the driver when he opened the regulator. A snatch would occur in any case even if the engine was not opened up, but this act, no matter how gently performed, only seemed to accentuate the snatch.

Having thus been presented with the bones of the problem I thereupon decided to try and devise a cure. Analysing what was happening through the length of the train, it soon became obvious that if the engine was kept pulling, even if very lightly, then the wagons would not buffer up. The trouble was, though, that speed had to be held down approaching the station. On the other hand, if one slowed too early time would be lost, and in any case this slowing in itself would cause an unwanted surge. The only answer seemed to lay in gradually easing the regulator some distance from the station so that there was a breath of steam on over the hump. Everything would have to be very finely judged in case the signals at Burton Station South were on, but I resolved to give it a try at the next opportunity.

This occurred the following night since it was my turn to drive. Our train was some 30 minutes late arriving, but at last we climbed aboard the usual 'Crab' and learned that we had 48 vehicles behind the tender, 18 of which were fitted. After

driving gently forward so that Les could relieve the guard, I replied to his hand signal and set off steadily down the goods line towards Derby station. Here we ran round the back of the platforms, and since we were usually held a short while before being turned out main line, it was advisable to proceed with caution.

As it happened on this occasion the road was clear, so opening up on to full first valve we pounded off towards Melbourn Junction in that distinctive wiggly way of those engines. 'Crabs' have a relatively weak first valve and any really hard work requires the regulator to be pushed well over, but they coped so effectively with these fitteds that the first valve sufficed to accelerate our lengthy train up the 1 in 435 gradient to Melbourn. From there, with the road virtually level, we soon started to rattle along at a handsome pace on no more than 20 per cent cut-off, and by the time we reached Stenson I was obliged to ease the regulator slightly.

These 'Crabs' were really magnificent engines on such duties, for although we were hauling 48 vans at something like 45-50 mph, she was only fractionally extended. Under such light working Fred had a fairly easy time keeping her steaming like an old kettle, seemingly tossing only the odd shovelful of coal into the firebox every few miles or so. Although the distants were off, in accordance with my predetermined plan I started easing the regulator still further at Clay Mills, which was some 2 miles out from Burton station. Gradually our speed began to fall on the level road, but by Wetmore Sidings I had to make fur-

During their lifetime 'Crabs' did their fair share of passenger duties, but by the late 'fifties they had been largely relegated to what was to prove their ideal niche - middle-distance fully or semi-fitted freights. I learned to respect these efficient locomotives from both sides of the footplate when working the heavy Hull-Birmingham fish trains from Derby North Junction. No 2903 is seen entering Saltley station on the down main with an evening local on 5 July 1947. Part of the Metropolitan Cammell Carriage & Wagon Works can be seen on the right beyond the up and down Camp Hill lines. *F. W. Shuttleworth*

ther reductions since our pace was rather higher than desirable.

At North Stafford Junction my nerve nearly failed because we still seemed to be going fairly fast, and as yet I could not see if the road was clear to Leicester Junction. Concentrating ten-tenths, I tapped down the regulator handle so that it was just cracked open and even wound back the gear lever to give less than 15 per cent cut-off. It was very tricky at this stage, balancing things to give just sufficient delivery of steam to keep the couplings taught while at the same time keeping speed down so that we could stop in case the signals were on.

Then all of a sudden we were into the station and I could see that the road was clear. A quick assessment of our speed showed that we could have indeed stopped in time had the necessity arisen, and I realised that with the brake power of a semi-fitted I could use this technique with confidence in the future. It only remained to be seen if by keeping steam on in this manner a snatch had been avoided, and I could hardly wait until we got to Washwood Heath to find out. After detaching our train we were sent off light engine to the shed, but we always waited a few minutes while Les and any other passengers who had travelled home in the brake walked up to us.

I was just fixing our tail lamp when he arrived. Les, always the gentleman, invariably thanked me for a pleasant ride, provided of course I had given him one, and having passed this complimentary comment, I quickly asked if he had noticed the usual snatch at Burton.

'Now that you come to mention it,' he said with slow deliberation, 'I don't believe that I did.'

I went on to explain that I was experimenting with a different technique to try and eliminate the snatch and that I would be very grateful if he would take particular note at that point and let me know of the results.

Two nights later he was able to confirm that the brake-van had traversed the hump as smooth as silk, and from then on I was able to develop my method to a fine art with confidence. As with everything else, practice makes perfect, so as time went on judgement of speed and where and how much to ease off became second nature.

The reward for the concentration put into this exercise came about one winter's night late in the year. Widespread fog blanketed most of the northern counties resulting in many delayed and can-celled trains. Although conditions were reasonable between Derby and Birmingham, our own train was over an hour late and a number of Saltley crews waiting in the cabin at Derby North had scant prospect of finishing without excessive overtime unless they travelled home with us. Strangely enough one of the drivers faced with this problem was my old mate Percy Trotter. Never keen on overtime, 'Piggy' had been chomping at the bit since we arrived, and after making repeated vociferous requests to the Control, finally obtained permission, along with two other sets of men, to return to Saltley in our brake.

Since visibility was too poor to see the brake lights I had to judge the length of the train, then give them a minute or two to climb aboard, but having started off we found the distants were in our favour. The fog was just sufficiently thick to keep me on my toes without actually proving too much of a problem, although the run up to Burton Station with steam on did cause some tense moments. However, everything went as planned and being aware that my colleagues at the rear end would be passing judgement on my driving, I pressed on as fast as I dared and with as much delicacy as I could muster.

We arrived at Washwood Heath without incident, and with a very crowded footplate slowly travelled through somewhat murkier conditions the odd mile to Saltley loco. Only Les had as usual passed comment on the smoothness of the ride. Later as we cycled home together he broke into conversation.

'Were your ears burning tonight?'

'That,' I replied, recalling eyebrows and hair encrusted with frost collected as a result of being forced to keep my head stuck out in a slipstream of freezing fog, 'was the last thing I was likely to have.'

'Well, you see,' he went on, 'I just happened to say as we were approaching Burton that you were the only driver to go through there without giving a snatch, and in fact you were so gentle that the main problem was keeping awake. Percy then started singing your praises saying that it was he who had taught you all you knew. Whereupon Horace [another driver who was almost as garrulous as Piggy] said that whatever Percy might have taught you, it certainly wasn't gentleness and everyone knew how he drove and most still bore the scars to prove it. Well, you can just imagine it after that - they were at each other's throats all the way back to Washwood Heath, so nobody got any sleep. Still, it was a very nice ride all the same.'

Knowing Percy so well I could readily picture the near riot that would have taken place, and no doubt the finer points of my efforts had passed unnoticed, but at least Les appreciated them, and that after all had been the original object of the exercise.

Early in January an amusing little interlude took place that serves to illustrate the erroneous impression even a railway enthusiast has of what it is like to ride on the footplate. Derek Bayley, an old school friend of mine who was then working as a chemist in the laboratories of Fort Dunlop, had for some time been badgering me to arrange a trip for him on an engine. His departmental chief had invited him to write an article for the work's magazine, and since railway topics were still of great interest to many people, he thought that a first-hand description of footplate life would be rather unique and gain wide acceptance.

Unfortunately, official footplate passes were so hard to come by that he did not even bother to apply, therefore I was duly approached in order to devise some clandestine scheme. The problem was of course that such a ruse would have to take place under cover of darkness, since for all our sakes we must avoid detection. All our regular turns involved long and uncertain hours coupled with the inevitability of frequent exposure to many grades of staff. However, we did have one job in the link that was absolutely made-to-measure.

This was our solitary passenger duty, which came round only on one Sunday night every 12 weeks. It could not have been better since we departed from Birmingham at 7.45 pm, invariably with a 'Jubilee', and arrived at Derby 1 hour later. After uncoupling, the engine was then left for the disposal men on Derby loco, and after walking back to the station we relieved the 9.20 express that terminated at New Street. This meant that we were back at our starting point only 2 hours 35 minutes after setting out, and in ample time for my friend to catch his bus home. Just in case some prying eyes should spot a third man on the footplate we arranged for Derek to be disguised as a Traffic Inspector by clothing him in my macintosh and a felt hat, the official uniform of one of those gentlemen.

The night in question found Fred and I standing at the end of No 7 platform while Derek was trying to make his languorous 6 ft 4 in frame inconspicuous by lurking in the shadow of a supporting pillar. At 7.40 pm a filthy looking 'Jubilee', which turned out to be *Rooke*, trundled in with much clanking of side rods and juddered to a halt halfway under the bridge.

'She's a bit run-down,' commented the Bristol driver as we exchanged places, then as he disappeared from sight I ushered Derek to my side of the cab.

'Just stand behind my seat, old lad,' I said. 'You'll be out of the way there while I put a bit on.'

Having flashed a dozen shovelsful round the box, I just had time to point out the principal controls and gauges before the guard's whistle blew. Answering with a raucous hoot, I then crossed to Fred's side to see the train out.

As I came near to him I spoke softly in his ear. 'Pull her well up mate - after all, we want to give Derek something to write about.' (It may be recalled that a rough engine always knocked more violently when run on a short cut-off.)

With 13 coaches behind the tender Fred was obliged to take a fairly hefty handful of regulator, and on New Street's perpetually greasy rails *Rooke* slipped. The cacophony this created startled even me, so you can well imagine the wonders it did for Derek. The term 'panic-stricken' might be a shade too strong, but in the glare of an already white fire I saw him grab the nearest handrail with both hands while he glanced fearfully around with an expression registering shock and alarm.

This initial slip and the subsequent thunderous gallop down through the tunnels left us in no doubt of what was to come. Poor old *Rooke* was just about as run-down as any locomotive I had had the misfortune to work on, and was obviously at the upper mileage limit and more than ready for a major overhaul. In fact, by the time we reached Derby I was quite prepared to believe that the last one had been missed and she was going round for the second time.

She rocked, she rolled, she waggled and she oscillated in a most spectacular and uncomfortable manner, while the excessive play in the big-end bearings caused three tremendous crashes to shake her from stem to stern at every revolution of the driving wheels. Sitting down was out of the question and Fred, instead of linking her well up to make her knock, ran with the longest practical cut-off in an effort to subdue this defect. Derek in his naivety had intended to make notes of our

'Jubilee' No 45660 *Rooke*. This locomotive gained fame during special test runs including the Settle to Carlisle section in October 1937 when it is reputed to have developed extremely high indicated horsepower figures in excess of 1,800. When I fired it from Birmingham New Street to Derby one Sunday evening 20 years later it was so rough that I would have been prepared to believe that it had not been shopped since then.

progress, but as far as I can recall he never relaxed his grip on the handrail for the entire journey, not even when we came to a standstill in Burton station for our brief halt.

I must admit that I had my work cut out firing her at speed, and this particular feat seemed to fascinate Derek above all else.

'I cannot understand,' he said afterwards, 'how you manage to fire coal through the mouthpiece, let alone place it accurately on the grate when the firehole has moved to an entirely different position in space by the end of your swing from that when you started it - quite incredible.'

His scientific brain had tried to work out a regular pattern of motion for he felt sure that I could not have done it without being able to predict the various movements. However, *Rooke*'s wildly cavorting footplate followed no set formula and, as I explained, success was due to nothing more than years of practice, a feeling of what was happening being transmitted through the feet, and split-second reflexes.

We could not have given Derek a worse first ride if we had planned it, and after suffering an hour of that treatment we were all heartily glad to drop *Rooke* on Derby shed.

I did nearly walk away with the exhaust injector steam valve control wheel as a souvenir, though. The banging and crashing had caused many cab fittings to become loose and one of these was the aforesaid control wheel. The bally thing kept shaking off its spindle and rolling around the footboards. Having become thoroughly tired of playing 'hunt the slipper' every time I wished to operate the injector, I took to keeping it in my jacket pocket, hence the near oversight.

Despite the fact that the 'Black Five' was also below average, our return journey was a much smoother affair by comparison and both Fred and Derek were able to sit down for most of the way. We arrived back at New Street practically on time and a somewhat deaf and numbed but infinitely wiser Derek, looking like a cross between Al

Jolson and one of the Harlem Globe Trotters, tottered off into the night. His article, when it came into print, made footplate life seem like some fiendish, perpetual torture, but then he did have a very rough ride.

The happy periods in one's life pass all too quickly, and that glorious year with Fred was no exception. May came round again and once more I was torn between wishing to stay on with him and wanting to progress to higher things. Since these higher things included the prospect of working the much venerated Carlisles, which had been my burning ambition since first signing on as a cleaner, I found our eventual parting less painful than I formerly imagined. As it turned out I went into the Bradford link, which contained four weeks of Carlisle jobs, and when the notices were duly posted I suddenly realised that at last I was one of the elite. I did not know my future driver Les Field, but Fred assured me that as far as the Carlisles were concerned I could not be with a better mate.

'You will not expend an ounce more energy than is strictly necessary with Les,' was his parting shot.

It was ironical that I was to expend more energy with him over a concentrated period than at any other time of my life, but I could not have even guessed at the circumstances then, and therefore suitably reassured I joined the Bradford link with a happy confidence.

The year with Fred had enabled me to considerably extend my road knowledge, but even this was but a cock stride compared to the marathon Carlisle run. However, my driving experience had given me a much greater appreciation of the problems and ideals to aim for when working steam locomotives, and this was to prove a great benefit during the coming year.

15
THUNDER OVER AIS GILL

At Saltley the Carlisle turns were surrounded with a certain awe and reverence in no way even approached by any other duty. The sheer magnitude of the job in terms of mileage alone was a daunting prospect to driver and fireman alike, for there were no booked stops at which to take a rest. Indeed, if all went well and the train ran to schedule, it meant seven hours of undivided concentration for the driver, and an equal amount of time with a shovel in his hands for the fireman. When not infrequent delays occurred, this ordeal could well extend to ten hours or more, and, on the outward-bound trip at any rate, this fearsome task was made all the more difficult by the fact that the really hard work started at Skipton, some 5_ hours after booking on, and some 140 miles from Water Orton. Here, already tired, with a fire well past its best and the coal at the back of the tender, one had to gird one's loins to tackle just about the most demanding 87-mile mountainous stretch on British Railways over the Settle and Carlisle line. It was little wonder then that on many occasions even healthy young giants of firemen had to be literally carried from the footplate at the end of such herculean labours, rigid with exhaustion.

Much has already been written about how the Settle and Carlisle line came into being. Suffice to say that it was born out of blood and sweat in an era of unparalleled human endeavour, hacked out of some of the most wild and barren moorland to be found in England, at great expense and cost in human lives. That it was all worthwhile lives on in the gifts to posterity offered by such superb constructions as Ribblehead and Dent Head Viaducts, and Blea Moor and Rise Hill Tunnels, fittingly set amid the grim grandeur of the Pennine Peaks. The challenge of that stupendous climb up to Ais Gill was exciting enough, but added to this was the barren isolation of unpopulated mountains, which the weather lashed in quickly changing moods with a fury that I have never experienced anywhere else. Every trip was a unique adventure and no two runs were ever the same. So many variables could come into play over such a long journey, and even the climate was totally different up in the fells 180 miles north of our starting point.

This paramount job had a long and regal lineage, for the development of the Birmingham-Carlisle service came about during the reign of Victoria in the year of her Golden Jubilee, when the 4.30 pm loose-coupled express freight train from Lawley Street to Derby was extended through to Leeds, conveying important North and Scotch traffic from Birmingham and district. The train was given the unofficial title of 'The Jubilee' by railwaymen having dealings with it, and was referred to as such for many years.

In 1931 Scotch traffic had grown considerably and the decision was taken to run a semi-fitted Class D freight at 4.30 pm from Lawley Street through to Carlisle, for Scotch traffic only, followed at 4.40 pm by 'The Jubilee', running from Lawley Street to Leeds as an express freight. Special authority was given in the Classification and Marshalling of Freight Trains circular for the 4.30 pm train to be double-headed when required to convey a maximum of 60 vehicles, and the train ran under this authority on many occasions, especially during the very heavy fruit season, with vans emanating from Evesham. A subsequent development of this arrangement was for a train to be booked through from Evesham to Glasgow during the main fruit period.

In 1936, to enable better connecting services to be given, a more intensive marshalling programme was introduced with these northbound and other

A general view of Skipton station. When the Birmingham-Carlisles arrived here they had already covered 140 miles. With the fire getting dirty and the coal well back on the tender, a tired fireman had to gird his loins in preparation for the long and formidable climb up to Ais Gill.

trains, and experience showed that this extended marshalling could be undertaken with much greater facility at Water Orton Sidings. This resulted in a re-arrangement of the connecting services into the trains. These trains then commenced their journey to the North from Water Orton at 4.40 pm to Carlisle and 4.50 pm to Leeds.

The demands for express freight services grew, so that by 1946 a 3.50 am semi-fitted freight from Water Orton to Carlisle was introduced to give a speedy transit to traffic that had accumulated during the night period in Water Orton, and to avoid such traffic having to wait for the afternoon services. A further improvement was introduced in 1952 by the running of the 4.45 pm Water Orton to Glasgow, which, in addition to Glasgow traffic, took wagons for Edinburgh (Lothian Road) and Dumfries perishable traffic.

Even in the early 1950s occasionally a 'Crab' found itself heading this crack train, and sometimes a Class '4F' 0-6-0 has been known to take over from Leeds in the event of an engine failure, but happily while I was in the link a 'Black Five' or '9F' was always rostered.

From my earliest days in the Shed link I had listened to many tales of exciting exploits on the Carlisles. They were like folklore, handed down to succeeding generations, and I tended to regard them as such, for some were so far-fetched as to be hardly creditable. Most of these stories concerned the ferocity of the weather over the Settle to Carlisle stretch and, although no doubt somewhat embroidered with each subsequent telling, I later

discovered at first hand that little exaggeration had crept in over the years.

Who could imagine a train being blown to a complete standstill by the force of the wind at Ribblehead? Or snow so deep as to bury telegraph poles? Or cold so intense that injectors froze solid? I personally did not believe that large lumps of coal could be stripped from the tops of tenders like so much dust, or that securely roped wagon sheets could be blown away as if they were tissue paper. The story of the guard who was left clinging desperately to his hand brake wheel after the very fabric of his van had disintegrated around him sounded to me very much like the inventions of an over-fertile imagination. However, seeing is believing and I duly came to experience some of these wild conditions before the year was out.

When I joined the link the limit of my knowledge was Sheffield, a mere 90 miles away, and although I was confident that I could work at full effort for up to two hours, how would I cope over a journey of 226 miles, involving maybe eight or ten hours of continuous labour? It was something of a relief, then, to find that I had three weeks with Les before our initial run to Carlisle came up, and I used this time to prepare myself for the task. Providentially our first job together was nothing more exacting than a local tripper, which gave us plenty of opportunity to discuss what I honestly considered were the only important turns in the link.

Les Field was of medium height and build, neither fat nor thin, and he dropped nicely into the classification so commonly termed 'average'. He looked his

57 years and had the usual thickening around his middle for a man of that age. He always wore a cloth cap that was long overdue for an oil-change and often a tweed sports jacket that likewise had seen better days, believing that these items of apparel gave him a more respectable appearance when popping into 'the local' to lay the dust after a run. Les liked his pint and also got through a fair quantity of Capstan Extra Strong cigarettes, but never allowed either habit to interfere with his job.

As a driver he was superb and, from the point of view of technique and route knowledge, undoubtedly the best I ever rode with. He never used an ounce more steam than was absolutely necessary, having the happy knack of using regulator openings and cut-offs to keep the engine always running at optimum efficiency. Les Field's driving was the model of consistency, which made firing for him a real pleasure, for one was never caught out by a sudden change of mood or display of temper. He could, however, drive as hard and as fast as anyone if the occasion demanded, and on the Carlisles this was sometimes necessary to gain or retain a favourable path.

As a companion, however, he had certain shortcomings. His reticence to hold a conversation meant that I had to pump every piece of information from him, and at times this was both discouraging and also hard work. He was not a very happy soul either, rationing himself to about one laugh, two chuckles and three smiles per week. If something cropped up that really amused him, and as a result he used up his quota on the very first day, then the remaining six were very dry indeed. In addition Les never offered to take up the shovel, but then I for my part had far too much to learn about the roads north of Sheffield to entertain any ideas of driving.

In order to familiarise myself with this unknown marathon, I obtained from Les a list of all the principal places, mileages and ruling gradients for the whole route to Carlisle. I laboriously wrote these out during the first week with the idea that I could consult this chart during the run and quickly obtain some notion of my whereabouts and what to expect. It did in fact prove very useful in as much that I could plan out in advance when I should require a heavier fire, when I could expect to be busy and for how long, when I could get coal forward and when I could reasonably snatch the odd sandwich.

Therefore by the time that first trip to Carlisle came along I had a little knowledge of what to expect, and Les fortunately supplemented this with some practical advice. For example, he suggested that I carried double rations of food and drink, for one never knew what was going to happen over such a distance. He also recommended that I select a new firing shovel, run it in on other jobs then put my name on the handle, so that it could be kept in the stores for my exclusive use. Furthermore, he pointed out that it was a good idea to carry a second shovel, two coalpicks and twice the normal complement of fire irons, then if by accident I lost or broke some item of equipment we would not be in trouble.

It was an undeniable fact that everyone at Saltley leaned over backwards to help when they knew that you were working the Carlisles, and the storemen were no exception. These fine fellows guarded new equipment as devotedly as if they had paid for it out of their own pockets. When I asked for a new shovel to break in for the Carlisles, I was immediately invited into that holy of holies and told to pick one out from a row of brand new 'Bulldogs'. After working my way through a dozen or so, I found one that possessed just the right balance and feel, and thereafter it was kept for my own exclusive use.

New shovels are not particularly pleasant to work with, since both blade and handle are rough and unpolished. A lot more effort is required to throw coal any specified distance, while the handle drags in the hand, making it difficult to execute those little twirls and flicks that were part of the virtuoso's repertoire.

However, after a few weeks of work I had the blade gleaming like stainless steel, while the handle was as smooth as a test match cricket bat. Admittedly I helped things along with a sheet of emery cloth and a drop of linseed oil, but the shovel turned out to be a real beauty and was at its best when I finally left British Railways.

For our first week's work on the 4.45 pm Glasgow we were required to book on at 3.55 pm on Monday, work up to Carlisle, then return on the 4.03 pm, which was scheduled to arrive at Washwood Heath No 2 at 11.33 pm Tuesday night. Wednesday was a rest day, and on Thursday and Friday the whole performance was repeated once more. We were paid on a mileage basis and, although we only actually worked four days, it was the equal in terms of pounds, shilling and pence to a full week of nights, but in terms of concentration and sheer physical effort it was the equal to just about any other two weeks' work in the link.

My preparations for that first momentous day were as thorough as I could conceivably make them. I arrived at the shed a full hour before I was due to book on, and to my delight discovered that we had No 5265, then one of the best 'Black Fives' at Saltley. She was standing on the back departure road, coupled to the locomotives for the Carlisle and Leeds, both of which accompanied us to Water Orton. The shed men had made, as always, an excellent job of preparing her. A mountain of best-quality coal rose high above the cab roof, making a mockery of the 9-ton nominal load, while the firebox already contained a well-built-up fire, just nicely alight. The cab had been hosed down, and even the windows had been cleaned.

I next examined the tools and fire irons, and, finding them all satisfactory, set off to obtain a second coalpick, a bent dart and a long clinker shovel to supplement those already on board. Having done this, I collected my own firing shovel from the stores and was just sweeping all traces of sand and char from the framing when Les arrived. As usual he did not have much to say except that he was glad to see that we had a good engine and, after stowing his belongings, carried out a thorough examination of all and sundry, including testing the sanding gear. While he was there I operated both injectors, making use of the water supplied by the exhaust one to hose down the over-filled tender. When all this was completed, we still had 10 minutes or so before ringing out, so

Les went off to mash our first can of tea. He told me that this would have to last until Skipton South Junction, where we were booked for examination and water at 9.00 pm.

The tea Les brewed was strong enough to start with, so that by the time it had stewed for five hours on the drip-tray, it was positively vitriolic, quite capable of burning holes in the footboards, in fact. I therefore only partook of one lidful at Water Orton while it was still fresh and, even then, I was forced to dilute it with milk from my own supply. For the remainder of the run I satisfied my thirst with orange juice or water, leaving the tea for Les and his own cast-iron innards that were, after all, far more used to it than mine.

Dead on time the shed signal dropped and, with our guard as passenger, all three engines chugged over Duddeston Road bridge amid much hissing of steam from open cylinder cocks and the respectful stares from colleagues who always gathered to watch the most important departure of the day. This was a proud moment for me, one I had waited eight long years for, and now that it had arrived I was finding difficulty in realising that it was not just another job. Here I was, about to embark on the longest run I could ever hope to make, and so far it felt just the same as dozens of others, but no doubt before the day was out the right impression would make itself felt.

Our quick run down to Water Orton proved that No 5265 was in fine shape, but the oscillations incurred by our speed shook down an awful lot of coal from that overfilled tender, so by the time we backed into the sidings the footplate was knee-deep in cobbles. It had been my intention to

No 45265 was one of the best 'Black Fives' at Saltley in June 1958 when I fired her on my first ever trip to Carlisle. Whenever possible only the finest engines were allocated to this marathon 226-mile run. Built by Armstrong-Whitworth in 1936, No 5265 is shown at Gloucester two years later. Note the crosshead-driven vacuum pump that was subsequently removed, and the code '5P5F' below the cabside windows.

fire the engine as lightly as possible, for I had already discovered how consistent Les was in his driving methods, but with so much debris lying on the footboards I was obliged to fill the box in the interests of tidiness.

With the headlamps correctly set and everything else in perfect order, we awaited our guard to advise us of the load, which happily on this first run turned out to be a fairly light one - no more than 29, equal to 32, in fact well within our limit. 4.45 pm came and, after being called out, we drew down to Water Orton station to await our signal. At precisely 4.50 pm it dropped, and with no more than a faint beat from our chimney we rolled gently into motion and headed out over the fast towards our far-off destination.

With Les there were no spectacular displays of pyrotechnics in getting away, just slight, almost imperceptible, increases in the regulator opening, coupled with an appropriately progressive shortening of the cut-off. Without any apparent effort we quickly accelerated our train so that by the time Kingsbury was passed we were rattling along at a good 50 mph. With so little steam being used I had a relatively easy time and was consequently able to enjoy the excellent ride provided by No 5265. The weather was also near perfect, being pleasantly mild and with clear visibility. By the time we stopped for water at Sheffield some two hours later, the coal was still falling down on to the shovelling plate, which was a good indication of how little we had used so far. Moreover, I felt in excellent spirits, but from now on I would be travelling over strange territory and would have to rely on Les for details of the road ahead.

I do not intend to detail the first trip since a fuller description of the route will follow, together with exact timings, of a memorable run with No 92137. Suffice it to say that we arrived at Skipton on time at 9.00 pm after an uneventful but nevertheless interesting journey. Here we were booked for examination and water, and while the tank was filling I walked over to the nearby cabin and made a can of coffee. By now I felt as though I had come a fair distance, but excitement kept fatigue at bay and I was really looking forward to the assault upon Ais Gill, which from all accounts was the best part of the run.

On returning to the engine I found that Les had cleared the fire from the back set of bars and he advised me to pull out any clinker to be found

there. With 33 miles of virtually unbroken uphill work ahead I thereafter always made a practice of so doing. With rocking grate engines it was of course no problem, and in any case I kept these relatively clean by frequent use of the intermediate rocking position.

Before departing at 9.17 pm I was able to pull some coal down, but there was still no necessity to keep the tender doors open all the time. In fact, it was not until we were approaching Ribblehead that I was forced to continually go into the tender.

The 14 miles from Settle to Blea Moor has a ruling gradient of 1 in 100, and even with only 29 vans in tow, Les had to give her a fair amount of stick. However, I do not recall many details of actually firing the engine at all; I was far too interested in absorbing the new panorama that unfolded at every bend in the track.

I have often recounted the benefits of changing links in May, but never was this more apparent than on the Carlisle run. As one progresses north and west in summer, so the actual time of sunset becomes later. I was therefore able to enjoy the glories of a magnificent sunset right up into the northern fells.

Seeing those great grey peaks and heather-covered moors for the first time, softened with continually changing shades of pinks and golds, was a sight I shall never forget. Then again, looking down from the top of Ribblehead Viaduct to the moor 169 feet below reminded me of all that I had read about the problems of its construction. As I was admiring this superb feat of engineering Les told me that this was the point where a westerly gale was most felt. The valley formed a funnel with its widest end opening out right on to the Irish Sea, and as the wind entered this its velocity increased until the full force was concentrated over the viaduct. It was hard to imagine such conditions on this calm summer's evening, but I was to find out for myself the terrible fury the elements could unleash later in the year. He also told me that a payment of 10 shillings was formerly given by the company to the local inhabitants for recovering wagon sheets blown away by such storms, a sure indication of the frequency and seriousness of this problem.

Blea Moor Tunnel, too, was a welcome sight, partly because this, at 2,629 yards, was the longest tunnel I was to journey through, and partly because it represented the end of our hardest climb. We had, of course, another 10 miles to travel until the summit of Ais Gill was reached, but this was an undulating course and the stiffest gradient against us was a mere 1 in 165. Moreover, a drop at 1 in 440 through the tunnel enabled us to gain sufficient momentum to overcome these short rises without undue effort, and only the last mile up to the 1,167-foot summit appeared a drag.

The stone portals of Blea Moor Tunnel looked innocuous enough in the soft failing light, but Blea Moor took on a totally different aspect in the depths of winter and, although I am digressing, I vividly recall one night standing on the top of our tender while taking water during a return trip the following November. It was heavily overcast, and save for the glimmer of an oil lamp in the nearby signal box, the blackness was complete. Not a single outline could be distinguished - it was just like being shut up in a coal cellar - and the feeling of utter isolation from the rest of civilisation was hard to describe. Never have I visited a blacker spot than Blea Moor, and it was also here that I had the unusual experience of sighting strange lights in the sky that may well have been UFOs.

This occurred during that same week in November on the outward run. We were hammering up the section from Ribblehead to Blea Moor and because the fire was now being allowed to run down somewhat, I was leaning out of my window taking a breather and staring out into the impenetrable darkness. Thick cloud cover obscured the stars so that it was impossible to ascertain where the mountains ended and the sky began, and of course in that remote area there were no reflections of street lights on the clouds. Suddenly I became aware of five orange lights, each about twice the size and intensity of Venus at her bright-

est, at an elevation of around 45 degrees, apparently keeping pace with us and formed into a diamond shape. This pattern then changed to that of an arrowhead, then elongated into a straight line.

I watched these manoeuvres for a few moments wondering what they might be, and frankly I was puzzled. As a frequent observer of the night sky I had never seen anything at all like it, and none of the usual explanations given for such sightings seemed to fit. They were certainly not stars, aircraft navigation lights, street lights, nor the reflection of car headlamps. In case they were in fact UFOs I called Les over to witness the spectacle, but he too could offer no valid explanation. I watched these fascinating lights until we plunged into Blea Moor Tunnel, but on emerging at the other end no trace of them could be seen. Thinking that someone else might also have made an observation, I scoured the papers next day and was disappointed to find no mention of any such sightings. I was therefore obliged to write it off as just another of those inexplicable happenings that come into everyone's life from time to time.

It was now becoming too dark to pick out features in detail, but I did manage to get an idea of the size of Dent Head Viaduct as we raced over its 200 yards length. On both sides of the line rose the vast black shapes of the fells, and I realised that I would have to wait until our return run before I could enjoy the scenery of this section.

Within minutes we were clattering into the 1,213-yard Rise Hill Tunnel, the exit from which provided a positive marker for dropping our water scoop into the famous Garsdale troughs, which, at an elevation of 1,100 feet, were the highest in the

Blea Moor signal box - always a welcome sight for the fireman from either direction. Travelling north towards Carlisle it was the end of the most arduous climb on the run from Water Orton. Going south, 14 miles downhill with a ruling gradient of 1 in 100 enabled the fireman to take a well-earned breather after the long haul up to Ais Gill. On a dark winter's night the blackness was complete at the this wild and remote spot. Note the heating arrangements for the water tank, and the substantial coal supply upon which the signalman depended when cut off by all too frequent blizzards.

world. I was also very interested to see the well-known turntable at Hawes Junction around which, so the story goes, a stockade had been constructed to protect it from the violence of the wind in that area. I had been amused at this tale of a forlorn engine and an even more forlorn crew being given a protracted merry-go-round ride on a turntable that was apparently unstoppable until the wind force abated. Whether authentic or not, the fact remained that I managed to glimpse that unique circle of sturdy timbers as we roared past.

Then began our last 2-mile climb up through the short Moorcock and Shotlock Hill Tunnels to Ais Gill where, framed against the darkening western sky, could be seen the black brooding mass of Wild Boar Fell. We breasted the summit at about 10.40 pm and, having been continually active for the past six hours, I was thankful to hear Les say that I could now sit down and take it easy for the next 15 miles. This section from Ais Gill to Ormside was virtually all downhill at a ruling gradient of 1 in 100, so I took the opportunity thus afforded to finish off the rest of my sandwiches as we coasted down through the mountains at speeds up to 60 mph. Most of the wild beauty of this area passed unnoticed in the darkness, but I did manage to make out Mallerstang Edge rising to a height of 2,328 feet in the east and the dim lights of the village far below.

This brief respite enabled me to reflect on how effortlessly a 'Black Five' performed its allotted task on this long run. The previous year I had come to appreciate the suitability of 'Crabs' on medium-distance semi-fitteds, but in terms of all-round efficiency and comfort they could not be compared to a 'Black Five'.

No 5265 was still steaming beautifully and I do not suppose that at this stage I had fired more than five tons of coal. With a similar load few other engines could have accomplished the journey with such economy of fuel and effort, while at the same time giving us a tolerably comfortable ride.

From Ormside it was back to the shovel, which unaccountably now seemed much heavier, for the undulating climb up to just beyond Appleby. From there we still had some 30 miles to travel until our destination was reached, although the gradients were mainly in our favour for the next 15 miles down to Lazonby and I was able to cope without undue effort. The stiff 1-mile climb at 1 in 165 out of Lazonby called for a bit of extra steam, as did the final haul up to Low House Crossing, but once this hump was surmounted I was able to run the fire down during the 7-mile run at 1 in 132 down to Carlisle.

Three minutes early and with everything looking as spick and span as when we left Saltley, No 5265 rolled into Petteril Bridge where we were relieved by an awaiting Carlisle crew. I must admit

Ais Gill signal box. At 1,167 feet above sea level this famous summit was the highest point on the Settle to Carlisle line. It was a formidable obstacle to overcome with any train in either direction. Southbound it was nearly 50 miles out from Carlisle, the last 15 miles from Ormside, mainly at 1 in 100, was particularly demanding on both engine and fireman.

that I felt much more spritely than I would have expected as we walked the short distance to 'The Barracks'. Perhaps the thoughts of a refreshing shower, a hot meal and a comfortable bed added a certain pep to my stride, for I found myself having to slow down a couple of times to enable Les to catch up as we climbed the steep slope to that very presentable establishment.

The lodge itself was large and modern, and in an entirely different class to the one at Sheffield. This perhaps was not surprising, since Carlisle was a natural relief point for the long-distance Anglo-Scottish traffic. The washroom was well equipped, having both baths and showers, while the canteen was designed on the self-service principle and provided a good selection of food right round the clock. The bedrooms, too, were a vast improvement upon what I had previously experienced, being relatively commodious, well soundproofed and having individual radiators. I also much appreciated the drying-room, since I frequently arrived at Carlisle soaked with perspiration, and without this facility I would have been obliged to don still wet clothing the following day.

After a satisfying meal and a congenial chat with crews from foreign parts, we retired to our respective rooms, where I for one slumbered soundly for a full eight hours.

One surprising point had arisen during the course of a conversation with a Camden fireman in the canteen. He was an old hand and several years senior to myself, but he had been quite sincere when stating that he did not envy us Saltley men on our run. When I asked why, since he had just fired a 'Duchess' over a considerably longer run, he pointed out the following facts.

The old LNWR route was for the most part much flatter, with Shap the only bank of any note. They worked the finest express engines in the country which, apart from giving a superbly comfortable ride, were equipped with coal pushers. This relieved them of the necessity of getting coal from the back of the tender - they only had to fire it. Furthermore, being an express passenger train they were virtually guaranteed the road, and in any case they were only on the footplate for five hours. We, on the other hand, travelled a route like a switchback with the formidable Settle to Carlisle section right at the end. Being only a fitted freight, our progress was much more subject to delays and we could be anything from seven to ten

hours on the footplate of nothing better than a 'Black Five'. With no coal pushers and the need to clean the fire en route, it amounted in his eyes to a good deal of hard work.

'I think you're a lot of bloody heroes, mate,' said he as a parting shot, and before I closed my eyes I perhaps unjustifiably felt one.

While we rested, our engine was re-fettled and left at the near-derelict Durran Hill loco shed. This was now only used for stabling engines such as ours, because of its close proximity to our starting point, Durran Hill Sidings. The following afternoon we signed on, did the usual checks, then topped up our tank before leaving the depot. Although we were booked for water at Appleby, only 29 miles on, Les preferred to have the tank as full as possible in order to save precious minutes once our journey had commenced. He liked to gain time if possible on the off chance that we might be slipped into an earlier path, for the sooner we arrived home the better.

The first part of our run from Durran Hill was quite a taxing affair, for although we again had only a moderate load of 32 equal to 36, it entailed a 7-mile climb at 1 in 132 from a cold start. Departing at 4.3 pm on a pleasantly bright afternoon I was able to see all the details I had missed the previous night, and the run up through the picturesque Eden Valley fully lived up to what I had expected. Thick woodlands and luxuriant pastures were to be found in profusion on the fertile soil, and it contrasted strongly with the barren fells further on.

We spent some 5 minutes taking on water at Appleby, then with the fire well built up and thoroughly hot, we set about the attack on Ais Gill. For the next 18 miles and 45 minutes the regulator was over on the second valve and, with the cut-off varying between 25 and 45 per cent, we hammered away in a most exhilarating fashion. At last I was able to see what had only been names on a route card and also obtain an idea of the gradients involved: 1 in 100 from Ormside to Griseburn Sidings, 1 in 166 to Crosby Garrett, 1 in 190 up to Kirkby Stephen, 1 in 100 to Mallerstang, then, after a half-mile stretch at 1 in 330, 1 in 100 all the way up to Ais Gill. Despite her exertions No 5265 was steaming beautifully and, with the exhaust reverberating around the mountains like a thunderstorm, I really enjoyed every moment of that truly wonderful 45-minute climb.

Carlisle men always made an excellent job of coaling Saltley engines with the best available for their return run. Understandably the lowest-mileage engines were allocated whenever possible in order to lighten the crew's burden somewhat over this very long haul. Standing at Durran Hill loco in June 1952, No 44966 has the look of a recent shopping as she awaits her crew for the 4.3 pm Carlisle to Washwood Heath. *Pat Webb*

The run along the high fells to Blea Moor took but 16 minutes, and we topped our tank up over the troughs as a precaution. Then, with the prospect of a 14-mile descent mainly at 1 in 100 before me, I sat down to view all the places of interest I had missed while firing on the outward trip. As on the day before, we were booked for examination at Skipton, but, having only been on the road for three hours, I did not attempt to clean the fire. I normally did this at Rotherham, where we were again booked for water at 9.3 pm.

The return run differed in as much as we travelled via Rotherham, rejoining the main line again at Tapton Junction. This little diversion took us past the countless collieries in that area

and, while aesthetically there was little to commend it, even on a bright summer evening the industrial activity was nevertheless interesting.

As the evening turned to dusk, familiar places and names began to slide past and I felt a sense of urgency in wanting to get home as soon as possible. It affected all of us, including No 5265, for she seemed to be now running better than ever. At 10.20 pm we passed Derby North, and it seemed incredible that only last year a trip to Derby represented a whole day's work. Having come all the way from Carlisle during the past 6 hours 20 minutes, this 40-mile run to Birmingham was now but the final lap.

Over the fast from Kingsbury I cleaned down

Kirkby Stephen station in Midland Railway days in 1905. It had changed little 50 years later when I thundered through with the Birmingham-Carlisle fitted freights. The section southbound from Crosby Garrett to Kirkby Stephen was somewhat easier at 1 in 190, but then up to Mallerstang it was 1 in 100, and following this, except for the half-mile stretch of 1 in 330, it was 1 in 100 all the way to Ais Gill summit, still some 7 miles distant.

the footplate and both Les and I washed away the traces of 226 miles of toil, so by the time we were relieved at Washwood Heath we looked clean and fresh, and even the appearance of the fire belied the fact that it had just burned five tons of coal.

Relieving the Carlisle at Washwood Heath may seem extravagant in the use of men, since we normally rode on the footplate to the shed in any case, but occasionally the Camp Hill loop was blocked and it was quicker to walk. Not wishing to delay our booking off any longer than necessary was, therefore, a further indication of the 'Red Carpet' treatment offered to the Carlisle crews.

Soon after I joined the link Class '9s' were substituted for the more usual 'Black Fives' as they became more readily available. Like many of the other drivers, Les was a little conservative in his attitude towards them and somewhat apprehensive about having his favourite engines usurped on this prime duty. However, as their finer points became better appreciated, the moans gradually died away and the fact that they always gave a superb ride while handling even the heaviest trains with consummate ease soon won the acceptance of all who worked them.

Generally speaking I found that on light and medium loads somewhat more coal was used than with a good 'Black Five', but this may have been partly due to Les not initially working them at their most economical settings. With further experience he discovered that a '9' could be effectively operated at shorter cut-offs than a 'Black Five', but this took time.

With heavier trains the '9s' were undoubtedly less troubled and this showed up in the coal consumed. It was noticeable, however, that if we were delayed and the time in steam considerably extended, a disproportionate amount of fuel was burned. This was not really surprising, however, when one considers the relative grate areas involved - 40.2 sq ft as to 28.65 sq ft for the 'Black Five'.

While on the subject of coal consumption, I well recall two occasions with Class '9s' when it was touch and go whether we made it to Saltley. Both were what we termed the 'morning job', which was scheduled to depart from Durran Hill at 11.45 pm, arriving Washwood Heath at 6.55 am. Unfortunately, this turn was more subject to delays than the others, particularly in winter, and on the first instance we arrived at the shed with no more than 2 hundredweights of dust in the tender. On the second occasion we cut it even more fine and, after a 10½-hour run I fired the last of our coal approaching Water Orton. Knowing that we had sufficient reserve in our boiler and firebed to get us to the loco, provided we did not encounter more undue delays, I brushed out and hosed down the tender so that it presented the appearance of a big, shiny empty bin. Doug Pinkerton and a young passed cleaner relieved us at Washwood Heath. It was not the first time that Doug had done so, and as he climbed on board and glanced approvingly around the spotless footplate he stated in his usual loud manner that he had just been telling his mate what a pleasure it was to relieve us.

'That's the way to bring 'em in, young feller,' he declared. 'Not a speck of coal lying about and the

While the 4.3 pm Carlisle-Washwood Heath usually ran on time throughout its journey, the 11.45 pm seemed far more subject to delays. Freight traffic was at its most dense during the early hours, and it only required one struggling mineral to displace a fitted from its correct path. When this happened things usually went from bad to worse - instead of arriving at 6.55 am it could be 10.00 am, which naturally resulted in a much higher coal consumption. On two such occasions with Class '9Fs' I completely emptied the tenders. Passing Burton loco some three hours late is Saltley 'Black Five' No 44805. *Pat Webb*

fire so clean you can see the bars.'

'There's not a speck of coal in there either, Doug,' I retorted, nodding towards the tender doors. He drew them aside, then reeled back in surprise as he surveyed the gleaming cavern thus exposed.

'Good grief,' he gasped, 'you have had a rough trip.'

His mate also goggled in awe, looking first at the empty tender, then at the shovel, and finally at me. His expression indicated how his mental processes were working. If this is what firing in the top link meant, he wanted none of it.

We were always allocated Class '9s' fitted with tenders capable of carrying 9 tons of coal and 4,725 gallons of water, the 7-ton variety being inadequate for the Carlisle run. Since they were invariably over-coaled, we went out with something like 10 tons on board, and because 5 tons of this had to be shovelled forward en route, I suppose I had shifted something like 15 tons of coal during the course of this run. Taking into account breaking up innumerable lumps in addition to one's other duties, it added up to a fair night's work.

Despite these strenuous labours I never felt particularly exhausted and must have appeared quite fresh since, on more than one occasion after such a run, colleagues in the lobby would ask whether I was booking on or off. While some firemen seemed to relish looking as if they had been down a coalmine for eight hours, I took the opposite view and tried to preserve a clean, smart appearance at all times.

Having proved their ability, Class '9s' were used more frequently on the Carlisle runs, and I accurately logged one journey I made in late July with No 92137. The run was quite typical in many respects, and shows how competently both Les and the engine handled a heavy load, although the weather proved to be exceptional in the form of violent thunderstorms, but then something different always seemed to take place on the Carlisles. This, apart from its arduous duration, made the turn so interesting - one never knew what was going to happen next.

After a week of unusually high temperatures and unbroken sunshine, I arrived at Saltley just after 3.00 pm. With the thermometer once again in the high 80s I was already perspiring profusely despite having cycled at quite a leisurely pace, and as I walked across to No 92137 standing on the back

departure road, not a breath of air stirred the layer of coal dust covering the yard in that area. Such smoke that came from the engines' chimneys coiled lazily up into the heavy atmosphere and any steam emitted evaporated almost immediately.

Struggling on board I became aware of an all-pervading sullen silence; human and animal activity seemed to be at a minimum and even the birds found it too hot to sing. The heat in the confines of the cab was absolutely stifling, and after depositing my kit I slowly went through the check routine. Every movement brought fresh rivers of sweat streaming from my brow, and I looked forward to the time when we could get into motion so as to generate a cooling air flow.

I had just finished trimming the coal when Les arrived looking a trifle like a boiled lobster just out of the pot.

'Christ, its bloody close today,' he gasped by way of a greeting. 'Won't be right until we have a good storm I reckon,' he continued. 'Looks as though we might get one too before the day's out.'

Les nodded towards the north where in the far distance I could discern not a few towering masses of cumulonimbus already building in an ominous fashion. I agreed with his observations, adding that if he thought it was close while standing on the ground, wait until he parked himself on the footplate. Having completed our preparations we sat in the shade of our engine, chatting to the other crews of our little group who likewise found conditions in their respective cabs intolerable. I had already downed a can of water when at last, and with great relief, we left the shed.

Although No 92137 had been out in service for some time now, she was still in excellent condition, and even the short sprint down to Water Orton proved this beyond all shadow of doubt. It also proved that at 50 mph sufficient wind force could be generated to revive a wilting form, providing that the head was stuck well out into the slipstream. This did not help the rest of the body very much, though, but I soon found that by holding a gaping sleeve out of the window and aligning my arms so as to remove any kinks, a forced flow of cooling air could be ducted up the right sleeve and around the torso, exiting via the left sleeve. During the following seven hours this simple technique did much to keep me in a reasonable state of efficiency.

Just when we could have done with a light train

to keep physical effort to a minimum, we found on arrival at Water Orton that no fewer than 48, equal to 52, awaited us. This was just about the heaviest train I can recall taking to Carlisle, and while it may make good reading for the record, it made me shovel an extra ton or two of coal at a time when I could have well done without the exercise.

Building up the fire while static in that heat was bad enough, too much in fact for Les to remain on the footplate in front of the open fire. However, this was nothing compared to the agonies I endured later when exposed to the wide area of searing white heat revealed by those huge fire-doors, and engulfed in a flow of hot air coming off the boiler casing - air, by the way, that had started out in the mid-80s. When actually firing, a thermometer in my overall pocket would probably have registered at least 140°F, and 226 miles of this had a more than somewhat debilitating effect on the system.

Despite everyone's obvious lethargy, we departed from Water Orton dead on time, accelerating rapidly over the fast on full first valve and 25 per cent cut-off. It was a sure indication of the high ambient air temperature that no steam was noticeable from our chimney, only a light haze of smoke. As can be seen from the table on page 236, although checking our speed for the 15 mph permanent way restriction at Branston we were exactly on schedule at Burton station. Here we encountered a series of signal checks all the way to Derby, but such was the reserve power of a Class '9' that we were only a minute adrift at Derby North.

By this time Les was driving in shirt-sleeve order, but because of the furnace radiation I was obliged to wear my overalls; however, these were now soaked right through, and were providing some cooling effect when exposed to a flow of air.

The steady climb from Derby North to Ambergate was accomplished in the scheduled 14 minutes, but over the more arduous drag up to Stretton an extra 5 per cent cut-off gained us 3 minutes, and the following quick dash down to Clay Cross added a similar amount. We therefore had no less than 6 minutes in hand when halted by signals. Unfortunately the London passenger train was running late, and we did not get under way again until 6.20 pm. Even then we were dogged by signal checks all the way up to Dronfield Colliery Sidings, and consequently No 92137 was not able to show off her climbing ability on the 1 in 100 bank. Moreover, no lost time was recovered on the descent into Sheffield, where we arrived for water 6 minutes late.

It seemed to be hotter than ever, but whether this was due to the atmosphere getting heavier and more electric or my physical exertions I know not. However, while our tank was filling I dived into the staff room on the end of the platform, quaffed a quick pint or two of water, then filled both my cans with this cool refreshing liquid. We set off from Sheffield at 7.00 pm and, after rattling down to Wincobank in the prescribed 8 minutes, Les opened up with sufficient purpose not only to pull back our deficiency, but also to gain a further 2 minutes over the rising gradients to Cudworth.

This was the beauty of a Class '9', for with so much power in reserve, even with a heavy load over adverse gradients it was so totally in command of the situation that time could be gained with no apparent effort. Normanton was passed dead on time, and here we noticed that an ominous coppery glow had spread across the northern skyline, silhouetting great dark grey masses of clouds that were piling up and thickening all the time.

A further series of signal checks from Stourton Junction to Wortley Junction pushed us 2 minutes behind schedule, but some spirited running then gave us 2 minutes in hand passing Shipley Leeds Junction. We had now run under the vast blanket of black clouds and it became so dark that I was obliged to light the gauge lamp. In this premature night at Keighley I saw in the distance the first flash of lightning reflected off the clouds. This was the precursor of what was to prove the longest and most spectacular thunderstorm, or rather series of thunderstorms, that I have ever witnessed in this country, and a fascinating spectacle it turned out to be.

Signal checks at Snaygill delayed us somewhat, so we arrived for examination and water at Skipton South Junction 5 minutes late. While the tank was filling I gave the fire a quick rattle, before nipping off to the relief cabin to make a can of coffee and obtain more drinking water. Once away from the engine I could clearly hear heavy and almost continuous thunderclaps rolling down from the hills, indicating that the storm could be no further away than Hellifield.

Les had lighted the headlamps during my

4.45 pm Water Orton to Glasgow College fully fitted freight
Engine: Class '9F' No 92137
Load: 48 (=52) wagons

	Booked time	Actual time	Remarks
Water Orton Station Junc	4.50	4.50	
Kingsbury Station Junc	4.55	4.55	
Tamworth	5.03	5.03	
Wichnor	5.13	5.12	
Leicester Junction	5.20	5.20	15 mph PW restriction (Branston)
Burton station	5.21	5.21	Signal check
Repton	5.27	5.29	Signal check
Stenson Junction	5.30	5.33	Signal check
Melbourne Junction	5.35	5.37	Signal check
Derby London Road	5.39	5.40	Signal check
Derby Midland	5.40	5.41	
Derby North Junction	5.41	5.42	
Ambergate	5.55	5.56	
Stretton	6.08	6.06	Signal check
Clay Cross	6.18	6.12-20	Signal check
Horns Bridge	6.24	6.27	Signal check
Chesterfield Midland	6.25	6.28	Signal check
Tapton Junction	6.26	6.29	Signal check
Bronfield Coll'y Sidings	6.36	6.41-42	Signal check
Sheffield Midland	Arr 6.48	6.54	Water
	Dep 6.55	7.00	
Wincobank Station Junc	7.03	7.08	
Cudworth	7.36	7.34	
Normanton North Yard	7.54	7.54	
Altofts Junction	7.56	7.55	
Stourton Junction	8.06	8.08	Signal check
Engine Shed Junction	8.10	8.12	Signal check
Whitehall	8.20	8.13	Signal check
Wortley Junction	8.13	8.15	Signal check
Shipley Leeds Junction	8.32	8.30	
Keighley	8.43	8.45	Signal check
Snaygill	8.56	9.00	Signal check
Skipton South Junc	Arr 9.00	9.05	Examination and water
	Dep 9.17	9.19	Collected linesman - block failure at Garsdale
Hellifield	9.40	9.40	Violent thunderstorms
Settle	9.45	9.50	
Blea Moor	10.22	10.20	Violent thunderstorms
Ais Gill	10.41	10.40	Linesman set down at Garsdale
Kirkby Stephen West	10.49	10.50	20 mph PW restriction at Ormside
Appleby	11.01	11.10	Signal check
New Biggin	11.10	11.20	Signal check
Lazonby	11.21	11.29	
Carlisle Petteril	11.40	11.40	

4.03 pm Carlisle Durran Hill to Washwood Heath No 2 fully fitted freight
Engine: Class '9F' No 92137
Load: 45 (=48) wagons

	Booked time	Actual time	Remarks
Carlisle Durran Hill Depot	4.03	4.08	Thunderstorms
Lazonby	4.33	4.39	Block failure due to storm
New Biggin	4.48	4.53	
Appleby	Arr 5.03	5.02	Water
	Dep 5.08	5.08	
Kirkby Stephen West	5.36	5.20	Signals at Mallerstang due to woman being killed on line
Ais Gill	5.54	5.48	
Blea Moor	6.10	6.05	
Settle Junction	6.30	6.22	
Hellifield	6.35	6.28	
Skipton North	6.50	6.44	
Skipton	Arr 6.52	6.45	Exam and water
	Dep 7.12	6.55	
Snaygill	7.15	7.00	
Keighley	7.27	7.12	Signal check
Shipley Leeds Junction	7.38	7.25	
Wortley Junction	7.54	7.43	
Whitehall Junction	7.56	7.45	
Engine Shed	7.57	7.49-51	Signal check
Stourton Junction	8.05	7.57	
Altofts Junction	8.17	8.07	
Normanton South Yard	8.19	8.09	
Cudworth Station	8.40	8.28	
Wath Road Junction	8.52	8.42	
Swinton Junction	8.54	8.44	
Rotherham Masboro'	Arr 9.03	8.55	Water
	Dep 9.10	9.03	
Masboro' South Sidings	9.14	9.05	
Beighton Junction	9.23	9.15	
Staveley	9.32	9.25	
Tapton Junction	9.37	9.30	
Chesterfield Midland	9.38	9.31	
Horns Bridge	9.39	9.32	
Clay Cross	9.46	9.38	20 mph PW restriction through tunnel
Stretton	9.53	9.43	
Crich Junction	10.02	9.52	
Ambergate	10.03	9.53	
Derby North Junction	10.21	10.09	Diverted to goods line to LNW Junc
Derby Midland	10.24	10.12	
Derby London Road Junc	10.25	10.14	
Melbourne Junction	10.28	10.17	
Stenson Junction	10.33	10.25	
Repton & Willington	10.36	10.28	
Burton station	10.42	10.32	15 mph PW restriction (Branston)
Leicester Junction	10.43	10.33	
Wichnor Junction	10.52	10.40	
Tamworth	11.05	11.00	Signal checks
Kingsbury Station Junc	11.13	11.10-11	Signal checks
Water Orton Station Junc	11.19	11.16	
Castle Bromwich Junc	11.23	11.20	
Washwood Heath Junc	11.28	11.23	
Washwood Heath No 2	11.33	11.25	

absence, and in near night conditions we departed at 9.19 pm only to be halted at Skipton North to pick up a linesman. He told us that a violent storm had been raging in the hills for some time and that he was being sent to Garsdale where lightning had damaged the block signalling apparatus. Les set off at a cracking pace, covering the 10 miles of mainly stiff adverse gradients up to Hellifield in 21 minutes. This, of course, kept me pretty busy, and the glare from the fire nearly polished off the poor linesman, who was already suffering some distress from the unaccustomed high temperatures in the cab.

Here we caught up with the storm. Jagged streaks of blinding fire, displaying all the colours of the spectrum, flashed and crackled all around at no more than 5-second intervals. In between these scintillating discharges the great black clouds intermittently blushed in a deep red glow as if trying to hide the electric violence raging within their interiors. Then came the rain - not cool and refreshing as rain usually is in this country, but an impenetrable deluge of warm steamy fluid that made one feel hotter than ever. It was like being hosed down with a slaking pipe.

Poor Les was soon as drenched as I, and, not being able to see much, lost 5 minutes in getting to Settle, but with the rain easing off as suddenly as it had started, we attacked the 14 miles of 1 in 100 up to Blea Moor with a display of pyrotechnics that would have been most spectacular had it not been for the far greater one raging overhead.

With having to drag coal forward between bouts of heavy firing, I was now continually busy and would have welcomed another deluge, but it did not come. However, I was able to snatch a few seconds now and again to gaze in awe at this fantastic electrical storm that grew in intensity as we proceeded. At Selside the flashes were almost continuous, for as one died away another occurred at a different point. Sometimes these enormous zigzag bursts of energy seemed to travel horizontally at almost eye level, entwining the hillsides in glorious webs of ethereal fire.

Approaching Ribblehead a full-grown pine tree was struck not 50 yards away, and suddenly exploded in a sheet of sparks and flame, while at such close range the accompanying thunderclap sounded and felt like the concussion from a 9.2 howitzer, and even in spite of the noise on the footplate it was loud enough to make all three of us nearly jump out of our skins.

For all the elemental distractions, No 92137 performed so vigorously that we arrived at Blea Moor 2 minutes ahead of time, and the long dark tunnel provided quite a contrast to the violence we had experienced during the past half-hour or so. At the other end we were met by torrential rain again, but Les battled on at such a pace through these unpleasant conditions that we breasted Ais Gill Summit a minute in front of schedule, even though we had stopped at Garsdale to put down the linesman. This was a tremendous effort considering our load and the foul weather.

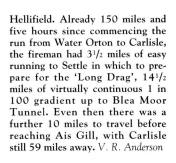

Hellifield. Already 150 miles and five hours since commencing the run from Water Orton to Carlisle, the fireman had 3¹/₂ miles of easy running to Settle in which to prepare for the 'Long Drag', 14¹/₂ miles of virtually continuous 1 in 100 gradient up to Blea Moor Tunnel. Even then there was a further 10 miles to travel before reaching Ais Gill, with Carlisle still 59 miles away. *V. R. Anderson*

Our long descent began, and although the lightning had abated somewhat, the rain still came down in sheets that obliterated visibility. Here Les was once more able to demonstrate his superb enginemanship and route knowledge, for at Kirby Stephen we were but one minute late. However, a 20 mph permanent way slack at Ormside and a stop for signals at Appleby put us back a further 8 minutes, but then with a clear road Les set about making up for lost time.

New Biggin to Lazonby took but 9 minutes, and from here Les really turned on the power. In the pitch-black conditions on that beautifully riding '9' I am sure that Les did not realise just how quickly we were travelling. The last 14½ miles from passing Lazonby to a dead stand at Carlisle Petteril Bridge took just 11 minutes, an average speed of 78 mph! So incredible did this seem when I came to analyse the timings that I double-checked with both Les and the guard, but all agreed that we arrived at 11.40 pm.

It will be recalled that the previous year, when driving this same engine, I had run at a very high speed between Stenson Junction and Trent using only 80 lbs per sq in in the steam chest and 10 per cent cut-off. Les on this occasion had used about 180 lbs per sq in and between 15 and 25 per cent cut-off, and furthermore the last 7 miles was down a gradient of 1 in 132, so perhaps we did attain the 90 mph necessary to achieve this average. Certainly it did not feel like it, but then No 92137 was an exceptionally fast and smooth-riding engine even for a Class '9'.

'Black Fives' always made the crew aware of the fact when travelling at over 70 mph, but '9s' were so deceptively smooth. I wonder just how many times fitteds have been near to derailment when pushed under circumstances similar to our exuberant dash.

Despite the thunder, which was still rolling continuously in the distance, and the lateness of the hour, the temperature had dropped very little. Every stitch of clothing I possessed was drenched with perspiration and, although I enjoyed a refreshing shower, I was obliged to dine in uncomfortably wet garments. Fortunately the drying-room was functioning and most of my outer clothes were nicely aired by the following day.

Once again the early afternoon heat was oppressive and we were not entirely surprised when another thunderstorm broke soon after we arrived at the shed. This gradually grew in intensity so that by the time we departed from Durran Hill 5 minutes in arrears, it was just as violent as on the previous night. A block failure due to the storm between Armathwaite and Lazonby delayed us further, but although we hauled a load only slightly lighter than that of the outward trip, 45-48, we arrived at Appleby 1 minute ahead of schedule.

Departing from there dead on time, Les used the power of the Class '9' to such effect on the 1 in 100 that we had gained no less than 16 minutes at Kirkby Stephen. Regrettably a woman had been killed on the line at Mallerstang, and we were halted by signals to be advised of this. Even so we reached Ais Gill with 6 minutes in hand, and, in spite of a signal check at Hawes Junction, passed Blea Moor 5 minutes early.

Even coasting, a further 3 minutes were gained during the descent to Settle and, despite the intervening 5-mile climb up to Otterburn, we arrived at Skipton still 7 minutes ahead of schedule. Slick work here gave us an added advantage so that Snaygill was passed 15 minutes to the good, and although checked by signals at Keighley we arrived at Leeds 8 minutes before time.

We ran some 10 minutes in front of time all the way to Derby North, where we were diverted on to a goods line as far as LNW Junction. Fortunately this was clear and did not delay us unduly, so that the 10 minutes' advantage was maintained. Severe signal checks at both Tamworth and Kingsbury did, however, cut this down to but 2 minutes, but some spirited work over the last 9 miles gained a further 6 minutes, so we finally arrived at Washwood Heath Number Two at 11.25 pm instead of the booked 11.33 pm; not a bad effort for an engine and crew that had already travelled well over 200 miles.

This run was typical of the fine performances Class '9s' could achieve. Apart from power, their main advantage over a 'Black Five' on longer runs was that the much larger grate area seemed to suffer far less from the build-up of ash and clinker. In other words, they were never short of steam, even at the end of a journey when large quantities of inferior-grade fuel had been consumed. Admittedly, a diligent fireman would make full use of the rocker grate equipment, but then this facility was also available on a number of later 'Black Fives'.

16
THE SUMMIT

Towards the end of the year quite a furore was created by the arrival at Saltley of No 92165, the first of three Class '9s' specially modified and fitted with American Berkeley mechanical stokers. These had, of course, been successfully used for many years by foreign railways on engines usually with firegrate areas of over 50 sq ft when firing rates in excess of the physical capability of a single fireman were demanded. In this particular instance the experiment was instituted in order to explore what increased output was attainable on a Class '9' by this means, although mechanical stoking for a grate area of only 40.2 sq ft was generally thought to be unnecessary in this country because of the relatively short journeys involved.

However, the Birmingham to Carlisle diagrams were the most arduous freight runs in the land, and we were therefore presented with the task of testing these engines on the road in normal service. That insufficient preparation had been done to provide suitable coal was not the fault of the design, since their diet was intended to contain nothing larger than small cobbles.

I for one was most enthusiastic at the possibilities offered by mechanical stoking. It was not so much the reduction of physical effort as the prospect of having more time available for road learning that appeared so attractive. Apart from the great length of the Carlisle run, there were some very complex sections, and when firing on the 'little and often' principle necessary to keep a clean fire, continuous observation of the road was just not possible.

The arrangement was robust and simple, consisting of a main conveyor screw lying in a trough at the bottom of the tender coal space, driven by a small, infinitely variable and reversible engine mounted on the tender front drag box. The screw,

working on the Archimedean principle, looked very much like a king-size mincing machine, and forced coal through a crushing grid that broke down larger lumps to a usable size. A secondary screw, known as the raiser screw, delivered the crushed coal to a distributor plate set just inside the firehole. Four separately controllable steam jets fitted below the distributor plate were arranged to direct fuel to the front and back of the left- and right-hand sides of the firegrate respectively. The controls to these steam jets were mounted on a panel in front of the fireman, and the valves for the stoker engine somewhat lower, at seat level. Below the main steam pressure gauge, three others showed the engine and jet pressures; black hands indicated the pressures to the back corners, while red hands showed the pressures to the front corners.

A standard-size firehole was fitted above the raiser screw housing, and access was gained by butterfly-type firedoors. This arrangement permitted normal manual firing, although in practice hand-firing was rendered extremely difficult for three reasons. Firstly, the firehole was much higher than normal, secondly the raiser screw housing obstructed the fireman's usual stance, and finally, because of a 'safety' barrier, coal did not drop on to the shovelling plate, but had to be extracted from the tender.

The other departure from standard on these three engines was by way of improved draughting and the fitting of double chimneys. Subsequent testing at Rugby showed that no greater evaporation rate proved possible than with hand-firing, for at 29,000 lbs of water per hour, 6,000 lbs of coal was being consumed by the stoker in place of 4,750 lbs with hand-firing. This discrepancy was due to the production of fines by the crushing grid, and the jets had to deal with both dust and cobbles up to 4 cm. The dust, of course, tended to be carried out through the chimney unburned, and just how this worked out in service I was soon to learn.

Quite out of the blue we were told to book on the following Monday morning for special training with the mechanical stoker. This was the first intimation we received that such an engine had arrived at Saltley, and when we learned that three Class '9s' equipped with these devices were to be used on the Carlisle runs, there was much speculation amongst the men involved.

It was arranged that these engines would be first used on Bordesley trippers for the dual function of running in and training the crews, or rather the firemen, in the use of this new equipment. Since Les and I were due for the afternoon Carlisle the following week, it was planned that we would work the initial run, and therefore we took the first turn on the training programme.

Mr Wood, the firing instructor, being in charge of tuition, was already on board No 92165 when we joined her in the shed yard. Apart from sporting a double chimney, there was little to distinguish her from a normal Class '9' externally. However, on gaining the footplate the modifications were very obvious. During the half-hour or

so before we rang off the shed, Mr Wood ran through the theory of mechanical stoking and pointed out the various components and their respective functions. It was all very interesting, for I had never seen a mechanical stoker before, nor had I ever considered the possibility of its application to British locomotives.

He explained that, pending the arrival of special fuel at Saltley, we would use passenger coal from the hopper. Since this contained larger lumps than was desirable, it would be dropped into the tender in small amounts and each layer would be broken up by a gang of cleaners acquired for the purpose. However, to eliminate the possibility of blockages during the training period, the tender would be only partially coaled and, if a jam did occur, this could be cleared by the means of an inching bar used as a sort of poker. This latter was a massive steel rod about 2 inches in diameter and some 5 feet in length, weighing the best part of 100 lbs. Needless to say, trying to clear a blockage with this mighty implement involved the expenditure of more effort and was far more tiring than firing half a ton of coal. He did go to considerable lengths, though, to point out that the bar must not be used with the stoker engine operating, since should it become caught in the conveyor screw, no end of

Three Class '9Fs', Nos 92165-7, fitted with Berkeley mechanical stokers, were sent to Saltley in the autumn of 1958 for testing on the arduous Carlisle runs. No 92165 arrived first and was used initially for crew training. Then came No 92166, and I was privileged to take this on its maiden run north. The stokers worked well enough but unsuitable fuel dogged the experiment, causing numerous blockages. Pictured here is the third of the trio, No 92167. *J. Coltas*

The fireman's view of the boiler fittings on No 92166. The battery of jet controls is within easy reach when seated, while their related gauges are arranged below the main steam pressure gauge. Note that the high butterfly-type firedoors leave no room for a drip-tray, hence the tea-can suspended from the gauge lamp bracket on the driver's side. *Author*

damage might result. The fact that one's foot might also be caught in the screw was not mentioned, but some small measure of protection was offered by a 3-inch-high transverse steel strip attached to the shovelling plate just below the tender doors. This was supposed to serve as a reminder that something quite nasty lurked on the other side of it. In actual fact, no problem was experienced in stepping or, for that matter, tripping over the thing, but it did prove a confounded nuisance by preventing coal from even a well-filled tender falling down on to the shovelling plate.

Steam to the stoker engine was controlled by a valve wheel as previously described, and this was sufficiently sensitive to achieve a very fine range of speeds to the conveyor screw. I soon found that it could be set to deliver just a gentle trickle of fuel at the minimum setting, or a veritable avalanche when fully opened. Unfortunately, with the lumpy mixture of coal we had in the tender the conveyor screw was never consistently loaded, so that the feed to the delivery plate was usually intermittent. This negated to some extent the fine control obtainable from the stoker engine, but I soon learned to detect whether it was feeding satisfactorily by the sound it made. When conveying coal the screw omitted a quiet, muffled rumble accompanied by a graunching sound as the fuel was pulverised against the crushing grid. When starved by a blockage, the screw rotated at a greater speed, giving off a higher-pitched ringing noise, and there was no graunching. An inspection flap at the top of the raiser screw housing enabled a visual check to be made of the actual flow rates, and a small hole in the firedoors proved useful in keeping an eye on just where the fuel was going. All these techniques were acquired later in the day, after some hours of practical operation, but initially I had to rely entirely on Mr Wood's guidance.

Having digested the theory and familiarised myself with the position of the controls and their respective function, we came to the actual operation. Opening the butterfly firedoors, he bade me inspect the fire. There was very little of it, just a thin layer barely covering the bars and surrounding several patches of apparently dead ash.

'It's best to build a thin fire by hand first,' he said. 'Make sure that you have a reasonable amount in the back corners because they tend to be starved by the jets.'

During the next 10 minutes I discovered just how difficult and exhausting it was to fire one of these mechanical stoker '9s' manually. Picking up the shovel I looked around for coal but found none in the usual place, for it was all dammed up behind that benighted footguard.

'You'll have to open the tender doors I'm afraid,' said Mr Wood apologetically.

Having done this another problem presented itself, because there was no flat surface to shovel off. The coal had to be dragged and scraped forward over the retaining strip, and I could visualise that, even with a full tender, getting coal on to the shovelling plate would be a strenuous business. As it was, the tender was now less than half filled with lumps broken down to a nice size for manual firing on a conventional engine, but it took far longer than normal to get 2 hundredweight forward on to the shovelling plate. At last it was done, but then I found that I could not take up my usual firing stance because of the thick trunking rising up from the middle of the footplate. I was forced to scoop up a shovelful of coal, then, holding it chest high, shuffle round the trunking on the driver's side, since this was not obstructed by damper wheels. The coal had to be delivered by an ungainly thrusting action with the arms held at virtually full stretch, and this after a short time proved a great strain on both arms and back. I was glad that only a thin fire had to be built up in this way, for I felt the need to sit down more than if I had just cleaned the fire on a Garratt.

'Right,' said Mr Wood after the fire had brightened up under the influence of the blower and a fully opened rear damper. 'We'll try the stoker.'

He first opened the stoker engine valve and, with the firedoors wide open, I watched as a 'river' of coal slowly poured over the distributor plate. Satisfied that this was moving at the desired rate, he then turned on the jet's main valve so that the gauges showed about 40 lbs per sq in for the front and 30 for the rear. Mr Wood had previously set the individual jet controls, but we subsequently adjusted these from time to time during the day as working conditions demanded.

As the jets came into action, the stream of coal falling over the distributor plate broke up and flew to all corners of the firebox, but even at this early stage of the proceedings I noted that, quite logically, the smaller particles carried further than the larger ones. Together with the action of the blast these small particles tended to build up in a solid bank under the brick arch, thus artificially reducing the active grate area by no small degree. It was a problem that was never satisfactorily overcome while standard coal continued to be used, although experience obviously lessened the tendency for this to occur. Even so, on the Carlisle runs it was necessary to periodically drag this fiery slurry back over the grate with a rake.

The blast of steam coming from the jets flattened the flames in the box so that accurate observation of the shape and condition of the firebed could easily be made while they were in use. This was one bonus that was not available on standard engines and most providential in view of the sometimes unpredictable distribution of fuel.

A few minutes' use of the stoker produced the equivalent of a light round of manual firing and, with a healthy column of smoke belching skywards, our steam pressure increased quite rapidly.

By the time we rang off the shed I had acquired the hang of things, and was left to experiment during the run down to Washwood Heath. I soon found that because of the small size of coal delivered by the stoker, it burned away very quickly and it was necessary to fire in short, frequent bursts in order to maintain any sort of firebed at all.

After backing on to our train prior to departure, we encountered our first jam, caused by some larger lumps riding on top of the conveyor screw and preventing any small coal from dropping into the trough. I then experienced the agony of using the inching bar. After only 2 or 3 minutes of vigorous prodding, every muscle in my body was quivering with fatigue. Mr Wood, too, was reduced to a sweating, inarticulate hulk after just 1 minute of showing me how it should be done. Fortunately our exertions were not in vain because after running the screw in reverse for a few seconds, a full flow of fuel was once more achieved.

Being able to reverse the screw was extremely useful in helping to clear jams, since it tended to push the offending lumps back out of the way, but the main problem was when coal interlocked to form a substantial arch over the trough. This then had to be broken down by levering and prodding, which was no easy matter when it was covered by several tons of coal, as I duly discovered on my first Carlisle run.

I was, of course, interested to see how she would steam when working hard up Camp Hill bank and, after the usual stop-go dawdle to Duddeston Road, we finally had a clear run. I think Les also wanted

to see what would happen because he opened up rather more vigorously than strictly necessary with 50 loaded mineral wagons, and soon had her at full regulator and 60 per cent cut-off.

I set the stoker engine at about 50 lbs per sq in, which was sufficient to give a fair flow of fuel, and the jet gauges showed 40 lbs per sq in for the front and 30 for the rear. Immediately great black clouds of smoke erupted from the chimney indicating that the coal was being spread around to good effect, and this abated little even when the firedoors were opened two notches. Unfortunately, the test was somewhat spoiled by another blockage just beyond St Andrews, but by then we had sufficient reserve in the boiler to see us safely into Bordesley without too much loss of pressure. The shape of the firebed was quite a revelation, though, for a substantial bank of small, half-burned particles of coal had built up under the brick arch. On the other hand, the rear part of the grate contained very little fire, while the centre section was actually bare.

On engines fitted with front and rear dampers it was usual to open only the rear, but with the stoker '9s' I soon found it expedient to use a wide open front damper and keep the rear almost closed. This allowed more air to the forward section of the grate, which in turn helped to burn away the excess of fuel that found its way there. Also, when the engine was working normally it was possible to fire the box much more evenly by periodically varying the jet pressures. This was easily achieved by manipulating the main shut-off valve, and in fact the jets could be dispensed with altogether for short periods. By so doing, a mound of coal built up at the back of the grate; however, care had to be taken so as not to block the jets under the distributor plate, although this in itself was not serious if quickly cleared. Later on I frequently used this technique when building up the fire at the start of a run, for when a large hump had been produced beneath the firedoors, I merely reached in with the firing shovel and spread it into the back corners.

Our second trip up the bank was rather more encouraging from the firing point of view. For one thing we did not get a blockage at the crucial moment, and for another further continual experimentation enabled me to control the jet pressures more effectively. The one disturbing factor was the regularity of blockages over the conveyor screw caused by lumps too large to fall into the trough.

Even so by the end of the day I was extremely enthusiastic about the project, particularly when I received Mr Wood's assurance that closer attention would be paid to the breaking down of lumps to a more suitable size during coaling operations. I had visions that if the stoker would work reliably, I could devote a lot more time to road learning, together with the added bonus of arriving at destinations considerably less fatigued than normal.

Les on the other hand was far less convinced as to the supposed benefits of mechanical stoking. It appeared to him as an unnecessary complication that could go wrong and lead to a failure of the engine. He did not say much at the time, but took everything in, particularly our strenuous jam-clearing efforts, which he regarded with mild amusement and toleration. In the event his judgement was to prove correct, but not, as it turned out, for reasons of mechanical breakdown.

The following week, as promised, we were booked a stoker '9' and, being the initial trip, Mr Wood had arranged to accompany us as far as Leeds. By then No 92166 had arrived, and since No 92165 was still being used for training purposes, it was decided, rather unwisely as it happened, to provide this later engine. Being well aware of the coal problem and also because any bad blockages would reflect upon himself, Mr Wood had personally supervised the coaling operation most fastidiously, and when I inspected the tender it certainly appeared that an excellent job had been done. The top layer at least was nicely broken to a uniform size and I remember thinking at the time if what lay beneath was exactly the same, we would not experience any trouble.

No 92166 was positively gleaming, fit for a Royal Train in fact, and even the paintwork still retained quite a pungent tang. I quickly ran through the usual checks, then operated the stoker engine in both directions to make sure all was well. The coal fed through very satisfactorily and, having dumped a fair load under the firedoors, I spread this into the back corners with the firing shovel. Then, by manipulating the jet pressures, I built up the fire into a reasonable shape without resorting to manual means. Les duly arrived, displaying no emotion either way, but after conducting his normal thorough inspection, returned to the footplate with a doubtful frown on his face.

'Doesn't seem to have done much mileage,' he muttered, half to himself. 'I'll have to check with Woody.'

The latter arrived soon after, complete with bowler hat and a small leather case containing his paraphernalia. Les wasted no time in broaching the subject of the engine's apparent nominal mileage, and Mr Wood had to admit that apart from running to Saltley, she had only worked for one day on a Bordesley. However, there had been no indication of undue tightness, since he personally had been in attendance all day. To these remarks Les rather scathingly pointed out that there was a slight difference between a Bordesley tripper and the Carlisle, when our first stop would be 90 miles away after running continuously at around 50 mph. It was therefore with a certain amount of doubt as to whether No 92166 would reach Carlisle without problems that we set off from the shed.

On arrival at Water Orton Les quickly dropped to the ground and felt all the bearings with the back of his hand.

'What do you think, Les?' enquired Mr Wood a trifle anxiously.

'Number 4 driver axlebox on my side seems a little warmer than the rest, but we will not really know until it's done some work,' he replied with a shrug.

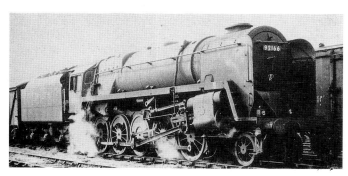

Stoker-fitted '9F' No 92166 stands at Water Orton waiting to depart on its maiden trip with the 4.15 pm Glasgow fully fitted freight. The well-filled tender shows a surface of finely broken coal belying the problems that lay beneath. *Author*

After changing the lamps I examined the said axlebox, but could barely detect any difference from the others so, hoping for the best, I returned to the footplate to complete my preparation of the fire.

We departed dead on time with 36 equal to 40 behind the tender and set off over the fast, accelerating at a fairly leisurely pace since Les obviously did not wish to press her too hard. I carefully adjusted the stoker engine and jets to deliver a light spray of fuel and soon a healthy trail of smoke was billowing from our chimney. I was very conscious that the future of these stoker '9s' depended much on how successful they proved to be on these first trips, and I was determined to do my part and make them work. I therefore devoted my whole energy to achieving the most efficient combustion possible and because I lacked practical experience at this stage I found it necessary to make frequent inspections of the firebed and adjustments to the controls.

Even so all went exceedingly well until Tamworth, when the screw 'ran dry'. This was the first of many blockages that spoiled what should have been an easy and comfortable journey.

In all fairness, Mr Wood immediately buckled down and did his share and with both of us prodding and poking, none of the jams proved too much of a problem. However, clearing them was very hard work and at times it was necessary to fire by hand, but the great thermal reserve in Class '9' boilers carried us over these difficulties.

We arrived at Sheffield more or less on schedule, and while we were taking on water Les hurriedly examined the engine. His face, on returning to the footplate, displayed concern.

'That number 4 axlebox is running very hot,' he exclaimed. 'We may have to fail her at Leeds.'

This was sad news indeed, for apart from the delays this action would incur, it was not the sort of start I had wished for on the initial run of the stoker '9'.

Departing therefore in an atmosphere of some anxiety, Les nursed the troubled engine as best he could and fortunately he was helped in this direction by a number of signal checks. Every time we actually came to a standstill, he would leap down to have a look at the offending axlebox, obviously trying to decide whether, and at what point, to telephone Control for a replacement engine. As luck would have it the easier going north of Sheffield allowed the bearing to cool somewhat, and by

Altofts Junction he announced to my intense relief that it appeared to have loosened up. He thought that we might complete our run in safety.

Although we arrived at Leeds some 15 minutes late, Mr Wood seemed quite confident that I could now handle the stoker unit efficiently, and, wishing us luck, took his leave as planned. Fate, as fickle as ever, contrived to produce more jams on the second half of the run than when Mr Wood was in attendance, but since the coal was now somewhat depleted they were a little easier to clear. Even so, on balance I used just about as much energy as I would have done firing a standard engine manually.

At Skipton I gave the grate a good rattle and levelled the ridge that had built up under the brick arch so as to ensure maximum efficiency for the climb up to Blea Moor. This was the place to test the stoker on the sort of work it was designed for, namely continuous high output, so the 14 miles of 1 in 100 from Settle to Blea Moor should give us some idea of its worth. Fortunately with fuel feeding reliably into the screw I experienced only one or two minor starvation problems, and the stoker performed exceedingly well over the entire ascent. Les, sensing that I was in command of the situation, gave her a fair bit of stick and pulled back several minutes on the climb.

Despite the fact that the boiler provided all the steam that Les could use, I gained the distinct impression that the mechanical stoker '9s' did not steam quite as freely as did the standard engines. However, the ability to accomplish the hardest part of our journey without having to get off my seat convinced me that we were on to a good thing and, with the correct fuel and further experience, the units should prove to be a godsend in the future. It was up to us as firemen, then, to overcome these early problems so that they would gain universal acceptance.

The 20-minute dash across the mountains to Ais Gill should have proved easy going, but for me it was far more strenuous than the preceding 14 miles. A number of larger lumps of coal became wedged over the conveyor screw and in the darkness I had considerable difficulty in locating and clearing them. A spotlight in the tender would have been most useful; as it was, I had to rely entirely on my sense of touch, which with a 100 lb inching bar was far from sensitive. As a result we breasted Ais Gill with no more than 180 lbs per sq in showing on the pressure gauge and half a glass of water.

During the ensuing descent to Kirkby Stephen I took the precaution of building up the fire manually, and this insurance paid handsome dividends, for I experienced a bad patch of blockages right through to New Biggin. However, from then on the stoker worked perfectly all the way to Carlisle, where we arrived practically dead on time.

My conclusions, as I lay in bed reflecting on the day's run, were that the stoker unit in general performed reasonably well. At maximum effort the engine did not steam quite as freely as the standard locomotive, due in part, no doubt, to the fact that the firebed could not be maintained in the same perfect shape as with manual firing. Also, it was undeniably less efficient since we had burned considerably more coal than normal with a train of this weight. This could, however, be largely accounted for by the wastage of fuel passing out of the chimney as unburned fines and was one of the debits that had to be accepted with mechanical stoking.

As far as I was concerned the real nigger in the woodpile was the lack of reliability caused by the presence of lumps of coal of a larger size than could be accommodated by the conveyor screw. Starvation could, and did, occur at any time with painful regularity, and this completely upset one's carefully calculated firing programme. With the correct fuel a run to Carlisle should have been a veritable joyride, but with things as they were, firing was very much a hit-or-miss affair.

Our return journey the following day was a little better in this respect. The Carlisle lads had been more punctilious in breaking up the coal and also, with the previous day's experience behind me, I tended to run with a somewhat thicker firebed. Furthermore, I took the precaution of operating the stoker engine at frequent intervals even on downhill sections just to make sure that it was still feeding, but even so blockages seemed to occur all too often when they were least welcome.

Two days later we had No 92165 on these runs, and things followed roughly the same pattern. Consequently our report at the end of the week stressed that while the stoker unit performed satisfactorily on a diet of small cobbles, far too many large lumps were finding their way into the tender, causing feed problems.

Other crews experienced exactly the same troubles, and it was just one of those unfortunate over-

sights in planning that a supply of suitable coal was not provided before the engines arrived. In point of fact a number of weeks elapsed before some ideal fuel was obtained, but even then this was only delivered to Carlisle, not Saltley. It took the form of screened chips 1-2 inches in diameter, and was apparently the coal used by Heysham-Isle of Man steamers, which were also equipped with mechanical stokers.

The reader may recall that earlier I stated that everyone achieves a peak of performance in any form of endeavour which is never surpassed. My own particular peak in terms of continual physical effort came about quite unexpectedly on our next afternoon Carlisle duty. The winter storms were now setting in, but high winds, although contributing to the problems, were not the cause of my excessive labours. Ironically it was on No 92167, the third of the mechanical stoker '9s', that I performed my feat of endurance.

As usual I was delighted to find that we were booked a stoker '9' and, on gaining the footplate, the well-coaled tender seemed to have received the full attention of the cleaning gang. However, I had been deceived before by the appearance of a well-broken top layer, so I quickly checked that the diabolical inching bar was lying in the fire iron compartment. After ensuring that the stoker engine and jets worked satisfactorily, I gave the still gleaming cab a final polish while Les conducted his usual tests.

Right on time we departed from the loco and, during the ensuing run to Water Orton, I operated the stoker two or three times to keep a reasonable fire in the grate. It worked perfectly and, as far as one could judge over such a short distance, No 92167 seemed to be the best of the three stoker '9s'. I therefore felt pretty confident when we backed on to our train of 43 vans equal to 45, and looked forward to a good trip.

Five minutes before being called out of the sidings, I built up a good bed of fire at the back of the box and, with a full boiler and 245 lbs per sq in showing on the pressure gauge, I relaxed on my seat with a lid of tea, eyeing the gathering winter darkness with the benevolent gaze of one who is snug and warm and well protected from a bitter north-west wind.

At precisely 4.50 pm the signal came off and, as Les pulled smartly out on to the main line, I instinctively opened the stoker engine valve. A

No 92167 passing Burton Station North signal box with the 4.45 pm Water Orton-Glasgow. I felt that this was the best of the three stoker '9Fs', and although later converted to manual firing, she survived until June 1968, thereby being the last of the class in service. *Pat Webb*

healthy graunching sound could be heard by an ear cocked for the purpose and, thus satisfied, I stood behind Les watching for our brake-van lights to appear. Having ensured that the train was in good order, I crossed back to my seat and was just about to sit down when the graunching changed to the distinctive ring of an empty conveyor screw.

'Blast,' I said, loud enough to cause Les to turn his head, and, after resignedly closing the stoker engine valve, hauled the heavy inching bar from its compartment. The mere act of holding this implement was effort enough, so a few seconds of prodding and levering at an obstruction buried under several tons of coal soon brought beads of perspiration to my brow. A minute later I decided to give the engine another try but, on opening the valve, only a small trickle of chips fell over the distributor plate, then it ran dry. I reversed the screw since this was often effective in clearing jams, but on running it forward again no more than a hatful of coal came through.

Once more I grasped the bar and attacked the compact mass until my muscles ached and I was gasping for breath, but with no more success than on the first occasion. The trouble was that I could neither see nor really feel what was causing the blockage due to the great weight of coal in the over-filled tender, and it was very much a case of luck whether the bar penetrated to the critical spot. Twice again I carried out the same procedure, each time more frantically than before, until I finally sank back on my seat with knotted muscles shaking with fatigue.

Meanwhile our steam pressure had fallen to 165 lbs per sq in and there was only a third of a glass of water showing in the boiler. Les, who had been regarding my efforts with a pensive eye, was now forced to intervene.

'You had better get some coal on or we'll soon be in trouble,' he yelled unsympathetically.

He was quite right, of course; I had expended far too much time and energy in trying to get the stoker to operate. Dragging my still panting and exhausted body upright, I looked into the firebox and was dismayed to find great patches of ash surrounded by precious little live fire. No engine but a Class '9' would have travelled this far with the fire in such a state. Determined not to cause the engine to fail through lack of steam, I set about the laborious business of extracting coal from the tender before shovelling it, equally laboriously, into the firebox. Had she been a standard Class '9', to cover the firebars would have been the work of but a few minutes. As it was, because of that accursed guard strip and the obstruction caused by the raiser screw trunking, it seemed to take ages to fire even a couple of hundredweight over the grate.

The boiler had already been mortgaged pretty heavily but I was forced to let it go even further in the interests of retaining steam pressure. By energetic and diligent use of the rake I spread live fire over the whole area of the firebars as it lit up and finally the downward swing of the pressure gauge needle halted at 150 lbs per sq in. With the water just in sight at the bottom of the glass, it was now necessary to use the injector in short bursts, but despite this and the very thin firebed, pressure slowly began to recover.

Stoically I worked like an automaton, first pulling out coal from under the tender doors with pick, shovel or even by hand, then, when there was sufficient lying on the footplate, shovelling it up and thrusting it awkwardly into the firebox. After closing the firedoors, a quick burst with the injector then repeat the operation over again. All the time muscles and sinews burned with the fiery ache of excessive fatigue. I longed to relax for even a minute, but there was no respite. The whole process was so inefficient that it demanded every ounce of effort I was able to muster.

Very slowly at first, then with gaining momentum, both steam pressure and water level rose until by Derby North they were back to where they should be. However, after an hour of expending so much energy at such a high rate I felt absolutely shattered. With blood sugar at zero, I suddenly remembered the supply of glucose I carried and promptly munched a few of those large tablets, washing them down with half a pint of cold water.

The prospect of another 180 miles of this sort of caper was pretty daunting to say the least, so, after hanging my head in the cooling slipstream for a minute, I tried once more to clear the blockage. Despite a prolonged and frantic attempt, the result was frustratingly negative and, with holes once more appearing in the firebed, I resignedly returned to the old routine.

The following 70-minute run to Sheffield was sheer hell, for although my back and arms were quite capable of normal shovelling at the rate of 2 tons per hour for seven or eight hours at a stretch without showing the slightest sign of stiffness, they were now, because of the unaccustomed awkwardness of the operation, a blaze of excruciating pain.

A diet of glucose and water undoubtedly helped to keep me going, but even the brief stop for water offered no relief, since I was fully occupied dragging coal out on to the footplate while the tank was filling.

Fortunately this task of extracting fuel was made somewhat easier by the fact that, with the release of pressure from the back of the tender doors, I was now able to open them. Even so, the conveyor screw remained obstinately blocked and my many attempts to clear it ended fruitlessly. For a further hour I endured the purgatory of hand-firing No 92167 until at Altofts Junction Les could restrain himself no longer.

With growing concern he had been watching me flog myself to quite unacceptable levels of effort and I was now obviously showing signs of the severe strain imposed by these dreadful labours.

'I think we had better fail her at Leeds,' he yelled above the noise. 'You can't go on like this all the way to Carlisle.'

I made no reply, partly because I had no breath to spare for talking and partly because he had phrased it as half question and half statement.

Since I did not wish to be personally responsible for failing the engine and the subsequent consequences this action might incur, I chose to regard his remarks as a statement of fact. His logic was undeniable, but I so much wanted to prove that these mechanical stokers were a viable proposition that I just would not admit defeat.

Grasping the inching bar, I plunged it into the coal above the conveyor screw with a fury born of desperation and disappointment. This time it penetrated deeper than on previous occasions and the tip seemed to lock under some solid object. I levered downwards with all my might and the object, whatever it was, moved upwards. Then a sudden jerk of the engine brought a small avalanche of coal down from the back of the tender, rendering further prodding impractical.

Half-heartedly I opened the stoker engine valve, then, wonder of wonders, I immediately heard the graunch of coal being broken on the crushing grid. Nor was it just the previous trickle, for on opening the inspection flap I perceived with great relief and immense satisfaction a full-blooded flow of fuel, falling over the distributor plate. Composing myself as much as one can compose a body shaking with exhaustion, I staggered over to Les and informed him that the stoker was once again operating and that I thought we could now manage.

'Well, it's up to you,' he said simply with a shrug of his shoulders, and immediately returned to his task of observing signals.

Always the opportunist, I grabbed a couple of sandwiches and greedily munched them while the jets were spraying in enough coal to cause the safety valves to lift from time to time. For 10 glorious minutes I was able to relax on my seat, allowing the stoker to actually build up the fire, then once more the screw ran dry. Coal, shaken down by the tender's oscillations, was again lying deep over the trough, so that no amount of prodding produced any worthwhile results. Reluctantly I gave up further attempts to get the stoker operating and returned to manual firing, having come to the cynical conclusion that the only mechanical stoker working that day was yours truly.

During that 10-minute break I had pondered the cause of our problems and it required no genius to conjecture that a pretty large lump of coal must be lying squarely over the conveyor screw, thus excluding the passage of the rest of the fuel as securely as a tailor-made lid. I would just have to be patient and wait until we had used up sufficient coal to expose it. Unfortunately we still had over an hour's run before we arrived at Skipton, and I now had doubts as to whether I could stand up to this murderous effort for very much longer. The hardest part of our journey started at Skipton, and if the stoker was not working by then, well, the prospect of hand-firing up the mountains to Blea Moor was too terrible to even contemplate.

In the event my worst fears were realised and the next hour proved a torture of endurance beyond anything I had previously experienced in my life. Despite several futile attempts, the stoker remained stubbornly inoperative and now, after four hours of incessant maximum activity, my whole body was racked with pain and fatigue. I hardly noticed our arrival at Skipton, and so distressed was my general condition that for the one and only time during our partnership, Les volunteered to go off and make a can of coffee while I attended to the watering. No doubt he did not wish to see me suffering, for the 15-minute halt was one of frantic activity.

Summoning up all my depleted reserves, I cleaned and levelled the fire, an exhausting enough task in itself when carried out in great haste. Then down to ground level to turn off the water, followed by a laborious scramble on to the top of the tender in order to extract the heavy hose. With my breath coming in rasping sobs, I made my way back to the footplate where, with failing strength, I desperately tried to dig out the obstruction. If only I could uncover the object I might stand a chance, and it was this driving thought that enabled me to extract, and fire, 5 or 6 hundredweight of coal before Les returned.

He regarded me quizzically for a moment in the firelight before asking the inevitable question.

'Is it alright now?'

I guessed that he meant the stoker engine and I shook my head, but quickly gasped that I had just started to uncover the obstruction. Hissing safety valves, a full boiler and a bright fire convinced Les that at least the engine was in good fettle and, after obtaining my nodding assurance that I was prepared to continue, he blew off the brakes.

As we drew out on the main line I automatically draped myself over the cab doors, watching to see that the train was complete while at the same time sucking in lungsful of cold refreshing air. Despite the fact that we were still in the shelter of a cutting, I could not help noticing how blustery the wind had become, for I was obliged to place a restraining hand on my cap before withdrawing inside again.

Although there was now a good body of fire on, Settle was only 15 miles distant, so the need to uncover that obstructing lump was most pressing. I therefore returned to the task without further ado. It is said that every black cloud has a silver lining, and on this occasion it took the form of the exposed end of that great slab of coal. The upper surface was smooth and flat and, despite the restrictions imposed by the confines of the tender, I had at last something suitable off which to shovel. Stupified with fatigue, my movements were slow and clumsy, but even so I was able to shovel coal out on to the footplate much faster than at any other time on the run so far. It was of course necessary to keep the footplate reasonably clear of coal, so the only place I could dump it was in the firebox.

Contrary to logic, therefore, considering my wretched state, I considerably over-fired the engine for the next few miles in a final attempt to expose the obstruction before my strength failed altogether. By Hellifield my mining operation had laid bare some 4 feet of the monster slab that was sitting so firmly over the trough, and I thereupon decided to shatter it in situ while I was still able to swing a pick. Staggering out on to the footplate, I collected the implement and on returning I was just about to commence the destruction of it when I realised that all was not as I had left it. Blinking unbelievingly through rivers of sweat, I saw in the reflected light of the fire that a fall of coal had almost completely covered the slab again.

I nearly wept with despair, for victory had seemed so near, and now it had been tantalisingly withdrawn at the last moment. Quickly this emotion changed to one of baleful resentment. To me, the successful application of mechanical stoking now appeared to be wholly hinged on the removal of this devilish obstruction, and I was not going to be beaten by a bally lump of coal. Once more I started shovelling with limbs now so weak that they would barely follow the brain's instructions. Had it not been for the years of built-in reflexes, they would doubtless have not worked at all.

Les was by this time thrashing the engine pretty hard for, apart from battling up the 1 in 100 gradient, we also had to overcome the force of a full-blown gale. Even so, No 92167 was still steaming beautifully; in fact, ever since the initial failure of the stoker, pressure had not dropped below 240 lbs per sq in, and because of my recent frantic efforts to use up fuel we had if anything an excess of it.

My little world inside the tender was now beginning to swim around in a most disconcerting manner and much to my annoyance I unaccountably kept losing my balance. Like all athletes, a top link fireman is the product of many long years of hard training. His strength and skills are acquired through thousands of repetitive exercises, while at the same time he learns to hold something back for the great effort when it is needed, rather like the finishing sprint of a long-distance runner. But so enormous were the physical demands this day that even my considerable reserves of stamina had been used up long since and for the past hour I had been running solely on that peculiar source of nervous energy that only the mind can produce, a mind so obsessed with the need to succeed that it totally refused to acknowledge the sad state of its body.

Gradually I cleared the area above the great slab again, but as I did so my angry frustration slowly diminished until eventually, unable to stand, I found myself working on my hands and knees, feebly pulling out pieces of coal with my fingers. I decided that this time I would try and lever the obstruction up and away from the trough, and taking a firm grasp heaved with all my remaining strength. Although it barely budged, the movement was sufficient to disturb the almost vertical wall of coal rising high above, and 2 hundredweights came crashing down from the top. It took me completely by surprise, and the first intimation I had that anything untoward had happened was the feeling that both hands had been suddenly amputated at the wrists, followed immediately by a violent blow on the forehead.

I reeled back as if kicked by a mule, the excruciating pain shooting up my arms and stinging my brain so acutely as to cause a myriad of coloured lights to whirl before my eyes. This was the last straw - if that blasted lump wanted to play it rough and have a fight then I would give it one. Gone was the cool, logical, efficient fireman, gone was the poor worn-out wreck of a labourer grovelling on all fours. A Hercules fired with the superhuman strength of the insane now stood with coalpick poised over the offending object. With the fury of a madman I unleashed a blow so violent that it might well have penetrated the very plating of the tender itself. The end of the lump disintegrated into a shower of fragments that ricocheted in all directions and cut into my face. I felt no pain, for the anger that possessed me did not permit distractions. Again and again the pick swung up and down. I did not so much break up the lump - I annihilated it. For a full minute the wild attack continued, until with a final shattering stroke, the last piece disappeared.

At once the blackness of the tender seemed to spread outwards and engulf me, and I felt myself falling down into a dark abyss; the sensation was not at all unpleasant, for a soft, relaxing peacefulness seemed to suffuse my whole body. I could hear the murmuring of water like that of a nearby brook, and it seemed that I was sleeping blissfully on the bank of some shady stream. Then I became aware of a vague rumbling that became more insistent and forceful with every passing second, and this I found was decidedly less pleasant.

A distant voice was calling my name. I opened my eyes and was puzzled to find myself looking up at an inky sky dotted with the brilliant pin-points of light from a thousand stars. The voice grew louder until the words began to register in my mind.

'Terry, are you alright, mate?'

I focused my gaze and saw the silhouette of Les standing out boldly against the white furnace light. With painful suddenness I snapped back to reality and with his help struggled to my feet. With the regaining of full consciousness came the awareness of agony, an agony that I had hitherto never experienced. Every part of my body hurt abominably and co-ordination of movement proved extremely difficult.

'It's OK, Les,' I heard myself say. 'I just over-balanced.'

A strong helping hand guided me firmly to my seat, where I slumped thankfully while fighting to regain my composure. I recognised Hawes Junction as it flashed past and realised that the sound I had heard a few moments ago must have been Les picking up water over the troughs. Of the long climb up to Blea Moor I could remember very little, but since fire, steam pressure and boiler level were all up to the mark, I concluded that I had somehow managed my duties.

If only my hands did not hurt so much, I thought, and with the idea of trying to relieve the pain, I began to gently ease off my gloves. I was surprised to see that they were badly torn and, as I pulled the tattered remnants free, I discovered why they had felt so soggy of late. The nail on the second finger of my right hand was missing, while long gashes ran very nearly the full length of my third and fourth fingers. My left hand had suffered slightly less but, even so, the skin across all four knuckles was split wide open. In keeping with my face, which sported a lump the size of a golfball in the centre of my forehead, both hands were a mass of congealed blood and coal dust.

Les, who was now looking closely at me, was aghast at the mess.

'Good God lad, whatever have you been doing? Just sit there for a minute until we're over the top.'

I needed no second bidding, and in a detached way I was also quite content to watch him top up the bucket with warm water from the slaking pipe and then, after obtaining a piece of towelling from his own haversack, bring them both over to me. Displaying a sympathy that belied his gruff exterior, he carefully bathed my face, cleaning coal dust out of the cuts with all the thoroughness of a trained nurse. In between quick bouts of looking out for signals and adjusting the brake, he also helped me to wash my hands and, when properly cleaned, dressed the wounds with makeshift bandages made up from two spare handkerchiefs.

'You know, you are a bloody young idiot,' he said quietly as he tied the final knot. 'You should have let me fail her at Leeds. I would not have come past Derby myself without the stoker working, and to be perfectly honest I've been expecting you to give up ever since.'

I thanked Les for his attentions, which had certainly made my hands feel a little easier, although of course they still throbbed and burned like the very dickens, and sought solace in a good drink of coffee and my first cigarette on the run. The combined effect of these stimulants, coupled with 10 minutes complete rest did much to make me feel human again.

With the stoker engine operational once more, the remaining 32 miles from Appleby to Carlisle proved relatively easy, which was just as well, for the mere act of holding the firing shovel proved both difficult and painful. Admittedly I did have to venture into the tender on several occasions in

order to push coal into the conveyor screw trough, because with only about one ton of fuel left at the back of the coal space, it would not shake down by itself. Fortunately I was able to accomplish this by means of my feet rather than the more usual way with coalpick and shovel. I even found sufficient time to clean down the footplate, so that when we were relieved only some 2 minutes behind schedule, all was looking more or less as spick and span as ever.

As I dragged myself slowly up to the lodge I was comforted by the thought that I had managed to fire some 8 tons of coal into a mechanical stoker's firebox by hand, a performance equivalent in sheer effort to three or four times that amount on a standard Class '9'. However, I knew then that I would never again achieve such a high level, nor for that matter indeed attempt it. This was to be my peak, a peak that, apart from providing some personal satisfaction and extracting a surprising response from Les, turned out to be of little practical value in furthering the cause of mechanical stoking. On arrival at the lodge I showered and had my injuries properly dressed, but I felt too exhausted to tackle a square meal and therefore promptly tottered off to bed to sleep the clock round.

It would be dishonest to say that I awoke feeling 100 per cent fit, for my back was abominably stiff and, apart from the cuts, my hands were black with bruises. Nevertheless, yesterday's marathon now seemed like a nightmare best forgotten, so when Les suggested that it might be prudent for me to return home as a passenger, I protested so strongly that he did not bring up the matter again. Fate produced another of its illogical quirks by providing only 18 vehicles for the homeward journey and, as if by way of compensation, I only had two or three minor blockages, which were easily cleared. After the best run yet with a stoker '9', I arrived back at Saltley feeling much perkier, although it took a few weeks for my hands to become normal once more.

Strangely enough we did not have another run on a stoker '9' after that. A number of problems developed that took one or other out of service just at a time when, ironically, the correct size fuel had been provided at Carlisle. This, as previously mentioned, took the form of small chips as used on the Isle of Man steamers, and a number of wagons had been sent to Durran Hill expressly for our use. It would have been ideal, of course, since this 1½-inch diameter coal 'flowed' rather like dry sand and jamming was impossible. Obviously it was equally unsuitable for standard engines, but since this coal had been provided exclusively for the Carlisle-Birmingham, the Carlisle-Birmingham had to use it.

We first discovered this problem on the next morning tour of duty. Winter had set in with a vengeance and, after several days of intermittent snow falls, a large high-pressure area over Scandinavia was bringing arctic winds down over all the country. As was often the case with the morning turn, we had a 'Black Five', and departing from Water Orton at 3.50 am the frost was just about at its most severe. Under a setting moon, the snow-covered countryside looked superb, but even with the effort of firing I was none too warm.

Surprisingly, the further north we travelled the thinner the snow became, until by Derby it petered out altogether. However, the cold, if anything, seemed more intense, and despite thick clothing Les was visibly suffering, for his trips to toast himself before the fire became more and more frequent. Leeds had received more snow than anywhere else, since it lay a good 8 inches deep, and I looked forward to seeing some impressive drifts over the mountains. In this respect, though, I was to be disappointed, because no more than a thin layer covered anywhere north of Skipton; however, a brilliantly clear morning made the climb up to Ais Gill one of the most memorable with regard to scenic delight of the whole year.

By the time we retired to bed the winter sun was already sinking fast and, despite its day-long sojourn, the temperature had at no time even approached freezing point. After the cosy warmth of the lodge, stepping outside later that night was certainly a shock, for the air was bitterly cold and, although walking at a lively pace, by the time we arrived at the shed our teeth were beginning to chatter.

My second shock occurred when I mounted the footplate and found it knee-deep in stoker chips! It took the best part of 15 minutes shovelling before we could actually see the footboards and, realising the problem I was going to experience, I hunted around for some old firebars. The act of inserting these brought forth another avalanche,

but this time it had to remain there, for the firebox already contained sufficient unburned coal.

Topping up at the water column produced yet another surprise. The tank lid was frozen solid, and it took several sharp clouts with the coalpick before I could gain access. Needless to say I left it open thereafter.

The fire burned up remarkably quickly, partly due to the small size of the coal and partly due to the fact that our engine was fitted with a rocking grate and the hopper ash-pan doors did not close securely. Despite leaving the firedoors wide open (an action much approved by Les), we proved to be a noisy nuisance until actually departing from Durran Hill.

Once under way I was able to fully appreciate the problems in dealing with this fuel. Under the action of a fairly substantial blast, it burned away almost immediately, giving off a fierce heat. This was grand as far as steaming was concerned, but with a standard firing shovel, even working continuously, I could barely keep pace with consumption. The action of firing was of course made doubly difficult by the river of coal flowing about one's ankles over the footplate and the necessity of keeping the footboards clear. Right up to Ais Gill I was kept working flat out, sweating profusely and cursing yet another of life's ironies.

At Skipton the coal ceased to fall from the tender on its own accord and, with the major hill-climbing behind us, life became a little easier. Even so, such was the rate of burning that I was using the original Saltley coal long before we reached Sheffield. One bonus accruing from these chips, though, was that it was only possible to retain the thinnest of fires. Consequently it remained exceptionally clean and on arrival at Washwood Heath even some of the bars were showing bare.

This miniature Ice Age that had descended upon Britain steadily intensified so that when we made our outward trip again two days later the air was noticeably colder. Once more we had a 'Black Five', and although Les arrived dressed more like an Eskimo than an engine driver, he suffered extreme hardship over the whole journey. For my part, working busily in front of the furnace and only looking out at odd times, I was comfortably warm, fully compensating for the agonies of heat endured in the hot summer months.

So cold was it in the mountains that it came as

no surprise to find Garsdale water troughs completely frozen over. I did in fact drop the scoop on emerging from Rise Hill Tunnel, but only collected a few ice chippings for my trouble. It was obvious that obtaining water might prove something of a problem in these extreme conditions.

That night, as we walked from the lodge, the frost was indeed cruel. The air was so cold that the act of inhaling resulted in an acute pain at the top of one's nose, while ears and extremities soon felt decidedly frostbitten. We did not know it at the time, but the air temperature at Carlisle later fell to no less than 39°F of frost. That is just about as low as I have ever experienced in this country, while up in the mountains it was anyone's guess.

It was fortunate that our tender tank was full for, despite a brightly burning brazier nearby, the shed water column was solid. Again, we were well coaled with the 'steamboat' chips, but this time the Carlisle preparation crew had fortunately inserted three firebars beneath the tender doors, thus leaving only the minimum shovelling space and preventing the footplate from being swamped. Appreciatively glancing around the clean cab, I noticed a platelayer's shovel standing in the corner. This no doubt belonged to the shed steamraiser who preferred it to a firing shovel. I was just about to pitch it off when the idea occurred to me that this might prove to be a much more effective implement for handling small chips. The blade area was double that of mine and it was less than half the weight. I tentatively tried a few swings and found that the firehole could just accommodate the full width. Furthermore it carried twice the quantity of coal with considerably less effort. It was of course impossible to obtain the accurate direction so easily achieved with the correct tool,

but it was possible to dump a lot of coal into the firebox in a very short space of time, and I thereupon decided to take it along with me.

Les conducted a rather more hasty than usual inspection of the engine and, when all was ready, we shunted across the main line and backed into Durran Hill Sidings. Travelling tender-first, even for that short distance, provided an eye-watering experience I did not wish to indulge in too often.

During the 10-minute interval before departure I built up a substantial fire, using both shovels alternately. This restored my circulation nicely, but it did little for Les who was now looking somewhat blue. Unfortunately, an efficient anti-glare shield interposed betwixt driver's seat and firehole was just as efficient in blocking heat, so that he received very little warming radiation unless actually standing in the middle of the cab.

Immediately prior to leaving the sidings, I swilled down the footplate and filled the bucket with boiling water from the slaking pipe. Then, having seen our train of 32 vehicles nicely under way, I settled down to what I knew was going to be almost continual stoking. No 4666 steamed so well that I found it unnecessary to close the firedoors. This had the dual advantage of allowing the maximum amount of radiated heat to come out into the cab, while at the same time permitting me to fire without continually manipulating the firedoors.

Having built up the correct firebed shape, I found I could execute the bulk of my firing with the broad shovel merely by dumping chips just inside the mouthpiece, where the action of the blast completed distribution in a most satisfactory way. From time to time I did have to resort to the firing shovel in order to cover specific areas, mainly at the front and sides of the grate, but on the whole it was much easier than the previous run.

At precisely 12.45 am we arrived at Appleby for water and, so as to top up the boiler as quickly as

'Black Five' No 44666 seen here at Crewe just after completion in 1949, and not yet fitted with a shedplate. It was duly allocated to Saltley, where it proved a very popular locomotive. One of the last batch built at Crewe, it featured forward top-feed plus Ivatt modifications, rocking grate, hopper ashpan, self-cleaning smokebox and, although fitted with return-bend superheater elements, it retained plain bearing axleboxes. This locomotive was still in excellent condition when I experienced a hectic run from Carlisle during an exceptionally cold spell in the winter of 1958-9.

possible, I attempted to use the live steam injector in addition to the exhaust steam one that I had been operating since Carlisle. We had tested both injectors before leaving the shed and knew it to be in good order, but now it was frozen solid. The water column, too, was in the same condition. We could neither pull the arm round nor turn on the water valve, despite the frost fire alongside belching forth a healthy flame.

Without wasting further time we set off with the 7 minutes watering time in hand. We needed every second of it, for with Garsdale troughs frozen, the next column was Blea Moor and Les would now have to nurse our engine very carefully. This was not an easy task when faced with a ruling gradient of 1 in 100, but in such a situation Les Field's superb enginemanship came into its own and by judiciously 'losing' those 7 minutes we breasted Ais Gill dead on time, having used not a whisp more steam than was absolutely necessary.

Shovelling merrily away in front of that white-hot furnace for nearly two hours had left me, if not exactly done to a turn, certainly pleasantly warm. Not so poor Les, for when he drew his head in, I could see frost and little icicles hanging from his eyebrows, twinkling comically in the glare of the fire. Had he not wound a scarf around his head he would probably have lost his left ear through frost-bite.

However, one of the best indications of how cold it was at these higher altitudes came to light when I tried to sweep the footplate. I often kept my handbrush in the bucket of water during cold weather. When sweeping up, this enabled me to lay the dust without making the floorboards as wet as when using the slaking pipe. The bucket had been left in its usual position standing at the back of the footplate alongside the cab doors. It was of course being subjected to the draught blowing under these doors, but at the same time it was little more than 6 feet from a white-hot fire radiating heat directly at it. I was therefore somewhat surprised when on grabbing the brush, the bucket came up with it. A quick jerk after a few seconds'

examination in front of the fire pulled 2 gallons of ice out in one piece - like a jelly from a mould. Had I not seen it with my own eyes I would have found such an occurrence hard to believe.

At Blea Moor we received another nasty shock, for this column too was immovably frozen. Although our tank was very low on water and we still had 27 miles to travel until we reached Skipton, there was now no other choice but to proceed. Fortunately most of it was downhill and we could coast for the first 14 miles. With a clear road Les really let the train run down to Settle, faster in fact than I can recall on any previous occasion.

Having no firing to indulge in, it was now my turn to become cold, and subjected to icy draughts, seemingly blowing in from all directions, I soon came to appreciate the extreme discomfort Les must have been suffering.

We halted at the Skipton water column with no more than a couple of hundred gallons of water in the tender, and I must admit that I was fully prepared to drop the fire there and then. As luck would have it this column had been in frequent use, so although the bag was stiff with ice, I was able to swing the arm round and water actually flowed. While the train was being examined, Les and I lit a fire under our live steam injector with the aid of hot coals from the firebox and some oil-soaked waste, and just prior to departing managed to get it functioning once more. Thereafter I used both injectors alternately and experienced no further trouble.

The remainder of the journey through that icy night was straightforward enough, although Les was literally stiff with cold and I did a devil of a

Appleby station looking north on a dreary August day in 1951. Thirty miles from Durran Hill, the Carlisle-Birmingham fitted freights were booked for a water stop here before tackling the formidable climb to Ais Gill. The water column, which on one winter's night we found frozen despite the roaring frost fire, was located at the end of the platform just behind the camera.

lot of shovelling, so that by the time we arrived at Saltley we were both very glad to get off.

It took some weeks for the coal supply position at Carlisle to revert to normal, and it is now past history that all three stoker '9s' were eventually converted back to standard engines.

The basic concept of mechanical stoking was sound enough, but on the journeys in this country it showed no particular advantage and was in fact wasteful on coal. With the correct fuel a fireman should have been relieved of much physical effort and should therefore have been able to devote more time to road learning. In the event I personally had been involved in a lot of extra effort, both with the stokers and afterwards when using up their special fuel on standard engines. It was an interesting experiment and, despite the various setbacks, I was very glad to have played a part in it.

We did not have the deep snows I had been led to anticipate that winter, but we did experience our share of heavy gales. The worst point invariably seemed to be Ribblehead Viaduct, and although we took the usual precautions to protect ourselves from the ravages of these hurricane-force blasts, the unexpected often happened.

On one particularly wild night we were pounding slowly over the viaduct on a 'Black Five', hauling no more than 30 vehicles, when Les resignedly pointed out that if it blew any harder we would come to a standstill. The engine was already fully extended and I was being kept very busy indeed. The cab doors were wedged with a fire iron to stop them blowing open, since the normal retaining spring was quite inadequate against the force of this particular gale.

I was in the middle of swinging yet another shovelful of coal into the fire when, due no doubt to constant vibration, the fire iron slipped out of position and the doors blew wide open. Instantly the cab was transformed into what felt like a wind tunnel. I clearly remember watching 20 lbs of cobbles disappear from the blade as if by magic, while the shovel itself was nearly torn from my grasp. My cap, which I had pulled down until painfully tight, was snatched from my head as I staggered to retain my balance. Unbelievable, you might think, yet it took the combined efforts of Les and myself to close and secure those doors again. Having these pressures to contend with over the whole length of the train, it was no wonder we could only manage about 10 mph flat out!

With the winds came also the rain. Rains that only mountain dwellers can appreciate. Rains that travelled horizontally and even upwards in continual sheets, driving into every corner of the cab until we were drenched to the skin. Every drop lashing in with such fury that it stung the face like an air gun pellet.

Despite the discomfort brought about by these extreme climatic conditions, battling with the elements only added more spice and sense of achievement to the Carlisle runs. Even on those rare tranquil nights there was always some excitement to stir the blood. For example, on departing from Carlisle at 11.45 pm we always made as much haste as possible in an effort to cover the greatest practical distance before being overtaken by the London-bound express sleeper.

Usually, if all went well, we were turned inside at Mallerstang and as soon as we had halted I knocked back our steam pressure to keep the engine quiet, then listened. Almost immediately in the prevailing silence one could hear a faint rumbling roar modulated by a fickle breeze. This roar gradually grew in intensity until it could be heard as a distinct pounding beat reverberating from the mountainside. Looking down the track we were then able to pick out the tiny twin dots of headlamps surmounted by a column of red sparks, shooting skywards like streams of tracer bullets. With individual beats only just distinguishable, the volume of sound quickly increased to an ear-splitting crescendo as a re-built 'Royal Scot' blasted by, while blazing particles of coal fell like rain for several seconds. A fleeting glimpse revealed in the brilliant white firelight a fireman toiling with his shovel and the regulator invariably right across. Just what cut-off they were using was anyone's guess, but I imagine that it was at lease 35 to 40 per cent.

What superb engines those re-built 'Scots' were, seemingly revelling in the terrific thrashing they received on that long climb. Watching them performing over this section was a most thrilling spectacle. How dear old Tommy Charles would have loved to work the 'Scots' up there, and I, too, for that matter.

Over the past year or two certain pressures both external and also of my own making had been building up. Pressure, I regret to say, arising from good sound reasons for departing from British

Railways. . . Although at this time life for me was happy and exciting on the Carlisles, promotion was going ahead so rapidly that in all probability I would be called upon to take my driver's examination within a couple of years. While this might appear to be a highly desirable situation, it must be borne in mind that when once a driver, I would have to return to the bottom rung of the ladder again - the Shed link. The prospect of several years of shed work followed by a lengthy stay in the Control was not one to send a fellow doing cartwheels in ecstasy. Moreover, with dieselisation and electrification already going ahead apace, it was very much on the cards that by the time I came out into the road links again there would be no more steam engines left to drive. To me the fascination of railways began and ended with steam locomotives. Take away these and there was very little left. Only a few trips as a passenger on diesel railcars were quite sufficient to convince me that I did not want to become a mere 'tram driver'.

For many years there had been an atmosphere of growing discontent, particularly among the senior drivers. In their heyday the work of an engine driver had been surrounded by a certain glamour and had commanded the position of prestige now afforded to airline pilots. They were also paid a salary commensurate with the high regard in which they were held, and this took them comfortably above average earnings. Since the war both status and relative pay had slipped steadily down the national scale and this, coupled with deteriorating conditions and continual line closures, gave rise to an understandable disquiet.

Despite grandiose schemes for modernisation, many felt at that period that British Railways was a dying industry and the advice form the majority of older drivers was 'Get out, young man, while you still can'. Split shifts, long and uncertain hours, getting up when everyone else was going to bed and working during holidays was extremely onerous and a tremendous disruption to family life. I had no children then, but my wife, along with all other wives of railwayman, was forced to suffer hours of loneliness and only the barest minimum of social life.

When, therefore, the opportunity to 'make a break' arrived in March 1959 I was already in a suitable state of mind to make a decision. In keeping with my life-long interest in fast, exciting and noisy machinery, I had developed a great fondness for cars, especially vintage, sport and racing cars, and had, during the previous year, become quite friendly with the proprietor of a garage in Solihull specialising in such vehicles. To work with and be surrounded by the machines that were now my principal hobby was a chance too good to be missed, so in April, just over nine years after signing on with British Railways, I handed in my notice.

However, as may be expected, I timed this so that my final week went out in a blaze of glory, so to speak, working the 4.45 pm Glasgow.

Looking back over those nine years one is bound to ask the inevitable question - was it all worthwhile? The tremendous physical strain, the acquisition of a vast amount of specialised knowledge, the dirt, the privations, the battle with the elements, being roasted, soaked or frozen and, above all else, the long hours of working all round the clock.

The answer always comes out the same. Yes, it most certainly was. The rapid demise of the steam locomotive only serves to emphasise this, for such an opportunity can never occur again. Few other occupations offered the same excitement, satisfaction and sense of achievement as that of operating a steam locomotive, and added to this was the wonderful spirit of comradeship that existed on the footplate. Furthermore, the work developed an iron self-discipline that, once acquired, stood one in good stead for the rest of one's life.

I must admit that, having once departed, I gave little thought to railways until 1968, when my brother sadly pointed out that steam traction for all practical purposes had ceased to exist in this country. The shock of this realisation was as sadly traumatic as losing an old and dear friend, since from my earliest memories there had always been steam engines and I tended to suppose that there always would be.

Fortunately, dedicated enthusiasts all over the country soon got together in an endeavour to rectify in some small part this tragedy and preserve an element of our great steam heritage. It is to these tireless and far-sighted individuals that I dedicate this book, and if they derive some small measure of pleasure and inspiration from these pages, then I consider the effort will have been well worthwhile.

INDEX